A National Flag for India

A National Flag for India

Rituals, Nationalism, and the Politics of Sentiment

Arundhati Virmani

With a Foreword by

Jacques Revel

permanent black

Published by
PERMANENT BLACK
'Himalayana', Mall Road, Ranikhet Cantt,
Ranikhet 263645
perblack@gmail.com

Distributed by
ORIENT BLACKSWAN PRIVATE LIMITED
Bangalore Bhopal Bhubaneshwar Chandigarh
Chennai Ernakulam Guwahati Hyderabad Jaipur
Kolkata Lucknow Mumbai New Delhi Patna
www.orientblackswan.com

First paperback printing 2016

ISBN 978-81-7824479-2

Typeset in Adobe Garamond
by Guru Typograph Technology, Dwarka, New Delhi 110075
Printed and bound by Sapra Brothers, New Delhi 110092

Foreword

This book comes well in time. It will surely contribute to a debate that has acquired increasing importance over the last generation. It does so in new terms by proposing an original reflection based on a vast collection of new material. We have been waiting for it ever since Arundhati Virmani first sketched its plan in a notable and noted article published in the British journal *Past and Present* in 1999.[1] Since then the author had time to nourish this programme with serious research. An Indian historian living in France, she had occasions to discuss her work with colleagues in India as well as in Europe and in the United States. It is not pure coincidence therefore that this very personal inquiry she today proposes to her readers enters so fully into the current historiographical debate.

It might come as a surprise to see this presentation by a historian of Europe, moreover one who is notoriously incompetent in contemporary Indian history. Even so, I believe that the problems examined by the author are very much relevant to our disciplines and on this basis are likely to retain our attention well beyond our personal specializations, if only because they prompt us to take a critical distance in relation to our habitual thoughts and acquired convictions since they are raised in a particular framework. They constrain us to a kind of 'estrangement' whose heuristic effect is a welcome reminder that our most familiar experience is not the only available or possible reference. I therefore suggest that *A National Flag for India* be read as it was conceived and written: as a specific contribution to a general problem whose importance cannot be underestimated.

[1] Arundhati Virmani, 'National Symbol Under Colonial Domination: The Nationalization of the Indian Flag, March–August 1923', *Past and Present*, 164, 1999, pp. 169–97.

There is not doubt that national phenomena, nationalism, its multiple expressions and its roots have re-emerged among the main preoccupations of historians. The quasi-simultaneous publication in 1983 of three major books can here serve as a symbol. Their proposals are essential to Arundhati Virmani's reflections, as they have been to a whole generation of historians. The works are unmistakably Benedict Anderson's *Imagined Communities*, Ernest Gellner's *Nations and Nationalism*, and Eric Hobsbawm and Terence Ranger's *The Invention of Tradition*.[2] Far from constituting a common project, together they restored all its problematic importance to a set of phenomena that a historiography hitherto more attentive to the social than the national had somewhat let fall by the wayside. One can, indeed one must, evidently examine the reappearance of this thematic from the 1980s, which, in most Western countries, overlapped an obsession with memorabilia on an unprecedented scale. As these ancient societies saw their certainties shattered, they once more initiated a search into the depths of the past for the reasons that could hold them together and that were so painfully lacking in these times of dormant crisis. But this version is only one among many others that would need more time to examine. In all this part of the world that the West had lazily come to designate as the Third World, the national preoccupation found other justifications and based itself on other arguments as these new (but in fact often very ancient) political entities affirmed their existence and their ambitions.

Works that illustrate the return of the national phenomenon share a number of common characteristics beyond their diversity. To begin with, they break with the old organicist imagery that dominates the nineteenth and first half of the twentieth century and which accompanies the affirmation of the nation-state, particularly in Europe. This earlier, formative approach conceived the nation (and probably lived it, to a degree still hard to grasp) as an ontological, transcendent entity, inscribed in a framework of history that was necessary to its culmination

[2] Benedict Anderson, *Imagined Communities: Reflections on the Origin and Spread of Nationalism* (London, Verso, 1983); Eric Hobsbawm and Terence Ranger (eds), *The Invention of Tradition* (Cambridge, Cambridge University Press, 1983); Ernest Gellner, *Nations and Nationalism* (Oxford, Blackwell, 1983).

and whose essential role would be to reveal the nation, in the sense of the old model of the Christian revelation—as in Ranke but also in Michelet. Instead, today an approach that could be qualified as constructivist compels recognition. It seeks to describe the conditions in which the nation was 'imagined', 'invented', or rendered necessary by transformations in the social world. To the evident nature of the nation, which had been so long accepted by historians as also by their contemporaries, was substituted a critical perspective that questioned the conditions, the means, and the resources with which such a construction was, and remains, possible. Whether we enlist it in a functionalist perspective, roughly that of Gellner, or accentuate the modalities and manipulations associated with the production of imagery and with national sentiment, the nation becomes an element of a bigger game in which it is the spoke, the product, and the stake all at once: in a word, it is an artefact related to particular circumstances.

Contemporary to what has often, in a term that is a little too sweeping, been called the *cultural turn*, this generation of studies has continuously been attentive to forms and symbols of national sentiment: they first questioned, then interpreted, iconography, collective rituals, 'places', and objects of memory. The flag as a leading symbol must naturally find its place in this repertory even if it has not been the most scrutinized object by historians; others who ventured forth in this inquiry have often limited themselves to the fairly obvious. On the contrary, Arundhati Virmani's research with its significant and stimulating results seems to me to reveal the crucial potential of the subject. No doubt this is partly due to her talent as a historian trained in several historiographical worlds, and one who knows how to use what each world has to offer with such effect. But partly, it seems to me, this is also due to the object she has chosen to study, to the particular experience this object refers to and whose importance she reveals in this book so well.

The Indian national experience is recent, even if, like many others, it has often hunted for precedents and resources in a glorious past. It took form and acquired significance in the context of the British colonial domination, that is to say, in a framework largely chosen by the colonial power. It had to overcome the disparity and profound diversity of an immense country, and was confronted very early with the problem of concrete coexistence within a community projected into the future—an 'imagined community' in Benedict Anderson's terms—of different and sometimes antagonistic entities. The disputed history of the Indian national flag describes this long and difficult history. And because the sources are abundant for one who has been able to find them, the study casts new light on the national elaboration of contemporary India. In its turn, it raises a set of new questions for our own particular national experiences. Even when the voluble protagonists of this history who are abundantly and usefully quoted in this book, evoke the past or the factor of historical necessity, it is always in the present that they do so. It is in this present that they exchange or counter reasonings, and elaborate—with others or against them—the argumentation that accompanies the affirmation of a national demand. In the typology he recently proposed, the German historian Hans-Ulrich Wehler elaborates the concept of *Transfernationalismus* ('adopted nationalism' or 'exported nationalism') to qualify the more recent national identity affirmations, which, according to him, can be understood as adaptations of European models. The formula is not entirely convincing: less because it perpetuates an abusively Eurocentric version—for, after all, as A. Virmani reminds us, a number of protagonists of the history she retraces kept an eye fixed on the West, if only to challenge their pretensions—but rather because it carries the risk of depreciating the specific context for each experience. On the contrary, this context is essential. One of the major interests of the analysis presented here is precisely that it permits us to grasp at the ground level the convictions, strategies, and various tensions that rendered a common formula acceptable to a larger number. We are led to understand a process, a history in the making that is possible in all its complexity and its details. But this is only the first aspect of the programme the author proposes.

The long and difficult elaboration of the Indian national flag, the diverse and sometimes contrary expectations that built up around this object during half a century with their stakes profoundly rooted in the social world: these essential aspects of the historian's work are masterfully unravelled in this book. This complex history must however be properly understood. Even while the author insists on the divergences, rivalries, and necessary negotiations, she never minimizes the symbolic value or emotional investments in this emblem. This sensitive identification, as A. Virmani recalls in the very first lines of her book, was expressed well before the flag even came into existence. On the morrow of the First World War, the poetess Sarojini Naidu felt its absence as a lack of recognition of her country, of its humiliation, as a personal wound. This emotional experience, whether individual or collective, accompanies the entire history that is presented here. First endured as a dispossession and deprivation, it would be infused with expectations, hopes, positive values, all of which this book allows us to follow in their powerful and complex affirmation.

In undertaking to retrace this history for us, the author adheres to a history of emotions, which has repeatedly been the object of new approaches in recent years—without however stabilizing under one single formula. One of the most interesting aspects is no doubt the project of accounting for the 'coherence of sentiment' to better understand the mechanisms of conviction and the resources of collective action within a given society.[3]

The difficulties of such an attractive programme are well known: the principal risk here lies in rationalizing that which has come to exist. Thus, from a permanent symbolic or ritual repertory we infer what anthropologists have often termed its 'effectiveness' that one takes as acquired. Yet, this conviction can hardly be taken for granted. Besides the fact that the life of the symbolic repertory is most often related to a specific time period, the capacities of decoding and identifying are also modified over time. All cultures, national or other, are thus encumbered by fossilized symbols or symbols that have become unreadable and consequently weak mobilizers. Some are subsequently inert but continue to be preserved on patrimonial grounds. Others can be exposed to subsequent reappropriations, often at the cost of significant deformations, perhaps retained for the benefit of reinvented traditions. They can then frequently become the object of a real retranslation. This simply means that these symbols have value only in relation to the uses to which they can be put, and the contexts in which they are mobilized. Sources often leave us few traces of these

[3] See Alain Corbin, *The Village of Cannibals: Rage and Murder in France, 1870* (Cambridge, Mass., Harvard University Press, 1993; French edn, 1990).

uses. When we reconstruct the political symbolism of medieval Europe or the logic of a monarchical ritual in the sixteenth century, what are we talking about? Do we dwell on the intentions of the learned scholars who elaborated the programmes? On the uses of these resources by the powers? Are we looking for the ways they could be perceived and understood by heterogeneous publics, to whom they were offered on display? Are we considering the interpretive virtuosity of historians, sociologists, or anthropologists, who long afterwards, and from the vantage point of other cultures, set out to describe and interpret them? The question, we must agree, at least deserves to be raised. One of the major merits of A. Virmani's inquiry is to raise it. Her approach to the history of the Indian flag through its debates during the pre-Independence decades has allowed her to measure the nature and depth of emotional investments, to grasp how a symbol was collectively affirmed and became performative across the shifting play of positions and actors. The lesson retained will not only interest historians: I hope that it will be heard by other specialists of the social sciences, such is its value.

In a passage that is little remarked, in *The Court Society* (1933, 1940), the German sociologist Norbert Elias suggested that, in order to understand the mechanisms of any form of social aggregation, it would be important to understand the 'formula of needs' that links men together within a specific social formation. Symbols obviously form part of these shared needs. This, it seems to me, is a major message of this successful book. Without imprisoning itself within any established formulae, it enriches our understanding of an essential moment of India's history by trying to explain the reasons and the sentiment that made it possible. More generally, it invites us to think in new, methodical, and clear-cut terms about the social construction of collective identities.

JACQUES REVEL

Contents

PART III

Black and White Illustrations

Colour Illustrations
(between pp. 86 and 87)

Acknowledgements

Many of the questions debated in this book were developed in seminars and conferences at the University of Bordeaux, SHADYC Marseille, EHESS Paris, the Department of Political Science at the University of Florence, and the Programme of South Asian Studies at Cornell University. I am grateful to these institutions, in particular to the Centre of South Asian Studies, Cambridge, for its facilities and technical support—above all, to Lionel Carter, Rachel Rowe, and Kevin Greenbank.

To those who have offered me their presence, support, and encouragement through these years this brief mention is quite inadequate. I would nevertheless like to thank Jacques Revel who followed this manuscript from its first painful beginnings down to its last version. I have not always been able to follow his suggestions but this work has certainly benefited from his comments. My gratitude goes to Pami Singh, who has never failed to be there, helping to organize, welcome, and promote my research. In a very different space, Marcello Verga provided me a platform to articulate and argue my ideas. Michael Porch helped me resolve some problems in digitalizing documents.

My greatest debt remains to my family, and above all to Jean Boutier who has accompanied me in this research in more ways than one.

Abbreviations

AICC	All India Congress Committee
AMAE	Archives du Ministère des Affaires Etrangères, Paris
CAOM	Centre des Archives d'Outre-Mer, Aix-en-Provence
CSAS	Centre of South Asian Studies, Cambridge
CWMG	*Collected Works of Mahatma Gandhi*
NAI	National Archives of India, New Delhi
NMML	Nehru Memorial Museum and Library, New Delhi
OIOC	Oriental and India Office Collections, British Library, London

Preface to the Paperback Edition

A decade is both too short and yet perhaps sufficient to assess the contribution of a work to questions that surround the study of nationalism. *The National Flag: Rituals, Nationalism and the Politics of Sentiment*, finished in 2006 and published two years later, proposed an unorthodox approach to the study of nation-building in India. It held at a distance the preponderance of institutional politics, agendas, party strategies, and decision processes to focus on the mechanisms and dynamics of national symbolic elaboration and reception that shaped broad-based collective emotional norms and systems of feeling for the nation. Without ignoring the many regional approaches to anti-colonial struggles, it considerd the scale of empire as more appropriate to this object of investigation.

Combining both national operations with individual and local experiences over the long time span of a century, it opened the study of nationalism to integrate a key symbol of the nation as a mutually constructed sign by nationalists and colonialists, an eminently hybrid product rather than a derivative product of Eurocentric political arsenals. I took the flag as a vector through which social and cultural dissemination of political qualities could take place, and national agendas fixed, both at the top and by individual appropriations and tinkerings. It operated within ritualistic-ceremonial frames to create a common symbolic language and shared practices that served to build a large emotional community beyond the many fragmentary identities, rooting the nation in the hearts and minds of Indians. It acted as a medium to project a collective 'will' that could be plebiscited by ordinary Indians. Thus, it became an open project to accommodate diversity and vernacular pluralities alongside each other without hierarchical distinctions. The cultural turn in the study of nationalisms that underscores the nation's links with art, its ties with commonplace material objects and its performative actions, its capacity to penetrate into everyday practices, has widened the framework of rational, strategic processes of nation-building to tap the sphere of emotions and sentiment.

Eight years later, not only do the main thrusts of the arguments advanced in this book still stand, but they have been considerably consolidated by other research on the Indian national flag itself by political scientists and historians (Roy: 2006; Jha: 2008; Pai: 2009). Equally, the approach I followed has been prolonged by later works on official emblems, ceremonies and rituals in parliamentary functioning (Rai: 2011; Rai and Johnson: 2014) and the continually expanding literature on the emotions in politics (Rosenwein: 2006; Eustace: 2008; Matt & Stearns: 2014) and the new practices of citizenship. These perspectives are more open to a comparative analysis of nationalism.

This field of research is still vibrant and promising. Social scientists have much to explore in understanding the capacity of nations to endure despite the growth of multiple and rival political or religious commitments. More decentralized approaches to nationalism are required that connect national processes to vernacular strains or top-down inquiries to quotidian cultural and social practices, strategies of marginal communities or group actions, as well as relationships between gender and national engagement. Some of the dimensions explored in the book would merit further development. The symbols of political power used in the princely states and their role in the invention of local and political languages hold particular interest for the analyst of contemporary political behaviour. Despite the contemporary pulls of globalization and the force of interconnected commercial world networks, the power and sway of nations remain strong. Nations and national identities have not vanished, on the contrary they are enduring political structures, sustained and nourished by national symbols like the flag, which curiously has gained in public visibility and increased its hold on collective passions, serving as a beacon of solidarity, previously in the United States on the morrow of the September 2011 attacks and today in the aftermath of the Paris terrorist massacre in November 2015.

The book stopped at the 2004 Supreme Court ruling that recognized every Indian's fundamental right to hoist the national flag on all days of the year. In one respect, the judgment recognized and confirmed the flag as a collective national property, a 'custom in common'. Today, the flag overwhelms other signs of community subjectivities and group identities. State hoistings of the flag on occasions of collective national significance like Republic Day or Independence Day are intensified by aggressive media representations and its intrusions into society through a plethora of trivial objects, from *tiranga barfis* and koftas to saris and *dupattas*. In the traditional anti-colonial strain, it continues to be wielded as a symbolic arm against the state in the cause of improving citizens lives. Recently, Sasi Perumal, an agriculturalist, made forceful use of the national flag in the public space to accentuate his demand for prohibition in Tamil Nadu. Other instances could be identified that would reinforce this demonstration (*Frontline*, 4 September 2015).

Simultaneously, regular invocations of the Flag Code and the Prevention of Improper Use of Emblems and Names Act of 1950 by the public reflect a general anxiety and feeling of outrage at what is sometimes perceived as a desecration of the national symbol. A series of court cases registered for insult to the national flag shows celebrities as special targets. A case was filed in 2007 against the cricket champion Sachin Tendulkar for cutting a tricolour cake during the West Indies tour. In 2008 the tennis champion Sania Mirza was accused of insulting the flag by putting her feet in front of the flag. In 2015 the Bollywood actor Amitabh Bachhan and his son were attacked for wrapping themselves in the national flag at the India–Pakistan world cup in Adelaide, Australia. Popular opinion decried the prime minister, Narendra Modi, for autographing the Indian flag for President Obama: 'That's our national flag; you can't just sign it like a napkin.' The general secretary of the Dalit Sena in Puducherry filed a police case against the prime minister for insulting the national flag during the International Day of Yoga celebrations in Delhi, by wiping his face with the national flag (*Indian Express*, 23 June 2015). Flag controversies seem to arise from the most innocuous actions, articulating an anxiety about the country's sovereignty. They gather greater heat in frontier states where migrant populations' national loyalties are easily questioned. The flag then becomes a litmus test of belonging, a sign of roots in a national territory, a mobile borderline that can penetrate every village and region.

At the same time, since 2004 there has been a vigorous privatization of the flag, which seems to have entered a phase of commodification. While individual collectors and vexillogists have always been part of the landscape, the emergence of a private foundation monopolizing the national flag is a new development. One such non-profit organization was set up in 2002, headed by the industrialist and member of parliament Naveen Jindal who had fought for the end of state monopoly of flag usage. Jindal's Flag Foundation of India has been extremely active in projecting the national flag from its status of a national political common good to a cultural commodity. Under the foundation's aegis, the flag has metamorphosed into a glossy coffee table product through hardcover books like *Tiranga—A Celebration of the Indian Flag* (2005). A sophisticated marketing strategy, exploiting the possibilities offered by the internet, invests the flag with a heightened aesthetics that is in harmony with the contemporary expanded world of commodities. The book features images of the flag by well-known professional photographers and artists, Reena Saini Kallat, T.S. Satyan, Raghu Rai, Avinash Pasricha and some amateurs, emphasizing the long road the flag has travelled from 1916 when Pingally Venkayya published his little book presenting possible designs of a future Indian flag (cf. pp. 64–6 and illustration III in this book). In comparison with Venkayya's designs, these images propose an aestheticized, shiny representation of the flag on smooth, brilliant paper. The foundation has commissioned artistic visualizations of the flag for art exhibitions in different cities, in particular the India Habitat Centre, New Delhi, the Jaipur Virasat Festival, Jaipur, and the Jehangir Art Gallery, Mumbai. Such representations are a far cry from the exhibitions mounted by government institutions like the National Museum in the 1980s and 1990s, which concentrated heavily on the flag's historical past and its place in anti-colonial struggles and social movements.

In addition, Jindal's foundation has instituted flag ambassador certificates and Tiranga badge awards for school students. At the same time, the evocation of national responsibility, service to the nation and community replicates a discourse of the state though in a more attractive, consumer-friendly form. The flag is here disconnected from its traditional cadre of khadi *bhandars* where it was sold after Independence, and surrounded by the aura of high society. At the same time, its national meanings are promoted. The foundation even moved the New Delhi Municipal Council (NDMC) to instal the national flag in Central Park, Connaught Place, a major commercial venue in New Delhi. After approval by the Delhi Urban Art Commission (DUAC), the 207-feet-tall flagpole holding a 60 × 90-feet-flag was planted in March 2014. It is the highest in the capital and perhaps in the country, easily dominating the single-storey arcaded circular complex of shops and standing as an illuminated beacon at night, powered with 2000-watt lights. Its material of knitted polyster fabric manufactured in Mumbai by the 'Flag shop' marks a clean break with its handspun, handwoven khadi origins, upholding traditional techniques. It is still too early to judge the effects of this commodification and fetishization of the flag.

Alongside this privatization that corresponds to the contemporary commercial age in India, the flag's absorption into social movements and its incarnation of citizenship shows itself to be more problematic. Civil society's involvement with the struggles for direct democracy and its concern with elaborating a new grammar of politics has produced some significant public campaigns in recent years. In 2011–12, the flag's omnipresence in Anna Hazare's anti-corruption movement in reaction to the numerous spectacular scams (Commonwealth Games, dubious distribution of telecom licences, illegal sales of mines in Karnataka, Adarsh Housing Society scam), seemed to announce the national symbol's absorption of new moral meanings dear to civil society. The tricolour occupied a central place in the iconography of this citizens' movement. Media coverage transformed the flag into a brand, marketed as a symbol of Team India, drawing on the image of corporate Indian cricket teams, linking it with a particular kind of nationalism that, on the ground, took on a masculine, high-powered and market-friendly form. This weakened the flag's initial links with clean government, a renewed engagement with ethics, responsibility, transparency, and accountability. While it made the tricolour an easy expression of a politically correct public posture, it simultaneously alienated minorities, women, and citizens who looked askance at the aggressively jingoistic uses of the flag. Many young women admitted to staying away from the protests because of the threatening tone of nationalist flag-waving and loud slogan-mongering around *Bharat Mata* and *Vande Mataram* by men on motorcycles in public protests. The flag was noticeably absent in the spontaneous protests across urban India against the gang rape of a young girl in Delhi in December 2012. Instead, participants wore black clothes or covered their mouth with a black cloth. Its noticeable retreat before the green, brown, blue colours of the environment movements signifying deforestation, air pollution, and water pollution, could be read as an indication of a break between a national symbol and citizen-relevant questions and struggles.

Does this signal an emotional shift in the flag's trajectory, from an icon representing unity and national sacrifice to an artefact of consumption, or is this simply a pessimistic and dark foreboding? Is the flag, caught up in the triangular state–market–media network, open to privatization and commodification, becoming a mere aesthetic annexe, an urban-oriented symbol that is being readjusted to fit in with India's global profile and the needs of its growingly influential and visible diaspora, in the process excluding minorities, effacing diversity, and replacing traditional techniques of production? It is too early to draw conclusions about this new chapter but not too late to reflect and engage collectively in these changes.

Marseille, 28 November 2015

References

Eustace, Nicole, 2008, *Passion is the Gale: Emotion, Power and the Coming of the American Revolution*, Chapel Hill, University of North Carolina Press.

Jha, Sadan, 2008, 'The Indian National Flag as a Site of Daily Plebiscite', *Economic and Political Weekly*, vol. 43, 2008, pp. 102–11.

Josh, Bhagwan, 2012, in Patrick Olivelle, Janice Leoshko, and Himanshu Prabha Ray (eds), *Reimagining Asoka: Memory and History*, New Delhi, Oxford University Press, pp. 394–408.

Matt, Susan J. & Peter N. Stearns, 2014, *Doing Emotions History*, Chicago, University of Illinois Press.

Pai, Sudha, 2009, 'The National Flag', *India International Centre Quarterly*, vol. 36, pp. 38–47.

Rai, Shirin, 2010, *Ceremony and Ritual in Parliament*, London, Routledge.

———, and Rachel Johnson, ed., 2014, *Democracy in Practice, Ceremony and Ritual in Parliament*, London, Palgrave-Macmillan.

Rosenwein, Barbara H., 2006, *Emotional Communities in the Early Middle Ages*, Ithaca and London, Cornell University Press.

Roy, Srirupa, 2006, 'A Symbol of Freedom: The Indian Flag and the Transformations of Nationalism, 1906–2002', *The Journal of Asian Studies*, vol. 65, pp. 495–527.

Introduction

'We've a war and a debt, an' a flag; an' if this Ain't to be inderpendunt, why whut on airth is?'—James Russell Lowell, *Biglow Papers*, 2nd Series, IV (London, Trüben and Co., 1864), p. 146

'I have suffered the most terrible moments of anguish in free countries, because India possessed no flag', confessed Sarojini Naidu, the well-known poet actively involved in the national struggles, to the Constituent Assembly on 22 July 1947 when it adopted the national flag of independent India. This surge of emotion expressed the culmination of a deep frustration endured during decades of political activity—she was the first woman president of the Indian National Congress—which she now recalled through some intense though imprecise memories. At the signing of the peace at Versailles after the First World War she had suddenly realized for the first time, amidst the rejoicing of all nations celebrating the victory, that India, which participated side by side with the Allies in the war, now seemed excluded from the festivities. Among the forest of flags draping the Opera House in Paris the absence of an Indian flag would have brought tears to the eyes of an Indian compatriot, and it led Sarojini Naidu to vow: 'the time will soon come when we shall have our own Flag and our own Anthem'. At the peace celebration in New York, the absence of the 'Flag of Free India' among the flags of the forty-four nations at an 'Assembly of Free Nations' (the League of Nations? the United Nations Organization?) convinced her that the Indian flag 'would become the most historic Flag of the world in the not distant future'. Later, at the Women's International Conference in Berlin, the programming of a national flag parade finally pushed her to drastic action: 'at my suggestion, some Indian women delegates tore strips from their saris, sitting up till the small hours of the morning to make the Tricolour Flag so that our country should not be humiliated for the lack of a National Banner'. Despite this somewhat 'flagrant' and quite informal arrangement, the absence of India's symbolic existence continued to haunt her for years: she experienced her 'worst anguish' a few months before independence, when Indians still could not display their tricolour at a meeting of the nations of Asia at Delhi, though it had been recognized since 1931 by the Indian National Congress as the national flag of India.[1]

Naidu's discourse came at the finale of a key moment a few weeks before the official proclamation of independence. India was adopting the symbolic arsenal without which the country could not appear as a nation. Preceding her, Jawaharlal Nehru had presented the history of the Indian flag as a national epic built of heroic battles and collective sacrifice. In contrast to this rather conventional and expected narrative, Naidu's testimony advanced a surprising perspective: the history of a pain that, once unmasked, would persist for decades, the feeling of being deprived of something the rest of the world possessed. She described her experience of the national struggle not as a heroic, positive exaltation, but as a living trauma caused by the symbolic non-existence of her country. The national flag was thus placed at the heart of a major political experience.

Naidu's emotional approach was not a simple response to a highly charged political conjuncture. Nor were the memories that she evoked an agile rhetorical device, aimed at intensifying collective feelings of solidarity. Already in 1928, writing to Gandhi from the United States where she had been sent on a tour to propagate the Indian cause, she had expressed the same sentiment: taking the floor at the World Alliance for Peace Banquet in New York in October 1928 she shared her unease at not seeing India's flag 'on the walls of the banquet hall . . . decorated with the flags of the free nations', seventy in all. Symbol of a complete nation, the flag encapsulated all their political objectives. 'The only guarantee of abiding world peace was a free India and till they could hang India's banner dyed in the red of hope, the green of her courage and the white of her faith among other world symbols of liberty, there could and would be no more peace in the world', she

[1] B. Shiva Rao (ed.), *The Framing of India's Constitution. Select Documents* (New Delhi, Indian Institute of Public Administration, 1966), vol. 1, pp. 507–8.

proclaimed.[2] From this perspective, the intensely emotional experience that was the nationalist movement could not be reduced to a simple political process, nor political emotions confined to exceptional moments like riots or Partition.

For a long time, the struggle for independence has in fact been presented through a scholarly and learned account of a 'real story' unfolding through a combination of political projects, strategies, negotiations and resistance; collective action is presented as a natural response to economic and political contexts and urgencies. This reductionist approach is all the more astonishing in light of the enormous literary, artistic, and ideological production around the nation, which contributed across individual but also collective experiences to a feeling of belonging through 'bonds of affection'. Building on Sarojini Naidu's experience of the flag, we can see that it overtakes individualized representations to generate a new kind of emotion. While being an intimate perception, more and more people repeatedly share it, and the accretion of emotion it solicits during collective demonstrations gives it the capacity of political organization.

It is this capacity of the flag to create political realities through emotions that is at the heart of this book. From this point of view it can be considered a contribution to a historical anthropology of emotions such as has been recently developed by William Reddy among others.[3] But the study of this specific political process, close to what the French historian Alain Corbin has termed the 'coherence of sentiment' with respect to collective action, proves to be a very challenging exercise. At least three reasons account for this.

First of all, for a long time historians did not consider the flag worthy of interest. Despite the huge erudition that it has invited under the name of 'vexillology',[4] it remained an object of curiosity for practitioners

[2] Makarand Paranjpe (ed.), *Sarojini Naidu. Selected Letters, 1890s to 1940s* (Delhi, Kali for Women, 1996), p. 215.

[3] Among the now abundant literature on this subject, William Reddy's work can be noted for its coherence and its proximity to the object studied here: *Navigation of Feeling: A Framework of the History of Emotions* (Cambridge, Cambridge University Press, 2001).

[4] The term 'vexillology' seems to have been coined in 1957 by Whitney Smith, one of the founders of the Flag Research Center, Lexington (Mass.), USA; in 1969, an International Federation of Vexillological Associations was created.

in very specific fields—such as the navy[5]—or for collectors of military objects. In this frame, since the second half of the nineteenth century, numerous studies have been devoted to the 'flags of the world', studies which are limited to inventories, even if large and detailed. These provide an accurate description of flags as symbols of sovereignty—which permitted an identification of territories, military forces, and ships—and give the precise etiquette for the display of flags in public locations; they focus on the meaning of flags, their colours, their designs and their forms, through a knowledge of their origins, their authors, and the context of their elaboration.[6] Assembling an impressive array of factual information, these accounts were often linked to contemporary political debates developing around new political regimes or emerging nations. However, in reducing the inquiry to an archaeology of origins, and in fossilizing its supposedly unique meaning established at birth, they refused to consider the flag as part of broad political processes. From this perspective the French medievalist Michel Pastoureau's sweeping statement that 'the flag still awaits its historians and its ethnologists' is not far wrong.[7]

The second reason is that the study of this object calls for the reformulation of political history by resituating the national movement as part of the elaboration of a political culture by both British and Indians. This political culture concerned not only public space but equally the private sphere, entangling nationalist agendas with the intimate world of family traditions, community memories, and oral narratives. It thus calls for the analysis of objects that are not forcibly, directly, and

[5] Vice Admiral Gordon Campbell, I.O. Evans, *The Book of Flags* (London, Oxford University Press, 1950; 7th edn, 1974), for example. Written by an English admiral, this gives a large quantity of information on the technical and normative uses of flags, especially in the navy and army. The book of the admiralty librarian W.G. Perrin, *British Flags, their early history and their development at sea; with an account of the origin of the flag as a national device* (Cambridge, Cambridge University Press, 1922), concentrates even more on British naval flags, seen as the main point of departure of the British system of political symbols.

[6] For a bibliographical inventory of this vast production, cf. Whitney Smith, *The Bibliography of Flags of Foreign Nations* (Boston, G.K. Hall, 1965); the Flag Research Center has published a journal, *The Flag Bulletin*, since October 1961.

[7] Michel Pastoureau, 'Drapeaux', in *Dictionnaire des couleurs de notre temps. Symbolique et société* (Paris, C. Bonneton, 1992), p. 60.

immediately political—statues, national anthems, postage stamps, associations, festivals, and rituals, and situating them as central resources within the nationalist process.

Lastly, questions around the flag do to some extent coincide with the interrogations and objects dear to post-colonial approaches. The flag could no doubt be considered as another 'fragment' of discourse on the nation, given the status of a text and deconstructed to reveal hidden agendas. But such an approach can prove to be too rigid to accommodate the ambiguities in the positions of both colonizers and colonized. That which I have chosen, though equally critical of an official national discourse elaborated before and after independence, uses the analytical tools developed by new cultural historians and social anthropologists. The institution of democracy in France during the nineteenth century thus led a historian like Maurice Agulhon to study the elaboration and reception of the symbolism of the French republic in the nineteenth and twentieth centuries. He devoted a significant part of his work not to the flag but to the allegory of Marianne incarnating France since the Revolution. In a different way, the French medievalist Michel Pastoureau, through his interest in symbols but also in the complex language of colours, broadened the questionnaires and opened the study of national political symbols to their more material dimensions.[8] Among those who undoubtedly developed one of the major tools for a renewed study of the flag as an essential political element was Raymond Firth who identified the flag as a 'master symbol' not only in so-called 'primitive' societies but also in contemporary societies, serving as 'instruments of expression, communication, knowledge and control'.[9] He thus proposed a veritable programme of study for the flag.

Flags are, to begin with, manufactured objects made of specific cloth, colours, and designs, answering to well-established norms and conventions which 'uniformize' their final form: the creation of this national symbol thus takes place within strict material constraints. Secondly, public displays of flags are regulated by a set of rules and legislation or customs which lay down the specific places, moments,

[8] On these works, see the first section of the present book's bibliography.

[9] Raymond Firth, *Symbols Public and Private* (New York, Cornell University Press, 1973).

and manner of their uses, variable from one country to another. Given these structural constraints, Firth did not consider the immediate political dimensions of flags as primordial, though he did not dismiss them entirely either. His interest lay in their social impact, their determining role in fashioning identities, behaviours, and emotions, both individual and collective. His proposals can thus constitute the point of departure for studying the complexity of flag symbolism from a larger anthropology of political sentiment and passion. Flags 'must be regarded not primarily as signals conveying information, but as symbols representing ideas or objects of value, often in a very general and emotional manner.'[10]

In appearance, Agulhon's approach to political culture and Firth's symbolical anthropology are hardly compatible: the former is more concerned with the processes of political modernization, the latter seeks to highlight the primitive elements of contemporary realities—the values attached to these pieces of cloth and the social acts related to these. Yet, at a deeper level, Agulhon and Firth share a common conception of political symbols: for both, the flag is not the pure and simple expression of a pre-existing national and political culture; its importance flows from its central position in the production of a nation in both its cultural and political dimensions.

These programmes allow the demystification of a unanimous, teleological official state discourse on the flag in favour of an analysis of contradictory and heterogeneous processes that lead to approximate agreements and compromises. By identifying the contradictory interests of British and Indians, it leads to a renewal of the discussion on the meanings and interest of 'derived discourses' in political constructions that are part of colonial situations.

Through a study of the elaboration and reception of the national flag, this book seeks to contribute to a cultural history of the construction of the Indian nation around three distinct but closely inter-related inquiries.

The first is a precise political narrative imposed by the nature of the symbol itself. This narrative examines the many successive projects, discussions, conflicts and decisions on both the British and Indian

[10] Ibid.

sides; it considers the role of a great variety of actors, from ordinary people to political parties and representative assemblies, and the impact of an important range of publications, from letters to the editor in newspapers to public speeches and pamphlets. It follows the flag's complex genesis through discussions in the public space. At the same time, such an exclusively political narrative—while providing a rich and precise description of the decision-making process—envisages the flag from a very reductionist perspective. The flag's graduation from this plane of relative obscurity to a level of national familiarity required a mobilization of cultural meanings, practices, codes and colours borrowed from international conventions (in its rectangular form and standard dimensions, for example) but reworked through Indian cultural traditions.

The second dimension of this book is cultural. The elaboration of a sense of belonging to a nation through the medium of the flag was not based on the political use of invented or real Indian political traditions. It implied the elaboration of a new symbolic language allowing the constitution of a new political culture produced during the national movement. In a way, the flag allowed a rupture with a political past while giving the impression that it included both Western and Indian traditions. The modes of individual and collective appropriation of this new type of symbolic object for India demand quite a different treatment from that contained in a political narrative approach. The cultural narrative principally mobilizes anthropological methods devoted to the uses and perceptions of colours and symbols as well as the organization and implementation of private and public rituals.

The third inquiry brings us back to the flag itself. It raises the question of the capacity of this material object to nourish and provoke feelings and emotions. It considers this emotional charge progressively infused into the flag from a dual perspective, first through the politicization of the object, then paradoxically through its depoliticization when included in very familiar and intimate practices. As a politicized object it was capable of strengthening collective mobilization and, at the same time, disciplining individual behaviours and organizing group action. A certain success led to its use in more private spaces, which in their turn reinforced its impact. It is no longer possible to treat the flag as an annexe to other projects, movements, and agendas;

its specific dynamics often imposed particular forms of collective action, independent of political slogans, goals, and stakes. In a country as strongly divided as India on religious, linguistic, community, and ethnic lines, it offered a common meeting ground and political grammar to all Indians, irrespective of their origins, gender, community, class, or age. It proposed a novel way for the co-ordination of political passions.

1

An Imperial Identity for India?

The Indian government reconstructed the history of the national flag—*Our Flag*—after independence in a small illustrated booklet destined for schoolchildren and republished continuously until today. The flag was here presented as a deliberate, self-conscious, persistent quest of nationalist leaders, beginning with the Bengal partition in 1905 and ending in its unanimous acclaim by the Constituent Assembly in July 1947.[1] According to this official version of India's independence, the struggle for freedom was accompanied by the search for and emergence of successive versions of a national flag until it matured to its final, finished form, popularly recognized and accepted as the national symbol of all Indians. This presentation of the flag as a natural, logical response of Indians to imperial domination, an almost intuitive expression of their profoundly distinctive identity, understandably satisfactory from the government's point of view, rests on a linear and unanimous schema or a success story marked by the absence of any questionings or doubts, failures, and rejections which inevitably characterize the history of national political symbols. The success of one national emblem has also to be understood as the failure of so many others which could not impose themselves on a national level, or on the national psyche, as the story of those that never made it to constitutional recognition. A striking example among others is Germany, where the figure of 'German Michael' never struck root in public consciousness, mainly because of his pacific qualities, which

[1] 'The evolution of the Indian National Flag reflects the political developments in the country during the twentieth century.' This is the line proposed since the first government publication in 1950 of *Our Flag* (Government of India, Ministry of Information and Broadcasting, Publications Division, revised edition, New Delhi, 1989, p. 1; 1st edn, 1950; 2nd edn, 1963).

were largely unappreciated in the political climate of the late nineteenth and twentieth century—a period marked by German preoccupation with international status and power. Similarly, in France the battle to impose Marianne was not won in a day but lasted nearly a century.[2] So, not only does the Indian official version of the flag efface or dismiss the role of a host of other more obscure Indian actors and antagonists, it also repudiates the part played by the British. Paradoxically, it was certain Britishers who first broached the issue of a flag for India at the turn of the nineteenth century, and the flag can be said to have been the outcome of a metropolitan debate.

The Symbolic Stakes of Edward VII's Coronation, 1901–1903

British attention turned to the need for a distinctive Indian flag at a particularly eventful juncture in the history of the British Isles. Queen Victoria's death on 23 January 1901 entailed the ritual of a royal coronation that had almost been forgotten during her long reign of sixty-four years. The domestic relevance of this event was heightened by its even greater imperial significance. For her son Edward VII acceded not only to the throne of England but also inherited the title of Emperor of India, as well as the additional status of Emperor of British Dominions beyond the seas. The ceremonial implications of these titles of the British monarch required the elaboration of new procedures and etiquette, rules of royal protocol and proprieties unknown at Victoria's coronation in 1837. How were the British dominions and colonies that lay at the heart of British identity to be now represented in the rituals of monarchical succession?

Great Britain's relationship with her overseas dominions had been a matter of some concern since the Boer War. Critics of her imperialist ambitions at home and a growing patriotic public opinion in the empire pressed for its redefinition. Against this background, the question of representing empire in coronation ceremonies was brought to the fore, from the point of view of monarchy and of the metropolis but

[2] Tomasz Szarota, *Der deutsche Michel. Die Geschichte eines nationalen Symbols und Autostereotyps* (Osnabrück, Fibre, 1998); Maurice Agulhon, *Marianne into Battle. Republican Imagery and Symbolism in France, 1789–1880* (Cambridge, Cambridge University Press, 1981).

equally from the perspective of the sentiments and distinctive identities of the dominions and colonies. Whereas Victoria's coronation had been a largely domestic affair, over the long period of her reign she had slowly but surely accumulated an impressive array of imperial titles that she now bequeathed to her successor. For the first time, a king of Great Britain was crowned with the Imperial State Crown instead of the St Edward's Crown, as his predecessors had been.[3] Thus, Edward VII's coronation had markedly ostentatious imperial overtones. J.E.C. Bodley's commissioned official account of the succession presented it as a great imperial event destined for 'the conservation of the imperial idea'. The title of this historian's work, *The Coronation of Edward the Seventh: A Chapter of European and Imperial History*, is self-explanatory. Newspapers trumpeted the imperial might of England in self-congratulatory terms, a fact that was sure to be 'instinctively recognized by the people as a sign of the new place we have in the world.'

The arrival in London of a large number of dignitaries from dominions and colonies received particularly widespread media coverage; the spectacular presence of thirty-one Indian princes and princesses, with their stately retinues, gave the Indian empire a particularly prominent place. Above this visible diversity of the British empire, the coronation sought to manifest its fundamental unity of aims and outlook: 'Whatever be the differences of race, or of history, or of creed between them, they are our people with a common inheritance, a common mission and a common duty. They are found to preserve the fabric of British polity and of British civilization.'[4] How could this union be expressed during the imperial ritual without suppressing an evident diversity, itself a sign of Britain's political power? The coronation thus became the occasion that opened an unforeseen public debate on appropriate symbols for the British nation and her dominions, a debate that has until now almost entirely escaped the attention of historians. This debate extended well beyond the ceremonial moment—originally fixed for 26 June 1902 but postponed to 9 August because of Edward's appendicitis operation. It was in this new context, at once British and

[3] The point is made by Jeffrey Richards, *Imperialism and Music. Britain 1876–1953* (Manchester, Manchester University Press, 2001), pp. 101–2.

[4] *The Times*, August 1902. Also quoted by Jeffrey Richards, op. cit., p. 103.

imperial, that, for the first time, the political question of a flag for India was explicitly raised.

Some weeks before the coronation, in May 1902, the India Office in London received an unusual enquiry from one William Coldstream, a nondescript retired British officer of the Indian Civil Service living in London. Thirty-three years of service in the Punjab province, from 1861 to 1894, and a family tradition of serving the empire (his son was even then in the British Indian army), explained the interest this former civil servant retained in the relationship between Britain and her Indian empire, which, in his view, would be ensured by a considerate regard for Indian sentiments.[5] His letter expressed a particular concern for India's identity within the British empire.

> I trouble you with an enquiry which I ventured to think you will not deem out of place under present circumstances. Briefly is there any flag or heraldic device which can be used on a flag bearing proper sanction, which can be to represent India, as the flags of other parts of the British Empire represent them? Scotland, Ireland, Wales and I believe the Colonies or some of them have their proper flags or heraldic blazons and some of them are embodied in the Royal Standard. I am not aware that any such has been sanctioned for India: but if it be so, we'll be greatly obliged if I can be informed on the subject. If there is no flag, or heraldic device capable of being used on a flag proper to India—I humbly submit the suggestion that it would be eminently appropriate and desirable that such should be devised and sanctioned by the proper authority. I suggest to embody the idea of the unity of India with the British Empire. It is unnecessary perhaps to add that the present moment would be an obviously fitting occasion to inaugurate the use of an appropriate and special Indian flag or blazon. London is full of Indians; their numbers will greatly increase during the next few weeks and I venture to think that our fellow subjects from the East would regard with much satisfaction the free use of such a symbol in the coming rejoicings. I also think that Anglo Indians would willingly adopt it and use on such an occasion as the present in loyal regard to the great and growing country where their life work has been mostly done.

[5] The biography of W. Coldstream is practically unknown; the principal facts can be found in *Who was Who in India? 1897–1996. One Hundred Years of Biography* (London, A.&C. Black, 1996).

P.S. It may be too large and difficult a question to decide at once (if there is no flag such as I suggest); in that can I submit that some device might be temporarily or tentatively sanctioned for present use as the opportunity is a very important one and I submit the need pressing. I venture to think that it is possible or even probable that happy results (hardly to be measured indeed by a visible standard) would flow from the subtle influence of the display of a symbol of this kind on such an occasion. It is pertinent to note that the symbolism of a flag is appreciated in India perhaps more than in England.[6]

This astonishingly long and unique letter allows us to discover some of the preoccupations of the period which do not appear so clearly in political accounts. Coldstream aimed to convince the government on one single point: it was immediately necessary to give India a strong and distinct political symbol. If a close reading of the letter highlights the occasion of the coronation ('an obviously fitting occasion', 'a very important opportunity') as responsible for the formulation of the problem, it also reveals that the situation could itself contribute to its resolution. Certainly, even if the evidence is missing, it would not be wrong to suppose that such a strongly worded argument reflected a preoccupation in some Anglo-Indian circles about the political equality of the various dominions and colonies, and the fitting manner of rendering this symbolically visible. More than that, it would serve to build a consensus between colonizers: here principally the 'Anglo-Indians'; and the colonized—the Indian princes present in London, and, more generally 'our fellow subjects from the East'—a consensus that would surely contribute to the cohesion of the empire. Coldstream's intuition led him to understand the importance of ritual for the Indians present in London: indeed, one of them, writing a few days after the coronation in a similar vein, expressed his strong desire to 'symbolize relations so unprecedented . . . which have grown up between our Sovereign and his Indian Empire'.[7]

If Coldstream insisted on the necessity of finding a solution, even temporary, as soon as possible, he nonetheless underlined the difficulties

[6] OIOC, L/P&J/6/602, William Coldstream to India Office, London, 31 May 1902.

[7] *The Times*, 14 August 1902, 'India and the Ceremonies of Empire', p. 6.

of the task: he no doubt had a sharper knowledge of this complex subject, since he referred to the royal standard, and never to the Union Flag, as if aware of the unresolved ambiguities of the latter and of the plasticity of the former, which, for many people, 'shares the position of the national flag with the Union jack'.[8] Indeed, every new sovereign had upon his succession the possibility of redesigning his own standard, according to the current political situation.[9] One possible solution in the light of custom to Coldstream's query could have been that Edward VII include a reference to India in his own royal standard. The only major factor Coldstream could hardly have predicted was the 'so lively and discursive a discussion.'[10] This began in the months that followed the coronation, from September 1902 to the end of 1903, and centred on the nature and meanings of the symbolic representation of nation and state in Great Britain.[11] The stakes involved in this discussion conditioned the answer to Coldstream's demand.

In the climate of national euphoria created by Edward VII's succession, bursting through the formal confines of conventions and ceremonies, and lingering on after the event, the British flag appeared everywhere and anywhere, from house façades to street displays to shops and tea packets and playing cards. But what did it stand for? From the beginning the debate questioned the uncertain nature and the 'misconceptions' of the 'Union Jack', as it was popularly known: was it the flag of the sovereign or the flag of the nation, with its three crosses evoking the union to England of Scotland (1707) and Ireland (1800)?[12] If it was the flag of the sovereign, could it then represent the

[8] This is the interpretation given by E.M.C. Barraclough, *Flags of the World* (London, Warne, 1950; 7th edn, 1971), p. 23.

[9] For the 'royal standard', see W.G. Perrin, *British Flags*, op. cit., pp. 74–6.

[10] So the debate was described by a correspondent in a paper titled 'The Union Flag. Its Earlier History', *The Times*, 30 September 1903, p. 5.

[11] This debate has been followed through articles, editorials, and letters to the editor published in one of the major dailies of the period, *The Times*. Despite its obvious limits, this examination highlights the principal stakes and positions on the issue.

[12] A number of booklets and songs on the flag printed in this period testify to the public interest in the subject. For example, *Our National Flag: What it is and what it is not, by an old naval officer* (London, editor unknown, 1902, known re-editions in 1903 and 1909); William Marshall Hutchison, *Under One Flag.*

whole of the territories subject to Edward VII, that is to say, the British empire?[13] A century earlier, in 1800, on Ireland's union with England, a similar query had been addressed by a British citizen to Whitehall, relating to the official uses of the flag in the empire. Were the flags used in the East India Company's various dependencies in India the colours of the British nation or those of the Company, asked a certain John Meheux. For the secretary of East India House the fact that they were the 'British colours' had appeared self-explanatory and sufficient.[14] If the same question now resurfaced in the public arena with even greater force it was because, as one reader explained, 'the sentiment which the flag inspires is of modern growth' and, using the same argument as Coldstream, 'because for fifty years there had been no great national emergency to call it forth.'[15]

Among the motley collection of queries that appeared in the press, at least three sets of questions can be distinguished. The first, hardly unexpected, concerned its origins and questioned its progressive emergence and evolution from a navy flag to a problematic emblem of national identity. The second, seemingly quite trivial, excited perhaps the greatest passion and remains an open issue even to the present day. Letters to the editor poured in on this subject from October to December 1903, particularly from navy officers and general readers rejecting or defending the term 'Union Jack' with passion and conviction. The absence of juridical norms encouraged readers to disagree in their exposition of details and information. They expounded on the exact naval meaning of 'jack' as being the name for the Union Flag only when flown at the main masthead,[16] whose use is noted at least from 1633,[17]

March introducing the . . . Song (P.F. London, Jeffery, 1898); *Our Flag! Patriotic Song, written and composed by S. Bath* (London, Weekes & Co., 1902); Mervyn Edwar, *Our British Flag. March* (London, E. Ascherber & Co., 1901); Renwol Malcolm, *Our Empire Flag. Patriotic Song* (London, Vincent Music Co., 1906).

[13] *The Times*, 10 October 1902, p. 6; 11 October 1902, p. 9; 13 October 1902, p. 15; 30 September 1903, p. 5.

[14] OIOC, H/787, 12 November 1800, letter from John Meheux to East India House.

[15] *The Times*, 13 October 1902, p. 15.

[16] E.M.C. Barraclough, op. cit., p. 12.

[17] W.G. Perrin, op. cit., p. 61; Gordon Campbell and I.O. Evans, in *The Book*

or, according to other authors, from the reign of Queen Anne.[18] Readers of *The Times* thus learnt that this fundamental technical distinction had been lost sight of, and that there was a general misapplication of the term 'jack'. When in 1603 James I proclaimed the union of the St George' Cross and the St Andrew Cross on ship flags, no name was given to this unified flag. It appeared to have been first called the 'British flag'. The word 'union' only surfaced in 1625, when it was mentioned in the list of flags and banners used at the funeral of James I.[19] The title 'Union Jack' for the flag would then have been used along with 'Union Flag'.[20] These same terms were still mentioned in the Queen's Regulations of 1899. In short, 'if any one contends that Union Jack is only a vulgar misnomer for the Union Flag, he is manifestly flying in the face, not only of history and usage, but of Royal authority, and to all appearance of direct official prescription'.[21]

The third and for us most relevant inquiry pondered over its relevance for the empire's subjects. Could they be satisfied with the current pattern of representing them through a small annexe in the Union Flag? It was this last aspect that was most directly linked with the question of India, and which must be considered here.

Briefly, the British system followed the simple principle of representing its dominions and colonies by using the Union Flag with the distinctive badge of the particular dominion or colony. This practice had its roots in a decision of 1866—that all ships employed in the service of British colonies should fly a blue ensign with the seal or emblem of the colony concerned shown on the fly. Later, the blue ensign

---

of Flags, op. cit., p. 17, define the 'jack' differently—as a 'small flag at the bowsprit . . . or stem of a ship'. Barraclough, op. cit., pp. 12–13, indicates that the second practice was substituted for the first.

[18] Gordon Campbell and I.O. Evans, op. cit., p. 17.

[19] One example among many others of the prevailing uncertainty: according to W.G. Perrin, op. cit., this union of the English and Scotland signs 'excited little attention, except from those directly concerned with shipping', p. 58.

[20] This imprecise terminology was partly due to the fact that after the seventeenth century, 'the Union Flag was rarely seen at sea in any other position making the misapplication of the term Jack almost universal', W.G. Perrin, op. cit., p. 73.

[21] *The Times*, 1 October 1903, p. 13, 'The Union Flag. Its Present Form' (From a Correspondent).

was replaced with the red ensign. This served to represent the sovereign and her representatives. In 1869 Queen Victoria authorized the creation of such a flag for Canada by the inclusion of a special badge in the centre of the Union Flag. The design of this badge, containing the quartered arms of the four founding provinces in maple leaves and surmounted with a crown, was approved on 16 July 1870.[22] South African colonies under British administration followed this system: the coat of arms of the Cape Colony and the seal of Natal-Transvaal presented by a landscape with trees and a lion, and the Orange River Colony a springbok on a mound upon the British flag.[23] Malta, which came under British protection in 1814, had a new flag—a shield halved vertically in white and red with a red and white cross overall—probably since the 1870s.[24] New Zealand had already drawn attention to the range of possibilities in the political spectrum between empire, Commonwealth and independent nation. As early as 1834 the British Resident of New Zealand had proposed that it should have a national flag, which was chosen by the Maori chiefs: the cross of St George on white with four stars on the left upper quarter.[25] In 1901 the six states of Australia (New South Wales, Victoria, Queensland, South Australia, West Australia, and Tasmania) united in a federation of the Commonwealth of Australia, with a new flag, the Southern Cross under the Union Jack.[26]

So the British voiced their attachment to this symbol for which 'we have spent 200 millions and thousands of our best lives for it' and claimed their right to display it as they willed, and defined its meanings and relevance—for 'the crosses have been dyed a deeper red, the white

[22] Conrad Swan, *Canada, Symbols of Sovereignty* (Toronto, University of Toronto Press, 1977), p. 76.

[23] *Flags, Badges and Arms of the British Dominions beyond the Seas* (Part I—Flag and Badges) (London, HMSO, 1910) (copy preserved in the Royal Commonwealth Collection, Cambridge).

[24] E.M.C. Barraclough, op. cit., p. 149.

[25] Gordon Campbell and I.O. Evans, op. cit., p. 101.

[26] Nora Hewett, *Peeps at the Union Jack and Other Principal Flags of the British Empire* (London, A. & C. Black, 1928), pp. 58–61. On the use of flags, badges, and arms of the British dominions, one of the rare pamphlets available was published only in 1910, *Flags, Badges and Arms*, op. cit.

field has been kept clean, the sea power on which the glorious combination rests has been maintained and all as the manifest result of the common effort of a united people'.[27] And simultaneously, the dominions too were witnessing the growth of a new flag patriotism that was particularly in evidence since the Boer War in Australia and New Zealand, to the point of being inculcated in schoolchildren through a regular drill of salutation.[28]

Whereas in one sense this debate was quite inconclusive—for questions were raised and many answers were proposed without any single one being legitimized by public consent or official decree[29]—in another sense it was not so much the answers as the inquiries that were of the greatest significance. The discussion itself seems to have died a natural death after 1903. No royal proclamation or parliamentary ruling regulating the status of the national flag or its use by private citizens or official representatives in England was issued. Thus, throughout the century the two labels 'Union Jack' and 'Union Flag' continued to be used in official documents, the British government of India often using the term 'Union Jack'.[30] But the discussion had drawn attention to a dimension of the flag that was of particular interest in the actual political conjuncture. This was its potential for depicting qualities of citizenship and identity. Edwardian England was rediscovering a new expression for Englishness. Paradoxically, a ceremony destined to project the monarchy as the source of power and unity had inadvertently drawn attention to the flag's capacity for representing a national and imperial identity.

[27] *The Times*, 13 October 1902, p. 15, Letter to the Editor from G. Wheatly Cobb.

[28] Anne Bloomfield, 'Drill and Dance as Symbols of Imperialism', in J.A. Mangan (ed.), *Making Imperial Mentalities, Socialisation and British Imperialism* (Manchester, Manchester University Press, 1990), pp. 74–95.

[29] In answer to a demand for a more precise legislation defining the 'correct flag' to be flown on land by civilians, atop public buildings and schools in Great Britain and in the colonies, Balfour answered in October 1902 that the government did not intend to introduce any new legislation: 'It is a matter which is best left, as hitherto, to the guidance of custom and good taste', in *The Parliamentary Debates. Session 1902*, vol. 13 (London, Wyman and Sons, 1902), pp. 466–7.

[30] On the use of 'Union Flag' and 'Jack', cf. E.M.C. Barraclough, op. cit., pp. 20–3.

Colonial Nationalism *vs* Imperial Patriotism

At the time when Coldstream was expressing his apprehensions about the lack of an adequate and satisfactory representation of the unity of India and the empire, Richard Jebb, a British journalist of Irish origins, was voicing the same sentiments with far greater vigour in a paper entitled 'Colonial Nationalism' published in the *Empire Review* in August 1902.[31] One of the foremost advocates of a deeper imperial partnership, nourished by the respect of their partners, Jebb was a product of Oxford, that bastion of 'sentinels of Empire'.[32] His aspirations to enter the Indian Civil Service had been thwarted by the unexpected death of both his father and brother and he found himself instead taking over the direction of the family estate. Nevertheless, he had not entirely abandoned his university passion for the Athenian and Roman empires, and, though fate had prevented him from pursuing his academic interest in the empires of the past, he now transferred this interest to the contemporary British empire. From 1899 to 1902, in precisely the critical years preceding Edward's coronation, he undertook a 'grand tour' of England's dominions, beginning with Australia and New Zealand, and going on to Canada and South Africa, in order to study developments in the empire from the perspective of the dominions. In a grand survey of what he dared to call 'colonial nationalism'—a combination of two notions that a priori excluded one another—Jebb asserted: 'The nationalist movement, led by Canada and Australia, is defining rapidly the limitations which an imperial union must respect. The popular habit of alluding to "the British nation" in a sense inclusive of colonial peoples already is an anachronism. It has become evident that the fundamental principle of any real advance towards closer union must be the frank recognition of independent national instincts in the four principal self-governing colonies, in varying stages of evolution.'[33]

[31] John Eddy and Deryck Shreuder (ed.), *The Rise of Colonial Nationalism. Australia, New Zealand, Canada and South Africa first Assert their Nationalities, 1880–1914* (Sydney-Boston, Allen & Unwin, 1988), p. 94; for a biographical presentation of Jebb, ibid., p. 64.

[32] The expression is that of Richard Symonds, *Oxford and Empire. The Lost Cause?* (Oxford, Clarendon Press, 1986).

[33] Richard Jebb, *Studies in Colonial Nationalism* (London, E. Arnold, 1905),

Jebb's lectures and articles during his tour through the dominions emphasized that the growth of national sentiment necessitated a corresponding change in the colonial connection. He foresaw the risk of emerging nations being repelled by the restrictiveness of the imperial system and drifting apart altogether. The idea of a mere alliance, he warned, was no longer satisfactory, and commercial or defensive interests would not suffice to hold the empire together. For the dominions, he insisted, loyalty to empire could not be expected to mean subservience. What was required to weld them together was a 'sentimental sanction'.[34] Jebb was really pleading for the cultivation of an imperial patriotism as a check to the rising tide of colonial nationalism and while Coldstream was not worrying about the problems raised by the growth of national self-consciousness in India, both expressed a similar concern for a suitable consideration and valorization of the dominions' and colonies' distinctiveness.

Even if the reflections on empire by these two Englishmen were not widely shared in the early twentieth century, they expressed an approach to the imperial question by non-specialists that acknowledged the need to strengthen the emotional bonds between Britain and her colonies. Their proposition of developing the ties of sympathy and sensitivity—in short, of rendering imperialism more humane—could be seen as a redefinition of empire following the denunciation of imperialism proposed by J.A. Hobson's *Imperialism*, published in the same context, in 1902, in reaction to the South African war. The preoccupation with integrating the British empire more closely was a topical question in these years: thus it formed the principal agenda of the colonial conference organized by Joseph Chamberlain in June 1902, a few weeks before the planned coronation.[35] Infusing colonial domination with a spirit of mutual co-operation was an idea that was also making inroads in Milner's kindergarten—the staff of young Oxford graduates recruited by Milner for the reconstruction of South

---

p. 273. Cf. John D.B. Miller, *Richard Jebb and the Problem of Empire* (London, Athlone Press, 1956).

[34] Richard Jebb, *Studies*, op. cit., pp. 277–9.

[35] Phillips Payson O'Brien, 'The Titan Refreshed: Imperial Overstretch and the British Navy before the First World War', *Past and Present*, no. 172, August 2001, pp. 146–9.

Africa when he was a British high commissioner there from 1897 to 1905. Reconciliation and consensus instead of supremacy and coercion were the key words for these imperialists.[36]

Nonetheless, Jebb's and Coldstream's propositions did not evoke widespread sympathy or even win them great notoriety. Coldstream's letter, it is true, had a certain impact within the closed circuits of India Office and the bureaucratic corridors of the Government of India, but it received absolutely no publicity or media exposure. Nor did Jebb's book fetch him much popularity. His reflections and analysis developed during his travels through South Africa and Canada, instead of winning him converts on the field, more often than not aroused hostility amongst his readers and audiences. A concept, which looked at empire from the perspective of the colonies and recognized their desire for self-identity to the extent of legitimizing it through a new term, 'colonial nationalism', was still too marginal and odd. In manuscript his *Studies in Colonial Nationalism* was rejected by Methuen and when it was finally accepted by Edward Arnold it was only because the publishers felt it would 'be novel and interesting to most English readers'.[37] It is not known whether the publishers' decision met with the approbation of readers. Yet, though no widespread echo of Jebb's views was to appear in the studies of imperialism, either at the time or later,[38] they were nonetheless noted by Milner's kindergarten, as revealed Lord Selborne's remarks to the Governor of Natal, Manfred Nathan, in 1908: 'I have always believed that the best chance for its [the Empire's] future lies in fostering what Jebb calls colonial nationalism.'[39]

However the political practice of reinforcing the sentimental bond between Britain and its colonies that was the basis of 'colonial nationalism' was one of the classical instruments of British colonization, at least after 1857. It had justified Queen Victoria's elevation to Empress

[36] Saul Dubow, 'Colonial Nationalism, The Milner Kindergarten and the Rise of "South Africanism" ', 1902–10', *History Workshop Journal*, no. 43, 1997, pp. 53–86.

[37] Richard Jebb, op. cit., pp. 64, 94, 193.

[38] It must be noted that this notion was ignored by historiography until the 1980s and the publication of John Eddy and Deryck Shreuder (eds), *The Rise of Colonial Nationalism*, op. cit.

[39] Saul Dubow, *Colonial Nationalism*, op. cit., pp. 66, 82.

of the Indian empire,[40] and the grant of high-sounding titles to the Indian princes and dignitaries on the occasion. All this aimed to ensure the 'sympathetic and cordial allegiance' of the native aristocracy to the crown.[41] The sentimental bond was at the heart of official celebrations such as the 1887 durbar marking the jubilee of Queen Victoria's accession to the throne or her diamond jubilee in 1897. Sentiment for monarchy and through it to the empire was built up by the tours of the Prince of Wales to Canada in 1860, India in 1876, by the Duke of Edinburgh's visit to the Australian colonies in 1867, and by the Duke of Cornwall and York's visit to Canada in September 1901.[42] They were all aimed at impressing and dazzling the popular imagination with a sense of their closeness and solidarity with the mother country. But the idea of expressing this relationship in a form other than the monarchy and by means other than those of pomp and circumstance, pageantry, frills, and royal magnificence was something new. Jebb and Coldstream had advanced the idea that perhaps, after all, the empire could not depend forever on 'ornamentalism' with its roots in the metropolitan social commitment to hierarchy and status, ostentatious display and monarchical exhibitionism of titles, ceremonial rituals, and royal status.[43] Something else was called for.

While monarchy still remained the focal point of attention in imperial ceremonies and celebrations, an organized movement around

[40] On 28 April 1876 the bill declaring Queen Victoria Empress of India was passed in Parliament. For Disraeli's role, Queen Victoria's own position and Lord Lytton's views, cf. L.A. Knight, 'The Royal Titles Act and India', *The Historical Journal*, XI, 1968, pp. 488–507.

[41] Lord Northbrook to Queen Victoria, 4 May 1876, in P.N. Chopra (ed.), *Secret Papers from British Royal Archives* (Delhi, Konark Publishers, 1998), pp. 29–32.

[42] On the uses of royal symbolism to build sentiment for empire, cf. David Cannadine, 'The Context Performance and Meaning of Ritual: The British Monarchy and "the Invention of Tradition", *c.* 1820–1977', in Eric Hobsbawm and Terence Ranger (eds), *The Invention of Tradition* (Cambridge, Cambridge University Press, 1983), pp. 101–64; Phillip Buckner, 'Casting Daylight upon Magic: Deconstructing the Royal Tour of 1901 to Canada', *Journal of Imperial and Commonwealth History*, XXX, 1, 2003, pp. 158–89.

[43] The word, taken from the title of David Cannadine's book *Ornamentalism. How the British saw their Empire* (London, Penguin, 2001), announces the

the Union Jack was born which asserted that the flag was the unifying symbol of an imperial identity. This was the Empire Day movement, one of those public rituals of propaganda seeking to modulate the opinions of individuals that were to characterize political regimes in the twentieth century.[44] Its elaboration in England in 1903 by the twelfth Earl of Meath, Reginald Brabazon, was not a sudden decision. Since 1892 he had been urging the London County Council to adopt a pedagogy of instilling a spirit of patriotism among schoolchildren. In 1896 he had suggested in *The Times* that the Queen's birthday, 24 May, designated 'Empire Day', be made a holiday—after a morning ritual of singing the national anthem in schools and a salutation of the flag, athletic displays, drills, parades, and gymnastics. From the perspective of empire it would help renew the imperial commitment in the British dominions, crown colonies, and its Indian empire. The idea made some inroads in British dominions like Canada, where the county of Ontario decreed 24 May a school holiday in 1897 and an act of 1901 made it a legal holiday throughout Canada. Then, in 1902, Earl Meath urged Joseph Chamberlain to seize the occasion presented by the arrival of the various colonial prime ministers and governors in London for the coronation. This was 'an ideal moment to bring the subject before them and involve them in spreading the movement throughout the empire'.[45] In 1903 the earl founded an organization to promote Empire Day, and the first public observance in England was held in

author's emphasis on the pivotal role of monarchy, its style of tradition and values of privilege, status, and hierarchy in the maintenance of empire.

[44] The strong emotional impact of political parades had already been grasped by French revolutionaries as early as the eighteenth century, especially Rousseau, although their use to further national unity through the elaboration of a new liturgy of songs, military displays, and colourful processions was a progressive development under the Second Empire in France or in Bismarckian Germany. George L. Mosse underlines the emergence and manipulation of a new terrain of political debate dominated by public national festivals: *The Nationalization of the Masses. Political Symbolism and Mass Movements in Germany from the Napoleonic Wars through the Third Reich* (New York, H. Fertig, 1975).

[45] John M. Mackenzie, *Propaganda and Empire. The Manipulation of British Public Opinion 1880–1960* (Manchester, Manchester University Press, 1986), pp. 231–3.

1904.[46] Around the two symbols of the national flag and the anthem, the ritual sought to emphasize 'imperial virtues' of loyalty, patriotism, courage, respect for laws, and the subordination of personal interests to the general, collective interest.[47] Sustained by the Church and Boy Scouts of England, the movement gradually swelled into a wider national tradition from the narrower public school tradition where it had taken root.[48] While the virtuous notes of duty and responsibility lent themselves particularly well to sermons,[49] those of obedience and heroic patriotism appealed equally to Scouts, more concerned with Britain and the British than with England and the English.[50] The imperial catechism of 'one King, one Flag, one Fleet and one Empire' drummed up the imperial catchwords: responsibility, duty, and sacrifices.[51] Empire Day could be celebrated at the same time in different places just as the ancient 'Te Deum' had been sung in parishes all over France to celebrate the king's victories and good fortune. But, unlike the latter, which depended on royal 'successes' and was therefore impossible to schedule with regularity, Empire Day once fixed, would be as regular as a natural season.[52]

The widespread success of Empire Day clearly shows that as far as the relationship between Britain and her colonies was concerned, the exaltation of empire had greater appeal than the nascent desire of overseas Britishers to win for their new country some of the attributes of a nation. However, the two paths were not incompatible.

[46] *Report on the Empire Day Movement*, 1937, p. 43 (copy in the Royal Commonwealth Society Collection, Cambridge University Library).

[47] Speech delivered by the Earl of Meath on 24 May 1905, in Marie Blanc, *The Empire Day, 24 May 1908* (Port Louis, Mauritius, 1908), p. 1.

[48] J.A. Mangan, 'The Grit of Our Forefathers. Invented Traditions, Propaganda and Imperialism', in John M. Mackenzie (ed.), *Imperialism and Popular Culture* (Manchester, Manchester University Press, 1986), p. 134.

[49] Rev. M.H. James, *Our Great Inheritance. A Plain Sermon for Empire Day* (London, Skeffington & Son, 1909), p. 9.

[50] Sam Pryke, 'The Popularity of Nationalism in the early British Boy Scout Movement', *Social History*, vol. 23, no. 3, October 1998, pp. 309–24.

[51] M. Blanc, op. cit.

[52] Its origins and diffusion in England are examined by J.M. Mackenzie, *Propaganda and Empire*, op. cit., pp. 231–3.

Mr Coldstream, the Viceroy, and the Indian Flag

Coldstream's proposal indeed contained both perspectives, the distinctiveness of the colony and its necessary union with the empire. Hence his interest in 'a flag proper to India' which, at the same time, could also 'embody the idea of the unity of India with the British Empire'. The renewed vigour with which the imperial question imposed itself in 1902 in the metropolis as well as in the colonies gave Coldstream's letter an importance that it would probably not have achieved in other circumstances. The problems it raised drew the attention of the secretary of state, who forwarded it almost at once to the viceroy of India. An official file was opened which was to pursue the Government of India for the rest of the half century.[53] In the immediate moment, through the summer to September 1902, letters, notes, memoranda went back and forth from the secretary of state in London and the viceroy in India. An initial minute paper on the question opened the debate on Coldstream's question. By the beginning of July the secretary of state, Lord Hamilton, had already received a succinct report on the state of heraldic devices or coats of arms in India. At the end of the month he insisted on a response to Coldstream's inquiry:

> In connection with the preparations for celebrating His Majesty's Coronation, my attention has been drawn to the fact that India has no distinctive flag and the suggestion has been made that on grounds of expediency and sentiment, as well as for ceremonial purposes, a flag and perhaps armorial bearings should be prescribed, embodying the idea of the unity of that great dependency with the British Empire . . . I commend this question to His Excellency's consideration and shall be glad to receive an expression of your view upon it.[54]

His letter caught the Government of India unawares. In fact, no

[53] The correspondence on the question is to be found in the Oriental and India Office Collections, London (OIOC), L/P&J/602, and in NAI, Delhi, Home Public 1902, nos 271–2.

[54] NAI, Home Public 1902, nos 271–2, Secretary of State, Lord George Francis Hamilton to Governor General of India in Council, 25 July 1902.

thought of 'representing India' had worried the viceroy or his cabinet. The question was clearly an offshoot of a recent debate in the metropolis. If a similar discussion had animated British circles in India in the preceding decades, it had not been expressed in such overtly political terms. The problem of the symbolic affirmation of the British presence in India had come up during the discussions on the best and most suitable architectural forms for official buildings, unleashing a veritable 'battle of styles'.[55] For some, it was necessary to faithfully duplicate British architectural traditions and forms in India, while for others the British had to take into consideration India's own culture and continue the indigenous traditions bequeathed by the Mughal emperors. For the former, the display of difference and distance would strengthen their domination by affirming their superiority and mastery, while for the latter proximity and complicity masked the foreign nature of colonial power. The question of the flag transposed this former debate in other terms, without for all that changing positions and stakes: in order to affirm the imperial power, was it better to refuse or reinforce the Indian cultural tradition?

Consultations were now begun with the various government departments in India. During the next two months it became clear that, like most matters of the British government, the practice of flags and their uses was buried in dense fogs of tradition[56] The government's first step was to ascertain which department had jurisdiction over the matter. Each ministry then tried to bounce the ball away. The political department cleverly wrote that while a flag for India certainly ought to be prescribed, they knew nothing about flags or the method of authorizing them. It suggested that the Herald College in London had best be consulted.[57] The home public department then argued that the element of ceremonial really made it a concern of the foreign department, whereas

[55] Thomas R. Metcalf, *An Imperial Vision. Indian Architecture and Britain's Raj* (Oxford, Oxford University Press, 1989).

[56] On this, see Arundhati Virmani, 'Drapeau colonial, drapeau national. De la "Star of India" au "Swaraj flag", 1863–1921', in Christophe Charle, Jacqueline Lalouette, Michel Pigenet, and Anne-Marie Sohn (eds), *La France Démocratique. Combats, mentalités, symboles. Mélanges offerts à Maurice Agulhon* (Paris, Publications de la Sorbonne, 1998), pp. 409–18.

[57] OIOC, L/P&J/602, 2 July 1902.

the latter retorted that it was primarily a matter for consideration by the home department. They would of course be open for consultation on 'the subsidiary point' of the use of such a flag with suitable additions or variations by the native states.[58] Having thus been cornered, the home department then expressed regret that it was 'absolutely impossible to bring the question of a distinctively Indian Flag under any of the heads of business which are relegated to this Department under rules of business.'[59] The public department betrayed the government's complete ignorance of the existing state of flag protocol and ceremonials in India by asking the military department for information on the subject and on the flags used by Indian princes.[60] However, once these technical niceties had been sorted out in what was by government standards a short delay of two months, the Government of India did manage to establish some facts with certainty which revealed, contrary to the initial impression given by Coldstream, that there well and truly existed a complex system of political symbolism mounted by the British for their Indian possessions.

First and foremost, they could all agree on the fact that there had been nothing specifically associated with India in the arms of the East India Company. To begin with, the East India Company had been authorized by Charles I to commerce under the Union Flag 'which our own ships and none but the ships employed in our particular service ought to bear, notwithstanding.'[61] In the seventeenth century the East India Company flag consisted of nine to thirteen alternate red and white stripes. In the upper corner near the staff was a canton containing the red cross of St George on a white field. Probably, the flag derived from that used by Portuguese merchant vessels, these bearing alternate green and white stripes with the Portuguese royal arms superimposed. The English had continued the Portuguese system of granting passes to native vessels sailing under their protection. Although the latter permitted country junks to use their commercial flag minus the

[58] OIOC, L/P&J/602, J.B. Wood, Foreign Dept, 1 September 1902.

[59] OIOC, L/P&J/602, A. Williams, 11 September 1902.

[60] NAI, Home Public, 1902, nos 271–2, Note of H.H. Risley, 16 September 1902.

[61] OIOC, H/39, Special Grant of Charles I, 12 December 1635.

royal arms, the English distinguished their own ships by the use of the national emblem in the canton. In 1707 Queen Anne issued an Order-in-Council under which the Union Flag with the St George's and St Andrew's crosses was to be substituted for the St George's cross in the canton of the Royal Navy's ensign.[62]

Secondly, from the evidence available it is also clear that no arms with special application to India had been substituted for the arms of the Company during the takeover of the Indian empire by the crown in 1858. Indeed, the question had never been raised seriously.[63] When the crown assumed control, the question arose of giving its Indian empire some kind of royal device. Thus, the first symbolic expression of India was from the perspective of the royal monarchy. After a debate that dragged on for three years, a consensus was finally reached on the Star of India in 1861. First proposed as 'the Star of Honour for England and India' or 'The Eastern Star of Honour' by Sir Frederick Currie and Sir John Lawrence, the word 'Honour' was held to be too reminiscent of the famous French decoration. The symbol of the sun was also ruled out for it was felt to be too closely associated with Persia, and various animals and flowers, such as the elephant (too close to the Order of the White Elephant of Denmark), and the thistle or 'Le Saint Esprit', were contemplated but dropped. Prince Albert, who by this time had stepped out of the imperial obscurity of being a mere husband of Queen Victoria and was in all senses a close observer and active participant in the business of government, had followed the discussion with interest.[64] He suggested 'the Eastern Star' but astronomers objected. Moreover, the word 'Eastern' was considered too close to the mutiny begun by the Bengal army and Lord Canning was assured that western India did not think highly of its Eastern neighbours and would not appreciate such a title. 'Western Star' was rejected as well for it was held to suggest the decadence of a heavenly body.

Finally, the civil service stepped in and a five-pointed star was envisaged. This of course raised the heraldic objections that a five-pointed star

[62] C.G.H. Fawcett, 'The Striped Flag of the East India Company', *Mariner's Mirror*, XXIII, 1937, pp. 449–76.

[63] OIOC, L/P&J/6/602, Minute Paper, Public Department.

[64] Lytton Strachey's reconstruction of Albert's emergence from a decorative prince consort to a statesman offers an insight into Victorian politics from a fresh perspective; cf. *Queen Victoria* (London, 1st edn, 1921; 3rd edn, Penguin, 2000).

was a mullet and not a star at all, but the design was retained nevertheless. Further protests from the lord chancellor, Lord Campbell, followed when it was called 'The Star of England and India' for he saw the name as a slight to 'natives of Scotland' who had played such a crucial role in Indian affairs. Yet it could not simply be called 'The Star' or 'The Celestial Star' as the prince consort suggested, for were not all stars celestial? Nor could it be 'The British Star' for the prince consort pedantically maintained there was no such star in heaven. As for the 'Star of Peace', translating that into Hindustani reduced the word only to rest or sleep. No end to these discussions seemed in sight until, finally, the cabinet arbitrarily decided that it would be the 'Star of India'. The motto 'Heaven's Light our Guide' was the translation retained of the Latin 'Lux Coeli Dux Noster' proposed by the prince consort, for Lord Canning had insisted that he would not go down in history as the viceroy who imposed Latin on his Indian subjects.[65] A decision in 1875 decreed that the same device—Union Flag with the Star of India surrounded by a garland on a blue shield and surmounted by a crown[66]—was to be borne on the flags of governors, lieutenant governors, and chief commissioners.[67] Meanwhile, the red and white striped flag, which the East India Company had received in 1668 when Charles II sold Bombay to it, still remained in use on ships of commerce, whether colonial or Indian, according to the Colonial Defence Act of 1865.[68] Military flags on shore would use the Union Flag.[69]

A third and last piece of information which came to light through this circulation of notes and minutes from one department to another made it evident that India's position on the matter of flags to be used was exactly the same as that of the other dominions, although its status within the empire was of course very different from theirs. Dominion flags too had originally been sea flags only, intended to distinguish the vessels of the different colonies.

[65] Sir Malcolm C.C. Seton, *The India Office* (London, Putnam, 1926), pp. 180–3.

[66] OIOC, L/P&J/6/602, Despatch of Lord Salisbury, 28 January 1875.

[67] NAI, Home Public, 1902, nos 271–2, Despatch of H.H. Risley, 21 September 1902.

[68] C.G.H. Fawcett, op. cit., 1937, p. 450; OIOC, L/P&J/6/1720.

[69] NAI, Home Public, 1902, December, nos 271–2, F. Cardew, 17 September 1902, Marine Regulations, India, vol 1, part 1.

At the end of six months of discussion—from July to December 1902—Curzon finally dismissed Coldstream's proposition. In December 1902 his government informed the secretary of state in London that it saw no reason to change the existing situation. Curzon had already announced his personal opinion since September: 'I cannot see that either sentiment or expediency require any alteration to be made, nor can I think of any alteration that would be for the better.'[70] The coming months simply reinforced his views: a satisfactory system for symbolically representing India had been working since decades without creating any difficulty. He referred to Lord Salisbury's decision in 1875, which had laid the ground for representation of India's union with the empire. 'We think', he elaborated, 'that the introduction of a more distinctive and consequently altogether new flag would only give rise to the inconveniences which necessarily result from a multiplication of flags. For example, the merchant vessels of British India would also have to adopt the new flag.' And finally: 'We feel that there is no good reason for a change in the flag currently in use in India [. . .]. As far as arms are concerned [. . .] we prefer the royal arms such as they are currently used.'[71]

The complexity of the British symbolic system contributed to making the debate sometimes uncertain and even ambiguous. On some points Curzon and Coldstream give the impression of being in agreement—on the use of royal arms, for example. But underneath such apparent convergences their stands differed clearly on one issue: Coldstream wished for a real Indian flag, Curzon categorically rejected the idea.

Lord Curzon's Victorian Stability

Curzon was soon to give a more spectacular political demonstration of his position through the organization of a durbar in Delhi to celebrate Edward VII's coronation.[72] This double coronation of the

[70] NAI, Home Public, 1902, December, nos 271–2, Calcutta, 23 September 1902.

[71] Idem, 11 December 1902, Viceroy's Council to Secretary of State for India.

[72] On this subject see Bernard S. Cohn, *An Anthropologist among the Historians and Other Essays* (New Delhi, Oxford University Press, 1987). The institution

king in London and then, represented by his brother the Duke of Connaught, at Delhi on 1 January 1903, he justified by the force of Indian tradition: 'Every sovereign of India or of parts of India did it in the old days, every chief in India—the illustration may even be carried as far as the titled noblemen and zamindars—does it now and the Installation Durbar is an accepted and acceptable feature of ceremonial life from one end of the country to the other'. Apart from serving as a 'form of cohesion', the durbar, claimed Curzon, would inspire a sense of 'fellow-citizenship of the same Empire' and furthermore give the Indian princes, British administrators, soldiers, and civilians from different parts of the country an occasion to meet and exchange ideas.[73] His ardent advocacy of this monarchical ritual, inaugurated in India in 1877, its emblems and insignia, whose character, meaning and evolution he associated with the system of Oriental symbolism,[74] continued the colonial government's firm belief in the power of this ostentatious ritual to enthuse loyalty and strengthen an imperial identity.[75] He defended the expense of the enterprise—negotiated, although unsuccessfully, with the secretary of state—as a gesture of largesse from

---

of the durbar was designed specifically for the Indian situation, though it was also introduced in other British colonies where similar pre-colonial traditions existed. Sir Frederick Lugard thus introduced it in Nigeria in 1911 when he was governor general there. It resembled a traditional ceremony in some parts of Nigeria, known under the name of 'bata' or 'tawar', which marked the last stage in the mobilization and training of volunteers for the army, before the troops embarked on military campaigns. The ceremony continued to be held after Nigeria's independence (1960, 1972, 1977), reincorporating traditional chiefs and other local elements like processions of musicians and singers, which the British had eliminated. Cf. Abdullahi Rafi Augi, 'The History and Performance of Durbar in Northern Nigeria', *Nigeria Magazine*, 1978, pp. 8–39.

[73] Speech in the Imperial Legislative Council at Simla, 5 September 1903, in H. Caldwell Lipsett, *Lord Curzon in India 1898–1903* (London, R.A. Everett & Co., 1903), pp. 122–6.

[74] Marquis Curzon of Kedleston, *British Government in India. The story of the Viceroys and Government Houses* (London, Cassell & Co., 1925), 2 vols, vol. 1, pp. 217–18.

[75] Philip Buckner looks at the Canadian reception of the British monarchy as one of the ways of promoting a sentiment of solidarity with Britain, in 'Casting Daylight . . .', op. cit., pp. 158–89.

the British government that would impress its Indian subjects, such as the reduction of the salt tax and a rise in the level of income tax exemption, and dedicated himself untiringly to the organization and layout of the Durbar.[76] These acts of royal pageantry and spectacle would inevitably dazzle and mesmerize Indians, in particular the Indian princes, by creating an illusion of belonging to a much wider family of aristocracy, headed by the king, to whom of course they were expected to owe allegiance.[77] The argument that the British were only following pre-existing patterns and conventions of rule was generally accepted in official circles. If this allegiance to the same sovereign were to be removed, the theory went, the one universally uniting element of empire would be lost and the nations would be but allies.[78]

The Indian princes, who even more enthusiastically pointed to the political necessity and happy effects of the ritual, welcomed his efforts. The maharaja of Jaipur described the impact of Edward VII's coronation in London as having 'made the deepest impression on my mind, and . . . on the minds of all my brother chiefs who were present there. The great gathering at Delhi will celebrate the same occasion, and I feel it would be a great mistake were so important an event to be ignored

[76] A detailed description of Curzon's organization of the durbar is to be found in David Gilmour's *Curzon* (London, John Murray, 1st edn, 1994, 2nd edn, 1995), pp. 239–46.

[77] The fact that the British recognized status and acknowledged and perpetuated hierarchy in their colonies cannot belie the truth that they also treated the Indian princes as a group to be educated, trained, and always controlled. In this sense, Cannadine's assertion that the British sense of class-consciousness, of superior and inferior social rank, saved them from being a racial imperialist power is a little too rosy. The acceptance of the princes' social superiority in the Indian structure was not a problem for the British. In fact, it added to the lustre of their empire. However, it did not stop them, particularly Curzon, from treating the princes as incapable and unfit to rule. Cf. David Cannadine, *Ornamentalism*, op. cit., p. 126. It is interesting that the new India Office Library in the British Library, London, still prominently displays the portraits of the Indian princes in its Reading Room, and that these constitute the most catchy item of display for visitors' tours through the library.

[78] Bernard Holland, 'The Crown and the Empire', in *The Empire and the Century. A Series of Essays on Imperial Problems and Possibilities by Various Writers* (London, John Murray, 1905), p. 35.

or only superficially honoured in my own dear country.'[79] Another Indian prince corroborated this view: 'In the symbolism which marked the great ceremony we of India see a significance deeper than do other subjects of the British Monarch—all that was done in this respect being in accord with Indian tradition and practice, and being matters to which we attach the highest importance.'[80] Curzon's unrestrained display of royal splendour and magnificence in this durbar translated his firm belief that the sentimental bond between Britain and India could best and indeed exclusively be resumed through the central pivot of the monarch and the crown. There was no place and no need for a flag representing India in this symbolic system.

The 1903 durbar at Delhi thus rivalled if it did not surpass its predecessor of 1877. To his critics—who doubted the money was well spent in a time of some economic distress and who dubbed it the 'Curzonation'—he explained: 'We brought home to them [the people of India] at Delhi that the Prince was now their ruler, and that in his rule were their security and salvation. We touched their hearts with the idea of a common sentiment and a common aim. Depend upon it, you will never rule the East except through the heart, and the moment imagination has gone out of your Asiatic policy your empire will dwindle and decay.'[81] They were all, he proclaimed, the viceroy, the British officers or the Indian princes, actors of the ceremony. It was their king-emperor whose coronation was being celebrated.[82] But Curzon's own imagination was stuck in the past. His belief in the invincible power of rituals of sovereignty checked him from envisaging any manner of portraying India's identity other than through the existing symbolic system and its central ritual of the durbar. He was content to continue with the old practices of royal display, splendour, and magnificence.

Driven by this imperial logic, Curzon's refusal to accommodate any new element or innovation in the durbar made his response to Coldstream's idea outdated, even though it was rooted in long official and

[79] H.C. Lipsett, *Lord Curzon in India*, op. cit., p. 220.

[80] 'India and the Ceremonies of Empire', Letter to the Editor from 'One of the representatives from India', *The Times*, 14 August 1902, p. 6.

[81] H.C. Lipsett, *Lord Curzon in India*, op. cit., p. 41.

[82] Ibid., p. 225.

traditional scepticism about the existence of an Indian nationality or an Indian nation. Had not British administrators like Alfred Lyall,[83] or historians like John Seeley and John Strachey, long confirmed that there was no 'feeling of nationality' of the modern European type in India?[84] From this perspective, which strongly coloured British Indian policy, where was the need for a symbol to express this non-existent germ of Indianness? Curzon's rigid commitment to the political formula of rituals of sovereignty, whose ancient European and Indian lineage and recent enactment in London could be considered sufficient guarantee of its success, thus blinded him to the possible advantages of new demands and proposals.

While 1903 can be read as a political move by Curzon to prove the strength and superiority of his own imperial logic before the naive sentiments expressed by Coldstream, its success was uncertain. Curzon's vision of governing India, centred on an appeal to what he perceived as the Asiatic need for kingship through means of the durbar, no longer convinced all his compatriots. The cabinet had taken umbrage at Curzon's highhanded behaviour. For some Britishers, demonstrations like the durbar 'made no impression on India in general'. They were perceived as England's way of showing her power and she was not loved any better for doing so.[85] Worse, it was arousing vehement criticism from some Indians. A section of public opinion was enraged at the vast expenditure involved and disappointed at the absence of a concrete grant of privileges (the reduction of the salt tax had been refused by the cabinet). It was doubtful whether durbars or royalist sentiment were capturing the minds and hearts of Indians. Certainly, it was undeniable that as a political practice the limits of the durbar ceremonial were as

[83] Sir Alfred Lyall had noted: 'the European observer—accustomed to the massing of people in great territorial groups and to the ideas (now immemorial in the West) contained in such expressions as fatherland, mother-country, patriotism, domicile and the like—has here to realize the novelty of finding himself in a strange part of the world, where political citizenship is as yet quite unknown . . .', *Asiatic Studies* (London, Watts, 1882), p. 152.

[84] Sir John Strachey, *India. Its Administration and Progress* (London, Kegan Paul, 1st edn, 1888, 3rd edn, 1903), pp. 4–9.

[85] Edward F. Elwin, *Indian Jottings. From Ten Years' Experience in and Around Poona City* (London, John Murray, 1907), p. 151.

glaringly obvious as were its glitter and pomp. While its extravagance and splendour could daze spectators and beneficiaries into awed or opportunistic compliance, the rigid, mechanistic, and formal ceremonial lacked the capacity to reach out beyond the spatial precincts of Delhi's Red Fort and the select public of princes and elite. Criticism in India indicated that perhaps very different kinds of sentiments were being generated by this imperial ceremonial than the desired 'community of interest between a sovereign and his people', or between Indians and the rest of the empire.[86] Even some British political observers felt 'the Indian public so used to the splendour of their own kings and courts . . . only find this ceremony wanting and would consequently form a poor opinion of their British masters.' Margaret Noble, known as Sister Nivedita, who had come to India in 1894 as a disciple of Swami Vivekananda and subsequently taken up the cause of India's national revival, confirmed this reaction, quoting the words of a resident of one of the native courts: 'Our impression is that all our Princes have been humiliated in an extreme degree. So India has gained, in the twenty-five years since the last durbar (1877), a good deal of political penetration. They say that the Bengali-English papers criticised everything in a vitriolic style.'[87]

Coldstream's forecast that 'happy results would flow from the subtle influence of the display of a symbol of this kind . . .' showed some political insight in light of the criticisms and reactions that welcomed the 1903 durbar. On the other hand, Curzon's response, formulated after a studied consideration of British imperial practices of symbolic representation, particularly so in India, led him to adopt a position that was politically insensitive and way off the mark. It was all the more astonishing considering his recognition of their mutual need and the importance he attached to the imaginative handling of Britain's relationship with India. Since his arrival in India he had not hesitated in urging Indians to develop a spirit of patriotism for the empire, whose roots would be 'embedded in the traditions and the aspirations of an Eastern people', but which would be 'aglow with the illumination

[86] H.C. Lipsett, *Lord Curzon in India*, op. cit., pp. 121–3.

[87] Letter to Albert and Hollister, Calcutta, 28 January 1903, in Sankari Prasad Basu (ed.), *Letters of Sister Nivedita* (Calcutta, Nababharat Publishers, 1982), vol. 2, p. 539.

of the West'.[88] He would continue to see loyalty to the principle of nationality and to the British empire as consistent and in no way paradoxical in relation to the notion of an Indian identity: 'As nationality is larger than race, so is empire larger than nationality . . . How to adjust race to nationality, and how to reconcile nationality with empire, that is the work which will occupy the British rulers of this country for many a long year to come. I am one of those who believe that it can be accomplished without detriment to race or nationality, and with safety to the empire. I want the Indian people to play their part in this great achievement and to share the results.'[89]

Yet this vision that placed India within the empire ruled out the idea of acknowledging her distinctiveness through a symbol specific to her. Consistent with this policy, Curzon's government responded with similar restraint to Lord Meath's request that the government apply itself to the propagation of Empire Day in India, by declaring 24 May a holiday. Here, he resorted to a more technical argument, namely the difficulty of declaring a holiday in the middle of the school vacations and the lengthening list of holidays that would affect government efficiency. But underlying these reasons lay the belief that rituals of sovereignty were best suited to the Indian context. Discussed by the various departments and local governments during 1904, the main objection advanced was that unity with the empire could be built on loyalty to a common sovereign and not on an impersonal idea of economic coherence or achievement that characterized British imperial possessions. After the traditional round in the education department and consultations with Madras, Bombay, and the Central and United Provinces, the government rejected the proposition. Curzon, in his habitual unambiguous fashion, declared the ritual 'quite unsuited to India', a country where few persons of British descent lived; those that did already had several celebrations connected with the royal family or empire, mainly, 1 January (the anniversary of Victoria's proclamation as Empress of India and the coronation of Edward) and 26 June (the king's birthday):

[88] *Lord Curzon in India. Being a Selection from his Speeches as Viceroy and Governor General of India. 1898–1905* (London, Macmillan, 1906), Speech at the Convocation of Calcutta University, 15 February 1902, p. 489.

[89] Ibid., Speech at the Convocation of Calcutta University, 11 February 1905, pp. 498–9.

> I have always been an entire disbeliever in this project . . . Lord Meath is an excellent enthusiast, who thinks that India is governed by the same sentiments as Canada or New Zealand. India does not want an Empire Day at present; and in so far as it has one, is quite content with January 1, the anniversary of the Proclamation of Queen Victoria and of the celebration of the Coronation of King Edward. The native community does not connect the late Queen with empire, but with motherliness and mercy. Moreover, if her birthday after death is to be celebrated as Empire Day, what is to become of the birthday of King Edward when he dies? According to present symptoms, that will become Peace Day. Then another virtue will have to be connected with his successor, and so on.[90]

Curzon remained convinced that India's consciousness of being part of a larger British union was based entirely on loyalty to a common sovereign. Introducing the note of imperialism was certain to incite dissension.

But while the idea of a flag for India was thus determinedly condemned to the archives of the British government, the search for more appropriate symbolic systems to express 'our true Relationship with India' continued to pursue the British. It surfaced in the form of a cautious warning in Sir Francis Younghusband's Rede Lecture at Cambridge University in 1905. The leader of the Tibet expedition of 1904 suggested that the British management of India be not on 'paternal or fraternal' lines, nor of 'conqueror and conquered', but that it be guided by the fundamental idea of 'a relationship of comradeship'. If the British sacrificed this element for efficiency in civil and military administration, he warned, they would find India only loosely bound to them in times of trouble.[91] Though not articulated in the same terms as Coldstream's, the idea behind these words inevitably raised the question: how was this 'relationship of comradeship' to be satisfactorily articulated and symbolized in the future?

In 1908 another Britisher living in India offered a solution that resurrected Coldstream's proposal. No apparent connection seems to have linked the two Englishmen. Yet, Reverend Richard Burges now

[90] NAI, Home Department, Public Deposit, January 1905, no. 17, Note by Curzon, 18 December 1904.

[91] B. Holland, *The Empire and the Century*, op. cit., pp. 617, 619.

urged the British government to devise a flag for India. Analysing the causes of the unrest in India following the announcement of the Bengal partition in 1905, the Reverend stressed the need to cultivate a sentiment of patriotism for the empire. The durbar method, 'so spectacular and Oriental', he wrote, 'is going out of fashion'. He counselled the adoption of a flag as a first, necessary step in this direction. The problem, in his opinion, was that India had no flag of her own. 'Surely', he wrote, 'the country which contains one-fifth of the human race and three-fourths of the British empire should have at least a special design woven into the Union Jack, as was accorded to other British dominions. In every school the children might be taught not only to distinguish it from others, but that it is theirs and their countries. The educational value of a flag and a cheer, practically unknown now in Indian schools, is very great.'[92] This proposal, published in a modest journal showed the failure of Curzon's political understanding and the solution he had imposed. Despite the official resources the viceroy had mobilized both in India and in Britain to promote his imperial vision in the form of the durbar, the question raised by Coldstream remained. Without any publicity, condemned to obscurity, it nevertheless persisted, resurfacing in another corner of British India with even greater clarity and force. Where Coldstream had been politely suggestive, Burges was categorical in his defence of India's right to be treated on equal grounds as other dominions. Six years earlier Coldstream had deemed a flag for India desirable for the specific political occasion of the coronation. Well after the event, the idea of the 'educational value of a flag' persisted in spite of Curzon's determined effort to prove that it had no place in the British system of representation.

Nowhere was the Government of India's royalist vision, its convictions that the principle of kingship was an idea as old as India and therefore best suited to the subcontinent's political traditions and practices, more apparent than in its systematic refusal to consider any changes in the symbols laid down since the middle of the nineteenth century. They showed a remarkable continuity and loyalty to their predecessor's ideas in this matter, undeterred by changing political

[92] Rev. Richard Burges, 'The Unrest in India. The Adolescence of an Empire', *The Hindustan Review*, July 1908, pp. 32–6.

contexts and developments at home or abroad. Curzon's notes and the 1902 file became the reference point for later viceroys when the question of a flag for India resurfaced in 1917, 1923, and 1931.

Consolidating empire had emerged as one of the key words that inaugurated the Edwardian period. Yet, despite the uninterrupted continuity of the Hanoverian line of royalty, a significant change had crept in. It was not that royalism was going out of fashion, or that monarchy was losing its powers of appeal, but the idea that imperial identities could be forged in other spaces, around other symbols, was slowly making headway. Three developments lay behind this shift. Firstly, the patriotic aura of the flag as a symbol of a collective common effort and values uniting the peoples of Britain with the dominions had been greatly emphasized since the Boer War. Secondly, the historic occasion of the coronation provided an ideal context for a debate on the British flag. The third significant milestone had been the emergence of a new ritual of propaganda, 'Empire Day'. But the Indian government refused to entertain the idea of letting these developments infringe on their territory. Was it because of the fear that this would open the doors to the swell of colonial nationalism? Or was it that monarchy and Victorian symbolism appeared a more reassuring guarantee for strengthening imperial identities? In 1902, admitting a distinctive Indian symbol into the Union Flag was far too big an admission of Indians into the imperial family on grounds of equality. Curzon's implacable Victorian conservatism was in this respect perhaps his most enduring legacy to his successors.

2

Failed Nationalist Images

Despite Coldstream's affirmation that 'the symbolism of a flag is appreciated in India perhaps more than in England', political interest for a symbol that could represent India seems to have been practically absent from the preoccupations of groups and nationalist movements at the beginning of the twentieth century. When on the morrow of independence the Indian Republic traced the genealogy of the Indian flag, it presented a succession of projects as if there had been contiuous reflection, a rich and open debate among Indians on this subject. When re-examined closely, these first proposals in fact appear isolated and discontinuous, linked more to marginal individuals and small groups than to a mainstream Indian movement. For years, British and Indians followed two parallel paths until they eventually encountered each other during the Home Rule movement. As against this, after 1917 they were more closely bound in a tighter dialectic. Even if they cannot be considered as steps in a unique symbolic process, we cannot ignore these initial and unsuccessful tentative moves. They participated in a reflection that would be mobilized in the inter-war period, when the necessity of a symbol for the Indian state became apparent.

Old Flags: A Past Without a Future

If Coldstream's statement did not pertain to the contemporary stituation in India, it was probably because it was a reference to more traditional practices. Flags had long been well-established symbols of royal power, besides being used as markers of group identity in political and social traditions. References in ancient texts like the *Mahabharata* described the royal *dhvaja* or banners in their military, political, and psychological functions, as a medium of divine help and intervention, and as royal insignia. Numerous references to banners could be traced in Hindu mythology, such as the flag of victory, or the evocation of a 'cock flag'. Capturing the enemy's dhvaja was equated to depriving him of divine protection. More concretely, in the fifth century some Gupta coins also displayed a banner.[1] At a more prosaic level, flags were used by communities and professional groups to affirm their distinct religious or cultural identity. From fleeting acknowledgements of their presence in pre-colonial societies, it appears that different castes, originally organized on the basis of craft guilds, carried their own device as emblematic of their trade.[2] The Salagama weavers, for example, are noted to have had their own flag, which went back at least to the fourteenth century. Hindu castes like the Vellal used a flag at weddings, while Muslims used flags of different patterns and sizes, but with an identical emblem, i.e. a sun and a crescent.[3] Tribal banners distinct from caste guilds also existed. Temples had their own flags, which varied according to the deity to whom the temple was dedicated. In 1717 the British government decreed the exclusive display of St George's flag in public processions in St Thomé, Madras, following conflicts between left-hand and right-hand divisions over the usurpation of this distinctive mark. Furthermore, in 1771 the governor prohibited the use of caste banners entirely in public spaces.[4] A monograph on flags in neighbouring Ceylon shows that they were used on Hindu temples or

[1] Uma Prasad Thapluiyal, *The Dhvaja. Standards and Flags of India. A Study* (Delhi, B.R. Publishing Corporation, 1983), p. 54.

[2] Arjun Appadurai, 'Right and Left Hand Castes in South India', *Indian Economic and Social History Review*, vol. 11, nos 2–3, 1974, pp. 216–59.

[3] The presence of the sun motif in Mughal royal standards is attested to by François Bernier, *Travels in the Mughal Empire* (London, Oxford University Press, 1916), p. 266. In the Sufi tradition it represented the source of Divine Light. Tipu Sultan adopted it in his flag, coins, and official documents. Cf. Kate Brittlebank, *Tipu Sultan's Search for Legitimacy. Islam and Kingship in a Hindu Domain* (Delhi, Oxford University Press,1997), pp. 147–9; the Mughal emperor Muhammad Shah granted Joseph-François Dupleix, governor general of the French possessions in India, a flag that represented golden pomegranates surrounding a sun. Cf. Pierre C. Lux-Wurm, *Les Drapeaux de l'Islam de Mahomet à nos jours* (Paris, Meta Editions, 2001), p. 125.

[4] Niels Brimnes, *Constructing the Colonial Encounter. Right and Left Hand Castes in Early Colonial South India* (Richmond, Curzon, 1999), pp. 72, 82–3.

hoisted on flagstaffs once a year during festivals, when the images were taken in procession round the temples.[5] However, the complex purposes and functions of flags in everyday life in these societies or in the state structures of power still remain to be analysed not only by historians but equally by anthropologists who have been strangely reticent about taking them into account, despite their fascination for totemic objects.[6]

References in contemporary chronicles to the Mughal emperors' flags confirm their status as one of the symbolic attributes of royal power along with the throne (*awrang*), the umbrella (*chhatra*), the fan (*sayaban*), the two globes (*kawkaba*), and the emblem of the sun (*shamsah*).[7] Two standards in particular are mentioned by medieval chroniclers, the black standard of the Abbasids, the ruling caliph of the period to whom the Muslim world owed allegiance, and the red standard of Ghor, a Turkish dynasty from Afghanistan that conquered the Ganges valley, founded Delhi in 1193, and set up the first slave dynasty (1206–90). The grant of banners (*alam*) signalled royal approval of nobles who had distinguished themselves in war.[8] The practice of conferring these standards to rally support became so common by the fourteenth and fifteenth centuries that, under the Tughlaqs, a separate state department called the Alam Khana was responsible for the

[5] Edward W. Perera, *Sinhalese Banners and Standards* (Colombo, Colombo Museum, 1916), pp. 6–7, 39.

[6] One of the rare anthropologists to have done so was Raymond Firth, *Symbols Public and Private* (Ithaca and London, Cornell University Press, 1973). A more recent work by S.A.A. Saheb analyses their role and function in rituals of collective worship in South India. ' "A Festival of Flags". Hindu-Muslim Devotion and the Sacralising of Localism at the Shrine of Nagore-e-Sharif in Tamil Nadu', in Prina Werbner and Helene Basu (eds), *Embodying Charisma. Modernity, Locality and the Performance of Emotion in Sufi Cults* (London, Routledge, 1998), pp. 55–76.

[7] Studies of Mughal symbols of imperial sovereignty have most often turned around the examination of court protocol with its accompanying systems of gifts and titles or coins. Cf. Andrea Hintze, *The Mughal Empire and its Decline. An Interpretation of the Sources of Social Power* (Ashgate, Variorum, 1997), pp. 50–7; John S. Deyell and R.E. Frykenberg, 'Sovereignty and the "Sikka" under Company Raj: Minting Prerogative and Imperial Legitimacy in India', *Indian Economic and Social History Review*, vol. 19, no. 1, January–March 1982, pp. 1–27.

[8] U.P. Thapluiyal, op. cit., pp. 94–5.

manufacture and upkeep of the standards, with a special custodian of the royal standard and emblems, the Qur-Begi. The chronicler Al Badaoni mentions Ibrahim Lodi's liberal grants of standards to all the nobles who joined him: 'to some two hundred amirs, Ibrahim had given royal tents and standards, and it frequently happened that to anyone who came and brought with him ten or fifteen horsemen he gave a sort of make-shift flag staff with a bit of red rag wrapped round it, simply to gain favour and to attract people.'[9]

The principal standard of the Mughal state was made of scarlet or green cloth with the royal emblem embroidered in gold fringe. Paintings of this period depict flags that are triangular, square, or oblong. The *Babur-Nama* mentions a military custom of consecrating the standard before marching into battle. Abul-Fazl Allami (1551–1602), Akbar's official chronicler and historian, distinguished between the royal insignia '*Alam*' and the Indian flag '*jhanda*', without however explicitly listing the differences between the two:

> When the king rides out, not less than five standards are carried along with the *Qur* (a collection of flags, arms, and other insignia) wrapped up in scarlet cloth bags. On days of festivity and in battle, they are unfurled. The *Chatrtoq*, a kind of *Alam*, but smaller than it, is adorned with the tails of Tibetan yaks. The *Tumantoq* is like the *Chatrtoq*, but longer. Both insignia are flags of the highest dignity, and the latter is bestowed upon great nobles only. The *Jhanda* is an Indian flag. The *Qur* necessarily contains a flag of each kind; but on great occasions many are displayed.[10]

French forces in the subcontinent under Governor General Joseph-François Dupleix were accorded a banner by the emperor, Muhammad Shah, in 1742. This was triangular like the Mughal standards and dotted with golden pomegranates surrounding a sun on a white background.[11] As rival powers and dissident feudatories rose up against the

[9] Al Badaoni, *Muntakhab-u-Tawarikh* (Delhi, Renaissance Publishing House, 1986), vol. 1, p. 543.

[10] Abul-Fazl Allami, *The Ain-i Akbari*, 3 vols, translated by H. Blochmann (ed.), D.C. Phillott (Calcutta, 1927), 2nd edn, vol. 1, p. 52.

[11] It was transferred to the museum of France d'outre-mer at Vincennes in 1938; cf. Pierre C. Lux-Wurm, op. cit., p. 124.

Mughal state, flags increasingly became a medium of reflecting fresh political balances and strategies.[12] In the 1780s Tipu Sultan chose the tiger and the sun as emblems for his flag, establishing a symbolic continuity through the sun with the medieval dynastic kingdoms of South India, such as the Cholas, the Vaishnavas, and the Hoysalas; and through the tiger with royal traditions, notably in Bengal, Rajasthan, and the Deccan, as well as with the Islamic world—which was familiar with the motif of the tiger stripe.[13] The British victory over Tipu at Srirangapatnam on 4 May 1799 was marked by their seizure of his taffeta olive-coloured silk banner with the design of a tiger head and a purple silk banner of the same dimensions with a sun emblem with stripes of green at the corners. Both were transferred in the form of a trophy to the Museum of the East India Company in London.[14] While Tipu's flag thus receded into oblivion, another flag of resistance against the British had been raised. The Maratha orange-coloured banner, *bhagwa jhanda* (sacred flag), symbol of the powerful Maratha confederation, fared better. It would be appropriated by Hindu nationalists as part of their symbolic traditions and it thus continued well beyond the political and military eclipse of the Maratha chiefs.[15] However, this was an exception. Most regional kingdom flags did not survive their demise, while the princely standards elaborated by the British government for the 1877 durbar failed to take root in popular imagination.

[12] Haider Ali Khan, raja of Mysore (1761–82), made a prominent use of flags in his state functions.

[13] This connection is indicated by Kate Brittlebank, *Tipu Sultan's Search for Legitimacy*, op. cit., pp. 140–5; '*Sakti* and *Barakat*: The Power of Tipu's Tiger. An Examination of the Tiger Emblem of Tipu Sultan of Mysore', *Modern Asian Studies*, XXIX, 1995, pp. 257–69. A two-paise copper coin of Tipu, minted at Chitradurga in 1788 also displayed the sun flag. The dimensions and detailed descriptions of Tipu's flags confiscated by the British are given by Mohammad Moinenuddin, *Sunset at Srirangapatam. After the Death of Tipu Sultan* (Delhi, Orient Longman, 2000), pp. 54–8.

[14] OIOC, H/787, List of Standards in the Museum of the East India Company. The rectangular banner measured 122 cm by 97 cm.

[15] A contemporary account of the Maratha campaign of Bassein in 1739 has an entry for 22 May mentioning the expense for hoisting the flag of victory; cf. P.K. Gode, *Studies in Indian Cultural History* (Hoshiarpur, Vishveshvaranand Vedic Research Institute, 1960–9), vol. 5, pp. 120–1.

Even the banners of revolt raised in 1857—among which a dark green standard with a sun in gold, Bahadur Shah Zafar's banner with the lotus flower and chapatis on a green and gold field, and the Rani of Jhansi's triangular silk flag with Hanuman holding a mountain on his left palm—did not leave many traces.

Incontestably, flags were integrated elements of state symbolism, but their close and almost exclusive relation to the monarch's power circumscribed their force. There is little evidence to show that they served as a strong signal of identity or belonging to a broader community.

Impossible Symbols

Notwithstanding this long tradition, Coldstream's assessment seems to have been more a political argument to convince the British government than a faithful description of the Indian political situation. Since the beginning of the British empire in India, this tradition had not given rise to the widespread political use of flags as symbols of resistance or integration. The few examples known to us had no large and durable impact. On the collapse of the Mughal empire, Indians resorted to flags for opposed purposes. On the one hand, Indian rebels raised the green standard of the Mughal empire as a symbol of resistance in 1857 to rally their compatriots behind the Mughal emperor Bahadur Shah Zafar.[16] On the other hand, after the British victory, some Indians, probably in Bengal, proposed reviewing the symbolic representation of India in the imperial system. Their proposal to include the lotus flower in the British Royal Standard, which already carried a rose, a thistle, and a shamrock, was recorded by George Cowell. The famous Sanskritist living in Calcutta at the time described the arms of the empire in these terms in a family correspondence. The proposal made no headway, either because it was not strongly supported by Indians, or because of British reluctance and suspicion of Indian loyalties.[17]

[16] C.A. Bayly, *Rulers, Townsmen and Bazaars. North Indian Society in the Age of British Expansion, 1770–1870* (Cambridge, Cambridge University Press, 1983), p. 365.

[17] This information is mentioned in a unique letter of George Cowell to his mother, Calcutta, 22 October 1859, in *Life and Letters of Edward Byles Cowell*

No other evidence of an Indian flag appears in the following years, until 1883, when a national flag featured on the front cover of a book published in Lahore. Written by a certain Srish Chandra Bose, it was entitled *Indian National Songs and Lyrics*. The flag design consisted of a sun, a symbol already utilized as we have seen, both by ancient Hindu and Muslim monarchs, and accompanied by the caption 'Our National Standard'.[18] It was certainly this flag that was paraded in Lahore by members of the Indian National Society, founded that very year in the city to foster Hindu–Muslim unity, which would explain the choice of the sun as a common symbol.[19] Subsequently, we have no other information about this flag being used. It would nonetheless be misplaced to consider it as an abortive event. In fact, this association was a branch of the Indian Association that had been created in Calcutta in 1876 and in which Surendranath Bannerjee, the Bengali lawyer, was then playing a very active part.[20] As we will see, Bannerjee would occupy a central role in the display of a flag during the partition of Bengal in 1905. Parallel attempts by Burjori Nawrosji, editor of the *Hindi Punch*, suggesting designs for a national flag in his cartoons on the Indian National Congress, produced no reactions.

Clearly, towards the beginning of the twentieth century, while the idea of an Indian national identity was making headway, flags as

---

(London, Macmillan, 1904), p. 165. George Cowell was a proficient Sanskritist who had, inter alia, in 1851 translated *Vikramorvasi*, the play by Kalidasa. In India since 1855, he was teaching English at Presidency College, Calcutta. Despite the tense situation succeeding the revolt, he was in close touch with Indians, in particular with Calcutta pandits, whom he described as 'the only luxury in India . . . that you can't get in England', p. 167.

[18] Published by N.R. Nund, Manager of the National Book Society, Lahore, 1883; its title page was reproduced in the *Modern Review*, October 1930, p. 481.

[19] K.V. Singh, *Our National Flag* (Delhi, Publications Division, Ministry of Information & Broadcasting, Government of India, 1991), p. 20; the source is not quoted.

[20] Anil Seal, *The Emergence of Indian Nationalism. Competition and Collaboration in the Later Nineteenth Century* (Cambridge, Cambridge University Press, 1968), pp. 214–21.

strong political symbols had far more importance for the British than for Indians. Coldstream's affirmation that 'the symbolism of flags is more appreciated in India than in England' reflected neither the existing political climate nor immediate Indian preoccupations very accurately. Indian interest in the subject of an imperial identity was focused more on their material rights as imperial citizens than on 'being British at heart'. While the British were thinking of the imperial relationship in terms of a sentimental attachment, Indians were more concerned with finding expressions for their own distinctive national identity.

The young Bengali Hindu character Binoy in Rabindranath Tagore's novel *Gora*, articulated the nationalist quest of these years: 'Tell me', he asked his friend Gora, 'is India very real, absolutely clear to you? India is in your thoughts day and night, but in what way do you think of her?' Tagore could find no other answer to place in Gora's reply except the enthusiastic declaration that India was 'in my mind at all times'.[21]

This, in short, summed up the nationalist predicament as it took shape in the last decade of the nineteenth century. The concrete problem they confronted was the kind of representation that could render this abstraction of India accessible and appealing. It absorbed their energies and dominated their reflections, giving rise to a significant production and diffusion of pictorial and literary forms.[22] The visual frames in which India was envisaged in the 1890s were strongly invested with religious references, predominant among them being the cow or Bharat Mata (Mother India). Henceforth, the continued political utilization of these symbols is taken as proof of their being one of the keys to the understanding of Indian nationalism under colonialism and in contemporary times.[23] They have become well

[21] Rabindranath Tagore, *Gora* (London, Macmillan & Co., 1924), p. 17.

[22] See Tapati Guha-Thakurta, *The Making of a New Indian Art. Aesthetics and Nationalism in Bengal, 1850–1920* (Cambridge, Cambridge University Press, 1992); Partha Mitter, *Art and Nationalism in Colonial India 1850–1922* (Cambridge, Cambridge University Press, 1994).

[23] Jackie Assayag examines these forms of patriotic imagination in *L'Inde. Désir de Nation* (Paris, Odile Jacob, 2001).

examined territories from the various perspectives of 'cultural artefacts', 'metaphors', or 'essentializing' projects of colonial knowledge and 'derivative discourse'.[24] These religious signs were developed to provide an iconographic and emotional unity to India's diverse communities within a Hindu matrix. While they allowed the integration of a large pantheon of gods,[25] their divisive potential was quickly apparent, sparking Hindu–Muslim riots and violence in the United Provinces.[26]

A less discordant icon, rooted in traditional conventions and values, was also being tapped simultaneously. Across the image of the 'Mother', Bengali writers like Bankim Chandra Chatterjee, political activists like Aurobindo Ghosh and Bipin Chandra Pal, saintly figures like Vivekananda, artists like Abanindranath Tagore,[27] and southern poets

[24] Sugata Bose, 'Nation as Mother: Representation and Contestations of "India" in Bengali Literature and Culture', in Sugata Bose & Ayesha Jalal (eds), *Nationalism, Democracy and Development. State and Politics in India* (Delhi-New York, Oxford University Press, 1997), pp. 50–75, esp. pp. 52–5; Jasodhara Bagchi, 'Representing Nationalism: Ideology of Motherhood in Colonial Bengal', *Economic and Political Weekly*, vol. 25, 20–27 October 1990, pp. WS65–WS71; Tanika Sarkar, 'Nationalist Iconography: Image of Women in Nineteenth-century Bengali Literature', *Economic and Political Weekly*, vol. 22, 1987, pp. 2011–15; Indira Chowdhury Sengupta, 'Mother India and Mother Victoria: Motherhood and Nationalism in Nineteenth-century Bengal', *South Asia Research*, 1992, pp. 20–37.

[25] Fed by and in turn sustaining the parallel cow-protection movement, this form of representation has been a favourite object of investigation. See Jackie Assayag, 'Le Corps de l'Inde. La carte, la vache, la nation', *Gradhiva*, 22, 1997, pp. 15–29; Christopher Pinney, 'The Nation (Un)Pictured? Chromolithography and Popular Politics in India, 1878–1995', *Critical Inquiry*, 23, 1997, pp. 834–67, esp. pp. 841–6; Anand A. Yang, 'Sacred Symbol and Sacred Space in Rural India: Community Mobilization in the "Anti-Cow Killing" Riot of 1893', *Comparative Studies in Society and History*, 22, 1980, pp. 576–96.

[26] The appeal of this image and its capacity to mobilize in urban and rural areas is analysed by Peter Robb, 'The Challenge of Gau Mata: British Policy and Religious Change in India, 1880–1916', *Modern Asian Studies*, 20, 2, 1986, pp. 285–319; Sandra B. Freitag, 'Sacred Symbol as Mobilizing Ideology: The North Indian Search for a "Hindu" Community', *Comparative Studies in Society and History*, 22, 1980, pp. 597–625.

[27] Nivedita welcomed Abanindranath Tagore's painting '*Bharat Mata* as the first masterpiece in which the artist has actually succeeded in disengaging . . . the

like Bharati,[28] to mention only a few, infused the nation with familiar—both domestic and cosmogenic—connotations of mother as nourisher or protector. Yet, despite the power of this idea of nation-mother which combined a parental relationship with a divine, sacred element—be it Kali, Durga,[29] Bhavani, or 'Bharat-Mata'—it failed to provide an entirely satisfactory political response that the representation of the nation seemed to need. While its emotional force was in no doubt, what was missing was a political edge. Nivedita, living in Calcutta since 1898, summed up the problem: India's depiction in the form of 'Bharat Mata' (Mother India) was but 'a step towards distinguishing definite symbols under which to think of nationality and the civic ideal.'[30]

Somewhat removed from this type of representation was the depiction of India through maps. These geographical representations of the country went back to pre-colonial times, when maps had been circulating as utilitarian objects for pilgrims, sailors, travellers, and

---

spirit of the motherland', in *Select Essays of Sister Nivedita* (Madras, Ganesh & Co., 3rd edn, 1911), pp. 1–6, reproduced from 'India the Mother', published in *Indian World.*

[28] Subramania Bharati in 'Bharat Mata', 'Our Mother', or 'Our Wild Mother', called his compatriots to worship this land which had nourished them, hailing her as goddess, noble queen, and Aryan queen. 'Whose was the dread bow, that destroyed the Lanka hoardes? It was our terrible Mothers. The Arya Queen, Mother Bharat.' For Bharati, the concept of 'Mother India' was merged with the concept of a Mother Goddess. Cf. Prema Nandakumar, *Subramania Bharati* (Mysore, Rao & Raghavan, 1964), p. 45. A terracotta statue (61 cms) of Bharata Mata was conceived by him and three of his associates, made in Pondicherry in 1917 and brought to British India. Cf. Subramania Bharati, *Chosen Poems and Prose* (New Delhi, National Book Trust, 1968), pp. 21–38.

[29] Sir Valentine Chirol noted that the point of departure of the anti-Partition demonstration of the Calcutta crowd was the Kali temple in the city, *The Modern World. A Survey of Historical Forces*, vol. 5, *India* (London, Ernest Benn, 1926), p. 117. Members of the revolutionary Anusilan Society, founded in 1906 by Pulin Behari Das to fight for political freedom, took their oaths in the presence of an image of Kali. All political assassinations were considered by them to be a sacrifice to the goddess. Cf. Gordon Johnson, 'Partition, Agitation and Congress: Bengal 1904 to 1908', *Modern Asian Studies*, VII, July 1973, pp. 572–5.

[30] *Select Essays of Sister Nivedita*, op. cit.

military generals. The practice was continued with renewed vigour by the British state.[31] As a matter of fact the logo of the 'Anti-Circular Society', founded in Calcutta in 1905, was a circle incorporating a map of India around which was inscribed 'For God and Motherland'.[32] While the nationalization of Indian space in opposition to the colonial enterprise was certainly rendered more accessible through the 'swadeshi' agitation of 1905, emphasizing home-made handloom (khadi), it proved just one of the various paths of national representation without acquiring a distinct edge or a decisive advantage over other forms.[33]

Other efforts included the revival of a pantheon of Indian national heroes and the propagation of their national cult across the country. Shivaji festivals[34] initiated by Bal Gangadhar Tilak, were part of this spirited movement to provide India with an inspiring national genealogy of great men and women.[35] So too was Tilak's revival of the Hindu

[31] Cf. Kapil Raj, 'Connexions, croisements, circulations. Le détour de la cartographie britannique par l'Inde, XVIIe–XIXe siècles', in Michael Werner and Bénédicte Zimmermann (eds), *De la comparaison à l'histoire croisée* (Paris, Seuil, 2004), pp. 73–98.

[32] Sumathi Ramaswamy, 'Maps and Mother Goddesses in Modern India', *Imago Mundi*, 53, 2001, pp. 97–114, esp. p. 101.

[33] The nationalization of concepts of territory, economy, and culture is analysed by Manju Goswami, 'Swadeshi to Swaraj in Colonial South Asia, 1870–1907', *Comparative Studies in Society and History*, 40, 1998, pp. 609–36.

[34] The Bengali journal *Yugantar* called on all Indians to wield the sword of Shivaji, while the wearing of turbans in the Shivaji style became fashionable among Bengali volunteers, as did the Maratha war-cry of *Hara Hara Bom Bom* (Glory to Lord Shiva), used as a slogan by the Dacca Samiti: Hiren Chakrabarti, *Political Protest in Bengal: Boycott and Terrorism 1905–1918* (Calcutta, Papyrus, 1992), p. 126. The slogan's appeal was confirmed by Nirad C. Chaudhuri who, as a boy in Calcutta, enjoyed shouting the Maratha war-cry 'Hara, Hara, Mahadeo' with his friends in their game battles against pretended enemies: *An Autobiography of an Unknown Indian* (London, Macmillan & Co., 1951), pp. 263–5.

[35] The path to the revival of Indian heroes had in fact been opened by the British, for in 1883 it was a British officer, James Douglas, who attempted to restore Shivaji's *samadhi* in Raigarh (the fortress in Kolaba district where Shivaji had been coronated *chhatrapati*—Hindu lord of the universe—and where he died in 1680), and actually succeeded in extracting money from western India's archaeological bureau. Tilak first projected Shivaji the liberator in a festival in

elephant god Ganapati through popular fairs and processions.[36] Though explicitly inspired by Western nationalism and its legendary figures, such as Napoleon or Joan of Arc, hero worship as a programme of national construction was short-lived.[37] Still, it was not without a certain impact in implanting the seeds of patriotism.[38] Rabindranath Tagore, after an initial interest in India's heroic heritage (he wrote a poem on Shivaji in 1897), turned away with disapproval from this particular path of national awakening in favour of a more 'spiritual nationalism' rooted in the peaceful bhakti tradition of western and eastern India.[39] It could, he suggested, be inspired by 'national saints' such as Nanak, founder of Sikhism (1465–1539); Kabir, poet and mystic from northern India (1440–1518); and Chaitanya (1486–1533), who spread the cult of Krishna in Bengal and around Mathura. All, Tagore pointed out, had proclaimed the essential unity linking people of different religious faiths and social origins. But this plea was drowned in the more spectacular, extrovert expressions of unity.

June 1897, which was the month of the Maratha leader's coronation and ten days before the diamond jubilee celebration of Queen Victoria's coronation; cf. Stanley A. Wolpert, *Tilak and Gokhale. Revolution and Reform in the Making of Modern India* (Oxford, Oxford University Press, 1981), pp. 81, 82; Sarala Ghosal, niece of Rabindranath Tagore, encouraged the revival of heroes like Pratapaditya. Cf. Indira Chowdhury, *The Frail Hero and Virile History. Gender and the Politics of Culture in Colonial Bengal* (Delhi, Oxford University Press, 1998), p. 151.

[36] An excellent analysis of Ganapati's potential as a useful political symbol for the nationalist movement was made by Richard I. Cashman in *The Myth of the Lokamunya. Tilak and Mass Politics in Maharashtra* (Berkeley, University of California Press, 1975), pp. 75–90.

[37] On the use of heroic models for national construction, see Pierre Centlivres, Daniel Fabre, Françoise Zonabend, *La Fabrique des Héros* (Paris, Editions de la Maison des Sciences de l'Homme, 1998).

[38] B.K. Nehru, *Nice Guys Finish Second* (Delhi, Viking, 1997), p. 20. The future Marathi lawyer M.R. Jayakar remembered his mother placing in his hands, at the early age of ten, short life-sketches of the historic figures of Maharashtra, among which was Shivaji's. Childhood stories highlighting Shivaji's patriotism, his daring exploits, his courage and the importance of the ideas of freedom and independence enthused Jayakar and his friends to form a group devoted to spreading the message of freedom.

[39] Hiren Chakrabarti, op. cit.

While pro-British newspapers scornfully dismissed 'the common worship of a few apotheosised heroes',[40] Muslims expressed their hostility to the glorification of historical figures like Shivaji and Hindu religious motifs. The former because his heroism had been directed against the Mughal emperors and the latter because they were alien and opposed to their own religious, cultural beliefs.[41] In the Amritsar session of 1906 the president of the All India Muslim League would chide the Congress leaders of the two prominent centres of nationalist activity, Poona in the west (bastion of Brahmin learning and culture epitomized by Tilak and his followers), and Calcutta in the east (home of the early nationalist movements), for expecting Muslims to rally to the cause of nationalism behind Hindu symbols: 'I ask the architects of Indian nationalism, both in Calcutta and in Poona, do they expect the Musulmans of India to accept *'Bande Mataram'* and the Shivaji celebration?'[42]

It is evident that the limited success of these symbols was due to their narrow, exclusionist qualities. Described by one contemporary witness as the 'Hindu revivalist ethos that had taken the upper hand over the liberal ideas inspired by the West',[43] this trend continues to be decried as a fundamental weakness in the Indian state even today. But it cannot be ruled out that the failure to rally round a common symbol was also partly due to a simultaneous, indeed uncoordinated, exploration of multiple possibilities and paths of iconographic representation.[44] All these forms from the cow to Bharat Mata, maps, khadi, heroes, and gods, jostled together in oral literature, prints, paintings, each promoted by distinct parties and groups—whether cow-protection movements or Bengali revolutionaries—poets and artists, economic thinkers or

[40] *Times of India*, 17 July 1907, 'The Shivaji Cult'.

[41] Sufia Ahmed, *Muslim Community in Bengal 1884–1912* (Dacca, Oxford University Press, 1974), p. 276.

[42] Sharif Al Mujahid (ed.), *Muslim League Documents, 1900–1908* (Karachi, Quaid-i-Azam Academy,1990), vol. 1, p. 336.

[43] Nirad C. Chaudhuri, *Autobiography*, op. cit., pp. 226–9.

[44] The use of 'Jagannath' as a symbol of Oriya identity was one example. Cf. G.N. Dash, 'Jagannath and Oriya Nationalism', in Ancharlott Eschmann, *et al.* (ed.), *The Cult of Jagannath and the Regional Tradition of Orissa* (New Delhi, Manohar, 1978), p. 365.

political leaders. Their very plurality operated against the idea of a single, united nation that they were intended to reflect, creating an ethos of competition and divided loyalties, group identifications and meanings, almost a war of symbols.

At the beginning of the twentieth century, none of these ways of representing India had succeeded in imposing themselves as a nationwide point of reference.

A 'Simple Curiosity'?

The summer of 1905 saw large demonstrations and processions in the streets and squares of Calcutta and its neighbouring regions in protest against the British government's formal announcement partitioning Bengal. In this tense political conjuncture a national flag was reported to have been raised as an emblem of Indian unity. Given that this moment is considered in post-1947 government accounts as the point of origin of this national symbol,[45] it merits precise and accurate reconstitution and analysis. Surprisingly, reconstructing its birth and trajectory during this period proves astonishingly difficult and elusive. Contemporary references to a flag are scarce and few details surface in newspapers,[46] or in administrative and police reports of the period.[47] It is difficult to affirm with certainty when exactly the flag was hoisted: at least two dates are proposed.

The first moment of its appearance in public is noted as October 1905, at the very moment when the formal announcement of the

[45] *Our Flag*, op. cit., p. 1, notes it to be the first national flag in India.

[46] The most precise but brief information is found in *The Tribune*, 9 August 1906, p. 1. According to K.V. Singh, op. cit., p. 24, other Bengali newspapers like *Yugantar*, *Sanjivani*, and *Vande Mataram* reported it, though *Yugantar* was the only newspaper to greet the event.

[47] Sumit Sarkar cites the following source: Abstract of reports from Bengal, August 1906, Enclosure A, Bengal Police Abstract no. 32, 11 August 1906, Home Public Progs B, October 1906, no. 13, *Bengalee*, 8 August 1906, in his *The Swadeshi Movement in Bengal, 1903–1908* (Delhi, People's Publishing House, 1973), p. 307. The government publication *Our Flag*, op. cit., p. 1, states that the source of information about the site and occasion of its hoisting is obscure.

partition of Bengal decided by the British viceroy was made: at Iswarganj in Mymensingh district, a procession of schoolboys is reported to have carried flags.[48] Then, in Calcutta, on 20 October 1905, an Indian national flag was hoisted by Surendranath Bannerjee in the compound of the proposed Federation Hall, opposite the University Science College on Upper Circular Road, with the bursting of crackers. The event was greeted with loud acclamations and shouts of *Bande Mataram*.[49] In fact, according to Bannerjee's memoirs, the ceremony would have taken place on 16 October 1905, the day on which the Partition was to take effect; the only difficulty lies in the fact that Bannerjee does not allude to the flag at all in his detailed description of that morning's programme.[50]

A second moment reported in newspapers of the day is the summer of 1906.[51] On 7 August 1906, flags, red, green, yellow, were 'in all hands', and the celebrations in Calcutta seem to have given place to a 'flags ceremony' in which Bhupendra Nath Bose presented the national flag to Surendranath Bannerjee, who unfurled it, declared it 'the emblem of unity', and asked the audience to salute it and renew the swadeshi vow.[52] A report by the chief of Central Intelligence, describing a large anti-Partition gathering held in front of the Anti-Circular Society building, College Square, Calcutta, stated: 'No speeches were made here, but a flag was hoisted half mast'.[53]

Inasmuch as the flag's design is concerned, the sources are more precise. Described as a red, saffron, green tricolour, carrying on the three bands, respectively, eight white lotuses, *Bande Mataram* in the Devanagari script in deep blue, and a white sun with a crescent and star, the flag is credited to Sachindra Prasad Bose, secretary of the Anti Circular Society (founded in 1905 to protest against the prohibitory

[48] *Amrita Bazar Patrika*, 17 October 1905.

[49] Binoy Jiban Ghosh, *Revolt of 1905 in Bengal* (Calcutta, G.A.E. Publishers, 1987), p. 100, no sources indicated.

[50] Surendranath Bannerjee, *A Nation in Making. Being the Reminiscences of Fifty Years of Public Life* (London, Humphrey Milford, 1925), pp. 197–9.

[51] Sumit Sarkar, op. cit., p. 307.

[52] *The Tribune*, 9 August 1906, p. 1.

[53] Hossainur Rahman, *Hindu-Muslim Relations in Bengal 1905–47. Study in Cultural Confrontation* (Bombay, Nachiketa Publications, 1974), p. 30.

circulars issued by the government of eastern Bengal), a close follower of Surendranath Bannerjee and son-in-law of the moderate Brahmo leader Krishna Kumar Mitra.[54] It was approved in a meeting at the Indian Association Hall, Calcutta. A suggestion was made that the eight lotuses representing the eight provinces of the country be placed according to their respective location on the map of India, instead of showing all eight in a row on the top green band of the flag. However, Bannerjee is said to have preferred the original design.[55] The three colours stood for Muslims, Hindus, and Sikhs, explained Sudhir Chandra Bandopadhyay—an academic closely involved in the events—in an interview to Dr Bhupendranath Dutt, editor of the Bengali newspaper *Yugantar*.[56]

One outstanding aspect of this flag is the persistence of emblems with strong religious associations, like the lotus, sun, and crescent. Beyond this first observation of the link with designs already utilized in the repertory of political symbols (discussed above), two significant novelties can be discerned. First and foremost, the structure of the flag. The juxtaposition of three horizontal coloured bands could be a possible echo of other symbols of political liberty: perhaps of the Dutch tricolour, the only horizontal tricolour raised as a flag of rebellion, but which is never recognized as a referent; more certainly of the French flag, designed at the beginning of the French revolution; no doubt this was a vertical tricolour but the political reference to the French revolution in the Bengal partition was more present in these years. Secondly, the simultaneous portrayal of symbols belonging to different religious systems was the first manifestation of their equal coexistence in Indian national space.[57]

In these very months of intense agitation, other projects for a national flag were taking shape. A flag with the emblem of a lotus was

[54] This account is given by B.J. Ghosh, op. cit., pp. 100–1. Ghosh says the colours represented Hindus, Muslims, and Sikhs.

[55] K.V. Singh, *Our National Flag*, op. cit., p. 23.

[56] Bhupendranath Datta, *Bharater Dwitiya Swadhinatar Sangram* (Calcutta, Aprakasita Rajanitika Itihasa, 1926), p. 229. I am grateful to Tim Pratt for helping me locate this work and to Shadhona Ganguly for her translation.

[57] Sumit Sarkar, op. cit., p. 307 considers the appearance of the flag an effort 'to evolve a truly non-sectarian and secular imagery'.

devised under the guidance of the vice chancellor of Calcutta University, Ashutosh Chaudhuri.[58] Was it the same flag or another? Impossible to say. One other project, designed by Nivedita, received slightly greater recognition. Though Nivedita had abandoned her Irish-British name on the direction of her spiritual master Swami Vivekananda after she came to Calcutta in 1898 in pursuit of self-realization, she was still mindful of the models and mechanisms of the British and Western political systems. More than her Indian contemporaries, she realised the value of this symbol in Western eyes for representing nationalist consciousness and the sovereignty of the modern nation. Nonetheless, Nivedita's project was quite different in its conception from that of her compatriot Coldstream's in 1902. True, she had carried forward his idea to its logical extension, by identifying a symbol that was truly Indian—the *vajra*, 'the thunderbolt as the national emblem of India', tracing it back to the Mahabharata and to the ancient Indian myths.[59] But her concern was not to express an imperial relationship. On the contrary her political sympathies lay clearly and radically on the side of the Indians and she was committed, like the authors of the Partition flag, to the furtherance of political unity and social harmony. In a letter to a friend in England she insisted: 'Nationality is the thought I am seeking by all means to popularise. It could appeal to both Hindus and Muslims . . . It is not an image and therefore the Mohammedan ought not to refuse it. And Durga holds it in one of her ten hands.'[60] Mobilizing the pupils of her 'Ramakrishna School for Girls', she concretized her design in a flag in scarlet and yellow with the sign of the thunderbolt. The flag was a red square, a choice of shape that marked a

[58] *Amrita Bazar Patrika*, 20 July 1923. Reporting on the flag movement in Calcutta at this moment, the article referred to a speech made by the Congress president at a public meeting in which he reminded his auditors of this flag devised in the swadeshi agitation of 1905.

[59] One of the myths explains the origins of the thunderbolt thus: The devas (gods) went to the sage Dadhichi and said that to help them and save their land he had to give up his life. He agreed and made the thunderbolt from his ribs. The thunderbolt is here the mark of selflessness and the selfless person the thunderbolt.

[60] *Letters of Sister Nivedita*, ed. Sankari Prasad Basu (Calcutta, Nababharat Publishers, 1982), to Miss J. MacLeod, 28 February 1906, 25 July 1906, pp. 791, 821–2.

voluntary break with the Western rectangular norms of national flags. It carried 108 *jyotis* (flames) all along the border and the thunderbolt in yellow at the centre with *bande* on the left and *mataram* on the right in the Bengali script.[61] (Illustr. I.)

No reference to this flag's appearance in the anti-Partition movement has been found, but it was certainly displayed in the exhibition of swadeshi crafts organized by the Indian National Congress at its annual session at Calcutta in December 1906.[62] So was the Partition flag as described many years later by the Marathi lawyer and Congress member Chimanlal H. Setalvad, who had attended this session: 'At this session, Dadabhai Naoroji (elected to preside over the Congress for the third time) unfurled the flag of *Swaraj* for India.'[63]

Over 1905–8, three flags existed, at least in Bengal: on the Indian side the Partition flag and the *vajra* flag, and on the British side the Union Flag. And yet, no clash, no confrontation occurred between these rival symbols. The only manifestation against the Union Flag was noted in an Arya Samaj school at Lahore where schoolchildren were encouraged to put the Union Jack in their shoes instead of waving it in the air, and shout '*Bande Mataram*'.[64] Henceforth, the contrast between them could not have been greater. Though the ritual of Empire Day, as we have seen, had been denied the status of an official holiday by Curzon in 1904, and by his successor Lord Minto, it was nonetheless celebrated at the local level from May 1905 onwards. Promoted by local British governments under instructions from the directorate of education, flag salutations and hoistings, accompanied by festivities and fireworks to dilute the propagandist effect, were regularly taking place in schools and universities of Punjab and Bengal in these years.[65] They brought home to young Indians, even in the

[61] These details are given by K.V. Singh in *Our National Flag*, op. cit. I have not been able to find such a complete description anywhere else, and unfortunately the author does not mention the source of his information.

[62] Barbara Foxe, *Long Journey Home. A Biography of Margaret Noble* (London, Rider & Co., 1975), pp. 172-3.

[63] Chimanlal H. Setalvad, *Recollections and Reflections. An Autobiography* (Bombay, Padma Publications, 1946), p. 279.

[64] OIOC, *Native Newspaper Reports*, Punjab, for the week up to 16 June, *Watan*, 8 June 1906, L/R/5/188, p. 150.

[65] NAI, Home Public-A, Proceedings August 1907, no. 45, 7 May 1907.

remotest parts of British India like Dera Ghazi Khan on the Afghan frontier, for example, their imperial identity and obligations through such key elements as the map of empire, the Union Jack, and the national anthem.[66] On the one hand the ritual diffused the presence of the flag down to the smallest villages, familiarizing Indians with a political symbol which they had until then associated with the exercise of colonial power. It was now projected as a symbol that could be used by them in certain circumstances. But on the other hand the nationalist press condemned the imperial rhetoric and political message as 'meaningless from the standpoint of Indians who enjoyed only nominal liberty and lacked the rights and privileges enjoyed by His Majesty's other subjects.'[67] Yet the Indian press did not go as far as using the contemporary proposals of flags to promote Indians' own symbolic alternative.

The three proposals for a flag for India described above invited no reactions. Each event was punctual. Beyond the Partition episode, no other observation or allusion to a public use of the flag in the streets of Calcutta has been found. It gave rise to no literary outpourings. The few precise evocations seem to have been confined to the Bengali press, like the well-known Bengali weekly *Sanjivani*.[68] This limited the flag's impact to a Bengali public, whereas as the symbol of the nation it was, by its very nature, destined to a national audience. Most astonishing of all is the complete blank on this subject by the large number of actors and witnesses of this widespread agitation. Surendranath Bannerjee himself, though caught in the maelstrom of Bengali swadeshi politics, did not emphasize its power of mobilization and significance in

---

A. Earle, Director of Public Instruction, Bengal to W.S. Milne, Secretary to Government of Bengal, General Education Department.

[66] Sir Malcolm Darling, *Apprentice to Power. India 1904–1908* (London, Hogarth Press, 1966), pp. 67–8, describes these rituals for 1907.

[67] OIOC, *Native Newspaper Reports*, Punjab, L/R/5/188, week up to 9 June 1906, p. 144; for other press reactions in 1906 to Empire Day in Madras, Punjab, and Bengal, cf. OIOC, *Native Newspaper Reports*, L/R/5/112, L/R/5/32; also *The Hindu*, 21 May 1906, 4 June 1906, p. 2; *The Mahratta*, 8 July 1906, p. 323, 7 October 1906, pp. 470–1.

[68] Bhupendranath Datta, *Bharater Dwitiya Swadhinatar Sangram*, op. cit., pp. 228–31, contained excerpts reproduced from a contemporary report which appeared in *Sanjivani*.

uniting Indians. In his lengthy description of these years of 'wild excitement and fervour . . . this strange upheaval of public feeling hitherto quite unknown', not once did he mention an Indian national flag. The same silence is apparent among other witnesses: the young Nirad C. Chaudhuri who made a particular note of this political movement and his own sentiments; and the British journalist Valentine Chirol touring India.

Nor was the flag re-utilized in subsequent political occasions. At a more material level, it did not register in a regular ritual. Congress annual sessions did not adopt it in the following years. Even groups which had been responsible for its birth did not follow up their initial enthusiasm. Bannerjee, it would appear, had on the eve of the famous 16 August ceremony given in to the insistence of a group of young Bengali political activists who then produced the flag during the night. His subsequent silence, especially from one deeply influenced by Mazzini and the republican form of struggle the Italian incarnated, can only mean that the national flag was not a significant stake for anyone except some impassioned Bengali youth influenced by the revolutionary French, Irish, and Russian traditions of political struggle and a marginal figure like Nivedita who was part of these Calcutta circles by 1906. She was in fact one of the council of five created by Aurobindo Ghosh to coordinate the political actions of the many revolutionary societies that had sprung up in Calcutta. In this circle of educated, idealistic, nationalist men, members of radical groups like the Anusilan Society or the Dawn Society, Nivedita contributed to the circulation of political literature and ideas, notably through her books on the Irish revolution, the Indian revolt of 1857, the American War of Independence, the lives of Mazzini and Garibaldi,[69] as well as through her writings and public speeches on the urgency of working for Indian unity and nationality. These links might explain the simultaneous elaboration of two Indian national flags by different sets of authors who were reacting to a colonial situation by methods borrowed from European revolutionary movements.

Nivedita's ideas on the flag found an outlet much later, in 1909, in the influential *Modern Review*, a Calcutta cultural monthly founded in 1907 by Ramananda Chatterjee. But her declaration, 'The question

[69] Barbara Foxe, op. cit., p. 169.

of the invention of a flag for India is beginning to be discussed in the press',[70] was a little optimistic, if not entirely wishful thinking.[71]

This overall silence in mainstream nationalism in both the Indian[72] and the Western press drove the flag into political obscurity.[73] No attempt was made to create a dramatic aura around its birth, surround it with a sacred halo, link it with the notions of sacrifice, honour, pride, dignity, in short, invest it with feeling and emotion. It was born and yet it was not a living object, attracting, mobilizing, clashing, and triumphing. It would indeed seem such a national flag lacked historical legitimacy, for the Bengali author Dr Bhupendranath Datta (Vivekananda's brother and subeditor of the Bengali journal *Yugantar*) maintained that when the 7 August flag ceremony was ridiculed by the opposition, its authors then described the flag as standing for 'Equality, Fraternity and Liberty'.[74] It had emerged at the height of a powerful political protest but remained cut off from the keywords of the movement.

[70] Sister Nivedita, 'The Vajra as a National Flag', *Modern Review*, VI, no. 5, November 1909, pp. 443–7. Except for this article, no other reference to her flag features in the principal Indian newspapers of the period.

[71] Nor was this contribution of hers particularly acknowledged in independent India except on some exceptional occasions. It was evoked by President Radhakrishnan in a speech at the inauguration of the centenary celebrations of Sister Nivedita in Calcutta. *President Radhakrishnan's Speeches and Writings. Second Series, May 1964–1967* (Delhi, 1969), 31 August 1966, p. 148. It must be noted that it is not mentioned in the Government of India publication *Our Flag*, op. cit.

[72] Charu Chander Ghose, a lawyer in the Calcutta high court, made no mention of the flag in his detailed account of the public agitation in Bengal in 1906: *The Partition of Bengal. A Plea for Reconsideration* (Calcutta, 1906), p. 5. Nor did another commentator, Syamacharan Ganguli, in his analysis of the 'Partition of Bengal. Its Annulment and Redistribution of Provinces', *Modern Review*, November 1911, reprinted in *Essays and Criticisms* (London, 1927), pp. 68–90.

[73] No more did it appear in news reports of the *New York Times*, which carried a notice, 'Bengalis in Mourning', describing how Bengalis went about barefooted; 30,000 participated in the demonstrations and took the swadeshi vow, *The New York Times*, 18 October 1907.

[74] Bhupendranath Datta, op. cit.

Of these two different flags that emerged during the Swadeshi movement, one fathered by some young Bengali boys, the other designed by a British woman, it was the first that crossed over to an international platform. Through the intermediary of one of the Bengali nationalists, Hem Chandra Da Kanungo, the Partition flag reached Bhikaji Cama, a Parsi woman nationalist living in exile in Paris because of her anti-British activities.[75] She brought it to the Twelfth International Socialist Congress held at Stuttgart in August 1907 in a session devoted to the colonial problem.[76] Her speech, denouncing the iniquities and atrocities of British imperialism, culminated with the display of a 'a silk red, saffron and green tricolour with a lotus and seven stars on the red strip, the words "*Bande Mataram*" on the saffron strip and the sun on the left and a crescent moon and star on the green strip'.[77] (Illustr. II.) To her audience she declared: 'This flag is of Indian independence. Behold it is born. It is already sanctioned by the blood of martyred Indian youths . . . I appeal to lovers of freedom all over the world to cooperate with this flag in freeing one-fifth of the human

[75] In his book *Banglay Biplab Prachesta* Hem Chandra Da Kanungo confirmed that he carried with him a small replica of the Calcutta flag and made a similar flag for Bhikaji Cama in Paris. He seems to have met her through the offices of another Indian revolutionary Khasi Rao whom he had encountered in Geneva. Khasi Rao's brother, a general in the army of the Baroda state, had gone to Switzerland for military training and there come in contact with Bhikaji Cama. A different version explaining Bhikaji Cama's acquisition of a national flag has it that her close associate, V.D. Savarkar, a young nationalist based in London and involved in the organization of the Free India Society, modelled on Mazzini's 'Young Italy', also designed another tricolour flag with saffron, white, and green. Cf. K.V. Singh, *Our National Flag*, op. cit., pp. 27–8.

[76] *Septième Congrès Socialiste International tenu à Stuttgart du 16 au 24 août 1907. Compte rendu analytique publié par le Secrétariat du Bureau Socialiste International* (Bruxelles, 1908), pp. 324–5. The unfurling of the flag of India's independence remained unrecorded in the minutes of the International Socialist Congress on the grounds that its intervention had not been announced but made at the last minute because of the British marxist delegate H.M. Hyndman's insistence.

[77] Walter Liefer, 'The First Indian Flag at Stuttgart', *Illustrated Weekly of India*, 26 January 1969, p. 19; A.C. Bose, *Indian Revolutionaries Abroad. 1905–1927. Select Documents* (New Delhi, I.C.H.R., 2002), p. 161.

race.'[78] It is possible this flag was later displayed during Bhikaji Cama's tour in the United States, in the autumn of 1907.[79]

From Calcutta to Stuttgart and then to London, the passage of the Partition flag from India to Europe assured it more publicity outside India than in. The same tricolour flag woven in silk and gold with the inscription 'In memory of the martyrs of 1908' was displayed by Bhikaji Cama at the Sunday meeting at India House in London on 2 November 1908. Then on 19 December, at a lecture on Indian nationalism by Bipin Chandra Pal, she stood up at its conclusion waving two flags in the air.[80] On 29 December 1908, the birth anniversary of Guru Govind Singh, the founder of Sikhism, two flags decorated the background of a meeting of Indian nationalists at Westminster, Caxton Hall, at which B.C. Pal, Bhikaji Cama, and Lala Lajpat Rai were present. One was the flag of the Sikhs, for which I have found no details. The second was the same tricolour flag.[81] After that, I have no evidence of its further use, with the exception of its appearance on the cover of the journal *The Talwar* created in 1910 by Virendranath Chattopadhyaya. The small world of Indian political exiles in Europe and their close contacts would explain the use of the red, saffron, and green tricolour by an Indian Independence Committee set up at Berlin by Chattopadhyaya after World War I and its presence among their volunteer force in Mesopotamia during the war.[82] At the same time, the Ghadar party, formed in the USA, also adopted a green, yellow, and red tricolour with crossed swords in the centre.[83]

Thus, the flag conceived in Bengal during 1905–6, which does not seem to have been utilized subsequently in India, was regularly

[78] K.A. Sethna, *Madame Bhikhaji Rustom Cama* (Delhi, Prakasana Vibhaga Sucana, 1992), pp. 1–2.

[79] Ibid., p. 74.

[80] Ibid., pp. 28–31.

[81] Ibid., p. 61.

[82] On Indian nationalist networks in Europe during the war, see Kalyan Kumar Banerjee, *Indian Freedom Movement Revolutionaries in America* (Calcutta, Jijnasa, 1969), pp. 20–6; Richard J. Popplewell, *Intelligence and Imperial Defence. British Intelligence and the Defence of the Indian Empire 1904–1924* (London, Frank Cass & Co., 1995), esp. pp.125–47.

[83] Gurdev Singh Deol, *The Role of the Ghadar Party in the National Movement* (Delhi and Jullundur, Sterling Publishers, 1969).

displayed in Europe though in small, select socialist, revolutionary circles during 1907–8. It was precisely in Europe, in November 1908, at India House, perhaps during the meeting already mentioned, that Tilak's legal adviser, R.P. Karandikar, discovered its existence. For this Maharashtrian nationalist, whose proximity to Tilak must surely have heightened appreciation of the importance of icons in creating a national consciousness, the meeting with Bhikaji Cama displaying a silk flag did not invite an enthusiastic response. Karandikar described it in a letter as a simple 'curiosity': if the term indicated that this flag had caught his eye, it suggested at the same time that such an object was of no political interest or utility.[84] From these accounts it is evident that nationalists in India were not using the same tools in these years as Indian nationalists in Europe.

War, Nation, Emotion

For the great majority of Indians the flag continued to be at best a curious feature and at worst an exotic element during the first decade of the twentieth century. This is confirmed by the future prominent nationalist and Congress leader Asaf Ali, who had embarked on his first long voyage by boat to England in 1909 as a young student. He recalled an experience that illustrates this point. The ship's passengers were a polyglot crowd and some French children, while playing, drew a French flag on the deck, which an English child of their age walked upon, or rather trampled. Offended, the French kids pulled the Union Jack, spat on it, and trampled it under their feet, causing a storm among the elders. But for Asaf Ali, who had played a part in the nationalist upheavals in Delhi as a university student, the incident provoked no reflection regarding its significance for these children and their parents, or its utility for India. Still, the experience marked him to the extent that he would note it in his memoirs many years later, though without any political comment.[85]

The flag's strangeness and uncertain status were surely reinforced by the fact that during these years this symbol was principally associated

[84] R.P. Karandikar, *Letters from England 1908* (Satara, 1935), p. 309.

[85] M. Asaf Ali's memoirs: *The Emergence of Modern India* (Delhi, Ajanta, 1994), pp. 66–7.

with political outcasts, radical revolutionaries abroad, political exiles, or uncommon and marginal figures like Nivedita and Bhikaji Cama. It was as if their unconventionality, proclaimed by the anglicized prefixes 'Sister' and 'Madame' of the names of the last two, almost hindered the flag from becoming truly Indian. As for the whiff of Western revolutionary antecedents like the French revolutionary tricolour, this added to its singularity, and even when promoting the very Indian symbol of vajra the flag failed to convince. Its genesis seemed to condemn it to the margins.

Such disinterest did not prevent a Congress volunteer from Masulipatam, Pingaly A. Venkayya, from publishing a small booklet entitled *A National Flag for India.* Financed almost entirely by Indians—a judge and some members of the viceroy's legislative council, who were more British government servants than Congress nationalists—the book urged Indians to wake up to the political importance of adopting a national flag and realize the primordial role of this emblem in uniting Indians behind a common idea and ideal. Venkayya presented no less than twenty-four designs for a national flag (Illustr. III) and invited the Indian National Congress to organize an exhibition in order to involve the people in this exercise of 'the greatest national importance'.[86] The work was the outcome of a long reflection pursued along a curious personal and political itinerary. This Andhra native was a descendant of a family of military commanders who had served under Maratha rulers in the eighteenth century and then migrated from Maharashtra to Kerala. He had entered the nationalist movement as early as 1906 when he attended the twenty-second session of the Indian National Congress at Calcutta presided over by Dadabhai Naoroji, in which the first Partition flag was unfurled. His family background coupled with his own army career in India, and his subsequent participation in the Boer War when he also met Gandhi, could well explain Venkayya's fascination with the power of emblems and banners. On his return to India he continued nationalist work, coming close to the 'Bal, Pal and Lal' trio and participating actively in Annie Besant's Home Rule movement. At this point he founded an Indian National Flag Mission with two other patriots from Bombay.[87]

[86] It receives no mention in the Indian government's version of *Our Flag.*
[87] P. Rajeswara Rao, 'Sri Pingaly Venkayya. Architect of our National Flag',

Venkayya's passionate promotion of the flag seems to have been a private obsession. At any rate, it was pursued without the official support of the Congress, for in 1916, discussions in the annual session of the Congress around the necessity of publicizing nationalist goals included no hint of the flag serving as a possible tool of propaganda. Instead they focused largely on the need for information bureaus and news agencies abroad to publicize the Indian cause.[88]

The twenty-four designs Venkayya presented as an argument, though conforming to Western codes in their rectangular form, were rooted principally in Indian and predominantly Hindu religious traditions as far as their designs were concerned. He quoted Vivekananda's injunction that India could be conceived only through her spiritual dimensions. He divided the symbols into four categories. The first proposed the images of Hindu goddesses—Durga, Saraswati, and Lakshmi—and saints like the Buddha; a second group represented events drawn from the Mahabharata like Bhisma on his deathbed of arrows, Arjuna in the field of battle, and Lord Krishna killing Kansa; a third group included Indian animals and flowers such as the snake, peacock, cow, elephant, lotus, and banyan tree; finally, a fourth category portrayed rather dated weapons of battle, like the bow and quiver and trident. Noticeable by their absence were two symbolically significant signs in the Hindu tradition, the swastika or *chaturbhuja chinha*, and the *chakra* or wheel widely represented in Hindu, Buddhist, and Jaina art.[89] Nivedita's flag with the thunderbolt was also included in his designs. A last notable feature of all the designs was a small Union Jack in the fly, revealing his own conception of nationalism.

Indeed, this last element was the only reference to the current political situation of India. Through this, Venkayya in all probability positioned himself in the movement demanding dominion status for India. The whole set of projects reflected an uneasy compromise

Triveni, Journal of Indian Renaissance, XXXVIII, 1969, no. 3, Mahatma Gandhi Birth Centenary Number, pp. 91–5.

88 NMML, *31st Indian National Congress Report*, 29 December 1916, microfilm, pp. 97–9.

89 Rai Govind Chandra, *Indian Symbolism. Symbols as Sources of our Customs and Beliefs* (New Delhi, Munshiram Manoharlal Publishers, 1996), pp. 51–64, 84–6.

between the desire to fix an entirely Indian icon and the parameters imposed by the colonial situation. Be that as it may, Congress party resolutions remained indifferent to these projects. Nor does the British government appear to have reacted. Yet Venkayya's enterprise corresponded to Coldstream and Burges' ideas for a distinctively Indian flag; except that, in his scheme, the Union Jack was now reduced to occupying a small place in the fly, with the Indian symbol taking up the largest place instead of the other way around.

Simultaneously, the Home Rule movement, founded in September 1916 under the direction of Annie Besant and Tilak, had designed its own flag.[90] Two very different descriptions are available. The first presents it as a tricolour for which a committee was appointed to consider a motif. I have found no trace of this committee ever having met to deliberate on the subject.[91] Such a design would establish a continuity with the Partition flag of 1905–7, placing it in a straightforward, unbroken evolution down to 1947. The second version describes the Home Rule flag as containing five red and four green horizontal stripes arranged alternately, with seven stars superimposed on them, as in Bhikaji Cama's flag. There was also a white crescent and star in one corner. In the left-hand top corner near the pole end was the Union Jack.[92] The partisans of Home Rule thus appropriated the symbolic arrangement of flags adopted by other British dominions since the beginning of the twentieth century to advance their own political claim, i.e. dominion status for India.

Through 1917–18 the Home Rule flag became part and parcel of numerous public political meetings and processions across the country. The movement gained importance in the south, in particular in Coimbatore and Erode, where a Home Rule flag was removed from Annie Besant's house on the order of the district magistrate, who found

[90] No information specifying who was at the root of this idea or the creator of the designs has been found.

[91] S.R. Bakshi, *Documents of Home Rule Movement* (New Delhi, Criterion Publications, 1989), p. 38.

[92] Christopher A. Bayly (ed.), *The Raj. India and the British 1600–1947* (London, National Portrait Gallery Publications, 1990), p. 343; the colours are indicated in *Our Flag*, op. cit., p. 2.

no other grounds to prohibit it than categorizing it as a criminal act.[93] The measure propelled the flag irretrievably into public space, on housetops, public transport, and even gardens. Already politically significant for Home Rulers, it now acquired a broader national meaning and following in all quarters, and among both Hindus and Muslims. The Bombay police reported groups of youngsters assembling in batches of thirty to forty and marching in processions to the town hall with posters and flags.[94] In Madras, the Indignant Group of the Home Rule League decided to popularize national songs, organize processions on national days, and induce householders to fly Home Rule flags.[95] It appeared in some reports as the emblem of 'India's future freedom',[96] or even as the 'national flag'.[97] Identified in this way, it assumed a familiar and intimate dimension, to the extent of being included in daily wear. The mother of the then imprisoned journalists, the Ali brothers, vowed: 'I shall now pin the Red and Green below the honoured badge of the Khaddama-i-ka'aba on my white Burqa or veiled mantle which I wear when going out.'[98] The internment of Besant and her colleagues Arundale and Wadia at Ootacamund reinforced its popularity. Annie Besant's release was acclaimed by an enthusiastic waving of the flag,[99] echoing her appeal to 'Keep the flag of freedom flying, to your last breath'.[100]

As a subject of public debate, it was projected as it had never been before, both as a 'sacrament' or the 'representation of a dream' by its

[93] OIOC, POS 3098, L. Davidson, Ootacamund, to Du Boulay, Sec., Govt of India.

[94] *Source Material for a History of the Freedom Movement in India*, 2 vols, *1885–1920* (Bombay, Government Central Press, 1958), vol. II, p. 719.

[95] OIOC, POS, 3098, Fortnightly report on the internal political situation for the first half of July 1917.

[96] *The Advocate*, 17 July 1917.

[97] *Amrita Bazar Patrika*, 22 September 1917.

[98] Abadi Bano Abdul Ali Begum to Sir Subramanyam Iyer, Chhindwara (Central Provinces), 4 September 1917, in Shan Muhammad, *Unpublished Letters of the Ali Brothers* (Delhi, Idarah-i Adabiyat-i Delli, 1979), p. 108.

[99] *Amrita Bazar Patrika*, 22 September 1917.

[100] Manmohan Kaur, *Role of Women in the Freedom Movement* (Jullundur, Sterling Publishers, 1968), p. 117.

partisans and scoffed by sceptics and critics as an affair that was 'puerile and [a] fad' mounted by a foreign 'theosophic trinity' (i.e. Besant an Irish, Arundale a Britisher, and Wadia a Parsi).[101] Counting on the people's sympathy in her fight against government persecution and censorship, Besant's newspaper *New India* undertook a pedagogical political instruction programme: 'What is the significance of the Home Rule flag? . . . We answer with a question: what is the significance of the Union Jack to the citizens of the British empire, of the tricolour to the citizens of the Republic of France? Our flag is to us exactly like the other flags in the world . . . the symbol of our National Ideal of Freedom and Self Rule.'[102]

Confronted with such repeated and persistent displays in public space, the British government was eventually forced to formulate a uniform policy regarding this political symbol, sometimes perceived as a substitute for the British ensign. The exchange of official notes from January 1918 reveals its large diffusion in British India (Madras, Bombay, Gaya, Delhi). Provincial authorities feared that their government's tolerance would convince Indian public opinion of their impotence and negatively affect government prestige.[103] In Madras the government opened a discussion with the principal spokesman of the Home Rulers, Kharpade, to discourage them from using it publicly. The latter, maintaining that everyone had a right to fly any flag he liked, declared it was 'an unwarrantable interference with private liberties' for government or any official to attempt to stop it. The Director of Criminal Intelligence affirmed, in his turn, that there were flags and flags: 'If Mr Kharpade sported the German flag for instance, he would find himself in a tight corner.'[104] In Delhi, Chief Commissioner Malcolm Hailey argued that since the Home Rule flag adorning the party office in the city attracted no attention from the public, a watchful policy of government inaction was the best response. There

[101] OIOC, *Native Indian Newspapers*, L/R/5/173, *Kesari*, 4 September 1917, *Priya Mitra*, *Parsi*, 5 September 1917, *Jam-e-Jamshed*, 3 September 1917.

[102] *New India*, 31 August 1917, p. 6.

[103] NAI, Delhi, Home Political Report, Deposit 10, March 1918, H. McPherson, Chief Secretary to Govt of Bihar and Orissa to S.R. Hignell, Secretary to Govt of India, 10 January 1918.

[104] Ibid., C.R. Cleveland, Director Criminal Intelligence, to Home Dept, 6 February 1918.

could of course, Hailey pointed out, be objectionable cases which might well call for action on the part of the local authorities.[105] The home department's final position was determined in light of British experience with the Irish Home Rule movement and its use of the Irish flag: the prohibition applied in Ireland had been a failure.[106] Consequently, the British government in India concluded that banning the Home Rule flag would inflate its importance and decided in February 1918 not to interfere.[107]

In 1917–18, for the first time, the idea of a 'flag for the Indian nation' ended by imposing itself in popular imagination. Its case was strengthened when the Congress annual session of 1917 displayed a rainbow-coloured flag designed by Venkayya, representing India's major religious communities.[108] The question of the national flag seems to have been formally raised in this session, although the party's official resolutions still made no mention of it.[109] Henceforth, it was to become a permanent element in the decor of the Congress annual sessions.[110] In England an Indian flag—there is no evidence that allows us to determine which precise flag was used—was hoisted in London in November 1918 to mark the participation of Indians in the First World War. The event was organized by Pincess Sophia Duleep Singh, the Egyptian wife of Prince Duleep Singh of Punjab, last heir of Maharaja Ranjit Singh and residing in England. However, the idea behind it was not to further the cause of Indian unity or nationhood but simply to highlight the contribution and sacrifice of Indian soldiers for the empire in the war.[111] Such use of the flag corresponded

[105] Ibid.

[106] NAI, Delhi, Home Political Report, Deposit 10, March 1918, H. McPherson, Chief Secretary to Govt of Bihar and Orissa to S.R. Hignell, Secretary to Govt of India, 10 January 1918.

[107] Ibid., S.R Hignell, 9 February 1918, J.H. Du Boulay, 12 February 1918.

[108] *New India*, 10 January 1917.

[109] This detail is noted by S.R. Bakshi, *Documents of Home Rule Movement*, op. cit., p. 38.

[110] A.M. Zaidi (ed.), *The Encyclopaedia of Indian National Congress*, vol. 7, *1916–20. In Search of a Creed* (New Delhi, S. Chand, 1980–1), pp. 23–4, 277; vol. 10, *1930–1935*, p. 73.

[111] *The Tribune*, 10 November 1918; the event was recalled in the months preceding independence, *National Herald*, 8 June 1947.

more to the preoccupations voiced fifteen years ealier by Coldstream than to existing nationalist proposals.

The Aftermath of the War: An International Symbolic Revolution

In 1920, to the newly acquired emotional dimension of the flag was added a more rational, constitutional logic imposed by India's participation in world official bodies. Indeed, if Home Rule had elevated the symbol from a 'curiosity' to a 'national emblem', the international conjuncture on the morrow of the First World War confirmed this shift. The war transformed the theory and practice of colonial participation in world affairs by privileging the idea of an international form of society and the theory of national sovereignty.[112] Its consequences for India were certain and immediate.

Britain's role in the international conferences at the end of the war introduced her dominions—Canada, Australia, South Africa—but also her colony, India, as original members of the League of Nations. All of them had already affirmed their international autonomy by their separate representation at international conferences. Thus India, just like Australia or Canada, had benefited from this right in the International Postal Union in 1906 and in the Conference on Electrical Units and Standards in 1908.[113] Moreover, India's contribution to the war effort placed her in the same league as the other dominions, and the country was thus represented in the imperial war cabinet set up to promote imperial co-operation and share the costs of the war and British plans of naval defence.[114]

[112] Significantly, it was at this time that Leonard S. Woolf was designated by the Committee of the Fabian Research Department to report on the growth of the system of international relationships and procedures of government, which was perceived by Labour circles as a means of preventing further wars. His report, the first comprehensive treatment of the development of international exchanges and regulations in diverse spheres, from trade and science to literature, labour, and social reform, was published as a book: *International Government* (London-Westminster, Fabian Society, 1916).

[113] A memorial to the soldiers of the British empire, dead in the war, in the cathedral of Notre Dame, Paris, includes India along with other dominions, Australia, Canada, South Africa.

[114] The Imperial War Conference of 1917 was attended by the secretary of

After the First World War, colonial delegates backed by President Wilson argued and won the right for separate representation at the Peace Conference with full voting powers, together with the right of representation in the council at the Peace Conference of Paris, despite opposition from Tory imperialists, France, and Italy.[115] India thus acquired separate representation in its own name besides being represented through the British empire. However, the country's new international and constitutional status altered neither its position of dependence nor its colonial status. Although self-government was a necessary qualification for admission to the League at the time, responsible government had been proclaimed the goal of Indian policy. The reforms of 1919 were being contemplated and it was generally considered that India's constitutional position was one of transition. The major difference with other self-governing dominions was that the members of the Indian delegation were appointed by the secretary of state for India and instructed by him. Therefore, the Government of India's views were subject to His Majesty's government, an anomaly Indian nationalists were quick to condemn.[116] But partly as a result of India's membership of the League and partly owing to resolution number IX adopted by the Imperial War Conference of 1917 recognizing the right of the Dominions and of India to a voice in foreign policy and foreign relations, the country was given the same right of representation as the dominions at all international conferences where the empire was represented by an empire delegation.[117] Furthermore, as India and not British India was a member of the League, the native Indian states were

state, Mr Chamberlain, accompanied by Sir Satyendra Sinha, the Indian member of the viceroy's executive council and the maharaja of Bikaner. Cf. A.B. Keith (ed.), *Speeches and Documents on the British Dominions. From Self Government to National Sovereignty, vol. 1, 1750–1921* (London, Oxford University Press, 1922), *vol. 2, 1918–31* (London, Oxford University Press, 1931), p. 5.

115 C.D. Allin, 'The International Status of the British Dominions with Respect to the League of Nations', *Minnesota Law Review*, vol. 4, 1920, pp. 190–218.

116 Surendranath Bannerjee protested that the Indians nominated were representatives of the British government in India, not of India. Cf. Annie Besant, *The Case for India* (Home Rule for India League, 1917), pp. 24–5.

117 OIOC, L/PO/6/28 ii, *Memorandum on India's Position in the British Empire*.

also included.[118] Indian delegates participated in the annual sessions of the International Labour Conference and in some fifteen conferences on special subjects held under the auspices of the League. In the 1920s India participated in the Washington Conference on Naval Armaments and the Geneva Economic Conference, besides being on several permanent League bodies like the Economic Committee, the Health Committee and the Committee on International Cooperation.

This was a development of no less significance than the concessions towards self-government. Montagu, secretary of state over 1917–18, described it as having 'put India so far as international affairs are concerned, on a basis wholly inconsistent with the position of a subordinate country'.[119] It much alarmed the British who dreaded the spectre of nationalists referring to the League of Nations for a resolution of India's problem concerning self-government, as indeed one swarajist, C. Vijairaghavachari, suggested.[120] Another factor of some worry was the resurgence of a national flag issue in other parts of the empire. In South Africa, J.B.M. Herzog, leader of the South African nationalist party, declared in a debate in parliament in March 1920 that they did 'no service to themselves, nor to England by bearing the Union Jack'. For him, this was 'merely a piece of cloth'. For South Africa to have its own flag, he announced, would lead to a better relationship with England.[121] In Canada a debate on the Canadian Nationals Bill spilled over to include questions on the implications for the flag of a change of status from 'dominion' to 'nation'.[122]

To add to British problems the colonial symbol of 'Star of India', customarily used within the limits of India but now projected to international platforms, no longer conformed to the norms of protocol. Already, in 1919, requests such as those of a Major Lane asking the librarian of the Colonial Office in London for a sample of the Indian flag—he was preparing a design of all signatures of British delegates at

[118] OIOC, L/PO/6/28 ii, *Confidential Memorandum supplied to the Simon Commission by the India Office, May 1928.*

[119] S.D. Waley, *Edwin Montagu, A Memoir and an Account of his Visits to India* (Bombay, Asia Publishing House, 1964), p. 194.

[120] Arthur Davies, 'Swaraj: India and the League of Nations', *The 19th Century and After*, vol. 106, 1929, pp. 433–42.

[121] *Journal of the Parliaments of the Empire*, vol. II, 1921, p. 686.

[122] Ibid., p. 341.

the Peace Conference—had announced the shift.[123] In September 1920 the British foreign office in Peking made a similar demand.[124] Two months later a telegram sent by the Indian prince Jam Saheb of Navanagar carried the demand further by asking for the use of an Indian flag by the Indian delegation to the assembly of the League of Nations at Geneva.[125]

Clearly, it was no coincidence that prompted Gandhi in December 1920, at the Congress session at Bezwada, to finally agree to Venkayya's persistent suggestions and ask him to design a new national flag with a spinning wheel on a red and green background. Gandhi's own explanation of this timing made no reference to the broader conjuncture: neither to developments in South Africa nor to the change in India's international status, nor to the political urgency of finding a symbol of unity for the Khilafat movement that he was then actively championing. His account dwelt exclusively upon one factor—the spinning wheel that could 'stir the nation to its depths'. From his nationalist perspective this was the crucial element that signified resistance to colonial rule, the Indian rediscovery of an economic and even moral self, and the recovery of dignity, pride, and above all unity. In the lengthy analysis he provided of its colours and design that was to become the ground for later elaborations and interpretations by him as well as others, he stressed the novelty of this icon and the meanings it promoted.

Compared to its predecessors, this was indeed a clear rupture. Gone were the juxtapositions and combinations of particular religious symbols like sun, crescent, and stars that had characterized the flags of 1905–7 and which, even while proclaiming the unity of the Indian people, did no more than put them side by side. Instead, Gandhi proposed a deeper unity through a single design representing all Indians. This unity was further emphasized in his eyes by the combination of red and green colours representing Hindus and Muslims. To that extent, he continued the logic of earlier flags. It was, he explained, one

[123] NAI, Home Department Public, 1920, Proceedings nos 175–6, Part B, Charles Niblett, Librarian, Colonial Office to Librarian, India Office, London, 17 February 1919.

[124] Ibid., B. Alston, Foreign Office to Curzon, 14 June 1920.

[125] OIOC, L/P&J/6/1720, E.S. Montagu to Governor General of India in Council, 13 January 1921.

Lala Hansraj of Jullunder's suggestion that the charkha should be included in their 'Swaraj flag' that convinced him to inject this national symbol at that moment into India's struggle for freedom. In three hours the flag was finalized, still too late to be presented to the All India Congress Committee. But it existed.[126]

Gandhi's 'Swaraj flag' could not be ignored by the British government, which would have liked to turn a blind eye and wish away the whole issue. But it was politically impossible to ignore what was obviously raised as a symbol of resistance that rivalled the 'Star of India' and dealt a serious blow to the imperial right to represent its colony. A month after Gandhi's 'Swaraj flag' was born, in January 1921, the secretary of state E.S. Montagu reopened the government file on a 'flag for India' for the third time, after 1902 and 1917, in light of [India's recent] admission as a state member of the League of Nations' and increasing demands for a flag for India.[127]

While the government deliberated, Gandhi wrote an article in his journal, *Young India*, explaining the meanings and possibilities of this new axis of the struggle, its capacity for uniting Indians behind a common ideal, submerging their differences and raising them beyond their particular, local identities as religious groups and regions.[128] Such a clear call for Indian unity behind its own banner was an obvious rejection of the British symbolic system. In the coming months, the Government of India was simultaneously and variously urged to act decisively and immediately against the Indian flag: from being conciliatory to modifying its existing colonial symbol to placate Indian demands and sensitivities—even to the extent of including the charkha in the fly of the current colonial emblem. Gandhi's flag finally involved Indian nationalists in a new exercise of elaborating a symbol that was pleasing and acceptable to both the government and its Indian subjects.

As in 1917, local governments pressed for the classic policy, i.e., a hardline response banning the flag. The second suggestion came in

[126] *CWMG, vol. xix, November 1920–April 1921*, pp. 561–2.

[127] NAI, Home Department Public-A, nos 25–6 & K.W., August 1921. E.S. Montagu, India Office, London, to Governor General of India in Council, 13 January 1921.

[128] *Young India*, 13 April 1921.

May 1921 from a British citizen, Mrs Chadwick Brown, living in Rangoon, Burma. She submitted a new design containing the Star of India with its motto in the upper canton on a red fly of the Union Jack, but now accompanied with a wreath of leaves of the peepul or bo tree and the motto 'Pro Axis et Focis' (For our altar and our hearths).[129] An explanatory pamphlet, 'Honour for Time for India and Burma',[130] stressed, just as Coldstream had done in 1902 and Reverend Burges in 1908, the importance of teaching patriotism, not through a colonial device which meant nothing to Indians, but through a symbol with deep religious meaning that would touch their souls and 'inculcate the Imperial idea'.[131] Pressure for change kept mounting from various quarters. Three months later, in August 1921, the home department received another demand for a flag of India from the International Agriculture Institute at Rome.[132] The British parliament in London too was confronted with the future of their system of symbolic representation. The peace treaty with Ireland in 1921 raised questions about the future status of the Union Flag in Ireland and the implications of the raising of the Irish flag for other British dominions. Chamberlain's reply that the question had not figured in the conference was greeted with sarcasm: 'Are we to understand that the Union Jack, as our national flag, was not considered important enough for the discussion?.'[133] Finally, the third and last idea came in September that year, from the Indian member of the viceroy's council, Munshi Iswar Saran. He urged the government to set up a committee of nationalists, which would include Gandhi, to decide a national flag for India. In that way the British would thwart the nationalist strategy of equipping their struggle with a symbol of resistance and recuperate them once more under the umbrella of colonial paternalism.[134]

[129] NAI, Home Department, Public, nos 342–3, Part B, Chadwick Brown to Earl of Reading, 9 May 1921.

[130] NAI, Home Department, Public, nos 342–3, Part B, 9 June 1921.

[131] Ibid., pp. 2–14, Chadwick Brown to Earl of Reading.

[132] NAI, Home Department, Public-A, August 1921, nos 25–6 & K.W., Home Department's Note, 15 June 1921.

[133] *Parliamentary Debates Official Report, House of Commons*, 5th series, vol. 149, 16, 19, December 1921, pp. 129, 281, 391–2.

[134] OIOC, L/P&J/6/1720, Official Report of the Legislative Assembly Debates, 20 September 1921, p. 580.

But the government remained immune to pressure from all these fronts, refusing conciliation, modification, and even prohibition. It dismissed Chadwick Brown's proposal, just as it had earlier done Coldstream's.[135] As for the idea of including the charkha in the colonial emblem for India, it could not be 'seriously contemplated'.[136] It rejected Iswar Saran's idea of establishing a bridge with the nationalists, saying the moment was inopportune. And finally, it made no move to prohibit the flag as advised by the Government of Bombay. Its justification for this inaction: constitutional reforms were being envisaged which might inaugurate a wider federative union, including the princely states. Elaborating a flag for British India at the present, only to change it later, did not make sense, for any accord concluded with the nationalists now could be questioned later by the princes.[137] Having considered the question from all these angles, the British government's reaction was marked by continuity, in almost complete disregard of the changed political context within India or abroad. Reading's answer did not vary from his predecessors'. The moment for a change of India's flag was 'not opportune and should be postponed for further consideration'.[138] In December 1921 the secretary to the Government of Bombay warned the government of nationalist plans to hoist Gandhi's flag in the annual Congress session at Ahmedabad that month, arguing that any accompanying speech or act of declaration of a republic or a civil disobedience movement must be answered with the prohibition of flying the flag under sections 42 and 54 of the District Police Act.[139]

In some twenty years, three moments of political tension had seen the formulation of projects for a national standard. During the partition of Bengal and the subsequent agitation of 1905–9, the flag remained a marginal element in a broad movement of protest. It was taken up and sustained in restrained circles of Indian revolutionaries

135 NAI, Home Department, Public-A, August 1921, nos 25–6 & K.W., H. Tonkinson, 11 May 1921.

136 Ibid., W.H. Vincent, 11 May 1921.

137 Ibid., 15 August 1921.

138 Ibid. Reading to Montagu, Simla, 11 August 1921.

139 NAI, Delhi, Home Political, F. no. 453/22, Sec. to the Govt of Bombay to F.G. Pratt, ICS, Northern Division, 12 December 1921.

living abroad. A simple curiosity, it stayed foreign to the Indian political dynamic. At the heart of the First World War, the Home Rule movement raised the flag wherever it succeeded in implanting itself and ended up after several months of increasing mobilization by having it recognized as a national symbol. But the flag did not survive the movement. Finally, the emergence of India at the heart of the concert of nations on the morrow of the war transformed the conditions and stakes surrounding its existence. When in December 1920 Gandhi called for a new proposal for this symbol, the question had, in a short time, become an important political issue for Indian nationalism, and even more for the British Government of India. In 1905–7, as in 1917–19, the force of political movements had overpowered the flag. Paradoxically, its evolution in 1920–1 continued without links with a strong political movement.

It was perhaps this that would permit it to take root in the long term.

3

Imposing a Consensus from Below

Hoisted a year after its birth—at the Congress session at Ahmedabad in December 1921—the 'Swaraj flag', a roughly stitched tricolour in *khaddar* with four *charkhas*[1] (Illustr. 1) was the tangible expression of Gandhi's promise to win full independence for India within the year. Its passage from the realms of an idea to formal hoisting within the precincts of a party organization, the Indian

Illustr. 1. Gandhi hoisting his Swaraj flag at the Ahmedabad session of Congress, 1921

[1] NMML, Report of the 36th Indian National Congress Session at Ahmedabad, 27–28 December 1921.

National Congress, already distinguished it from its predecessors. But it still had to be 'adopted by the public, perceived, received',[2] in short, its success was far from certain. The context in which it had emerged augured well for its survival and even popularity in at least four respects. First, the familiarity with this idiom of nationhood in India had lately increased thanks to the appearances and recent public polemic surrounding the Home Rule flag. The second element was Gandhi's personal imprint; he had already acquired a strong political stature and his astute choice of the symbol, the spinning wheel (charkha), that he was promoting as an instrument of resistance against the British, placed the flag in a larger movement of protest on a national scale. Third, it was not conceived in an exclusive relationship to a particular and limited political movement, which could lead to its retreat with the end of such a movement. And last, its fate hinged equally on the yet unknown reaction of the British government, although the Government of India's repeated refusals to accept any modification of the existing system of symbols for its Indian empire could lead to future confrontations. The flag's field of influence thus depended as much on nationalist operations as on British interventions.

Could Gandhi's flag shake the colonial system of political symbols and rituals that the British government seemed determined to maintain? Its name—the Swaraj flag, i.e. for independence—announced the opening of a battle against the colonial power symbolized by the Union Jack. As an 'object of idolatry' in a non-violent struggle, Gandhi hoped it would rally and coalesce the manifold political preoccupations of Indians. Both facets, the complex interplay between Indians and British and between the different political strains within Indian nationalism, were deeply interrelated. Its political trajectory in the 1920s and 1930s was marked by three waves which unfolded progressively and sometimes merged into one another.

The first task was to get the flag recognized as the unique national symbolic reference point for all Indians, in other words to nationalize it. The key moment was a movement of protest, more or less spontaneous, whose goal was to win the right to display the flag in public

[2] Maurice Agulhon, 'Politique, images, symboles dans la France post-révolutionnaire', in *Histoire Vagabonde*, vol. 1, *Ethnologie et politique dans la France contemporaine* (Paris, Gallimard, 1988), p. 314.

space. From April to August 1923 this satyagraha in the city of Nagpur canalized national attention and gave the flag a central position in collective actions and also in the individual imagination. The success of this operation opened the second phase. It allowed the marking of British India's geographical territory with the Indian flag during the late 1920s, and more so invested it with a larger dimension during the 1930s—once the Congress officially proclaimed the tricolour as the 'national flag'. Henceforth, by displaying their symbol from the smallest village to the biggest residencies and institutional structures, from district courts and schools to the viceroy's residence, Indians would be symbolically occupying and recovering their land.

Finally, the flag's appropriation by a large number of Indians—in a certain way, its nationalization —changed its status and transformed it into a political weapon. It led to an immediate rivalry with the British flag, which took the form in 1930 of an open symbolic war around a very explicit slogan: 'Up, up with the National Flag, Down, down with the Union Jack'.

Nationalizing the Flag: The Nagpur Satyagraha, 1923

Gandhi's call in April 1921 to Indians, 'Hindus, Mohammedans, Christians, Jews, Parsis and all others to whom India is their home—to recognise a common flag to live and to die for',[3] was taken up a week later by the local newspaper of Allahabad. It noted the widespread hope that this flag newly designed by Gandhi would float over the Allahabad district conference for the first time.[4] Another newspaper even proclaimed that if the standard of Swaraj were not unfurled by 25 December, there would be little meaning in convening Congress members for the annual session.[5] While Gandhians welcomed it as some kind of hallowed, empowering, divine 'mantra', the Indian National Congress continued to be preoccupied with what seemed more urgent political subjects, such as reconciling council entry with

[3] *Young India*, 13 April 1921, p. 116.

[4] OIOC, L/R/5/96, Selections from Newspapers Published in the United Provinces for the week ending 23 April 1921, *The Independent*, 21 April 1921.

[5] *Navjivan*, 6 November 1921, cited in S.R. Bakshi (ed.), *Documents of Non-Cooperation Movement* (Delhi, Akashdeep Publication House, 1989), p. 327.

non-cooperation, for example.[6] Despite these differences the flag's progress was unexpectedly rapid and quite spectacular. It was integrated in a host of local events, outside the political field, like a large fair near Patna (at Berhampur in Shahbad district) or an industrial exhibition at Bhagalpur in Bihar in February 1922.[7]

Through 1921 to 1922 the flag was integrated in local protests, picketing, and processions. One Assamese non-cooperator, imprisoned in 1921, remembered men and women thronging at the prison gates daily with the tricolour flag in hand, raising slogans, beating drums and demanding to be arrested.[8] A British civil servant in Patna reported the spectacle of small processions carrying flags and shouting 'Gandhi Maharaj ki Jai' in 1921.[9] Demonstrations of crowds, escorting persons accused of damaging tar trees, to the subdivisional officers' camp as part of the 'temperance' campaigns, integrated the tricolour into their existing arsenal of drums and trumpets.[10] All over the Central Provinces, Bihar, and Orissa the act of hoisting the flag on the town hall and other municipal buildings became a common occurrence.[11]

Though dispersed and uncoordinated, these acts, by their very repetition, established a political pattern of visually defying British authority. These appearances were of course reported in the press,

[6] Nonetheless, a report of the 36th Indian National Session of Ahmedabad included a photo of the event. NMML, Report of the 36th INC session at Ahmedabad, 27, 28 December 1921, p. 33.

[7] NAI, Home Political, F. no. 650, 1922, S.P. O'Donnel, Secretary to Government of India, Home Department to E. L. Hammond, Chief Secretary to the Government of Bihar and Orissa, 2 March 1922; extract from the confidential diary of the superintendent of Police, Bhagalpur, for week ending 9 February 1922.

[8] M. Tayyebulla, *Between the Symbol and the Idol at Last* (Delhi-New York, Allied Publishers, 1964), p. 38.

[9] G.E. Owen, *Bihar and Orissa in 1921. A Report of the Administration of Bihar and Orissa* (Patna, 1922), p. 154.

[10] Ibid., p. 152

[11] OIOC, L/P&J/6/1794, Report on Indian Papers Published in Central Provinces and Berar, 1922; NAI, Home Political, F. no 650, 1922, S.P. O'Donnel, Secretary to Government of India, Home Department to E. L. Hammond, Chief Secretary to the Government of Bihar and Orissa, 2 March 1922; extract from the confidential diary of the Superintendent of Police, Bhagalpur, for week ending 9 February 1922.

whether in brief headlines or in small recapitulations of main events. But they also provided the background for more detailed analysis and comments about the meaning of the symbol and its role in different political traditions, both Western and Indian. Gandhi's newspaper *Young India* wrote prominently and systematically on the flag from 1920 onwards, being the first to publish his explanation of this emblem. Gandhians like C.R. Rajagopalachari also promoted the symbol energetically, expounding on its power, its 'profound meaning and importance . . . that affect everyone, near and distant'.[12] The visible evidence of the flag in all kinds of contexts—formal political sites, festive occasions, and popular gatherings—coupled with a political discourse from national personalities as well as ordinary individuals expressing their sentiments was contributing to the creation of a set of images accessible to all. Thus, nearly fifty years after independence Annapurna Moharana, from an aristocratic family of Cuttack in present-day Orissa, remembered how as a young child she gleefully watched her uncle hoisting the tricolour on their house in 1922, despite warnings that the act was tantamount to sedition. 'Instead of being frightened', she narrated, 'we felt honoured'.[13] The fright was no doubt nourished by the British administration, which treated the emblem as taboo and reacted to its display with immediate censure. In contrast, nationalists exalted the sentiment of honour. The child's feelings reflected the effectiveness with which a system of emotions about the emblem was being put in place.

The first serious confrontation between the 'Swaraj flag' and the Union Flag took place a year later, at Jubbulpore in the Central Provinces. On 18 March 1923 the municipality greeted the arrival of a Congress committee, charged with examining the possibilities of launching civil disobedience in the city, by hoisting Gandhi's flag. The British immediately confiscated this when it was carried in a procession through the civil station and cantonment area and arrested the participants. Indian members of the municipal committee further attempted to hoist it on the town hall and, when prevented, fourteen of them

[12] *Young India*, 17 August 1922, 'Shanti's flag', pp. 340–1.

[13] Naveen Joshi (ed.), *Freedom Fighters Remember* (New Delhi, Publications Division, Ministry of Information and Broadcasting, Govt. of India, 1997), p. 127.

resigned on 20 March. However, an attempt by local Congress members to use this incident and the British order prohibiting the flying of the Swaraj flag in the city as a point of departure for a civil disobedience campaign proved difficult to organize.[14]

Nonetheless, on 1 April 1923 the Jubbulpore Congress Committee launched a satyagraha with the support of C.R. Rajagopalachari.[15] Appeals were launched to other districts and provinces for support,[16] without any official statement being issued by the All India Congress Working Committee. On that same day, the town Congress committee outlined a strategy for vindicating the honour of the flag; it set up several sub-committees to collect funds, enrol volunteers, organize media exposure and national publicity, and ensure the supply of provisions and medical aid. Furthermore, it began informing the public on the standard dimensions of the flag and the correct manner of using it.[17] Mobilization around the affair increased with the immediate publication of a leaflet on the history and importance of the 'flag affair' circulated by the secretary of the Central Provinces Congress Committee.[18] Neighbouring towns in the Central Provinces also witnessed similar demonstrations,[19] even seeing the standard raised on the district commissioner's bungalow.[20] Other local Congress resolutions called upon their municipal committees to hoist the flag in the town hall on a variety of occasions,[21] for example raising it in April on the meeting of the twentieth Provincial Rajput Conference at Bilaspur, Orissa.[22]

Clearly, in this initial phase, the flag was heavily championed by district and provincial Congress committees and workers pursuing local strategies to impose themselves or win control over municipalities, without any clear-cut directions from the central party leadership.

[14] *The Hitavada*, 28 March 1923.

[15] Iqbal Singh, *The I.N.C.—A Reconstruction*, vol. 2, *1919–1923* (Delhi, Manohar, 1988), pp. 465–6.

[16] OIOC, L/P&J/6/1794, Report on the Political Situation in Central Provinces and Berar for the second half of March 1923.

[17] *The Hitavada*, 11 April 1923.

[18] *The Mahratta*, 1 April 1923.

[19] *Young India*, 3 April 1923, p. 110.

[20] *The Hitavada*, 4 April, p. 5.

[21] *Young India*, 5 April 1923.

[22] Ibid.

This policy of using the emblem as an instrument for consolidating and widening networks of influence, while it certainly provided public exposure, also had the unfortunate consequence of arousing the hostility of non-Congressmen competing for local resources and power, particularly so in the bigger cities of Bombay and Calcutta. Nehru would later categorize such acts of easy display and exhibition of nationalist sentiments as 'pretexting nationalism', which only proved embarrassing to the Congress Party.[23] But in 1922–3, as a survey of the English press shows, the flag was clearly serving local Congress members as a means of reinforcing their control over municipalities. This inevitably invoked the ire of the British authorities. As evident from the Jubbulpore agitation, there was local, provincial pressure on the central Congress Party to take up the cause of nascent movements in defence of the flag. Public political meetings became a powerful propaganda tool aimed both at the central Congress organization and the British.[24]

But this provincial Congress enthusiasm to exploit the flag's potential as a symbol of anti-colonial protest and its effective mobilization of public support found no echo in the party's national echelons. An independent leading newspaper of the Central Provinces like *The Hitavada* also criticized the Jubbulpore incident as exaggerated and politically irrelevant, revealing the different political stakes and positions, as well as the lack of consensus on national goals and strategies. Critical press articles highlighted the weaknesses of a political movement that switched from one cause to another with a rapidity that could only leave the public bemused, whether it was the Sikh agitation to regain control of their temples, or the Khilafat movement, or the issue of council entry. Seen from this optic, the 'national flag affair' was a diversion from 'more tangible and useful activity on behalf of our motherland'.[25] In a more serious vein, the press interpreted the Jubbulpore agitation as raising two important questions. The first: when had the Indian nation adopted a flag for India? And the second: had

[23] *Rajendra Prasad Correspondence and Select Documents*, ed. Valmiki Choudhary (Delhi, Allied Publishers, 1984), vol. 3, January–July 1939, pp. 132–5.

[24] *The Hitavada*, 11 April 1923, 'National Flag'.

[25] Ibid.

the Congress ever officially decided upon any particular form of the national flag?[26] Both remarks were legitimate, for the flag was indeed Gandhi's creation and Congress had not yet adopted it by any official resolution. But these questions were swept away before the wave of sympathetic reaction against the British administration's prohibition of the standard, judged as 'hurting municipal freedom'. Every nation, seen from this perspective, had the right to hoist its own national flag and the British measure constituted an 'insult to national honour and self respect'.[27]

In London members of parliament considered the Jubbulpore affair a municipal rebellion. They asked if the under secretary of state for India was even aware that the 'revolutionary flag' had been hoisted over municipal buildings as a sign of welcome to the civil disobedience committee and that no action had been taken by the governor of the Central Provinces?[28] In fact, the Government of India, always conscious of the difficulties the British government had faced in a similar struggle with the Irish flag,[29] did not sway from its earlier policy reaffirmed a year before the Jubbulpore agitation. It remained opposed to 'any action which would give undue notoriety to insignificant individuals' and preferred to handle each incident as it arose.[30]

A new incident was to put this policy to test. Barely two weeks after the Jubbulpore affair, on 13 April 1923, a flag bearing procession at Nagpur, led by Gandhians commemorating the 1919 massacre at Jallianwala Bagh, was stopped from entering the civil lines area by the police. Immediately, the matter was seized by local Gandhians who saw it as a means to strengthen their electoral base in a constituency dominated by Tilak's Maratha followers. A month of intense political activity at all levels followed. In the city itself, from the middle of April,

[26] Ibid.

[27] *The Mahratta*, 1 April 1923.

[28] OIOC, L/P&J/6, Report on the Political Situation in Central Provinces and Berar for the Second Half of March 1923.

[29] Lucy Bryson & Clem McCartney, *Clashing Symbols. A Report on the Use of Flags, Anthems and other National Symbols in Northern Ireland* (Belfast, Institute of Irish Studies, 1994).

[30] NAI, Delhi, Home Political, 941/II, 1922, question no. 84, 27 November 1922.

public meetings, addresses, publicity, recruitment of volunteers, and fund collection mounted a convincing case of grassroots resistance against the colonial administration. On 1 May the struggle was formally begun in Nagpur, with small batches of six volunteers entering the prohibited area with the flag in hand, observed by crowds.[31] Local Congress cadres and Gandhians backed it, in particular Jamnalal Bajaj, the rich Marwari industrialist who was chairman of the Congress reception committee at Nagpur, and also treasurer of the Congress Party.[32] On 17 May Gandhi's secretary, Mahadev Desai, urged the Congress central leadership to approve and take up the cause of a fight, which the rest of the country could not look upon 'with indifference or even amused interest'.[33] Indeed, as the Indian *Daily Telegraph* declared, the national flag activities alone could save the country 'from acute Hindu–Muslim strife by directing popular attention to patriotism rather than religious fanaticism'.[34]

Such persistent projection of an issue that was quite novel compared to the more established forms of collective protest guaranteed it publicity within the city, the Central Provinces, and other states, thanks to the Gandhian mobilization. Gradually, a consensual climate in favour of nationalizing the 'Swaraj flag' through a local conflict was gaining ground. Sarojini Naidu joined Jamnalal Bajaj in pressing for an intensification of the agitation and the involvement of volunteers from other regions of India.[35] *Young India* of course did not let up, pointing

[31] For a detailed analysis of the Nagpur flag satyagraha, see Arundhati Virmani, 'National Symbols under Colonial Domination : The Nationalization of the Indian Flag, March–August 1923', *Past and Present*, no. 164, August 1999, pp. 169–97; the study has been prolonged from a different perspective by Sadan Jha, 'The Indian National Flag as a Site of Daily Plebiscite', 7th Subaltern Conference, 'Lives of Democracy: Peoples, Populations & Citizens in South Asia', 6–9 January 2004, Centre for the Study of Developing Societies, Delhi, unpublished typescript.

[32] *Young India*, 24 May 1923, p. 175.

[33] *Young India*, 17 May 1923. Mahadev Desai pressed the Congress Working Committee and the All-India Congress Committee to give the question the consideration that it deserved: 'The Issue in Nagpur'.

[34] OIOC, L/R/5/97, Native Newspaper Reports for the United Provinces, 30 June 1923.

[35] *The Hitavada*, 6 June 1923.

I Nivedita's 'Vajra' design for an Indian national flag
(*The Modern Review*, vol. VI, no. 5, Calcutta, November 1909).

II Bhikaji Cama showing her flag, *c.*1907.

III Some of Pingali Venkayya's designs for an Indian national flag, published in his *A National Flag for India* (Masulipatam, 1916), private collection.

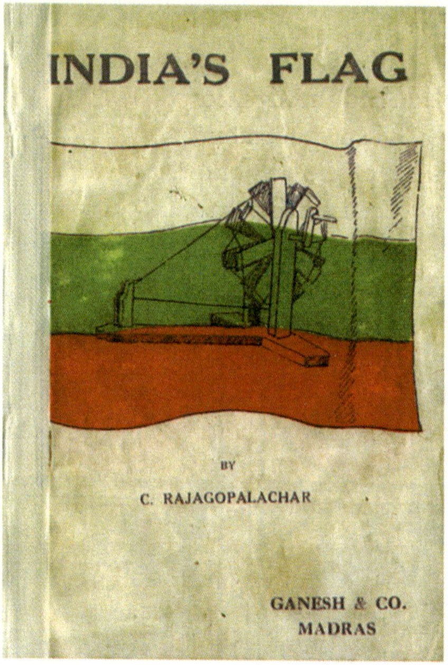

IV Cover of C. Rajagopalachari's *India's Flag* (Madras, Ganesh & Co, 1923), private collection.

V Lord Mountbatten's proposal for the Pakistan flag, 1947.

out that Gujarat and Tamil Nadu had already incorporated Nagpur as one of the items in their civil disobedience programme. This momentum forcefully advanced the question of the flag into the agenda of the next AICC meeting, despite some resistance from a small group led by Motilal Nehru and C.R. Das, already at odds with the main Congress Party line that rejected electoral participation. Far from effacing these differences and reconciling party men on fresh grounds or subjects, the flag became yet another bone of dissension. Motilal Nehru had already made his position known: 'You have seen the Jubbulpore incident in connection with the national flag and are no doubt aware of a similar venture being contemplated at Nagpur. I confess I do not appreciate either of these undertakings. The net result will, in my opinion, be the temporary loss of the valuable services of some of the most ardent workers. Do you take any of these things seriously?'[36] In the AICC discussion of 25 May, C.R. Das and members from Maharashtra and the Central Provinces like Sampurnanand and Abhayankar opposed the transformation of a local agitation into a national affair. They preferred first a larger, open debate on the national flag and its formal acceptance by the nation before undertaking such actions.[37]

On 25 May 1923, more than a month after the flag satyagraha had already been launched in Nagpur, the AICC meeting of Bombay finally gave its seal of approval. It formally opened the satyagraha in defence of the 'National flag' in Nagpur, delegating Sardar Patel to organize and co-ordinate the movement and calling upon all volunteers throughout India to be ready to join in the struggle when required. It further recommended all Congress provincial committees to observe the next Gandhi Day as Flag Day (18 July), instructing them to organize flag processions and displays.

In one concerted voice, Congress members were lined up in 'The Nagpur Battle'. All through the summer months of June and July the momentum was maintained: articles, editorials, reports, speeches, and statements by prominent figures—from Jawaharlal Nehru, Sarojini Naidu, C.R. Rajagopalachari, Hardayal Nag, and George Joseph, Kasturba Gandhi, Vallabhbhai Patel and Rajendra Prasad—built a

[36] *The Hitavada*, 9 May 1923.
[37] *Janmabhumi*, 6 June 1923.

national legend, a historical narrative showing the way in which the nation was being forged at that very moment. Curiously only Gandhi, who was in prison, cut off from the outside world and strictly following his vow to refrain from political reflection, said not a word on the flag that he himself had helped design. His letters of that year are full of advice and concern for the digestive problems of his ashram's inmates. On the other hand, many Congress leaders and public figures came to the city of Nagpur: Mahadev Desai (17 May), C.R. Rajagopalachari (31 May, followed by several visits in June), Hardayal Nag (31 May, 18 June), George Joseph (1–7 June, 20 June), Sarojini Naidu (12 July), Dadabhai Naoroji's granddaughter Miss Perin (3 August), Kasturba Gandhi (9 August), Vallabhbhai Patel (9 August), Rajendra Prasad (9 August). At a more abstract level, they offered a set of associations and images of what the flag meant for Indians. Dramatic headlines like 'The Battle of India' and 'The Flag Calls You' opened a veritable pedagogic crusade, with even schoolchildren under ten being mobilized in processions to the town hall to hoist the flag, singing national songs like *Bande Mataram* and *Hindustan Hamara*.[38] Nagpur, the geographical heart of India, was transformed into a centre of national pilgrimage,[39] attracting people from Gujarat, Calcutta, Madras, Wardha, Bombay, Mathura, Trichinopoly and of course the United Provinces and Central Provinces.[40]

In this sense it was one more addition to the geographical contours of protest and collective action being drawn for the nation since the beginning of the twentieth century: the Swadeshi movement in Calcutta, the Home Rule movement in Madras, Jallianwala Bagh in Amritsar, and now the flag satyagraha in Nagpur. Both in the specific moment and in the larger context of national struggle, Nagpur had already distinguished itself by its association with a symbol that was being affirmed by some Indians as incarnating the nation. It fuelled discussion on a national language and even a national dress.[41] This forceful insistence on common, shared signs increased in proportion

[38] *Bombay Chronicle*, 1 June 1923.
[39] *Young India*, 2 August 1923, p. 253.
[40] *Amrita Bazar Patrika*, 20 July 1923.
[41] *Young India*, 19 July 1923, pp. 242–3.

to the British emphasis on the differences that separated Indians, and the local party manipulation of a flag that appealed neither to Muslims and other religious communities, nor to broader social groups.[42] British arguments and the deployment of force against the tricolour were read as an acknowledgement of this symbol's significance. A series of articles by C.R. Rajagopalachari, published first in *Young India* from May to August 1923, and then collected in a 39-page booklet printed in the same year from Madras under the title *India's Flag*, aimed at canalizing and reinforcing the surge of sympathy and national sentiment that Nagpur had created. Carrying a coloured picture of the flag on the cover (Illustr. IV), the booklet sought to popularize the symbol by tracing its history, explaining its meaning (symbol, colours), and its stakes in the conflict with the British through labels like 'The flag calls you', 'The Nagpur Battle', 'The Battle of India' and 'Go to Nagpur'.[43] In order to sacralize it, Rajagopalachari attempted to associate certain virtues with the flag, such as 'honour', 'pride', 'dignity' and 'sacrifice', all presented and exalted as 'national'.[44]

The acceptance of these qualities and identification with them permitted individuals from different groups and regions to forge a common bond. This new reality was rendered visible through bands of volunteers coming on foot, doing 'twenty miles a day' according to *Young India* reports, or by train to Nagpur from the different provinces of British India. They diffused this 'national' message during their stops in villages. Explaining the flag movement, they proclaimed their journey as a pilgrimage 'in the service of India—Goddess and Mother'.[45] Many of them were arrested upon their arrival, and in the shared experience of imprisonment with other compatriots these bonds could be intensified. Rajagopalachari thus urged that this situation should serve to experiment with the use of Hindi as a unique 'national language' among the jailed volunteers.[46]

[42] British reactions can be found in OIOC, L/P&J/6/1794.

[43] C.R. Rajagopalachari, *India's Flag* (Madras, Ganesh & Co., 1923).

[44] From the beginning, Nehru also used the same terms: e.g. in an interview for the Hindi newspaper *Aaj*, 19 June 1923.

[45] *Young India*, 2, 9 August 1923, pp. 253, 266–7.

[46] *Young India*, 19 July 1923.

Three months later, the flag's 'all-India importance' was confirmed,[47] not only by the impressive number of 1099 convictions made at Nagpur—more than half of the volunteers being from other British India provinces[48]—but equally by the debate in the United Provinces legislative assembly and the British accord that the Indians had the right to display their flag. On 18 August 1923 the satyagraha was formally ended with a procession of eighty volunteers carrying fifty Swaraj flags through the town, led by Vallabhbhai Patel and Rajendra Prasad.[49] The satyagraha concluded amidst shouts of '*Rashtriya Jhanda ki jai*' (Long live the national flag).[50] It gave the Indian National Congress the opportunity to claim that 'Despite all the croaking and despair, the country is still loyal to the Congress'.[51]

What was at the beginning a simple little piece of 'tricoloured khaddar' acquired a sacred dimension at the level of India, through the trial and suffering of the Nagpur satyagraha.[52] It established the possibility for Indians to be united in a surge of emotions evoked by the flag, and to maintain this unity after the struggle, through the flag and thanks to it. This was its particular value, in contrast to other political struggles that also aspired to be national and to unify. As Gandhi had noted only a year earlier, in 1922, public memory was so short and the course of events so encumbered with issues and counterissues that the country could not vividly recall the intensity of the battles once they had receded. The flag was a reminder of their goal as well as of their struggles.[53]

The central position of the flag during the struggle led to the elaboration of a new ritual conceived in opposition to colonial rituals: the Flag Day, which I will discuss in chapter five. It is sufficient here to recall that it was first celebrated all over India on 18 June 1923. It installed a regularity and repetitiveness, creating a synchrony characteristic

[47] C.R. Rajagopalachari, op. cit., p. 30.

[48] *The Hitavada*, 25 July 1923, p. 3.

[49] *Young India*, 23 August 1923, p. 283.

[50] *Indian Annual Register* (Calcutta, 1923), vol. 2, p. 172.

[51] *Young India*, 26 July 1923, p. 249.

[52] C.R. Rajagopalachari's speech at Nagpur on 31 May 1923; *The Hindu*, 8 June 1923.

[53] *Young India*, 30 March 1922.

of all national ceremonies. In this way, it contributed to its diffusion through the simple gestures of hoisting and saluting the flag, singing flag songs, all hereafter a vital part of the nationalist repertory. If before Nagpur it had been possible to think and celebrate the nation through a variety of symbols, after Nagpur it was no longer imaginable to organize this struggle for independence without the flag.

Motilal Nehru's sentiments in the aftermath of the conflict outlined the change that had taken place. Though he had been hostile to the idea of organizing a protest movement around the tricolour in the spring of 1923, two years later he had become one of its ardent advocates: '(The flag) represents Swaraj of all Indians, Hindus, Muslims, Sikhs, Christians, Jews, Parsis and all other communities and religions to be found in India. . . .'[54] Muslim political personalities too acquiesced in this assessment. Journalist and militant leader Mohamed Ali, hoisting the 'flag of the nation' during the 38th Cocanada Congress in December 1923, though not a Congress member himself, urged his audience to forget their differences and stop thinking of themselves as Hindus and Muslims, 'for you are all of one faith in defence of the national flag'.[55] On the same occasion the unfurling of the Swaraj flag at the Independence Resolution moved by the Congress president Pandit Ram Prasad Misra confirmed its role in the fight for freedom.[56]

Lastly, 1923 reinforced the position claimed by the Congress of being sole administrative proprietor of the emblem of the nation. Since Nagpur it had begun with laying down the norms of how and when the flag should be raised and what it represented. G.T.P. Bracken, a British magistrate in Cocanada (Andhra Pradesh), noted this process of the Congress monopolizing the flag as its symbolic property. When motoring with some Europeans he found Swaraj flags flying over the Congress office. Congress workers, when ordered to remove them, replied that individual workers had no authority to do so, for they were hoisted at all times under Congress orders.[57] Such complete control of

[54] *Hindustan Times*, 28 October 1925.

[55] *Indian Annual Register*, 1923, Supplement, vol. II, op. cit., pp. x–xi.

[56] NMML, Report of the 38th Indian National Congress, 28 December 1923–1 January 1923, p. 123.

[57] M. Venkatarangaiya (ed.), *The Freedom Struggle in Andhra Pradesh*, vol. III, *1921–31* (Andhra Pradesh State Committee, 1965), pp. 249–50.

a symbol that the party had earlier neglected to take seriously proved the effectiveness of local pressure in imposing its agenda on the national party. The analysis made here clearly proves that the process had its roots in the initiatives taken by local Congress cadres. It was they who favoured and developed the movement at Nagpur in 1923, they who convinced the AICC, despite itself, to temporarily deviate from its programmes and to take a symbol seriously that in a certain way it had previously considered an appendage. That which had been taken as a form of 'patriotic exhibitionism' on the periphery of a political agenda now moved to the heart of the affray.

British hopes that the resolution of this local conflict would mark a return to colonial normalcy were belied by continued acclamation of the flag's national status from many quarters. They opened a second phase in the flag's progress, whose key strategy became the saturation of British India's geographical and institutional territory. In fact the tactics of symbolically possessing the official sites of British colonial power had already begun in 1921–2 in the euphoria of possessing a new political weapon. Now, the flag was hoisted in equivalent Indian sites: Congress provincial party headquarters, meeting halls, universities as well as municipalities. Congress district and provincial committees did not wait for an official resolution from their party confirming the flag's national status in all circumstances of protest, or for simply marking their possessions. The strike in Presidency College, Calcutta, on the Simon Commission's visit on 20 January 1928, for example, was characterized by singing *Bande Mataram* and wearing tricolour badges.[58] From 1923 to 1930 this dispersion in the geographical and political landscape aiming to strengthen its 'national' character inevitably plunged it in an open battle with the British flag of empire.

'Up, up with the National Flag, Down, down with the Union Jack!'

On 29 December 1929 at the Congress session at Lahore, under Jawaharlal Nehru's presidency, Purna Swaraj (complete independence) was

[58] Benjamin Zachariah, Subhas Rajan Chakrobarti, and Rajat Kanta Ray, 'Presidency College, Calcutta: An Unfinished History', in Mushirul Hasan (ed.), *Knowledge, Power and Politics. Educational Institutions in India* (Delhi, Lotus Collection, 1998), p. 349.

announced as India's political objective. At midnight, the Swaraj flag was hoisted on the banks of the river Ravi. Surrounded by a large crowd cheering enthusiastically and shouting 'Up, up with the National Flag, Down, down with the Union Jack', Nehru danced around the pole.[59] The combination of the slogan and the gesture gave a material perception to this major political claim: independence implied the disappearance of the Union Jack and its substitution by the Indian tricolour. The flag thus became a means of rendering visible and also realizing a political programme. This scene was widely reported in the Indian press as having moved 'a record crowd of over thirty thousand'. While women volunteers sang *Bande Mataram* and *Jhanda uncha rahe hamara* (Let our flag soar high), Jawaharlal Nehru took his stand below the flag on a raised platform and unfurled it amidst cheers and cries of 'Long Live Revolution' and '*Bharat Mata ki jai*'.[60] For at least one future Congress enthusiast and party member, Vejubhai Shah, a student of Science College, Karachi, who attended the Lahore session, this wave of collective euphoria and commitment to a common goal, epitomized by the slogan 'Up, up, down down', had a transforming impact: 'We returned from Lahore changed persons.' The experience convinced him to abandon college studies, leave for Ahmedabad to meet Congress leaders, and throw himself into the nationalist movement.[61]

Party workers were called to concentrate their efforts on the celebration of 26th January as India's Independence Day.[62] Provincial committees were instructed to hoist the flag in a formal ceremony accompanied by a speech delivered by a prominent political figure. An independence pledge was then to be read in the regional language.[63] The celebration of Independence Day in 1930 all over British India, with songs, salutations, hoistings, and speeches translated Congress instructions that the flag must be present in the smallest village and its daily display must be a permanent cue of the nation's existence and their demand for independence. (Illustr. 2.) From Poona in the west,[64]

[59] *The Tribune*, 17 January 1930, Margaret E. Cousins, 'The National Flag'.

[60] *The Hindu Illustrated Weekly*, 5 January 1930, p. 20.

[61] CSAS, Tape Recording of Shri Vejubhai Shah.

[62] *The Hindu Illustrated Weekly*, 19 January 1930, p. 19.

[63] S. Gopal, *Jawaharlal Nehru. A Biography, 1889–1947* (Delhi, Oxford University Press, 1975), vol. 1, p. 138.

[64] *The Hindu Illustrated Weekly*, 16 February 1930, p. 14.

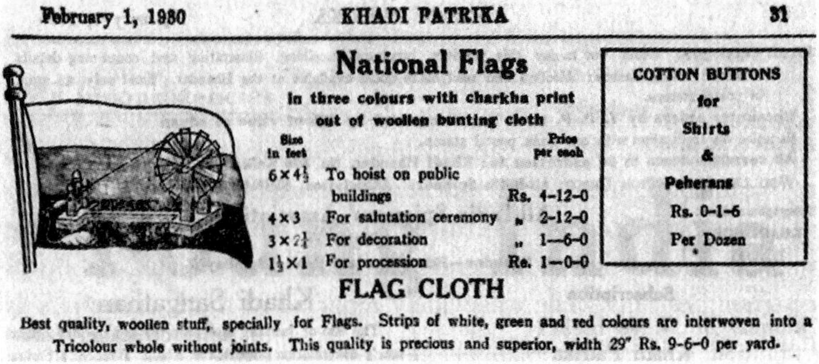

Illustr. 2. Advertisement for sale of flags in *Young India*, February 1930

through Gujarat, Punjab, Sind, Bihar,[65] and down to the Madras Presidency,[66] these celebrations represented not the nation that was but a nation that had to be completed. Children, women, tribals, and crowds of observers could participate in or witness the processions, sing or hear the songs and slogans like *Bande Mataram* and *Bharat Mata ki jai*. In her childhood reminiscences of the freedom struggle the Gandhian Usha Mehta recalled marching in a procession, shouting this slogan and singing '*Vijayi vishwa tiranga pyara, Jhanda uncha rahe hamara*' (World victory to our beloved tricolour, let our flag always be raised). The song had been written by Shyamlal Gupta Parshad in 1924 and first published in 1925 in a Kanpur weekly, *Pratap*.[67] When their flag fell during a lathi charge, they borrowed khadi and took out a procession dressed in white, red, and green, themselves having 'become the colours of the flag'.[68] G.F.S. Collins, secretary to the Bombay government, noted that during the demonstration of 26 January 1930 for 'Independence Day' a procession of 15,000 people had crossed the city demanding immediate independence, with banners on which was

[65] J.C. Jha, 'The Tribals of Bihar and the Indian Freedom Movement: 1940–42', *Indian Historical Review*, XII (1–2), July 1985–January 1986, p. 291.

[66] *The Tribune*, 28, 29, 31 January 1930.

[67] K.V. Singh, *Our National Flag*, op. cit., p. 102.

[68] Nawaz B. Mody, *Women in India's Freedom Struggle* (Mumbai, Allied, 2000), pp. 373–5.

inscribed the slogan 'Up, up with the National Flag, Down, down with the Union Jack'.[69] (Illustr. 3.) A contemporary observer of the political scene, Nirad C. Chaudhuri, later noted in his memoirs: 'The Hindus of India, who could not think that they would be independent in any foreseeable time, were keen to have the psychological satisfaction of declaring themselves free from British rule. From that date, every year, the day was celebrated with the hoisting of the national flag. The formula was 'Up, up with the National Flag, Down, down with the Union Jack'.[70] Through this move the Congress reinforced its claims to being a national party by attaching the flag to its political public

Illustr. 3. Kamaladevi Chattopadhyaya heading a flag procession during the 'Up up with the national flag, Down down with the Union Jack' movement, January 1930. Published in *L'Illustration*, Paris, March 1930. Roger-Viollet.

[69] OIOC, L/P&J/12/15, Bombay, G.F.S. Collins to Haig, 5 February 1930. A photo of the banner carrying this slogan appeared in *L'Illustration*, March 1930, p. 372.

[70] Nirad C. Chaudhuri, *Thy Hand Great Anarch, India 1921–1952* (London, Chatto & Windus, 1987), p. 276.

rituals, all the more important because the party's provincial organization was yet partial.[71]

The flag enabled a spatial occupation through processions and ceremonies until it became a persistent assault on the colonial state.[72] Its potential was not lost on Nehru who, recently back from Europe, sent a circular to provincial Congress committees encouraging them to propagate its use: 'It is not enough to have a ceremony in the district capital. Meetings must be held and flags displayed in as many villages as possible . . . it is strongly advisable that, even after 26 January, we encourage flag hoistings . . . Tongas and cars could have little flags on them. I suggest to your committee to lead a big campaign to carry these ensigns and small flag pins. The propaganda and psychological effect would be tremendous.'[73] He also placed the Congress at the apex of this action: 'When the Congress decides anything it should be done by the whole of the country on the same date. If all the people do it on the same date, you will be able to see your own power and your enemies will also see it.'[74] The point was not whether civil disobedience was a national phenomenon or not, but that it was felt to be one both by British and Indians. The moderate lawyer and nationalist T.N. Sapru took note, writing in a letter to Irwin: 'The Congress has undoubtedly acquired a great hold on popular imaginations. On roadside stations here until a few months ago I could hardly have suspected that people had any politics, I have seen with my own eyes demonstrations and heard with my own ears the usual Congress slogans. The popular feeling is one of intense excitement. It is fed from day to day by continuous

[71] On the structure and networks of the party, see B.R. Tomlinson, *The Indian National Congress and the Raj, 1929–1942. The Penultimate Phase* (London, Macmillan Press, 1976), p. 34 ff.

[72] On the mechanism of the popular demonstration and its role in the negotiation of political conflicts, see Pierre Favre, *La Manifestation* (Paris, Presses de la Fondation Nationale des Sciences Politiques, 1990), especially pp. 344–55.

[73] *Jawaharlal Nehru: Selected Works*, ed. S. Gopal (Delhi, Orient Longman, 1972–82), vol. iv, Nehru's Speech at Allahabad, 12 October 1930, pp. 203–4; 24 January 1930, p. 224.

[74] Public speech at Tangan, in Rae Bareli district in February 1930, ibid., pp. 245–9.

and persistent propaganda on the part of the Congressmen . . .'.[75] More than a simple imposition from above, as Sapru thought, the flag was a point of convergence for different forms of politics, both formal and popular.

As the flag's presence and display in British India became more and more widespread, the slogan 'Up, up with the National Flag, Down, down with the Union Jack' was given a new force with Gandhi's spectacular inauguration of Civil Disobedience on 12 March 1930. In this changed context, its position as rival to the Union Flag, already announced through dispersed acts of protest, was hardened. A salutation marked off its central role in Civil Disobedience. Only after this formal ritual was accomplished did Gandhi set off for his 240-mile 'salt march' from Ahmedabad to Dandi accompanied by a thousand volunteers and schoolchildren, carrying twenty-three national flags.[76] Simultaneously, flag parades took place in Delhi, Amritsar, and Allahabad.[77] The following scene, describing the future CPI general secretary P. Krishna Pillai's involvement in the movement in Kerala, could have taken place anywhere in the country: 'On 11 May 1930, about fifty volunteers marched to Calicut beach to violate the salt laws. The police swooped down on the volunteers. Heads were broken. Bones cracked . . . the leaders . . . fell unconscious . . . Only one man refused to yield . . . the dark lean figure in blood-spattered white khaddar cloth, holding high the national tricolour.'[78]

All along Gandhi's twenty-four-day salt march, the villages lying on his route were decorated with the national colours.[79] Over 1930–2 flag hoisting ceremonies and processions with patriotic songs became a regular occurrence, from town halls and district courts to schools and

[75] Judith M. Brown, *Gandhi and Civil Disobedience. The Mahatma in Indian Politics 1928–34* (Cambridge, Cambridge University Press, 1977), p. 147.

[76] OIOC, L/P&J/12/15, Secretary of the Government of Bombay, 18 March 1930.

[77] OIOC, L/P&J/12/18, Delhi; *The Tribune*, 14 March 1930.

[78] Robin Jeffrey, 'Matriliny, Marxism and the Birth of the Communist Party in Kerala, 1930–40', *Journal of Asian Studies*, vol. XXXVIII, no. 1, 1978, p. 85.

[79] Bipan Chandra, *India's Struggle for Independence* (Delhi, Penguin, 1989), p. 271.

universities, particularly where the Congress dominated.[80] These events were reported from all over British and even princely India, in particular at Aligarh, Ahmedabad,[81] Lahore, Bombay,[82] Allahabad,[83] Ratnagiri,[84] Srinagar (Kashmir),[85] Rewa and its neighbouring states of Central India and in Mysore,[86] in Bihar, Orissa, and the United Provinces,[87] in Bangalore, Hyderabad in the South, Ratlam, Nagod, Malhar,[88] in the Punjab countryside,[89] and in the countryside east of Calcutta.[90] British local governments appealed for special juridical powers to intervene without having to go through Indian municipal authorities, who, despite being told that they had no right to hoist the 'national flag' and that this was definitely an abuse of power conferred on them by law,[91] were increasingly taking a position in its favour.[92]

The historiography of the Civil Disobedience movement constantly alludes to the flag's presence as 'a common sight even in remote villages', outlining its political confrontation with the British 'jack' as between 'the flag of freedom and the flag of foreign domination'.[93] But this hasty, facile recognition, expressed as 'the power exercised by forms—visual or symbolic—which the nation takes',[94] condemns the flag to the margins of the freedom struggle of these years.[95]

[80] S. Theodore Baskaran, *The Message Bearers. The Nationalist Politics and the Entertainment Media in South India, 1880–1945* (Madras, Cre-A, 1981), p. 54.

[81] *The Tribune*, 7 September, 2 August 1930.

[82] OIOC, L/P&J/12/4, Bombay, Letter of G.F.S. Collins, Secretary to Government of Bombay, Poona, 9–17 September 1930.

[83] OIOC, L/P&J/12/22, United Provinces, January, July, December 1930.

[84] *The Mahratta*, 19 January1930.

[85] *The Tribune*, 15 March 1930.

[86] OIOC, R/1/1/2141, Important Events in Indian States.

[87] OIOC, L/P&J/12/34, United Provinces, second half of May 1931.

[88] OIOC, R/1/1/2142, R/1/1/2040, Reports by Residents of Events in Indian States in the first half of July and last quarter of December 1931.

[89] *The Tribune*, 26 February 1930.

[90] OIOC, L/P&J/12/2, Bengal, second fortnight of April 1930.

[91] *The Tribune*, 18 July 1930.

[92] OIOC, L/P&J/12/22, United Provinces, January, July, December 1930.

[93] Bipan Chandra, *India's Struggle*, op. cit., p. 278.

[94] David Page, *Prelude to Partition. The Indian Muslims and the Imperial System of Control 1920–32* (Delhi, Oxford University Press, 1982), p. 2.

[95] On the discussion of the flag's role over 1930–1, see Arundhati Virmani,

Acknowledging the flag's visibility in diverse forms of protest such as the non-payment of taxes, the illegal production of salt, the destruction and boycott of foreign cloth, or pointing to its integration by Congress in the paraphernalia of tools of political mobilization without an examination of its deeper psychological and political impact, denies its historical importance and the fact that an important transformation was effected by 1931.[96] The flag had evolved from an ideological symbol into a territorial one. When the Indians planted the flag atop a local municipality or a town hall as in Gujranwala (Punjab),[97] in Amraoti (Central Provinces),[98] on district council buildings as in Calcutta,[99] on the district court in Rohtak (Punjab),[100] on a police station or a court of justice, on the Bombay stock exchange,[101] and even on the viceroy's residence itself,[102] they were doing far more than 'metaphorically contesting British authority'.[103] Through daily, continuous, repeated displays of their own national symbol on official sites, Indians were appropriating the British colonial apparatus of political power and visually marking their nation. At the same time, they were demonstrating

'Up, Up with the Indian Flag, Down, down with the Union Jack' ! Le drapeau indien et le ralliement à la nation, 1930–31', in *Les Ralliements. Ralliés, traîtres et opportunistes du Moyen Age à l'epoque Moderne et Contemporaine* (Bordeaux, CROCEMC, 1997), pp. 215–37.

[96] Analyses of the symbols mobilized to enthuse a population make brief references to the appearance of this new ritual in Congress political practices. Gyanendra Pandey notes the use of songs in the salutation of the flag in a pamphlet of 1930: 'Mobilization in a Mass Movement: Propaganda in the United Provinces 1930–34', *Modern Asian Studies*, IX, 1975, pp. 207–9, 218; the use of patriotic songs in the local dialect and of theatre troupes to draw the tribals into the civil disobedience movement is also indicated by J.C. Jha, 'The Tribals of Bihar and the Indian Freedom Movement : 1920–42', *Indian Historical Review*, XII (1–2), July 1985–January 1986, p. 291.

[97] OIOC, L/P&J/12/21, Punjab, first half of February 1930.

[98] OIOC, L/P&J/12/2, Central Provinces and Berar, first fortnight of March 1930.

[99] OIOC, L/P&J/12/2, Bengal, 1930.

[100] OIOC, L/P&J/12/21, Punjab, 1930.

[101] *Hindustan Times*, 16 April 1930.

[102] OIOC, L/P&J/12, Bengal, second fortnight of February 1932.

[103] Nandini Gooptu, *The Politics of the Urban Poor in Early 20th Century India* (Cambridge, Cambridge University Press, 2001), p. 341.

that the end of their collaboration with the British, which constituted the basis of colonial domination, was no longer an abstract claim but a reality at the very grassroots. When in Calcutta the mayor declared: 'It is unnecessary to hide the fact that the Union Jack is an affront to national honour; when it is hoisted on our national institutions, it gives us great pain. I hold the flag of my country above any other',[104] the flag was also sketching out irreconcilable paths. It served as a catalyser, sharpening the struggle, concentrating attention on the symbolic collapse not only of colonial domination but also even more significantly of colonial collaboration.

This concentration of national rituals celebrating the sovereignty of the Indian nation through Independence Day and innumerable flag hoistings on state institutions or buildings presented a picture of an accelerated national momentum engineered by the Congress. Growing international interest in the Indian struggle was facilitated by the flag's presence at the heart of demonstrations and protests. Radio reports and photographs of the flag accentuated this novel feature in an Indian question, bogged down, as Penderel Moon (a young civil servant) was to describe, in a set of stereotypes: elephants and princes, thin, ill-clad peasants, Gandhi in his dhoti, cows in the streets, slow, heavy camels or an Indian crowd of men with and without turbans.[105] Instead, dramatic captions like 'India wild at Independence celebration', 'Violence accompanies demonstrations as Flag of freedom is unfurled', and 'Flag of Revolt flies over India', outlined the Indian struggle for a Western, particularly American, public sympathetic to a language and political codes turning around themes of 'Independence Day' and 'National Flag'.[106] It was the beginnings of photojournalism that enabled a democratic participation and consumption of distant events. Aided by foreign journalists on the spot, like George Slocombe of the *Daily Herald*, or Webb Miller, the European newsmanager for the United Press of America, or *The Times*, or the French magazine *L'Illustration*—to cite only a few—photographic reporting guaranteed the worldwide

[104] *Hindustan Times*, 27 January 1930.

[105] Edward Penderel Moon, *The Future of India* (London, Pilot Press, 1945).

[106] The Congress propaganda abroad is examined by Milton Israel in ch. 5, cf. *Connections and Power. Propaganda and the Press in the Indian Nationalist Struggle, 1920–47* (Cambridge, Cambridge University Press, 1994), esp. pp. 307–8.

projection of nationalist aims and was a rich source of propaganda for the Congress. It was *L'Illustration* which carried a black-and-white photograph of a line of Indian women holding up the banner 'Up up with the National Flag, Down, down with the Union Jack'.[107] When Gandhi was photographed preaching civil disobedience and non-violence to large crowds in the villages, it was with a big flag at his side; and when Patel was shown being welcomed after his release from prison by Bombay Congressmen, it was with two big flags.[108]

These photographs accentuated the flag's importance in public rituals; the photographer put the emblem at the centre of his cliché. In doing this the photographers, Westerners for the most part, were interpreting the 1930–1 Indian civil disobedience movement in the European frame of street demonstrations and public protests: since the nineteenth century their protest marches, revolts or revolutions, displayed flags (national, republican, socialist, communist) and banners with political or trade union slogans. When they photographed these demonstrations their focus on the flag reinforced its importance. The impact of such images, a novelty in political information, largely exceeded what the Congress' strategy of self-representation to the world was trying to achieve.[109] The flag appeared as the main factor assembling the group, lending it discipline, investing it with national purposefulness. Always held up high, when being saluted by a group of women for example, or raised by every demonstrator so that there seemed to be as many flags as there were protesters, it was shown to literally represent the goal to which they aspired. It dominated the crowd, reducing it in comparison, almost as if its force was leading the crowd. Sometimes, the charkha dominated, whilst in photographs where there were a large number of flags, it was their number which stood out rather than the design. Whether in the centre of the photograph or on the margins, at the head of a procession or accompanying every participant, the flag appeared omnipresent, leading and uniting—as in a

[107] 'L'agitation Gandhiste aux Indes', *L'Illustration, Journal Universel*, 22 March 1930, p. 144.

[108] *The Times of India*, 12 April 1930, p. 8; 3 July 1930, p. 12.

[109] A particularly inspiring study of photographs as a rich source of historical study is Alain Dewerpe's 'Mirroirs d'usine: Photographie industrielle et organisation du travail à l'Ansaldo, 1900–20', *Annales ESC*, no. 42, 1987, pp. 1079–1114.

group photograph of Gujarati, Maharashtrian, and Parsi women assembled under the Indian National Congress banner in Bombay.[110]

Official reports show the flag to be a common denominator in varying acts of disobedience throughout the country. It had become the leitmotif of the movement, its watchword and battlecry. Dressed in khaddar, all kinds of people could gather under it, singing patriotic songs, including songs about the flag, and participate in a collective experience which combined both the ideological and emotional aspects of a political symbol.[111] It explained why the police often attempted to seize the flag in the course of public processions, as in December 1930, when a group of women led a march in Azad Maidan, a public garden of Bombay; or when on the occasion of 'Gandhi Day' the police opened a veritable 'tugging competition' to get hold of the banner.[112] Some provincial governments like Madras applied section 144 of the Criminal Procedure Code that prohibited the assembly of five or more persons entirely in its administrative jurisdiction.[113] Others like the Punjab government imposed fines or rigorous imprisonment extending to nine months.[114] Occasionally, these battles could be pushed to ridiculous extremes, as in Satara (Gujarat), when a crowd of three hundred refused to give up the pole to which the national flag was attached and the magistrate ordered the police to seize it by force.[115] What could appear as a collection of miscellaneous items in fact highlighted the point that the flag, far from being a peripheral object in the national struggle had become the object of the struggle itself.[116] Indian

[110] C.A. Bayly (ed.), *The Raj*, op. cit., p. 355.

[111] On this duality, see Victor Turner, *The Forest of Symbols* (Ithaca, Cornell University Press, 1967), p. 30.

[112] *The Hindu Illustrated Weekly*, 14 December 1930.

[113] OIOC, L/P&J/12/31, Governor's Reports, Madras, second half of August 1931.

[114] *The Tribune*, 17 June 1930.

[115] *The Hindu Illustrated Weekly*, 14 September 1930.

[116] See Jim Masselos's analysis of the civil disobedience movement. He emphasizes this element in the huge processions, but unfortunately does not deviate from the interpretive model of seeing in them the transfer of the private and public religious idiom into the nationalist campaign. 'Audiences, Actors and Congress Dramas: Crowd Events in Bombay City in 1930', in Jim Masselos (ed.), *Struggling and Ruling. The Indian National Congress 1885–1985* (New Delhi, Sterling Publishers, 1987), pp. 71–86.

newsreels of Congress activities produced to strengthen the party's contacts with the masses seized upon the flag as a crowd puller. One of the earliest documentaries made by A. Narayanan's Srinivasa Cinetone Studios at Madras and Modern Theatres at Salem was 'Unfurling the National Flag'.[117]

Photographs dramatized the contrast between the forces of repression—policemen armed with lathis or riding horses, beating a crowd of peaceful women—and demonstrators walking in disciplined order. They shattered the protectively paternal, efficient image of the colonial state, inspiring confidence, obedience, and co-operation. The ultimate winner was the flag, whose visible humiliation could only be described by the Indian press as 'an insult to Hindus, Muslims, Sikhs and Parsis' and the attacks as 'an attempt to crush the awakened spirit of the country and strike at national solidarity'.[118]

Above everything else, the photographs gave the impression that the national movement was more cohesive and united than the British government wished to recognize or admit. While negotiations at London between Indian nationalists and the British government at the Round Table Conference in 1931 were revealing the difficulties of reconciling the political differences between Muslims, the Congress, the princes, and the untouchables,[119] photographs presented the image of a whole country moving in a wave of solidarity against the Raj. The national flag hoisted in opposition to the Union Jack mirrored Indians pitted against the British as a united people, not as separately constituted communities or groups. But the question was whether this unity was deeply implanted or only a photographic illusion?

Conflicts Around the Swaraj Flag

Widely though the flag might be displayed and hoisted,[120] the unity it was intended to assert was proving more difficult to realize in

[117] S. Theodore Baskaran, op. cit., p. 203.

[118] OIOC, L/R/5/99, Native Newspaper Reports, *Daily Pratap*, week ending 29 November 1930.

[119] Judith M. Brown underlines the lack of unanimity and absence of vision in the Congress about the goal of Civil Disobedience: *Gandhi and Civil Disobedience*, op. cit., pp. 80–4.

[120] On incidents of flag salutations and hoisting in 1931, see the fortnightly

political terms. Even as the Congress Party organization and directives pushed the flag to the centre of the struggle as a political objective in itself, this very management worked against the flag's unifying dimension. M.A. Ansari's reminder to Gandhi on 10 February 1930, not to judge the response to Independence Day as a true reflector of the support they could expect for real action, indicated a more troubled situation.[121] Rival political parties and groups were coming to see the flag as yet another means through which the Congress was denying them their share of political space and power. At the height of the civil disobedience movement, this Janus-face quality of the flag had already revealed itself. In the process of becoming national, the flag had also become sectarian, exciting political opposition, deepening differences, and encouraging the elaboration of alternative projects and models of a national flag. A symbol destined to create a symbolic unity at a moment when political differences between parties and goals appeared irreconcilable was becoming, in its turn, a field of dispute, attracting to itself all the existing conflictual visions of national goals and programmes. Its extended use inevitably begged the question whether the flag defined by Gandhi in 1921 could be the definite, final version of the Indian national flag. Did it truly represent the nation?

The Sikhs were the first to manifest their discontent with Congress political strategy and reject the flag hoisted by the Congress in December 1929. In March 1930, when Gandhi launched Civil Disobedience, the Sikh leader Baba Kharak Singh, president of the Shiromani Gurdwara Prabandhak Committee, refused to join the movement if the Sikh colour, saffron, was not included in the national flag.[122] The committee sent a deputation consisting of four Sikhs and three Hindus to meet Jawaharlal Nehru and urge him to include the Sikh colour in the national flag. They made this a condition of their alliance with the Congress.[123] A year later the problem remained, preventing 'the

---

reports of events in Indian states in OIOC, R/1/1/2140, R/1/1/2141, R/1/1/2142.

[121] Judith M. Brown, *Gandhi and Civil Disobedience*, op. cit., p. 84.

[122] J.S. Grewal, *The Sikhs of the Punjab*, The New Cambridge History of India, II-3 (Delhi, 1990), p. 169.

[123] OIOC, L/P&J/12/21, Local Government Fortnightly Reports on the Political Situation, for fortnight ending 31 October 1930.

majority (of Sikhs) from participating in the national struggle.'[124] The Akali Party (founded in December 1920 in Amritsar) made it a condition of its political alliance with Congress in the Punjab. This was a major problem for the Congress, which was, according to the British reading, 'desperate to obtain the cooperation of the Sikhs.'[125] In fact, in September 1930 the Punjab Provincial Congress Committee decided to replace red with saffron in all the flags hoisted in the province and asked the Congress national committee to take a similar decision for all of India.[126] The move provoked a long letter from Nehru, then in prison, stating that as long as the question of the national flag was open, the solutions could only be adopted in a national session of the Congress.[127] In March 1931 Sikh political leaders were still preoccupied with the question of the flag's colours and raised it before Gandhi, demanding either the inclusion of a colour representative of the Sikhs, or a national flag with one single colour.[128] The Sikhs' insistence on including 'their colour' in the flag before committing themselves to civil disobedience mirrored the importance which they accorded to this national symbol, perceiving it as a barometer of their relative position in the political spectrum.

An even greater resistance was manifested by the Muslim League, which, driven to define itself in opposition to the Congress, now refused to recognize the tricolour as a national flag. In the 1920s at several moments, Muslims had used a green flag with the crescent and star, in particular during the Khilafat movement of 1922–3,[129] but it seems to have represented more a religious than a national identity. Muslims promised their affiliation to Gandhi's flag at the All India Khilafat Conference in July 1921 at Karachi: 'if the British government

[124] *The Tribune*, 6 March 1931.

[125] OIOC, L/P&J/12/21, Punjab, 15–30 September 1930.

[126] *The Tribune*, 2 November 1930.

[127] Nehru's letter was published in *The Tribune*, 2 November 1930.

[128] *Searchlight*, 31 March 1931.

[129] The Ottoman sultan who bore the title of khalifa was considered the rightful successor of the caliphate. Though the Indian Muslims did not recognize the authority of the Abbasid caliphate as long as they had their own Muslim kings, they gradually integrated the name of the Ottoman sultan as caliph in the Friday khutba and Id prayers and regarded him as their spiritual leader after the end of the Mughal empire.

directly or indirectly, openly or secretly, fights the Angora Government, the Muslims of India will start civil disobedience and establish their complete independence at the next session of the Indian National Congress to be held at Ahmedabad and hoist the flag of the Indian Republic'.[130] Newspaper reports of these years describe the green flag as a symbol of Islam, a relic to be preserved in sacred places like Ajmer rather than paraded around the country as an exhibition piece, an act that would diminish Muslim reverence for it.[131]

Muslim sentiments of tolerance and acceptance of the tricolour were resumed by Mohamed Ali in December 1923 at the Cocanada Congress, as seen above. But this outlook was shortlived. The breakdown of the Congress–Khilafat alliance of 1922–3 opened the gates to growing Muslim alienation on issues like joint or separate electorates, reservation of seats in legislatures, and the separation of Sind from the Bombay Presidency. The flag now failed to act as a cementing factor. Muslims and Parsis were reported to be almost absent from the Bombay processions and meetings, which always concluded with slogans, most prominently 'Up, up, Down, down';[132] Muslims did not participate in the Independence Day functions in Bombay,[133] nor in Calcutta.[134] Their hostility even led them in Salem or Calicut to organize a counter-procession carrying the Union Jack.[135] The Khaksar movement, founded in 1931 in Lahore by Allama Inayatullah Khan Mashriqui, formerly in the Indian Educational Service, is noted to have carried its own flag.[136]

At the height of the civil disobedience movement in Karachi, a procession organized in memory of Mohamed Ali saw a veritable

[130] A.M. Zaidi, *Evolution of Muslim Political Thought in India*, vol. 2, *Sectarian Nationalism and Khilafat* (New Delhi, Indian Institute of Applied Political Research, 1975), pp. 550–1.

[131] OIOC, L/R/5/97, Selected Notes on the Press of United Provinces of Agra and Oudh for the week ending on 3 March and 17 March 1923.

[132] *The Times of India*, 27 January 1930, p. 9.

[133] OIOC, L/P&J/12/15, G.F.S. Collins to Haig, 5 February 1930.

[134] OIOC, L/P&J/12/2, Report on Bengal for second half of January 1930.

[135] OIOC, L/P&J/12/19, Report on Madras for second half of January 1930.

[136] Ian Talbot, *Freedom's Cry. The Popular Dimension in the Pakistan Movement and Partition. Experience in Northwest India* (Karachi, Oxford University Press, 1996), pp. 61–2.

battle of flags, with Muslims lowering the half-masted national (Congress) flag, tearing it to shreds, and hoisting the Islamic flag. Although the Muslim leaders present there condemned the incident and waved the national flag from the platform to shouts of 'Allah o' Akbar', the crowd refused to allow it to be hoisted.[137] Even if Muslims did not manifest any solidarity or identification with the flag chosen by the Congress, the Muslim League made no formal proposal for an alternative national flag. The Islamic flag was being raised more and more frequently in the 1930s. Seeing off Mohamed Ali's brother Shaukat Ali on the Bangalore city railway station, the journalist Nihal Singh was struck by banners with the star and crescent of Islam and volunteers carrying small flags blazoned with a star and crescent. It made him wonder whether India was going the Irish way towards a war of symbols; the tricolour of coarse homespun with the emblem of the charkha held above the heads of Congress volunteers would battle against the star and crescent waving above the Muslim heads.[138]

Other political parties, which kept their distance from the tricolour, were the Communist Party and the Rashtriya Swayamsevak Sangh (RSS). Indian communists rallied to the red flag as the banner that represented the interests of the working class beyond national boundaries and interests. The use of the red flag as a symbol of the Indian working class presented it, in Nehru's words, as 'a challenge to the national flag'.[139] After a confrontation between the Congress and the Communists in Bombay during the celebrations of Independence Day on 26 January 1930, Nehru was led to state: 'I honour and respect the red flag, for it represents the blood and sufferings of the workers . . . There is not and should not be the least rivalry between our national tricolour and the red flag of the workers.'[140]

But neither words nor good intentions could wish the rivalry away, for rivalry there was. During a meeting at a textile factory in Bombay in March 1931, fifty union members of the 'Girni Kamgar Union'

[137] *The Times*, 8 January 1931.

[138] *The Hindu*, 25 July 1931, p. 10.

[139] Jawaharlal Nehru, *The Unity of India, Collected Writings 1937–40* (London, Lindsay Drummond, 1941), pp. 108–9.

[140] *Selected Works of Jawaharlal Nehru*, ed. S. Gopal, op. cit., vol. 4, 28 January 1930, p. 232.

pulled down the tricolour flag and hoisted the red flag to cries of 'Down with Gandhi, down with the Congress'.[141] In a public battle, Congress volunteers burnt posters of the red flag.[142] Hostility broke out particularly at moments of discontent with Congress policy: for example, on Gandhi's departure for London to participate in the Round Table Conference, a parade of red flags was organized in Bombay.[143] Indian Communists stayed away from Civil Disobedience, manifesting their solidarity with Lancashire workers by wearing foreign cloth and 'insulting the tricolour' on Chowpatty beach in Bombay.[144]

One of the earliest political parties to raise its own version of the flag of the nation was the RSS. Considering the saffron flag to be the ancient emblem of the Hindus, the party, founded in 1925 in Nagpur, incorporated the banner almost immediately in its ceremonies. 'The *swayamsevaks* [volunteers] of the party meet every day for one hour every morning and evening. They sing patriotic songs, salute "*Bharat Mata*" and the ancient flag.'[145] No doubt, the party's regional implantation in the Central Provinces made this Hindu flag a less dangerous rival for the tricolour than, for example, the flag of the Muslims. When civil disobedience began, the RSS contented itself with admitting that the Congress too had independence as its political objective. Notwithstanding, RSS branches celebrated Independence Day by hoisting their own flag, that is, the '*bhagwa jhanda*' (sacred flag).[146]

One more body for which the national flag posed a problem was the group of princely states. Congress' non-interventionist policy towards these states left the liberty of using the national flag to the initiative of

[141] *Madras Mail*, 17 March 1931.

[142] *Bombay Chronicle*, 31 August 1931.

[143] Ibid.

[144] Minocheher R. Masani, *The Communist Party of India* (London, Derek Vershoyle, 1954), p. 42.

[145] Craig Baxter, *The Jana Sangh. A Biography of an Indian Political Party* (Philadelphia, University of Pennsylvania Press, 1969), p. 33.

[146] T. Basu, P. Datta, S. Sarkar, T. Sarkar, S. Sen, *Khaki Shorts and Saffron Flags* (Delhi, Orient Longman, 1993), pp. 21–2.

local movements. Jamnalal Bajaj, touring Indore in August 1931, did not fail to advise the public in meetings held in his honour not to hoist the tricolour as the states had their own flags.[147] Though princely states did not view civil disobedience favourably, they could not completely control popular reactions. On Nehru's visit to Bangalore in June 1931, a flagstaff was constructed and a flag hoisted, but soon after his departure its removal by the police provoked a public debate. The state government considered the tricolour an insult to the state flag, which alone could be the accepted symbol of its sovereignty.[148] A Bangalore judge cited this as a reason to prohibit hoisting of the national flag. Led by a Brahmin lawyer, K.T. Bhashyam, local Congressmen pressed for retaliatory action. So too did a number of letters to the editor.[149] To Gandhi, Bhashyam wrote: 'Public opinion in the state is so strong that it condemns our position of not hoisting the national flag immediately.'[150] But Gandhi recommended caution, pointing out that public pressure to hoist the flag revealed the symbol's real status and meaning for the people. In general, Congress was cautious not to antagonize the princely states, and party workers emphasized that the tricolour flag was intended to drive out the Union Jack and not oppose the state flags. Other states like Kashmir confined themselves to occasional prohibitions against the flag: for example, stopping cars carrying the tricolour from entering the state. They rejected the argument that since the tricolour was not formally prohibited in British India, it could equally be exhibited in the princely states.[151]

These signs of resistance reflected growing doubts about the national pretensions of what was only a 'Congress flag'.[152] Meanwhile, on 29 March 1931, Congress met in Karachi to endorse the Gandhi–Irwin or Delhi Pact, by which the British government released Gandhi

[147] OIOC, R/1/1/2141, Important Events in Indian States, Central India Agency.

[148] *The Hindu*, 14 July 1931.

[149] See *Madras Mail*, 7 July 1931.

[150] Bjorn Hettne, *The Political Economy of Indirect Rule. Mysore 1881–1947* (Stockholm, Scandinavian Institute of Asian Studies, 1978), p. 186.

[151] *The Tribune*, 19 June 1930.

[152] The British reports referred to the flag as the 'Congress' flag.

along with other political prisoners.[153] It finally agreed to participate in the Round Table Conference as the party representing the entire nation in its diversity, through Gandhi. But its creed of one party, one nation, one flag, was weakened by two factors. One, the increasingly apparent rivalry from flags of other communities and parties which threatened to diminish the status of the tricolour to a party flag; and two, the fact that the flag was not yet officially adopted by the Congress. Would not the Congress position in London be reinforced if it went armed with a national symbol, recently legitimized by a public consensus and officially adopted? It would give Congress an edge over the other political parties or princely delegates participating in the conference and conclusively show that it was truly a national party, as compared to others who represented only group or community interests. Furthermore, it would silence critics who maintained that a flag designed by Gandhi, promoted by the Congress, and now controlled by the party was hardly consensual, let alone national. The moment necessitated a public plebiscite. Opening a national debate on the flag followed by a formal adoption would not only put an end to growing questions about the flag, its design, and its colours, it could also be one of the means of rallying the discontented and alienated groups and identifying them with the cause of the nation.

Gandhi too had admitted that 'the more the National Flag is gaining in importance, the nicer become the questions that are being raised about its colours, size, the charkha, symbol etc. It should be remembered that the National Flag has become national only by convention and not by any Congress resolution.'[154] It was this logic that prompted Congress in April 1931 to name a seven-member flag committee representative of India's geographical, religious, and social heterogeneity. Headed by Pattabhi Sitaramayya (Madras), it included Vallabhbhai Patel (Gujarat), Maulana Abdul Kalam Azad (Muslim), Master Tara Singh (Sikh), J. Nehru (Central Provinces), D.B. Kalelkar (Maharashtra), and N.S. Hardikar (General Secretary of the Hindustan Seva Dal). Its

[153] It promised to concede the right to make salt for consumption to villages along the coast, return confiscated lands not yet sold, remit all fines not yet collected in exchange for discontinuance of the Civil Disobedience Movement, and Congress participation in the next Round Table Conference.

[154] 'The National Flag', *Young India*, 27 February 1930, p. 70.

task was to examine existing objections and recommend a flag to the Congress Working Committee by 31 July.[155]

The Sikhs, who had been asking for a redesigning of the flag to make it more representative, particularly welcomed the decision.[156] After three months of receiving designs, suggestions, and criticisms both from provincial Congress committees as well as individuals, the flag committee proposed a saffron colour flag with the charkha. The All India Congress Committee rejected the design and instead the existing tricolour was adopted with one change: red was replaced by saffron.

[155] NMML, AICC Papers, file no. 70, Congress Working Committee Resolution 1, 1–2 April 1931, Karachi.

[156] NMML, AICC Papers, file no. 58, 15 April 1931.

4

Colours for a New Nation

The decision in April 1931 to hold a plebiscite on the flag before its formal adoption revealed the limits of the nationalization that could be achieved by pitting the Indian tricolour against the British flag. A flag satyagraha in 1923 and a civil disobedience movement in 1930 had given the tricolour a definite advantage over other symbolic forms of the nation. Even so, this profile which determined its status also threatened to restrict its impact to the domain of a political symbol: worse, a party emblem. The risk was heightened by the appearance of other party flags, as well as by questions and uncertainties about the tricolour's official status. When the Congress decided to place the design for public discussion, its immediate concern was to proceed to the Round Table Conference with a legitimized national flag. But, more broadly, it had understood that simply controlling and displaying this symbol was insufficient when it did not touch the broader spheres of 'feeling' and personal identification. This was implicit in the short three-point questionnaire circulated to Congress provincial committees and the public:

1. Is there any feeling amongst any provinces in regard to the design of the national flag which should be taken into consideration by the Committee?
2. Have you any specific suggestions for the national flag?
3. Is there any defect or drawback in this design that demands attention?[1]

This invitation for suggestions, opinions, and criticism from all over India was in fact a call to Indians for a deeper investment in their

[1] NMML, AICC Papers, file no. 58, 1931.

national banner at all levels: from its material texture to its design and colours. By fixing public attention on these details and encouraging collective thinking and exchange on the drawbacks of the existing symbol, on the additions or modifications necessary to make it truly national, the process of weaving a more personal, subjective relationship with the flag was inaugurated. Moreover, suggestions, criticisms or refutations demanded justifications, whether in tradition, international norms, or national urgency, thus permitting the consolidation of a pyramid of meanings, feelings, and sentiments about the nation and the flag. It encouraged an emotional identification that was indispensable for the flag's nationalization.

A press statement issued by the convener of the Congress Flag Committee set up on 2 April 1931 declared that although 'the national flag now in vogue has gained in popularity by usage and convention', it aimed to review the objections which had surfaced regarding the perception of the three colours in the flag as having a 'communal basis'.[2] This admission revealed the difficulties of streamlining a mosaic of cultural, aesthetic traditions and references into one uniform model. Although the committee did not go as far as stating this principle in these terms, its statement betrayed a major problem: colours could not be taken for granted. Their meanings, codes, and values had changed over time and been fashioned by complex cultural interactions, political interferences, and events. For the Flag Committee, it was evident that behind their innocuous appearance lay a latent power of persuasion, attachment, and conviction that could be directed towards national purposes. It is also from this perspective that the study of colours acquires value in the construction of nationhood. Colours merit a treatment that extends beyond the stylistic interpretations of art and painting.[3]

[2] *The People*, 3 May 1931.

[3] Michel Pastoureau has made the most significant inclusion of colours in the field of social history: 'Vers une histoire sociale des couleurs. Couleurs, images, symboles', in M. Pastoureau, *Etudes d'histoire et d'anthropologie* (Paris, Le Léopard d'Or, 1989), pp. 9–68; 'Une histoire des couleurs est-elle possible?', *Ethnologie Française*, vol. 20/4, October–December 1990, pp. 368–77; *Bleu, Histoire d'une couleur* (Paris, Seuil, 2000).

Rivalry of Colours?

'Of all colours, red and yellow have the most power and of these the power of red is the greater', observed a British Indian civil servant in 1932 while studying Indian rituals and beliefs.[4] This note on the power of colours was misleading on several grounds. To begin with, it gave the impression of a uniformity of social practices, beliefs, and customs sharing the same significations across different cultural contexts and communities in India. For the author, these colours signified the same meanings of auspiciousness or omens for all Indians, whether Muslim or Hindu, whether from Sindh or southern India. Therefore, red for Hindus, he wrote, was associated with *sakti*, gods and goddesses, and marriage ceremonies and symbols from the swastika to the turban; whereas for Muslims it was integrated in magic rites, circumcision ceremonies, and the tombs of saints. Yellow, as in turmeric or saffron, carried power for both communities, being used in wedding rituals and to avert evil. In fact, not only did there coexist several codes of colour symbolism, but also colours were far from eternal, unchanging givens, with fixed absolute meanings. Thus, in the 1920s and 1930s Sikhs were divided about their preferred colour: some claimed yellow (more exactly saffron) while others affirmed it was black.[5] In fact, as part of social practices, colours were the result of a slower selection that accompanied the affirmation of social identities. Subject to historical change, they were also an active medium of expression and participation, of domination or resistance. In their turn, they could thus become the field of struggle themselves.

This was precisely what had happened with the three colours chosen by Gandhi in 1920 to represent the unity of Hindus, Muslims, and other Indian communities. In the space of ten years they had come to be perceived as exclusive to these religious groups. Instead of depicting the spirit of consensus and unity, which had welcomed the flag's

[4] J. Abbott Abbot, *The Keys of Power: A Study of Indian Ritual and Belief* (1932), reprinted as *Indian Ritual and Belief. The Keys of Power* (Delhi, Manohar, 2000), p. 281.

[5] In 1921 Gandhi referred to their demand for black (*CWMG*, vol. XX, *April–August 1921*, Ahmedabad, 1966, p. 107); for saffron, *The Tribune*, 24 May 1931.

inception and which the Nagpur flag satyagraha in 1923 reinforced temporarily, their meaning and suitability were being questioned and refuted. The following letter addressed to Gandhi in 1924 from a prominent group of Bengalis, including Suniti Kumar Chatterjee and Dwijendranath Tagore,[6] suggested that the current interpretation of the colour red as symbolic of Hindus was not faithful to the tradition of this culture. They had an alternative to propose before the presentation of the flag at the approaching Belgaum Congress annual session. In their opinion, ochre (*geru* or *gerua*), the colour of renunciation (*sannyasa*), sacrifice (*tyaga*), and non-violence (ahimsa), was a more satisfactory choice for representing Hindus.[7] Further proof of the colour's deep-rooted significance in Hindu civilization and culture lay, they pointed out, in its adoption not only by most Hindu religious sects—Brahmanical, Buddhist, Sikhs—but also by Hindu warriors like Shivaji. No doubt, their argument ran, red was used by some Hindu sects like the Saktas, but it was the colour of war and did not evoke the fundamental Hindu note of non-violence (ahimsa). Furthermore, red, white, and green were colours used by many countries and did not constitute a distinctive flag for India. Finally, the signatories proposed that either the Indian national flag could have red, ochre, and green; or ochre, white, and green—ochre for Hinduism, green for Islam, and white for other faiths and cultures. Or even all four colours, red, white, ochre, and green.[8]

Gandhi, though he published this letter in his journal, thus making it public knowledge, made no changes in his flag. But the letter announced the concerns that were to dominate the debate. Underlying these thoughts was the idea that if swaraj, a political goal embracing notions as varied as constitutional powers to complete independence, was to be clothed in a form suited to international practice, it must do

[6] Other signatories included Vidhushekhara Bhattacharya, Kalidas Nag, Nepal Chandra Ray, Bhim Rao Shastri, J.J. Vakil, Prem Sundar Bose, Marichi, N. Aiyaswami: *Young India*, 11 December 1924.

[7] Shahid Amin's analysis on the use of *gerua* by Chauri Chaura volunteers in 1922 also highlights its Hindu roots. Cf. *Event, Memory, Metaphor, Chauri Chaura 1922–1992* (Delhi, Oxford University Press, 1995), pp. 184–9, esp. footnote 194.

[8] The letter was printed in *Young India*, 11 December 1924.

so in respect of Indian philosophical and cultural traditions. It emphasized the weight of tradition, which gave gerua and not red the status of the colour representing Hindus. And second, it gave equal consideration to international norms by arguing that the Indian flag must be distinct from those of other countries.

On the one hand the letter's insistence on the idea that political ideals could be communicated through the colours of a flag was of course not new, in light of the powerful functional role of colours in Indian traditions for designating social status, denoting an inner condition or even effecting a change of state.[9] The term varna, designating caste, stood first for colour, hence the textual attribution of specific colours to the different castes, such as white for Brahmins, red for Kshatriyas, yellow for Vaishyas, and blue or black for Shudras.[10]

On the other hand the contention that ochre and not red was the colour that represented Hindu culture revealed that more than an aesthetic quarrel was at issue. This strong difference of opinion indicated that some significant shifts in the perceptions of these colours and their political status had surely taken place. Indeed, the questionings around red or ochre in 1931 referred to a gradual succession of past interventions and adjustments, reviving the memory of time-honoured practices, political innovations, and colonial intercessions. In refusing to acknowledge red as the colour portraying Hindus, the letter pointed to its imposition contrary to custom or social convention and sought to invalidate these encroachments.

In fact, traditional Indian usage tended towards broad descriptions to name colour. It evoked colour not in absolute, categorical terms of red or yellow, black or white, but by referring to an object or a natural phenomenon. Hence, an association of words qualified the precise

[9] C.A. Bayly, 'The Origins of *Swadeshi* (home industry): Cloth and Indian Society, 1700–1930', in Arjun Appadurai (ed.), *The Social Life of Things. Commodities in Cultural Perspective* (Cambridge, Cambridge University Press, 1990), pp. 290–1.

[10] On the multiple functions and significance of colours in Hindu India, the literature is either scant and discrete in its discussion or far too technical. Some reference to the system and symbolism of colours in ancient Indian literature is available in Serge Bouez, 'Une couleur de trop. Perception et dénomination des couleurs chez les Ho et les Santal (Inde)', in S. Tornay (ed.), *Voir et nommer les couleurs* (Nanterre, Labethno, 1978), pp. 401–21.

shade of colour: for example, *priyangu kalika syama* (dark like the *priyangu* plant) or *megha syama* (grey like rain clouds) or *karpura gaura* (camphor white). In the Indian systems, colours—auspicious or inauspicious—were attributes of inner states and qualities or indicators of social status and functions. The *Vedas* and *Rig Veda* hymns contain many descriptions for the sky, without specifying precisely that it is blue. Literary traditions tended to give more importance to judging colour according to its qualities of lightness and darkness. Thus, the use of multiple words for a certain condition of darkness could be used, making it impossible to affirm which colour was evoked with certainty. For example, such words as *krisna, nila, asita, syama, kala, mechaka,* etc. referred to black, dark blue, grey, or dark green. Words like *pandu, pandura, gaura,* and *arjuna* could mean white as well as pale yellow or even pink.[11]

The British civil servant Robert Taylor, credited with the task of designing heraldic blazons for the Indian princely states in 1877, undertook a survey of the colour preferences of the eighty-odd princely states. His enquiry was limited to a very basic interrogation addressed to British Residents posted in the states, about local histories and legends available in English, such as Tod's *Annals and Antiquities of Rajasthan* (1829, 1832), and Ferishta's *The History of the Rise of the Mahometan Power in India* (1829). On these grounds Taylor came to two conclusions, one that was predictable and another that was less well appreciated and acknowledged. The first inference was that the general favourite colours of Hindu princes could range from shades of light yellow, pink, light purple, and red, without any rigid attachment to one or the other tone.[12] This confirmed the traditional Indian approach mentioned above of not fixing colours within precise, exclusive boundaries. Thus, he noted that the southern states of Trivandrum and Travancore wanted their banners to be light yellow and red, the Rajput states, Rewa, Boondi, Bansda, and Mewar asked for a shade

[11] Sivapriyananda, 'Colour Symbolism and the "Tri-Guna Concept" ', *Journal of the Oriental Institute*, vol. 38, 1988, nos 1–2, pp. 33–41.

[12] Robert Taylor, *The Princely Armoury. Being the Display of the Arms of the Ruling Chiefs of India Prepared for the Imperial Assemblage held at Delhi on the First Day of January 1877* (Calcutta, 1902), p. 6. One copy is in OIOC, R/2/430/78.

of yellow or red, Central Indian states like Sindia and its tributaries and Dewas wished for red, while Porebundar in Gujarat asked for light orange.

But Taylor's second conclusion noted the flexible political uses of colours. He recorded the change in the Jat house's banner from green to red in the sixteenth century. Similarly, in 1550 Ali Adil Shah of Bijapur changed the colour of his royal umbrella and standard from yellow to green to defy Hossein Nizam Sham of Ahmednagar. Again, the princely banner of the Hindu states of Mandi and Garhwal was green. Thus, yellow or saffron in pre-colonial India was part of both Hindu and Islamic traditions, being the colour of renunciation for sufis as well as sanyasis. Tod's *Annals* referred to the Rajput chieftains' use of saffron-coloured flags, and the Maratha warrior chief Shivaji adopted a saffron standard in the seventeenth century. Red flags in ancient India were an indicator of power, royal or spiritual. From this arose the association of red with Kshatriya, the warrior or potential king,[13] and its use in rituals of royal consecration as well as rituals of regeneration of the universe.[14] But Mughal emperors too used red for royal tents. The umbrellas or *chattras* of Muslim rulers in the Deccan were red. The presence of red umbrellas among Mysore troops denoted the presence of officers of the highest rank.

Not surprisingly, given India's geographical size and variety of historical experiences, there was more than one interpretation of the power and significance of the colour red. Generally considered auspicious in the north, red was also perceived as being the colour of blood and danger, therefore more dangerous in parts of South India such as Mysore.[15] No doubt the Hindu social system accorded no place to green in its attribution of colours to the four social categories of priests, warriors, merchants, and lowest serving classes: these being white, red,

[13] C.A. Bayly notes that when used by kings, red was regarded as a sign of wrath. It was associated with power and energy in both the cults of pirs and the worship of goddesses. 'Origins of Swadeshi', op. cit., p. 291.

[14] This idea is reinforced by anthropological readings of red that in cosmological understanding denotes the light of the atmosphere, but also the light created by sacrifice, which brings about renewal.

[15] Even today, Brahman widows wear plain red saris in the South, and many fastidious vegetarians of southern Brahmin communities avoid tomatoes and beetroots because these are the colour of blood.

yellow, and blue-black. It was also true that the Mughals had used green; but then they had also used red. Other examples of Muslim kings outside the Mughal line adopting green for more political reasons could also be found. Green was used extensively by Tipu Sultan, ruler of Mysore over 1782–92, for decorating his buildings, and it was the colour of his campaign tent and his flag.[16] In short, Hindus and Muslims both used green and saffron flags in religious worship and festivals in South India, green standing for success and prosperity, and saffron to characterize divine offerings.[17]

This clearly indicates that there was little rigidity in the adoption of colours for the representation of political power. Red and green were used indistinctly by Hindu and Muslim monarchs. Although a single colour was the norm, green and red could also sometimes appear together, as in the triangular flag of Nagoda state in the nineteenth century. This malleability was later to be demonstrated by Venkayya in 1916 when he used red to represent Hindus, Sikhs, and Muslims but also green for Muslims as well as Sikhs.

Disregarding this tendency, Taylor settled on a straightforward scheme of granting red banners to Hindu princes and green to Muslim states. The other grand conclusion he reached was that Muslim princely states inevitably used green. For if Bhopal, Hyderabad, and Bhawalpur had green banners, this was, declared Taylor, because it was their sacred colour. Taylor's impressions were reinforced by Lockwood Kipling (the novelist Rudyard Kipling's father), whose professional post of curator at the Lahore Museum and interest in the indigenous traditions of craftsmanship and artistic schools lent added weight to Taylor's conclusion that Hindus preferred all shades of red, pink, yellow, light purple, and so on. It was Kipling who set Taylor on the path that green was the colour of Islam. Loyally subscribing to this idea, Taylor thus refused to give the Nizam of Hyderabad the gold colour he had asked for and instead gave him green.

Despite having enough information to show that symbolic allegiances could shift from red to green, Taylor thus ignored the suppleness of meanings and shades of colours in the Indian system as well as the simultaneous use by Muslims of red and green in their political systems

[16] Kate Brittlebank, *Tipu Sultan's Search for Legitimacy*, op. cit., p. 137.
[17] S.A.A. Saheb, 'A Festival of Flags', op. cit., p. 61.

and practices. He was accustomed to the British heraldic tradition of colours, characterized by continuity, not by shifting and multiple affiliations to different shades at the same time or crossovers and exchanges from one colour to another. The three red and white crosses of the Union Flag, representing Saint George, Saint Andrew, and Saint Patrick, stood for England, Scotland, and Ireland.[18] Taylor's schematization of red for Hindus and green for Muslims transposed a Western logic onto the Indian situation, which was marked by cultural adjustments and the coexistence of different colour systems and codes. Naturally, he found satisfactory technical justifications for rejecting saffron. It hardly corresponded to the Western heraldic tradition and so he dismissed the colour as 'embarrassing'. In any case, as Lockwood Kipling had pointed out, this was the most variable colour in the world: 'when new it is a bricky sanguine, but as the wearer washes it in many tanks and dries it in the sun it assumes according to the texture and original dye all kinds of tints.'[19] Taylor also cited the princes' general indifference to the colours of their banners, on the basis of information from British Residents. From Travancore, the British Resident wrote that the colours of princely banners had been determined in the past more by chance than by political precedents, whereas the Jat state of Bharatpur, wrote the British agent, had no national colour.[20] On such grounds a new system of state colours was instituted by the colonial state, though Taylor was honest enough to admit his ignorance: 'I am sorry to say', he wrote, 'I know nothing. Ousely was commissioner and could tell nothing.'[21] Finally, he attributed red exclusively to Hindu states and green only to Muslim states. This schematic codifying of colours in the system of princely banners seems

[18] Cumberland Clark, *The Flag of England, its History and the Flags of the Empire* (London, The Golden Vista Press, 1932), p. 3. Richard the Lionhearted chose the red cross of Saint George in 1190 as England's patron saint and the badge of his knights. In 1605, when James VI of Scotland also became King James I of England, the white Saint Andrew cross or saltire was added, forming the first Union Flag in 1606. And finally, the red saltire or the Saint Patrick cross was chosen to represent Ireland on the Union Flag in 1801. W. Francis Aitken, 'Our Flag. The Story of the Union Jack', *Overseas*, V, 3, 1918, no. 28, pp. 35–7.

[19] OIOC, R/2/430/78, Robert Taylor, *The Princely Armoury*, op. cit., p. 147.

[20] Ibid., pp. 145, 149.

[21] Ibid., p. 167.

to have been, on the whole, accepted unquestioningly by the princes, with brief exceptions like Cochin, which complained on being attributed black.

Curiously, in the early designs of the national flag in 1905–7 and 1917, nationalists continued this association of red with Hindus and green with Muslims. Juxtaposing red and green, with or without yellow, was of course a departure from the Indian traditional flags in only one colour. In cultural systems which valued appearances and where colour served to mirror social status, dignity, royalty, and rank, this combination of colours broke with the idea of colours standing for segregation. Instead, their union suggested a passage from one colour to the other, read in this case from one community to the other, each colour setting off the other by virtue of the strong contrast it established. By thus emphasizing both difference and proximity, they sought to accentuate the alliance and unity of the two communities. But such readings further enmeshed the symbolic meanings of the colours within narrow communitarian frontiers. Bengali intellectuals' insistence in 1924 that ochre was more representative of Hindus than red followed the colonial logic instituted by Taylor and Kipling of binding colours in a one-to-one exclusive relationship with an object, group, or usage. This was quite contrary to Indian political usage, which had manifested a certain elasticity in the use of colours. In the explanatory scheme advanced by Bengalis, the decisive and determining origins of the status and meanings of colours were sacred textual references, traditional practices and social codes, or some selected historical episodes such as the Maratha adoption of the saffron flag in the seventeenth century. This deep-seated conservatism marked the meanings attributed to specific colours from 1905 to 1907, in 1917, and finally by Gandhi in 1921. All remained captive to a rigid, sectarian interpretation of colours that had been advanced and promoted by the colonial government.

Colours as National Values

Few digressions from the predominant interpretation of red, green, and white as the colours of Hindus and Muslims were made by the 1930s. In 1909 an article published in *Modern Review* did suggest that gold, white and red, standing for victory, purity, and strength, be the chosen colours. It argued that these three principal qualities were particularly relevant to the Indian situation.[22] But on the whole, since the *Bande Mataram* flag, a narrow religious connotation of red and green had imposed itself upon what was intended as a national symbol of sovereignty. Even Venkayya's novel, militant enthusiasm for equipping India with an emblem of political modernity succumbed to his fascination for Swami Vivekananda's worldview, which exalted religion as the sole torch of true civilization. The reasoning was not incoherent in a period dominated by the rediscovery of India's spiritual and artistic traditions by Orientalists and by Indian nationalist artists who perceived the basic ingredients of Indianness as its religious maturity, indeed superiority. Nationalist sentiments were deeply infused with the ethos of religious devotion, and when Venkayya affirmed that Indians, being steeped in religion, could not have a political flag distinct and separate from a religious flag, he was echoing the prevailing mood of that decade. From this perspective the colours of the flag could only have a religious meaning. This idea found a broader echo: 'our nation is a union of three important religious parties—Mohamedans, Christians and Hindus and we also have a few more religious parties . . . When we go in for a standard to represent our nation, we should definitely allot one colour to each,'[23] affirmed a newspaper reader.

Gandhi's reflections in 1921 also emphatically insisted that red symbolized Hindus, green Muslims and white other faiths. Together the colours stood for the unity of all faiths of India. The political class immediately and widely echoed this emphasis. Motilal Nehru made a plea for unity in 1925 under the Swaraj flag in terms of its colours:

> It has three colours, white, green and red. White at the top is emblematical of the unity of all classes, races and creeds in India. As a beam of light is the blend of the colours it shows on passing through a prism, so is the white on the flag symbolic of the unity of all the diverse classes, races and creeds in India . . . Green and red placed below the white represent the three major communities, which form the bulk of

[22] Quoted in P.A. Venkayya, *A National Flag for India* (Masulipatam, 1916), p. 59.

[23] *Janmabhumi*, 6 October 1921, Letter to the Editor, signed 'an Andhra Scout'.

the population, namely the Muslims and the Hindus. The flag thus presents a united India.[24]

At the height of the Nagpur flag satyagraha, C.R. Rajagopalachari underlined this same unity of colours as the principal threat of the flag for the British government: 'The secret is that the Government do not like the combination of three colours in this flag. If an individual Christian or Parsee carried a white flag, a Hindu a red flag, or a Musulman a green flag, the government wouldn't have interfered . . . But if all these colours are put together in a flag there is a great danger to the British Empire.'[25] Similar public discourses propagated these associations.[26]

A single colour would perhaps not have evoked the idea of reconciliation and unity of India's groups so openly. Precisely this idea of unity had prompted Gandhi to insist on three colours: 'I would have had only one colour if there had been no quarrel between Hindus and Musulmans . . . The two colours red and green should be there to perpetuate the growing unity.'[27] From this logic, displaying the colours representing Hindus and Muslims together would lead to their eventual concord. The Hindi newspaper *Lakshman* contended that if all the communities in India recognized the three-coloured national flag, communal differences would cease to disturb the people.[28]

Contrary to this hoped-for harmony, the choice and association of colours had become another unexpected and unforeseen contentious issue, reinforcing existing differences. On the one hand the divergent opinions reflected a cultural sensitivity which attributed power to colours as mediums and reflectors of personal qualities and accomplishments. On the other hand they indicated that a fresh appreciation of

[24] *Hindustan Times*, 28 October 1925, in *Selected Works of Motilal Nehru, 1923–1925*, ed. Ravinder Kumar and Hari Dev Sharma (New Delhi, Vikas Publishing House, 1986), vol. 4, p. 272.

[25] *The Hindu*, 8 June 1923.

[26] Babu Bhagavan Das at a public meeting at the town hall in Benaras declared that, in his eyes, red represented Hindu religion and its derivatives, while green stood for Muslims. *The Hindu*, 3 August 1923.

[27] *CWMG*, vol. XX, *April–August 1921* (Ahmedabad, 1966), p. 462.

[28] OIOC, L/R/5/97, Native Newspaper Reports, United Provinces, *Lakshman*, 30 June 1923.

the role of colours in the building of a national unity was now being made. Simultaneously, criticisms about the communal interpretation of colours had increased.[29] The principal theorist on this subject was the Bengali linguist Suniti Kumar Chatterjee, one of the authors of the 1924 letter to Gandhi that had proposed ochre instead of red. Now, in a long article in English published in a Calcutta journal in 1931, he castigated Indians and asked them not to think in terms of different communities, or perpetuate a sense of communal distinctiveness. Any explanation of colours in the national flag as symbolizing Hindus, Muslims, Christians, and other communities, he declared, should be regarded as pernicious and anti-national.[30] But in fact the communitarian interpretations of these colours were proving difficult to efface. Newspaper articles repeated that red, green, and white stood for Hindus, Muslims, and minorities, that is, the aggregate population of India, and not the ideas of liberty, equality, and fraternity—just in case the French model should inspire people.[31]

Even if presented as symbolizing the unity of religious denominations, these explanations led to demands from communities that now felt excluded from this colour scheme. Sikh reactions confirmed the dangers of interpreting colours as representative of certain communities. The following letter to Gandhi by a Sikh, Sardar Charan Singh Shahid, summed up Sikh sentiments: 'When the three coloured flag idea was mooted by you, where is the harm of including the fourth colour? The Sikhs consider it a question of Panthic honour. Continued postponement of this question disturbs the average Sikh mind . . . their overwhelming majority is abstaining from joining the national struggle only for this reason.'[32] Even the Western press concurred with this view. The *New York Times* wrote:

> The only cloud on the Mahatma's horizon today has appeared in the form of a peremptory demand from Kharak Singh, the leader of the

[29] *The People*, 5 April 1931.

[30] Suniti Kumar Chatterjee, 'The National Flag', *Modern Review*, June 1931; later republished in Suniti Kumar Chatterjee, *The National Flag. A Selection of Papers Cultural and Historical* (Calcutta, Mitra & Ghosh, 1944), p. 2.

[31] K. Vyasa Rao, 'What the Flag Stands for', *The Hindu*, 16 July 1931.

[32] *The Tribune*, 6 March 1931.

Punjab Sikhs, to know why Mr Gandhi has failed to observe the promise he made at the Lahore Congress to change the red, green and white Congress flag into a four colour emblem to satisfy the Sikhs. Mr Gandhi may be too elated over winning victories in villages to worry about awkward colour schemes, but Kharak Singh's letter comes as a reminder to him that the Gujarat district is not the whole of India.[33]

The Sikh League's immediate reaction to the Swaraj flag had been to write to Gandhi inviting him to include their black colour in the flag. Black was commonly held to portend ill luck or disaster. Conversely, its ominousness was meant to avert evil and serve as a means of protection. Gandhi's conciliatory reply to this demand was that 'we must not be parochial, provincial or clannish'. He hoped the Sikh Leaguers would see 'the unpractical nature of their suggestion'[34] and considered that their agitation 'has no point' as the flag had not even come before the AICC for discussion and decision. Gandhi insisted that he did not propose to bring the flag's adoption before the AICC committee in view of the Sikh objections, at least not until he had convinced them of 'the unreasonableness of their demand'. He had 'not the shadow of a doubt that they should withdraw the objection.' Did not the colour white include all other colours, he enquired? In his eyes their demand for special prominence reflected a refusal to merge into the two numerically great communities. They must seek for points of contact. 'It is a dangerous thing to emphasize our differences or distinctions', he warned. He put down the Sikh nationalist demands to government agents in the Sikh camp who were making all kinds of mischievous suggestions to breed dissensions, but he concluded: 'The best thing is not to worry.'[35]

Despite Gandhi's reassurances, Sikh nationalists persisted with their claim through the 1920s. In September 1930 the Akali Dal General Committee renewed its intention of convincing the Congress central leadership to include the Sikh colour in the national flag. The Provincial Congress Committee formally wrote to the AICC, whose reply was expected by 8 October. Meanwhile, Sardar Kharak Singh

[33] *The New York Times*, 10 April 1930, p. 10.
[34] *Young India*, 18 May 1921, p. 154.
[35] *Young India*, 4 August 1921, p. 242.

warned Akalis in Amritsar that Congress could not be counted upon to consider their demands and their only way out was a stubborn display of the Sikh colour. He even refused to meet Pandit Madan Mohan Malaviya for any discussion on the subject. Malaviya suggested to the Amritsar Akali Dal leaders that if the AICC found it impossible to agree to their demand, they should be satisfied with the inclusion of the Sikh colour in the Punjab Congress flag. Not surprisingly, this idea was not well received by the Akalis.[36] They were noticeably missing among picketers at Lahore on 1 November 1930, after the disappointing return from Lucknow of a deputation sent by the Shiromani Gurdwara Prabandhak Committee. It had failed to interview Jawaharlal Nehru on the subject of including the Sikh colour, because of his arrest, and in the meantime the publication of the AICC's refusal to accept the Sikh demand in the press had not improved matters.[37]

Surprisingly, Sikhs were not very dogmatic about their colour. Earlier demands for black were now merged with calls for saffron. Both the Sikh deputation, which met Gandhi in December 1929, as well as the Lahore session of the Congress recommended saffron. The absence of saffron was now put forward as the major cause of Sikh abstention from civil disobedience.[38] But when Sikhs manifested their discontent and determination by hoisting a four-colour flag at Amritsar on Independence Day, saffron had no place in this flag. It included black with the already present white, green, and red.

A National Debate, April–July 1931

The Flag Committee's appeal in April 1931 for views on the question of the flag's colours and symbols offered Sikhs and other communities the opportunity to air their grievances and thrash out the merits or inconveniences of the existing colours— red vs. ochre, or white—or even advance other colours, justifying their deeper symbolism and meaning in the Indian cultural, social, and philosophical traditions.

[36] OIOC, L/P&J/12/21, Local Government fortnightly reports on the political situation, for the fortnight ending 30 September 1930.

[37] OIOC, L/P&J/12/21, Local Government fortnightly reports on the political situation, for the fortnight ending 31 October 1930.

[38] *The Tribune*, 1 April 1931, Hanwant Sahai, 'Our National Flag'.

Throwing open the debate to ordinary individuals, cultural organizations, political groups, and party spokesmen would permit the expression of divergent views; after which a gradual convergence of varied interpretations could eventually lead to a common understanding of colours in the specific context of the nation. It was an operation in national persuasion.

Similar processes had been launched in other countries during the past decade. In Canada a flag contest had been organized by a newspaper, *La Presse*, in 1926.[39] As for South Africa, where the flag issue had become a regular feature of political battles, the government instituted a public competition when it decided to adopt a national flag in 1925.[40] Unfortunately, in this case the exercise had proved futile: the final selection of a design did not have the desired result of creating a consensus. Instead, it unleashed an explosion of popular violence that effectively suspended the project.[41] The passionate and irreconcilable differences between Dutch and English groups in South Africa, between the Nationalist Party and the Labour Party, held many lessons for the Indian National Congress. However, no allusions to the South African experience or to the Canadian trials and tribulations come across in party documents or in the press of these years.

Letters, articles, and editorials written from early April to early July 1931 on the colours and design of the Indian national flag provide a variety of opinions of individuals or groups from all over India. The discussion seems to have been conducted largely in the main English-language Indian newspapers like the *Tribune* (Lahore), the *Hindu* (Madras), the *Amrita Bazar Patrika* (Calcutta), the *Bombay Chronicle*, and *The Mahratta* (Bombay). Few echoes are found in the Indian vernacular press. In fact, while the latter accentuated local events, the English newspapers aspired to be national dailies, aiming at an English reading élite in all provinces and therefore raising what were felt to be nationwide issues. Consequently, the corpus of letters examined

[39] Alistair B. Fraser, 'A Canadian Flag for Canada', *Revue d'Etudes Canadiennes*, vol. 25, no. 4, 1990–1, pp. 64–80, esp. p. 73.

[40] 'The Flag Question in South Africa', *The National Review*, vol. LXXXVII, August 1926, pp. 844–56.

[41] Drummond Chaplin, 'What is Known as the Flag Issue', *The Round Table*, vol. XVI, December 1925–September 1926, pp. 856–62.

reflects a limited cross-section of an urban élite's public opinion.[42] Without engaging in quantitative analysis, a few strong proposals can be clearly identified.

To begin with, there was a large demand for saffron. One of its most loyal defenders was Pandit Malaviya, the orthodox Hindu lawyer and politician from the United Provinces, vice chancellor of Benares Hindu University and future president of the Indian National Congress in 1932. Malaviya differed with Gandhi during the non-cooperation movement and now proposed an all-saffron flag to represent the united Indian nation and not simply one community, whether Hindus, Muslims, or Sikhs.[43] Another long article entitled 'The Indian National Flag. An Inquiry into its Colour' in Tilak's newspaper also defended this choice. Loyal to its strong Hindu inspiration, it suggested: 'The whole of India including all creeds and communities must find expression in a single symbolic colour and design.'[44] Jawaharlal Nehru himself was not averse to the idea and would back the case for saffron in July 1931. The All India Sanskrit Conference and the Gujarat Vidyapith in Ahmedabad, as well as the Sikhs, wished for the inclusion of saffron in the flag.[45] One argument favoured the replacement of white with saffron.[46]

The next-most-popular colour was red. It was proposed as the symbol of a class of living martyrs of the nation—peasants, labourers, artisans, and workers.[47] Sarojini Naidu's definition of red as the blood of martyrs and the nation's sacrifice in her speech at the National Flag Day celebrations in Bombay on 29 April 1928 was recalled in this context.[48] One letter from Nagpur defended red as the well-established

[42] Sixty-three letters, addressed directly to the Flag Committee by individuals and provincial Congress committees, are preserved in NMML, AICC Papers, file nos 58, 60, 61. More letters, used for this study, were published in newspapers as letters to the editor.

[43] *Searchlight*, 11 April 1931.

[44] *The Mahratta*, 14 June 1931, p. 317.

[45] NMML, AICC Papers, file no. 58, Gujarat Vidyapith to President, Flag Committee, Ahmedabad, 14 April 1931.

[46] NMML, AICC Papers, file no. 58, Suniti Kumar Chatterjee from Calcutta to the President Flag Committee.

[47] *The Tribune*, 10 April 1931, 'Our National Flag'.

[48] *The Tribune*, 29 April 1931.

colour of revolution.[49] A far more unusual reflection on these colours saw them as a means of depicting the geopolitics of the subcontinent, with British India being depicted as red.[50] Red was more generally interpreted as standing for states of being like sacrifice, triumph, passion, and hope.[51] None of its negative traditional associations was recalled, such as the fact that red was, for example, a marker of widows in South India. Nor were there attempts to draw meanings from traditional Indian systems, such as Ayurvedic medicine. Yet the latter's systematization of colours was well known, more particularly its view of red as a 'hot' colour with a strong effect on blood and vitality, and as increasing metabolic activity and stimulating the mind. The meanings attributed to red by the correspondents in 1931 were not linked to Indian systems or models. Nonetheless, they all proposed a significant shift from the sectarian readings of red made in 1905 for the *Bande Mataram* flag; or in 1916 by Venkayya;[52] and in 1917 with greater force during the Home Rule movement.[53] In this sense, the debate was already serving a political purpose by enlarging and publicizing the multiple, alternative, possible meanings of red, revealing its elasticity and allowing parallel, complex appropriations of the colour. Three proposals to the Flag Committee argued for an all red-flag, while eleven provincial Congress committee designs pressed for red as one of the colours of the flag.

Closely following red, green emerged as one of the colours in the flag, although there were no suggestions for an all-green flag. It had, as we have seen, come to be indissociably established as the Muslim colour in 1905, during the Bengal partition. This interpretation continued in Bhikaji Cama's flag of 1907 as it did in the Home Rule flag which fixed green for Muslims.[54] Gandhi maintained this association.[55] As the debate progressed through the summer of 1931, other

[49] *The Tribune*, 17 June 1931, anonymous letter.

[50] *The Tribune*, 10 April 1931, Letter to the Editor, Teja Singh.

[51] The Bengali linguist Suniti Kumar Chatterjee who wrote an article (op. cit.) on the national flag in *Modern Review*, June 1931, offered this interpretation.

[52] P.A. Venkayya, *A National Flag*, op. cit.

[53] *New India*, 1 September 1917, p. 9.

[54] Ibid.

[55] *Janmabhumi*, 6 October 1921.

dimensions and meanings of green came to be accentuated. One letter to the editor recommended green as the first band of the flag because it was a lively colour and held out hopes of ultimate success.[56] Still others attempted to correct the misconception that green was a Muslim colour by quoting the example of Persia and Turkey, neither of which had adopted green in their flags.[57] Green was linked to prosperity,[58] to hope and ambition,[59] to vegetation, life and growth, national wealth and courage.[60]

In contrast to the popularity of red and even green, colours like blue and black had few advocates. A reader who in 1920 visualized the flag design in the form of an isosceles triangle with a border of light blue colour on both sides to represent the Indian Ocean remained a lonely voice.[61] No evidence of futher recommendations of blue are found. It remained outside the hierarchy of auspicious colours despite its prominence in connection with the production of indigo in Gandhi's native province of Gujarat.

Some continuities with pre-colonial traditions can be discerned in this absence of blue. Taylor had noted that no princely chief had asked for blue in any shade on his arms or banner;[62] for him this fact emerged as most curious, coming as he did from a European culture in which blue had become the dominant colour since the Middle Ages.[63] The French traveller Polier had observed in 1788 that Hindus considered this colour to be inauspicious; in opposition to their beliefs, the Sikhs showed a particular penchant for blue as the symbol of royal power, following their founder Guru Nanak who adopted blue in order to

[56] NMML, AICC Papers, file no. 61, letter to the editor of *Swarajya Daily*, Madras.

[57] *The Hitavada*, 23 April 1931.

[58] NMML, AICC Papers, file no. 58.

[59] NMML, AICC Papers, file no. 58, Karnataka Provincial Congress Committee.

[60] Vishwanath S. Naravane, *Sarojini Naidu* (New Delhi, Orient Longman, 1980), p. 76.

[61] *Searchlight*, 22 December 1920, p. 6, by Babu Bindbasini Prasad Varma, Hajipur (Patna).

[62] Robert Taylor, *The Princely Armoury*, op. cit., p. 6.

[63] Michel Pastoureau, *Bleu*, op. cit.

highlight the absurdity of all religious prejudices.[64] In the same logic, Taylor recorded that the ancient state flag of the Jat Bumrowlia, a Sikh family, had been plain blue until 1760, but following a battle with the neighbouring chief of the Budhowrias they had adopted the latter's flag of gold cloth with a Hanuman in red at its centre.[65] Despite noting the absence of any demand for blue or black as curious, Taylor had nevertheless gone ahead and attributed the states of Rewah and Cooch Behar black banners. They of course considered this unlucky and complained to the British government.[66] Apparently Taylor was unaware that among the planets, which are all depicted by colours in the Hindu system, Rahu and Ketu (nodes of the moon) and Sanaiscara (Saturn), both considered inauspicious and harbingers of obstacles and failures, were symbolized by dark blue-green or smoke-grey. In addition, the kingdom of Yama, the lord of death, is black; and in the Puranas and Tantras black is the colour of darkness.[67] Interestingly, Venkayya attributed blue to the Jews, and indigo to the Christians.[68] While the Sikhs had by now largely abandoned their original inclination for black or blue, a few letters in 1931 continued to propose black.[69] Another instance of dislike for black was given by Kamaladevi Chattopadhyaya, who, enrolled as a volunteer at the Belgaum Congress in 1924, found the women volunteers' uniform of black saris with the flag colours on

[64] Quoted in Guy Deleury, *Les Indes Florissantes. Anthologie des voyageurs français 1750–1820* (Paris, Robert Laffont, 1991), p. 146.

[65] Robert Taylor, *The Princely Armoury*, op. cit., p. 141. Curzon, viceroy of India from 1899 to 1904, also noted that gold was the royal colour, referred to in Sanskrit literature as the scarer of spirits. Cf. George N. Curzon, *British Government in India: The Stories of the Viceroys and Government Houses*, vol. 1 (London, Cassell and Co., 1925), p. 218.

[66] Robert Taylor, *The Princely Armoury*, op. cit., p. 6. Blue and black were considered variants of the same colour in Indian classical texts like the Natyasastra: V.V. Vertogradona, 'Problems of Interpretation of Ancient Indian and Ancient Greek Theory of Colour', *Journal of the Oriental Institute*, vol. XXXVII, nos 3–4, 1988, pp. 321–8.

[67] Sivapriyananda, 'Colour Symbolism', op. cit., pp. 37–8.

[68] P.A. Venkayya, *A National Flag*, op. cit., p. 21.

[69] *Janmabhumi*, 6 October 1921, letter to the editor, signed 'an Andhra Scout'.

the borders too drab. When she was put in charge of the volunteers at the Madras session of the Congress in 1927, she changed the colour of the sari to orange.[70]

The 1931 flag debate reveals an inclination for lighter, brighter colours, as opposed to dark colours. In particular, white was retained as occupying a legitimate place on the flag. Several pleas even for an all-white flag were made in 1930–1.[71] Letters often justified this choice by quoting testimonies of foreign travellers describing the widespread use of white by Indians.[72] Paradoxically white, though associated with 'auspiciousness', 'abundance', and 'purity' among the Hindu and Muslim communities, was also a colour of mourning for Hindus, particularly a signal of widowhood in North India; but none of these negative connotations of white were evoked in the debate. Strangely, white had never been included in the earlier flags from 1905 onwards, despite the powerful promotion of white as the colour of khadi during the Swadeshi movement.[73] Nor had it found a very significant place in Venkayya's designs. The colour was also not very prominent in the pre-colonial princely system of heraldry, although there were instances of it being found in the flags of Hyderabad and Cochin. Taylor had not retained it in any of his designs. But once its political status was elaborated by Gandhi through his militant defence of khadi and its inclusion in the Swaraj flag, it became for its advocates a highly charged symbol of peace, non-violence, unity, austerity and truth, the colour which contained all other colours, and therefore representative of all India's communities.[74] Still, this position did not create unanimity: leading personalities like S.K Chatterjee, C.V. Raman, Ramananda Chatterjee (founder of the *Modern Review*), S. Radhakrishnan asked that white be replaced by saffron, without feeling the need to give

[70] Jamila Brijbhushan, *Kamaladevi Chattopadhyaya. Portrait of a Rebel* (New Delhi, Abhinav Publications, 1976), pp. 28–9.

[71] *The Tribune*, 7 February 1930; *The Mahratta*, 14 June 1931.

[72] The detail was noted in *The Tribune*, 7 February 1930. Chinese pilgrims to India had noted that the inhabitants commonly wore white colours. Cf. Sir Richard Winstedt (ed.), *India Art* (London, Faber & Faber, 1947), p. 180.

[73] C.A. Bayly, 'The Origins of *Swadeshi*', op. cit., pp. 285–321.

[74] Suniti Kumar Chatterjee, 'The National Flag', op. cit.; reproduced in *The National Flag*, op. cit., pp. 7–9.

any explicit reason.[75] In fact, this open debate does not seem to have thrown up any strikingly new colour schemes, for example, browns, purples, pinks . . . the discussions focused on the merits and drawbacks of the few colours inextricably associated with the emblem.

On the whole, two significant features stand out. First, a clear rupture had been made with the 'blue ensign' used by the British to represent their sovereignty in the Indian empire. This involved imposing a different colour scheme that could be used for nation building. But inconsistently this resolve to break away from the traditional British ensign did not lead Indians to justify their new choices in light of their own traditions of philosophy or social practices. There were no evocations of the status of colours in Indian treatises, literary texts, and artistic movements.[76] More pragmatic considerations, such as international norms or Western practices, seem to have prevailed over the classic connotations of social status or cosmological meanings, in justifying the choice of certain colours and not others.[77]

Secondly, an equally radical break was accomplished with the colonial logics inaugurated in 1877 by Robert Taylor that essentialized colours as symbols of groups and communities. This second breach involved a profound upheaval. It implied fixing a meaning for colours that could be read by every Indian, independent of his community, class, and linguistic or religious group. For the first time, therefore, explanations of colours in terms other than communitarian were highlighted. Sarojini Naidu had set the tone when, before a vast assembly

[75] *Bombay Chronicle*, 4 July 1931.

[76] A thirteenth-century text from Kashmir Shaivism, the *Guru Gita* (verse 140), associates white with light and purity, red with passion and action, black with darkness, each colour evoking emotional states and goals, both spiritual and material.

[77] Anthropological associations of red with *rajas* or with passion, black with *tamas* or inertia, white with *sattva* or truth and purity in sacred texts are interpreted to read: tamas, is first of all the earth and obscurity; *sattva*, the light of the sky; and finally, between the two there is *rajas*, the light of the atmosphere, but also the light created by the sacrifice which brings about renewal. Hence, the association of red with *kshatriya*, the warrior or potential king, and its use in rituals of royal consecration—which are also rituals of the regeneration of the universe. Serge Bouez, 'Une couleur de trop', in Serge Tornay (ed.), *Voir et nommer les couleurs*, op. cit., pp. 413–15.

in New York, at the World Alliance for Peace banquet, in which seventy nationalities took part in October 1928, she interpreted red as standing for hope.[78] There was of course nothing specifically Indian about such qualities. Very similar interpretations could be found for colours of other flags. To take only one example, in Italy, Giosue Carducci had also analysed the red in the Italian 'bandiera' in 1877 in terms of passion and the blood of martyrs and heroes, and green as the renewal of hope for a better future for Italy and the promise of success.[79]

Thus the debate accelerated a movement to break with the colonial symbolic system of colours—given the difficulties of nation-building on the basis of 'traditional' colours still linked with particular groups, which in no case could be recognized as shared symbols by all members of the future nation. Not only did this limit the possibilities, it also led to their interpretation in terms that could be presented as universal: that is to say, capable of eliminating all communitarian interpretation. In order to achieve a symbolic construction of the nation through colours it was in fact, necessary to 'denationalize' them.

Saffron: Plebiscited but Impossible

The Flag Committee's deliberations in July 1931 turned primarily around two possibilities.

The first option was backed by popular acclaim and pressure from the Gandhians. It implied retaining the flag's colours as they were, that is, the tricolour pattern of white, green, and red with the charkha. This model had been faithfully followed since the emergence of the first *Bande Mataram* flag in 1905, then in 1907 as well as in 1921. The only exception was the Home Rule flag with its five red and four green bands. Certainly, the tricolour pattern was a deviation from the Indian political, military tradition of one-colour triangular flags, or even the less frequent but familiar two-colour flags in certain princely states. Nevertheless, the *tri-guna* or tricolour concept was rooted in a Hindu philosophical creative principle of the universe. The *Chandogya*

[78] Sarojini Naidu to Mahatma Gandhi, Cincinnati, 19 November 1928, in Sarojini Naidu, *Selected Letters 1890s to 1940s*, ed. Makarand Paranjpe, op. cit., p. 215.

[79] Giosue Carducci, Mario Luzi, *Discorsi per il Tricolore* (Montichiari, Zanetti, 1999), pp. 11–12.

Upanisad saw the phenomenal word reduced to the three basic elements of fire, water, and food, represented by the three colours, red, white, and black.[80] In a more recent political tradition the tricolour scheme and rectangular shape was closer to the model of Western national flags, to which many letters referred in 1931. These referred to the flags of Germany, France, America, and Russia, which had also all undergone changes and alterations.[81] At the same time, they held up the examples of Persia, Bulgaria, Mexico, and Italy which all contained green, white, and red in their flags.[82] Whether as models to be imitated or rejected, Western precedents and norms were systematically evoked. There were comparatively few voices reclaiming a revival of the oriental tradition of triangular flags. Those who did so pointed to their use by both Muslim states and Hindu kingdoms. A further argument in favour of a triangular banner was felt to be the grace and symbolism inherent in the convergence of lines to a single point, in contrast with the complete absence of these qualities in the rectangular form specific to European national states.[83]

The second option open to the Flag Committee was to adopt a one-colour flag. Here, two propositions were made: an all-saffron flag with the charkha, or an all-white flag with the lotus.[84] Two sittings of the Committee were held on 8 and 9 July to discuss the designs submitted. Eight provincial Congress committees staunchly defended the existing Swaraj flag. Bihar, Utkal, Bombay, Andhra, Karnataka, Tamil Nadu, Uttar Pradesh, and Sind generally opposed change. The only modification that could be envisaged was voiced by Sind. It suggested placing the charkha in a small square at the top, with the figure of Gandhi at the wheel to give a more personal touch. According to the *Bombay Chronicle*, if a large majority desired to continue with the current symbol, the Committee had at the same time to take note of the growing communal interpretation of colours—which could not be tolerated. The proposal for an all-white flag with the lotus not being approved, the Committee suspended its final decision for the moment.

[80] Sivapriyananda, 'Colour Symbolism', op. cit., p. 34.

[81] *The Tribune*, 24 May 1931, 'Indian National Flag', Sardul Singh Cavershar.

[82] *The Tribune*, 17 June 1931,

[83] *The Mahratta*, 21 June 1931.

[84] *Bombay Chronicle*, 9 July 1931.

It finally submitted its report in the first week of August 1931. On the whole, it considered the moment inopportune for changing the design and colours of the flag, for powerful emotions had coalesced around the symbol. This argument, outlined by the secretary of the Hindustan Seva Dal, Madras, had been echoed by many: 'No one has any right to tamper either with its meaning or its significance . . . that has become sacred to all freedom lovers in the country.'[85] But in light of the continuing controversy about the communal meanings of colours, the Committee had been obliged to recommend a change and unanimously propose an all-saffron (*kesari* or *bhagwa*) national flag, with the charkha in blue on the top left quarter.[86] Noting that the 'concept of flag as a symbol of nationalism, national aspiration and sacrifice for national freedom' had installed itself through a decade of collective struggle, the Committee declared its decision to be taken 'from wholly an aesthetic, heraldic standpoint'. Clearly, it was hiding the true motives that lay behind its decision. A lengthy note, conserved in the committee papers,[87] suggests the pressure of arguments used by some orthodox Hindus and Sikhs to swing the choice in favour of saffron: the weight of an ancient historical tradition (without any precise historical data), the anticolonial dimension (saffron being considered to have been insulted by the British), the omnipresence of the colour throughout the country, and the scientific claim that saffron contained every other colour. To the eventual criticism against the religious dimension of the colour, the note answered by quoting Giuseppe Mazzini: 'You deluded yourselves with the expectation of success while you banished from your work the religious idea.'

As soon as the report was communicated, public reaction against an entirely saffron flag was explosive. No denunciation was made on the grounds that a single colour, without any element of contrast or even a thin border, was commonly held to be inauspicious—hence the use of plain red or plain white saris to represent mourning in southern and

[85] *Bombay Chronicle*, 6 August 1931, letter to the editor, signed K.S. Gopalakrishnan, secretary Hindustan Seva Dal, Madras.

[86] NMML, AICC Papers, file no. 60, from the Flag Committee to the President, AICC.

[87] NMML, AICC Papers, file no. 58.

northern India. Nor was it argued that a single colour perhaps had less impact than contrasting bands. The attacks against saffron were levelled entirely at its Hindu connotations.[88] To Muslims this was categorical proof that Congress was a communal body which had adopted the flag of the 'notorious bandit Shivaji'. Was not saffron the colour of the Hindu Mahasabha flag and of the ancient Hindu yogis and rishis?

> In no way does it represent the Indian nation [wrote one indignant Muslim]. By introducing this flag you have driven away thousands of Muslims from the Congress fold. It would have been better if you had introduced a blue or white flag with the *charkha*. But why should you? You think India belongs to the Hindus and therefore the flag should represent the Hindu community only . . . If you want to be impartial to all communities of India you will either reintroduce the former flag, beloved of all, or have some other flag, blue or white, but not this hated saffron colour flag.[89]

Gandhians were equally revolted at seeing the flag designed by their political leader, and by now nationally familiar, thus rejected. So too were organizations that had worked with militant fervour to publicize the tricolour. The secretary of the Hindustan Seva Dal, Madras, criticized the Flag Committee for arbitrarily changing its colour. The act, he affirmed, struck a death blow to the meaning and traditions of the flag and annihilated the significance that had grown around it through all the days of strife and struggle for freedom. Why, he asked, had the Committee chosen saffron and was it not preferable to give a more liberal interpretation to the meaning of the standard rather than change it? At least ten more years would be needed to popularize the new colour scheme, he warned.[90]

Instead of creating a consensus, the change threatened to deepen sentiments of alienation among Muslims, although the AICC president defended the Committee's choice by acknowledging that the proposal of a saffron-coloured flag had come from the Muslim member of the

[88] For a discussion of single colours and the changing perceptions and uses of stripes see Michel Pastoureau, *L'étoffe du Diable*, op. cit.

[89] NMML, AICC Papers, file no. 60, 6 August 1931.

[90] *The Hindu*, 6 August 1931.

Flag Committee.[91] Confronted with this public furore and differences within its own ranks (in particular, Pattabhi Satyamurti, K.M. Munshi, Purnachara Mitra, and N.S. Hardikar made a spirited defence in favour of the earlier white, green, and red colours of the Swaraj flag), the AICC almost immediately proposed a tricolour of saffron, white, and green.[92] Quite clearly, the choice of an entirely saffron flag was politically inappropriate in the face of growing Muslim hostility. The AICC's final resolution stated:

> The national flag shall be three coloured, horizontally arranged as before, but the colours shall be saffron, white and green in the order stated here from top to bottom, with the spinning wheel in dark blue in the centre of the white stripe, the colours standing for qualities, not communities. The saffron shall represent courage and sacrifice, white peace and truth, and green shall represent faith and chivalry, and the spinning wheel the hope of the masses.[93]

The move was widely acclaimed. The Sikhs, particularly the Central Sikh League, welcomed the new tricolour as a confirmation of their own earlier proposal made at the Lahore Congress.[94] Considering that at least one principal obstacle to national unity had been vanquished, the Sikh League now urged every Sikh man, woman and child to join the new national flag ceremony scheduled for 31 August. The *Bombay Chronicle* echoed a broader opinion, congratulating Congress for having settled the matter 'unanimously without much passion or bitterness', with the least possible change in the composition of the flag. All that remained now was for Congress committees to explain its significance and meaning to the people.[95]

But not all political parties were similarly appeased. The Muslim League showed no appreciation of the Congress decision not to adopt

[91] NMML, AICC Papers, file no. 60, 18 August 1931, President to Mohsain Bhai, Nagpur, U.P.

[92] *The Hindu*, 6 August 1931.

[93] B. Pattabhi Sitaramayya, *The History of the Indian National Congress, 1885–1935* (Bombay, Padma Publications,1947), vol. 1, pp. 482–3.

[94] The suggestion had been made by Master Tara Singh, Sardar Amar Singh, Gyani Gurumukh Singh, Sardar Bhag Singh, Vakil Sardar Teja Singh Jathedar.

[95] *Bombay Chronicle*, 10 August 1931.

saffron as the unique colour. Through the 1930s their discontent with the colours grew until the complaint about the 'Congress tricolour' became a standard feature of every Muslim demand. Some Hindus too persisted in their loyalty to saffron and the *bhagwa jhanda*, until the formal adoption of the tricolour by the Constituent Assembly in 1947.[96] A few advocates of red would continue to urge their cause to the bitter end. One of these, S.D. Kalelkar from Nagpur, in a note submitted to the ad hoc committee set up to determine the flag of independent India, argued that red, white, and green was the perfect distinctive combination 'against the background of the sky', with red symbolizing the 'non-violent revolution that we have witnessed in India.'[97] Despite this reticence and even rejection, the new meanings of the colours established in 1931 were no longer seriously questioned either at that time in the national press, or even debated in the 389-member Constituent Assembly which met at New Delhi on 9 December 1946. This was at odds with the attention given to the issue of the national anthem and indicated the broad degree of consensus that had been successfully created around the colours of the flag through the press, public speeches, and official party statements.[98] Both white and saffron came to be perceived as colours of nationalist resistance. White, through the medium of khadi and the spinning wheel, had been sanctified as the official garb of the Indian political battle. Saffron too was linked to the struggle for freedom. As one author noted: 'The Gandhi woman dons a saffron sari. In 1930 thousands of saffron saris were seen in Bombay policing the traffic, bringing order to mass meetings . . . breaking the salt laws . . . in the vanguard of a procession.'[99] The political transcription of saffron as a Hindu colour has in this sense been a development of the past few decades, both by Hindu

[96] *Hindustan Times*, 21 July 1947, letter to the editor from Hanuman Prasad Poddar, Gorakhpur.

[97] B. Shiva Rao, *The Framing of India's Constitution*, op. cit., vol. 1, pp. 494–5.

[98] Following its first official adoption by the Indian National Congress in 1931, a systematic policy to familiarize and educate the public on this principal emblem of the nation was undertaken. E.g. 'A Study in Colours', *Amrita Bazar Patrika*, 19 August 1931, p. 10.

[99] Krishnalal Shridharani, *My India, My West* (London, Gollancz, 1942), pp. 150, 153.

political parties and by the literature devoted to the study of the rise of right wing fundamentalism in contemporary India. These see saffron as an exclusively Hindu cultural and political heritage and underplay its broader, cross cultural meanings.[100]

Finally, in 1947 the adoption of the national flag by the Constituent Assembly did not provoke any profound divisions or opposition. Public responses to a special flag supplement issued by the *Hindustan Times*, showed a broad acceptance of these colours. Among a sample of more than seventy letters to the editor, no criticism or alternative demands were made. On the contrary their choice and meanings were further endorsed and sacralized at the moment of the flag's solemn adoption by the Constituent Assembly. Official discourses in the assembly accentuated the universal, humanist slant of these colours. The philosopher and future president Sarvepelli Radhakrishnan explained white as the colour of the sun's rays, the path of light, the light of truth and transparent simplicity. True to the ancient Indian literary tradition, which used adjectives and associations to describe shades of colours rather than establish rigid distinctions between them, Radhakrishnan brushed aside the distinctions between red, orange, ochre, saffron by encompassing red, orange, and the bhagwa colour in the same bracket as all representing the spirit of renunciation. By thus condensing and encapsulating them together, he rendered the distinction between saffron, red, etc. quite irrelevant. Finally, green in his view represented the relation to soil and the plant life on which all life depended. If Indians were to succeed in their enterprise of complete freedom, they must, he said, be guided by the higher principles of truth (white) while adopting the method of self-control and renunciation.[101]

In July 1947, in the climate of communal violence, the subject of colours provided a precious platform for the expression of ideals emphasizing a unity of thought and purpose, and the political and emotional reconciliation of all groups and communities. This was illustrated

[100] To quote only some of them, Thomas Blom Hansen, *The Saffron Wave. Democracy and Hindu Nationalism in Modern India* (Delhi, Oxford University Press, 1999); *Saffronised and Substandard. A Critique of the New NCERT Textbooks* (New Delhi, Sahmat, 2002); Tapan Basu, *et al.* (eds), *Khaki Shorts and Saffron Flags*, op. cit.

[101] B. Shiva Rao, *The Framing of India's Constitution*, op. cit., p. 505.

in a speech made by Mohammad Saadulla, leader of the Muslim League. He extended the interpretation of the colour saffron to meanings that went beyond history and community identity. Welcoming its inclusion in the flag, he described saffron as depicting the scorched condition of the earth caused by the torrid heat of the Indian sun. He explained that when crystal-clear white raindrops and water from snow-capped mountains and rivers came down, the arid areas were converted into smiling green fields whose crops sustained the people. Saffron was also the colour of all who lived the spiritual path, Hindus as well as Muslims. Therefore saffron would be a reminder that they should keep themselves on that high plane of renunciation, the realm of their sadhus and saints, pirs and pandits. As for white, he elaborated, it was the emblem of purity for Hindus and Muslims. Its presence in the flag was a reminder that they must be pure in word and deed. Purity should be the motto of their lives, individually as well as well as in connection with the state. Lastly, he pointed out that green had been the colour of the Muslim standard from the time of the Prophet of Arabia thirteen centuries ago,[102] and equally symbolized India's struggle for freedom since 1857. In short, it had particular sentimental and symbolic value for Muslims.

In a survey I carried out in 2003 among schoolchildren of Amritsar and Delhi, these very official meanings of the colours were echoed. Only one 8-year-old from a Delhi public school proclaimed that saffron was the colour of Hindus, but his classmates immediately booed him down. Even if this reflects institutional pedagogical coaching in some schools and by some teachers, it marks above all the success of a long-lasting operation which produced such a multiplicity of meanings that any restrictive communitarian interpretation was overshadowed. Moreover, the entire exercise of a public discussion of colours in 1931 and the Constituent Assembly speeches in 1947 permitted a more individual appropriation of the flag by expanding its symbolic capacities.

Colours Without a Symbol?

The exercise of representing India as a modern nation state had begun with the conception of a symbol. In the 1870s this was a primary

[102] Ibid., pp. 507–9.

preoccupation for Indian princes when the British government redesigned their state banners.[103] It was the difficulty of finding the right symbol that had also kept Gandhi from deciding a national flag for India. For many decades the main symbols selected had a strong religious dimension: lotus, moon, sun, stars, thunderbolt, and peepul tree all continued ancient patterns. For example, the Rajputs and certain other Hindu princes favoured the sun as proof of their solar descent. Taylor, in his inventory of the symbols of princely states, had observed the widespread tendency among Hindu states to depict gods on their banners (Porebundar and Rutlam, for example, had Hanuman). His own designs perpetuated these traditions, and the heraldic supporters he accorded to the princes were drawn from Hindu religious mythology—such as the eagle (Bhavnagar), elephant and tiger (Bharatpur), lion (Mysore, in use since the fifth century), Shiva's bull Nandi, and the lotus (Sikkim).[104]

The British did not explore the possibilities of adopting non-religious motifs, either in 1877 or later. And until 1921 the Indian search too continued within the logic of Hindu or Islamic religious traditions, even if it was with the idea of creating a unity of purpose and being. When Nivedita chose the thunderbolt, it was from this perspective.[105] Venkayya's numerous devices were also largely of religious inspiration: gods and goddesses like Buddha, Krishna, Kali, Omkar, Lakshmi, Saraswati; animals like the horse and cow, flowers and flora like the lotus or the plantain tree with flowers and shoots; sacred or historical places like Mount Kailas, the river Ganges, the Taj Mahal; or the miscellaneous collection of objects like the cross, conch-shell, trident, bows, arrows, and sword, and the sun, crescent, and stars. The only flag without any symbol whatsoever was the rainbow-coloured banner designed by Venkayya, which embellished the Congress session of 1917.

Gandhi broke this pattern in 1921 when he put the charkha on the flag: 'We must not', he wrote, 'have any religious symbols and we must find a clear and permanent rallying object. That is the spinning wheel,

[103] Robert Taylor, *The Princely Armoury*, op. cit., pp. 3–7.

[104] Ibid., pp. 41, 133, 151, 161.

[105] R.S., 'The Vajra as a National Flag', *Modern Review*, November 1909, pp. 443–7.

according to the vast majority who believe with me that we lose our liberty with the loss of the spinning wheel and we can only regain it when we have revived the spinning wheel and rejected foreign cloth'.[106] It was the missing element he had been searching for. Despite Venkayya's insistence on the need to adopt a national flag, there was nothing in his designs, Gandhi disclosed, which he felt could move millions. He himself had already proposed the spinning wheel as a panacea to India's 'growing pauperism' in his book *Hind Swaraj* in 1908. But his personal discovery of the spinning wheel as a material object had been long and complicated, and he had never really seen one until it was procured for him after a determined search by a woman called Gangabehn in Vijapur, Baroda state.[107]

Gandhi's adoption of the charkha reflected the political shift in Indian self-perception as independent and self-sufficient. The charkha symbolized the recovery of their inherent but lost dignity and self-consciousness. It had thus far no religious or communitarian association. On the contrary, it evoked a vision of practical, daily commitment and effort, recalling the collective goals of freedom and liberty. Gandhi's articles in *Young India* in 1921 gathered the myriad significances of the symbol in order to enlarge its significance and make it appealing to all communities, men and women alike.[108] He went as far as digging into unfamiliar Islamic texts and sources, distant from the Indian world. A Muslim friend, he wrote, had sent him a note from the work of Daem-ul-Islam compiled by Kazi Naman ben Mahomed, Chief Justice of Cairo in the third quarter of the tenth century. According to this text, reproduced at length by Gandhi in his journal, the Holy Prophet had proclaimed the charkha to be the best occupation for a woman believer. He quoted another Muslim writer, Shaikh Ebrahim Saufee, who had written in the *Kitabun Najah* 250 years earlier that

106 *Young India*, 18 May 1921, p. 154.

107 M.K. Gandhi, *An Autobiography or The Story of My Experiments with Truth* (Ahmedabad, Navajivan Trust 1995, 1st edn, 1927–9), pp. 407–12; *Hind Swaraj* (Cambridge, Cambridge University Press, 1997), p. 150.

108 Among the numerous articles published in his journal, the more important ones in which he developed his arguments are: *Young India*, 13 April 1921, p. 116, 8 April 1926, p. 130, 27 August 1931, p. 239; speech at a prayer meeting at Delhi, 20 December 1947, *CWMG*, vol. 90, 11 November 1947–30 January 1948 (Ahmedabad, 1984), p. 267.

the charkha's inventor had made it as a replica of the physical world. The wheel's circular form represented the heavens. Its revolutions indicated those of the planets, while the twelve spokes stood for the twelve constellations. Its two legs represented the north and south poles. The axis stood for the relation between the powers of the poles, while the spindle represented the medium through which the influence of the heavenly bodies was exercised on earth. Cotton signified the elements of mineral, plant, and animal products and the spinner represented God. The description, though fanciful, admitted Gandhi, nevertheless showed the ancient symbolism incarnated in the charkha.[109]

More significantly, his choice of a concrete material object like the charkha departed from the European heraldic tradition. It had nothing in common with the customary corpus of designs which characterized European national flags until the end of the nineteenth century—with their geometrically disposed colours, animal heraldry, and stars. Even before its portrayal on the flag, it had already become a familiar object of protest, part and parcel of public processions, paraded on banners or carried in demonstrations. For those who were against a nostalgic harking back to the 'ancient flags of *Bharathavarsha*', it represented an 'instrument of national emancipation' and the 'emblem of national striving and solidarity'.[110] At the same time, critics advanced some reservations, mainly that the charkha promoted an archaic image of Indians: 'Indians were mainly weavers by profession and that Indians' ideal was very low'.[111] Still others complained that it was far too cumbersome. Rabindranath Tagore was particularly sceptical of the moral and material power of change attributed to the charkha. It was not enough to say, he wrote, 'Let them spin.' Producing thread, he explained, would not bind people with the larger community or make them conscious that the 'welfare of the people was a synthesis comprised of many interrelated elements'. In fact, linking swaraj to the charkha distracted the mind of the country from the 'great and vivid picture of the country's well-being in its universal aspect . . . Heaps of thread and

[109] *Young India*, 6 July 1921, p. 213.

[110] *Janmabhumi*, 18 September 1923, p. 4; 23 October 1923, 'Under the banner of the spinning wheel'.

[111] OIOC, L/R/96, Selections from Newspapers for the week ending 23 April 1921, United Provinces.

piles of cloth do not constitute the subject of a great picture of welfare.'[112] Criticism of the charkha was aired with greater confidence during the 1931 debate. It was held to be unartistic, even 'extremely inartistic', of short-term relevance, reflecting a transient phase in Indian economic life and of doubtful staying power when India industrialized.[113] But none of these criticisms moved Gandhi from his position.

In contrast to the complex and detailed argumentation provoked by the colours, the rich variety of designs for the symbol, proposed from April to August 1931 during the debate launched by the Congress, were unaccompanied by justifications or even interpretations.[114] It was almost as if, for their exponents, the symbols were self-explanatory and required no further commentary, accessories that were a stable feature of a culture and civilization. This silence suggested both the existence of shared meanings and the absence of strong appropriations that could be the source of conflicts or disputes between groups. In addition, it revealed that they had not been integrated into either a strictly coded symbolic language similar to European heraldry since the middle ages, or to a European system of state emblems developed since the fifteenth century.[115] The only steps in this direction had been taken by Taylor, himself an amateur heraldist, but they had not succeeded in imposing a set of rules. In the absence of such conventions, treatises, orthodoxies, the embodiment of the modern nation state

[112] Rabindranath Tagore, 'The cult of the charkha', *Modern Review*, September 1925; quoted in Sabyasachi Bhattacharya (ed.), *The Mahatma and the Poet. Letters and Debates between Gandhi and Tagore 1915–41* (New Delhi, National Book Trust,1997), pp. 115–21.

[113] *The Tribune*, 24 May 1931.

[114] Three lists of the symbols proposed are available: a list first of forty-three suggestions was published in *The Tribune*, 17 June 1931; a second was printed in the *Bombay Chronicle*, 4 July 1931. Finally, a list of the sixty-four suggestions received by the Congress Flag Committee can be found in NMML, AICC Papers, file no. 58.

[115] Michel Pastoureau, *Traité d'héraldique* (Paris, Picard, 2nd edn, 1993); Alain Boureau, 'Etat moderne et attribution symbolique: emblèmes et devises dans l'Europe des XVIe et XVIIe siècles', in *Culture et Idéologie dans la Genèse de l'Etat Moderne, Rome, 15–17 Octobre 1984* (Rome, Ecole Française de Rome, 1985), pp. 155–78.

could proceed relatively unencumbered. Many symbols were easily identifiable as personifying an Indian culture, and were less conflictual.

Despite the possible multiplicity of meanings, the propositions can be regrouped into a few categories. One or two claims manifested a desire to resemble Western countries like America, hence the stars. Others sought to depart from the forms impregnated with ancient mythological and religious meanings, and instead proposed more functional, familiar objects rooted in India's rural world, like the plough, the spade, the sheaf of corn. But on the whole, many others like the lotus, wheel, or chakra, reflected the will to reinforce the modern nation's ties with its distant past. Focusing on the continuity of religious tradition was the swastika, an equal armed cross from ancient Hindu culture going back to the Indus valley seal-amulets, and one of the auspicious symbols for Hindus, Buddhists, and Jains.[116] In the same strain were the chakra—'the arm of our salvation'—and the Islamic crescent. All these symbols were a recurrent feature of the Indian historical and political scene since ancient or medieval times, and displayed an apparent continuity in India's evolution. It was in this framework that the prime minister of Mysore, Sir Mirza Ismail, made a special request for the adoption of the balance as the symbol of justice, a theme closely tied to the Mughal symbolic corpus.[117] Others drew upon mythological traditions to propose the elephant (perceived as the Indian symbolic equivalent of the unicorn and present in quite a few princely banners) the horse (unmistakably identified with its role in royal sacrifices) or the falcon. But, significantly, we do not find a

[116] Rai Govind Chandra, *Indian Symbolism. Symbols as Sources of Our Customs and Beliefs* (New Delhi, Munshiram Manoharlal Publishers, 1996), pp. 25–7.

[117] *The Tribune*, 17 June 1931, p. 4. The balance as a symbol of good morals and justice was a significant motif in the Koran and Hadith but there also existed an abundant literature dealing with balance and weights in commerce. Abd al-Rahman al Kazani's treatise dating from 1120, *Kitab miszan al-hikma*, was an encyclopedia of mechanics dedicated to the description of the ideal balance conceived as a universal tool of a science at the service of commerce. The so-called 'balance of wisdom' combined with the 'tongue of justice and article of meditation' made this symbol particularly meaningful for Muslims. Significantly, in 1947, the design proposed by Sind minorities for Pakistan's flag included a big balance signifying justice and fairness.

single letter among those published in 1931 that proposed the cow as a symbol on the flag. As an emblem the cow had featured on the flag of Karauli in 1877,[118] and subsequently become a subject of dispute among Hindus and Muslims in the nineteenth century, continuing to be so right up to independence and later.[119] Nor did any discussion take place on Bharat Mata (Mother India), another persistent and powerful motif since the beginning of the twentieth century that had (as we saw in chapter 2) given rise to a considerable artistic, literary, iconographic production. These symbols evoked a powerful emotion at par with Britannia, John Bull, and Marianne, but they were clearly not considered to conform to the emblematic requirements of a flag. Yet other symbols like the map of India (2 out of 43 suggestions printed in *The Tribune*), referred to the unity of the future nation—thus, one design proposed clasped hands, another a wheel signifying the celestial globe, circular motion and fortune, or India as a federal union; and yet another suggested a four- or eight-petalled lotus, standing for the idea of federation.[120]

Notwithstanding this variety of suggestions, the subject evoked less passion and polemic than the colours. It did not appear to question peoples' or communities' place within the nation. There was no similar clamour from each community for its own symbol as had surfaced for the colours: perhaps because, as noted above, no formal, technical rules had fixed their meanings in the past nor had this been accomplished in more recent times. Gandhi had clearly affirmed in 1921 that they could not have a religious symbol on the flag, whereas he had defined the colours in communitarian terms. None of the symbols suggested in 1931 was considered to be politically more appealing, or representative of India's distinctiveness by the Flag Committee. As one article put it, there was nothing to be said regarding the spinning wheel

[118] Robert Taylor, op. cit., p. 75.

[119] Hindus demanded the total ban on cow slaughter, equating it with untouchability. In 1994, the Delhi Agricultural Cattle Prevention Bill made the slaughter of cows, calves, and bullocks a non-bailable offence with imprisonment up to five years and a fine of Rs 10,000. Cf. Ernesto Noronha, 'BJP: Cow as a Political Symbol', *Economic and Political Weekly*, vol. 29, no. 24, 11 June 1994, pp. 1447–8.

[120] Suniti Kumar Chatterjee, 'The National Flag', op. cit., p. 2.

except that it ought to be retained. It was '. . . a messenger of common sense . . . the very elixir of our drooping economic life', the solution to the present world problem of 'capital vs. labour'.[121]

In 1931 the Flag Committee's choice of the spinning wheel marked a turning point in a tradition that had never strayed very far from an ancient symbolism. The AICC endorsed this choice. Only in 1947, on the recommendation of a second Flag Committee set by the Constituent Assembly, was it eventually replaced by a simple 24-spoke wheel, the Ashoka chakra.[122] Jawaharlal Nehru justified this change on aesthetic grounds, for the charkha could not be identically reproduced on the obverse side of the flag, and if looked at from the other side the spindle came before the wheel.[123] Of course, a very different explanation was that by 1947 many considered the tricolour with the spinning wheel as a 'Congress flag'. It was advisable that the symbol of independence rally the people to the nation, not to a party, and not carry the burden of a party's failures. Having accompanied the national struggle, the spinning wheel evoked its period of resistance. The country was now entering a new phase not only of political freedom but also of economic development, which was not ideally incarnated by the spinning wheel.

Such views were not expressed officially, although they surfaced in some newspapers. One writer claimed the change reflected the unpopularity of the charkha and the isolationist and unprogressive economic policy associated with it.[124] Opinions were mainly shared in letters to the editor on the occasion of the *Hindustan Times* July 1947 flag supplement. Through them an official consensual interpretation of the *chakra* or wheel was publicized. It had the double advantage, as the press reported, of being a part of the spinning wheel, thus conveying the nation's loyalty and gratitude to the source of that idea,

[121] *The Mahratta*, 14 June 1931, pp. 316–17, R.D. Tiwari, 'The Indian National Flag. An Inquiry into its Colour'.

[122] *Constituent Assembly Debates, Official Report* (New Delhi, Lok Sabha Secretariat, 1946–50), vol. IV, 22 July 1947, p. 737.

[123] This explanation was also advanced by Badr-ud-Din Tyabji, member of the Constituent Assembly, and the author of this idea, in *Memoirs of an Egoist* (Delhi, Roli Books, 1988), pp. 172–3.

[124] *The Madras Mail*, 14 July 1947, 'Charkha and Chakra'.

Gandhi, as well as recalling the Buddhist emperor Ashoka's emblem. It offered many layers of meanings for Indians as a whole, hungry for an ancient, powerful, united idea of India in the past. The wheel was a more unifying object at all levels—the spiritual, the ancient historical, and more indirectly the recent political past. It appeared an appropriate evocation of India's ancient genealogy. Significantly, in my enquiry among Amritsar and Delhi schoolchildren, a large majority expressed their satisfaction with the design of the chakra. For them it continued to stand for 'progress, dynamism'; it stood for the 'welfare of the masses', 'our great and glorious, vast culture and civilization', 'the heart of India', 'a reminder of King Ashoka', 'symbol of victory'; it 'implores us to move forward following the path of dharma and righteousness'.[125] Without agreeing entirely with Mircea Eliade's distinction between pre-alphabetic cultures capable of grasping symbols with a precision that Europeans could imagine only through the oral or alphabetical medium, it is certain that the complex symbolism of the wheel appealed in a social world that, as Eliade put it, sought to achieve the ultimate dissolution of the individual in the original whole before creation.[126]

Establishing a corpus of 'national colours' and a 'national symbol'—for a diversity of communities and groups accustomed to interpreting them in terms of their own specific religious, social, and cultural traditions—involved the creation of a fresh and broad political consensus on an issue that had largely been confined to the parameters of personal aesthetic experiences, group conventions, and political traditions. The process was punctuated by continuities and decisive turning points. Until 1877 the field of political symbolism offers a picture of unbroken patterns and practices, with progressive accommodations and slow adjustments. There was a continuous exchange between Hindu and Muslim practices or political representations, characterized by a flexibility (between red and green for example) and renewal with older symbols (Tipu's recovery of the tiger, for example, and Nivedita's use

[125] The school survey was conducted with ten-year-olds and sixteen-year olds in Junior Modern School and Victoria Girls Secondary School, Delhi and Ajanta Senior Secondary School, Amritsar.

[126] Mircea Eliade, *Sur l'érotique mystique indienne* (Paris, L'Herne, 1997), pp. 102–4.

of the thunderbolt); 1877 was a first rupture, introducing concepts drawn from a European system of heraldry and a redistribution of colours according to religious boundaries and beliefs.

A second break was made in 1931. The public debate held at this juncture brought to the surface not only the various demands of groups of people and their particular codes of belief, but also the layers of meanings and associations and historical experiences from ancient to colonial times that had been absorbed by colours and symbols. The process of producing a fresh vocabulary of colours more suited to the nationalist programme for the future Indian nation revealed that, though colours had no fixed, absolute meanings, they did nonetheless carry certain significations, both inherited and recently annexed. Other values and codes could be elaborated but within certain constraints. For example, no one affirmed that blue stood for non-violence, or that black was an auspicious colour. An entirely radical reversal of meanings and colour codes was not possible in such a short term. At best, what could and was achieved was a recoding of the colours in broader, humanist, universalist terms. This was both a 'denationalization', in the sense that it joined an international norm, and an 'Indianization', in the sense that it connected to an Indian philosophical strain of placing the individual and the nation in an integrative, united whole.

As opposed to the colonial state, the Indian objective was to make the colours and symbol, once chosen, nationally significant and appealing to the entire population. This reinterpretation marked a momentous rupture with the colonial tradition of a narrow communitarian reading of colours that had gradually and almost imperceptibly imposed itself from above in 1877 in the princely banners. The striking success of this colonial vision of Indian society was apparent in its progressive assimilation by Indians themselves, so much so that the Hindu, Muslim, and Sikh communities defined their collective identity through specific colours like red, green, or yellow, and black. Even the first nationalist uses of colours were unable to break with the colonial pattern and remained stuck with these significations, the most spectacular example being Gandhi himself. In 1931 a large-scale mobilization of public opinion was necessary in order to redefine and broaden the meanings of the colours, and align them with the imperatives of national construction, and coincidentally with the longer

Indian literary tradition of perceiving colours as reflectors of *rasa* (moods) and *bhava* (emotions).

Finally, the choice of the charkha signalled a conscious break with the long search for finding in India's past the resources to nourish the process of her national construction. In 1931 this symbol, conceived and imposed from above, placed the nation in the present moment of struggle against imperialism. Depicting non-violence and civil disobedience, the charkha fitted into its project to battle poverty. As the symbol of Indianness, it stood for India's ancient tradition—without being really so, for its rediscovery by Gandhi in 1920 had in fact shown it to be a largely forgotten, unused tool and it was his persistence that infused a contemporary, political value into what had become an antique, curious object. It defined India in terms that were actual, not derived from the past, and upheld values that announced the modern state it aspired to become.

5

Rituals Around the Flag

Political decisions and battles were without doubt crucial in bringing the flag to the forefront of national events. However, a fast sequel of political happenings and the succession of national causes worked as rivals for public attention. A different kind of ritual was required to ensure that the flag remained rooted in collective memory. The Indian National Congress's decision to institute a Flag Day in July 1923 reflected its intention to extend the flag's reach beyond moments of resistance or heroic gestures and acts, and to implant it in the permanent realm of the ordinary, even of non-political national awareness. This monthly public celebration devoted to hoistings and salutations was designed as a reminder of a common Indian identity, struggle, and goal. During the next two decades it was a permanent fixture, though performed with varying degrees of intensity. Its adoption and use by Indians in the national struggle invites at least two sets of enquiries.

The first turns around the origins and roots of Flag Day and attempts to trace the different sources of inspiration or interconnections with an international political culture and practices. Enclosing this national ritual purely in the framework of opposition to Empire Day would reduce it to yet another example of colonial transposition or imitation. Such an approach masks the sometimes more circuitous paths and less obvious crossovers that were taking place. Indeed, the system of imperial rituals, though an unavoidable reference, was not the only model available. If the possibilities and potential of this institution were quickly apparent to many Indians, the process of translating them into their own language and grammar was more complicated.

A second and equally crucial aspect was the propagation of such rituals that opposed empire and rivalled imperial ceremonies in a colonial space controlled by the British administration. The success of such an exercise required open involvement and active participation by all Indians. In the sense that Flag Day followed from a conscious, deliberate decision, it was part of a strategy of national integration, a kind of national engineering, a method of enforcing a political norm and affirming national authority and legitimacy. Its diffusion in national space and continued public mobilization need some examination. Since rituals for the flag came to occupy a central place in the anti-colonial movement from the 1920s onwards, their study can considerably enrich our understanding of the processes of Indian nation-building.[1]

In Search of a National Day

'Few things are so badly needed these days', proclaimed Tilak's newspaper, *The Mahratta* in 1905, 'as a national day for India.' Now that Indians had decided to observe a day of fasting and mourning on 16 October, the date of Bengal's partition, it was probable and indeed desirable that the day 'will spread throughout the length and breadth of the country and become established in our calendar as India Day, or the Day of the United Indian Nation . . . for when the attention of millions is concentrated at one moment in a common observance, the results must be significant.'[2]

The idea privileged a new type of ritual action, a national practice and activity that would promote group cohesion and solidarity without presuming a similarity of political beliefs.[3] The impression that engaging in a conscious act of collectively thinking of the nation

[1] There is little need to justify rituals as 'sites of resistance'. Historians have integrated them as one of the tools of struggle, a means of social inversion or protest: cf. Natalie Zemon Davis, 'The Rites of Violence: Religious Riot in Sixteenth-Century France', *Past and Present*, no. 59, 1973, pp. 51–91. In his study of the Aiyanar festival of '*kutirai etuppu*' that set the calendrical and cosmological agenda for the year's ritual cycle, Nicholas B. Dirks highlights the subversive nature of ritual practice that is patterned but reinvented, closed and yet open and unpredictable: cf. 'Ritual and Resistance: Subversion as a Social Fact', in Douglas Haynes and Gyan Prakash (ed.), *Contesting Power. Resistance and Everyday Social Relations in South Asia* (Delhi, Oxford University Press, 1991).

[2] 'National Day for India 1905', *The Mahratta*, 15 October 1905, quoted in *Source Material for a History of the Freedom Movement in India, 1885–1920* (Collected from Bombay Government Records, Bombay, 1958), vol. II, pp. 917–18.

[3] This approach to rituals as a tool of social integration and unity was first

everywhere in India at a particular chosen time would will the nation into being—We Do, Therefore We Are—lay behind the first nationalist tentatives to establish an all-India calendar of public celebrations or commemorations. A similar preoccupation had characterized new states and new regimes, from the French revolutionaries and the American founders to Australia and Canada. They too were eager to equip themselves with suitable political rituals focusing on either symbols of liberty or national heroes and national days. Eighteenth-century French revolutionaries inscribed national festivals in the 1791 constitution to preserve the memory of the revolution, and to build fraternal affection and attachment to the constitution, the country and its laws.[4] A similar desire marked Australian efforts in the late 1890s to establish a uniform celebration of Australia Day.[5] As David Kertzer has observed, the massive effort of symbolic construction that lies behind the creation of a new nation itself involves subverting local identity and loyalty and replacing them with national identity.[6] There were enough historical patterns and precedents and more immediate models for Indians to draw upon. The exaltation of the imperial idea and virtues in public rituals like Empire Day were, we have seen, unacceptable to many Indians. But the ideas propagated—of loyalty, of commitment and subordination to the ideal of empire— had to be redirected to forge a common bond of Indianness, transcending narrow group identities and ties.[7] What was at stake was

---

outlined by Emile Durkheim, in *The Elementary Forms of Religious Life* (London, George Allen & Unwin, 1915).

[4] Mona Ozouf's work examines revolutionaries' belief in the imaginative connection with the nation which, they felt, would produce irresistible political belief: *The Pedagogy of the Nation. Festivals and the French Revolution* (Cambridge, Mass., Harvard University Press, 1991, 3rd edn, 1994).

[5] Though celebrated under different names like Foundation Day, Anniversary Day, and Australia Day, it was finally made official in 1931. Some of the difficulties of elaborating a uniform ritual for Australia are examined by K.S. Inglis, 'Australia Day', *Historical Studies*, XIII, 49, 1967, pp. 20–41.

[6] David Kertzer, 'The Virtues of Ambiguity', in idem, *Rituals, Politics and Power* (New Haven and London, Yale University Press, 1988), pp. 66–76.

[7] In a study of Surat's local elites, Douglas Haynes analyses this group's uses of an imperial language and idiom of durbar to elaborate their own distinctive

the identification and articulation of a distinct Indian ritual around a symbol that incarnated nation as opposed to empire.

While in Maharashtra, at the beginning of the twentieth century, Tilak championed the cause of a National Day, in Bengal a strongly worded article by the militant journalist and nationalist Bipin Chandra Pal made an ardent appeal to his fellow countrymen to set aside a 'Nation-Day' to impress the Nation-Idea upon the minds of all and instil a genuine love of the motherland in them.[8] He explained that the colonial state had laid before them a rich repertory from which to borrow, adapt or reinvent. Empire Day had been instituted by the British for the commemoration and celebration of the empire, with the flag of empire being hoisted all over the land and the glories of empire sung and expounded by musicians and orators. In the same way, America had specific days dedicated to the nation idea, such as Independence Day (4 July), but also Lincoln Day and Washington Day. England had Nelson Day. France had been the first to institute feasts and festivals during the Revolution to perpetuate the ideals of the Republic. So too, he declared, Indians should elaborate similar celebrations, organize festivities and fairs in villages, sports, and athletic *jatras*, theatricals, and puppet shows—all centred on the theme of nation-building. Magic-lantern shows could present the geography of the motherland, speakers recite her ancient glories, orators expose inspiring elements of her culture and civilization, past achievements, and future possibilities. Exhibitions of local arts and industries would be a reminder of her traditions and distinctiveness. Finally, affirmed Pal, this civic religion would be incomplete without an adequate symbol. Indians must therefore fix a symbol of their motherland.

Tilak and Pal's response to Empire Day's propagandist aim of consolidating the British empire contained the seeds of a crucial element: the necessity of a distinctive political ritual around a national symbol that would finally allow Indians to assert their national identity through

---

public culture, *Rhetoric and Ritual in Colonial India. The Shaping of a Public Culture in Surat City, 1852–1928* (Berkeley, University of California Press, 1991).

8 Bipin Chandra Pal, 'Rakhi Day', 10 October 1906, reprinted in *Swadeshi and Swaraj: The Rise of New Patriotism* (Calcutta, Yugayatri Prakashak, 1954), pp. 281–2, 286.

their own signs and rites of power.[9] The search for elements that could constitute the heart of rites of power was, as we have already seen, marked by a succession of propositions that had a limited and short-lived impact. One of these was 'Rakhi Day', a private ceremony that had been converted into a signal, even a strategy, of political resistance by Rajput women during the Mughal conquests. 'Rakhi', originally a bracelet or charm to avert evil, was the thread Rajput women tied on their brothers' wrists in a mutual exchange of blessings and protection.[10] They could use the practice to seek the support of powerful nobles or sometimes neutralize rival princes by creating and personalizing a relationship. On this day, proposed Pal in 1905, Indians would 'meditate on the past, present and future of the nation, try to get at the soul of it and realise our divinely appointed destiny as a people.'

Thus, on the eve of the Bengal partition, this intimate, family ritual was transformed into a public act of hostility to the colonial government, when the people of Bengal manifested their unity by tying rakhis on each others' wrists. One striking particularity of this celebration of protest that stood in sharp contrast to the festive aspect of Empire Day

[9] The analysis of ceremonies and rituals of state power as mechanisms and fields of domination from ancient times to the modern period now constitutes a veritable discipline, extending from the study of symbols of power to the political impact of rites of power. In the works of the German and French medievalists Percy Ernst Schramm and Marc Bloch, the study of the role of rituals in political structures as well as the relationship between rituals and language or rituals and social structures, has been extended to modern political states by historians and anthropologists alike. On the role and function of symbols of sovereignty: cf. Benedict Anderson, *Imagined Communities. Reflections on the Origin and Spread of Nationalism* (London, Verso, 1983); Maurice Agulhon, *Marianne into Battle*, op. cit.; Ilaria Porciani, *La festa della nazione. Rappresentazione dello stato e spazio sociale nell'Italia unita* (Bologna, Il Mulino, 1997); Edward Muir, *Ritual in Early Modern Europe* (Cambridge, Cambridge University Press, 1997); Sean Wilentz (ed.), *Rites of Power: Symbolism, Ritual and Politics since the Middle Ages* (Philadelphia, University of Pennsylvania Press, 1985); Max Gluckman, *Politics, Law and Ritual in Tribal Society* (Oxford, Basil Blackwell, 1965); on the functions of rituals as safety valves, and as strategies for imposing political and social norms and formalizing behaviour, cf. Maurice Bloch, *Ritual, History and Power: Selected Papers in Anthropology* (London, Athlone, 1989).

[10] James Tod, *Annals and Antiquities of Rajasthan or the Central and Western States*, vol. 1 (London, Smith, Elder & Co., 1829), p. 581.

was the focus on sacrifice and austerity. Perhaps this conformed to the importance accorded to such practices in Indian traditions for the attainment of a higher goal. In his earlier writings Pal had already emphasized that patriotism was not mere love of the fatherland but an organized cult of patriotic rites and sacraments through which this love could be developed. The old patriotism, he pointed out, had referred to ancient heroes who were unreal, mythical characters, and, though the magic of their name worked somewhat upon the imagination, they failed to strike any profoundly real chord in the hearts and minds of contemporary Indians.[11] Moreover, Rakhi Day had an obvious drawback.[12] Its political significance was closely linked to the partition of Bengal. If the act were withdrawn, as they indeed hoped it would be, Rakhi Day also risked losing its relevance. Therefore, the celebration of the motherland had to be dissociated from a particular event and linked absolutely to a nation idea through a particular symbol transcending the event.

Parallel attempts to establish a pantheon of heroes or heroines from India's historical traditions also failed to work (as noted in Chapter 2). Neither Tilak's warrior models nor Tagore's more pacific devotional models of poet saints were taking root. But the theory of great heroes had not been abandoned for all that, and a new gallery of less problematic or divisive national heroes, produced by the contemporary struggle against the colonial state, was emerging. Tilak and Gandhi captured national attention; their defiance of colonial rule and bouts of imprisonment had made them national heroes whose birthdays were therefore occasions of rejoicing at par with those of Hindu gods like Krishna or Ganesh. Annie Besant's journal *New India*, also an advocate of the centrality of national imagery in the struggle for political rights, supported this idea. It noted: 'Anniversaries stir men's hearts and form a bond of union and serve as milcstones on the path of progress.'[13]

The first to propose a more civic ritual for the Indian nation was P.A. Venkayya. Despairing the complete absence of patriotic exercises and a national pedagogy, this singular champion of the cause of a national

[11] Bipin Chandra Pal, 'The Cult of Patriotism', 25 February 1905, in *Swadeshi and Swaraj*, op. cit., p. 13.

[12] 'The Hymnology in Bengal', ibid., p. 99.

[13] 'A National Flag for India', *New India*, 14 August 1917, p. 9.

flag for India argued for the institution of a national Flag Day involving all the people of India in a common ceremony around a national flag. This would, he pointed out, bring home to all people the idea of the nation. The only concretization of this idea was the organization of a Congress Day in 1917; the event had a certain success, as testified by the demands in the press to continue it.[14] However, it does not seem to have survived by 1918, and for the present remains ill known. Venkayya then developed his plan further by proposing that, once the flag was created, it be accompanied by a ritual celebrating its birth. He considered this rite essential to ensure the political success of the flag. His patriotic programme thus included distributing printed cloth flags and books along with a full sized 20–30" national flag to every Indian. Its possession, he argued, would allow a more personal appropriation of this symbol. People could hang it in a frame at the threshold of their houses, use it in processions or for hoisting on houses, make brooches containing the national flag in two-inch-square size to be pinned on the coat or on the dress, make small handkerchiefs and use it in all kinds of public decorations and conferences. Unfortunately, he lamented, none of the above patriotic exercises had been undertaken, despite the establishment of the Indian National Flag Mission in 1916 in South India under his own direction. He appealed to readers for financial contributions to realize some of this programme and ensure the free distribution of flags to various political and charitable institutions, including AICC members as well as members of the subjects committee of these assemblies.[15]

In spite of this, there was little public or official response to Venkayya's proposal for a ritual for a flag that would elicit complicity and eventually lay the ground for the installation of civic values available neither in history nor in the sacred texts and epics. Warmer reactions welcomed the introduction of national festivals like Tilak Day (1 August), probably in 1920.[16] It was the first to be celebrated. Ironically,

[14] *New India*, 10 January 1917; *The Hindu*, 14 November 1918.

[15] P.A. Venkayya, *A National Flag for India*, op. cit., pp. 31–2.

[16] Tilak's death on 1 August 1920 coincided with the date Gandhi had announced for inaugurating India's first satyagraha movement. Gandhi proclaimed it a day for fasting and prayer: cf. Stanley A. Wolpert, *Tilak and Gokhale: Revolution and Reform in the Making of Modern India* (Oxford, Oxford University Press, 1989), p. 294.

Tilak's dreams for a National Day took shape only after his death. Gandhi's birthday inaugurated Gandhi week from 2–8 October.[17] A new category of Indian martyrs was emerging from the succession of confrontations with the colonial government. The Bengal partition was succeeded by the Jallianwala Bagh massacre (13 April 1919): at Gandhi's initiative in 1920, the first all-India commemoration of these Punjab martyrs was held. Jawaharlal Nehru, as chairman of the Allahabad Municipal Board from April 1923 to April 1925, would apply himself enthusiastically to introducing a national calendar of public celebrations in his native city. He withdrew Empire Day from the list of public holidays, replacing it with Tilak Day and Gandhi Day (18 March—the anniversary of the day when Gandhi was sentenced to jail). He also made the singing of Iqbal's *Hindustan Hamara* (Our Hindustan) a part of the school curriculum.[18]

These commemorations and celebrations initially consisted of public processions and ceremonies with speeches, but were extended under Gandhi's direction to include spinning and what he termed the contemplation of 'national or civic virtues'. They had little of the joyous, festive aspect that characterized national festivals in Europe or in America. The emphasis was on a laborious learning of a grammar of nationhood that was gradually being defined through conscious and active manifestations of tolerance towards other Indians. Thus, these events became an occasion both for an orderly exhibition of solidarity and display of loyalty to a national programme. In 1921, Gandhi Day was changed to become a National Week, 6–12 April, giving him the chance to propagate his common agenda of national values and beliefs. M.R. Jayakar, member of the Congress and one of the founders of the Responsive Party, was sensitive to this change in their political culture, noting its first large-scale observance in Bombay.[19] The broad outlines of a national political calendar were thus progressively intertwined

[17] It is difficult to establish the precise date when these anniversaries were insitituted. They seem to have been progressively absorbed into the national chronology. One of the earliest references to National Week can be found in *Young India*, 31 March 1920.

[18] Sarvepalli Gopal, *The Viceroyalty of Lord Irwin 1926–1931* (Oxford, Clarendon Press, 1957), p. 92.

[19] Mukund Ramrao Jayakar, *The Story of My Life. 1922–1925* (Bombay, Asia Publishing House, 1958–9), vol. I, *1873–1922*, vol. II, pp. 4–5.

with the seasonal calendar. In April, July, August, and October, commemoration ceremonies around national figures served as reminders to Indians of their common political goal.

In fact, these celebrations focusing on personalities, even contemporary ones, were really perpetuating the old logic of the heroic origins of national histories—with their limits. They could at best serve as models to admire and venerate, but either their exceptionality made them unreal and therefore an obstacle to complete identification, or they did not contain the set of civic virtues that could form the basis of citizenship in the nation.

From National Day to Flag Day

Confronted with the lessons Empire Day offered about the effectiveness of state ritual and its emotionally manipulative qualities, Indians tried to conceive a swadeshi political ritual by idolizing leaders and heroes. This unquestioning loyalty to pre-colonial traditions prevented them from venturing into the more impersonal terrain outlined by Venkayya. If a decisive moment is to be identified in the collapse of this system of heroic adulation, it is the Nagpur satyagraha. Here, for the first time, the flag outstaged individual personalities and moved to the forefront of the national scene. During this movement, different rites were slowly elaborated around the flag: of collective protest, but also of adoration, salutation, and reverence. For a brief period Nagpur created a ceremonial space for the new national icon in the presence of the British authorities, and despite their refusal. It revealed the power exercised by a ritualized use of the flag on public imagination and the political desirability of maintaining and developing this dimension beyond the dramatic context of a particularly spectacular confrontation. But perhaps these lessons might have receded and not spilled over into a well-organized ritual of Flag Day if another, more distant, foreign prototype had not intervened—thanks largely to the efforts of one individual, hitherto absent from the Indian political scene.

Dr N.S. Hardikar, a Karnataka Brahmin from Bombay, returned to India after a lengthy sojourn to study medicine in the United States from 1913 to 1921. Hardikar's meeting with Lala Lajpat Rai shortly after his return propelled him into the nationalist struggle at the precise moment when Gandhi's recently designed Swaraj flag was beginning to carve a space in the municipal landscape. When reconstructing his subsequent political itinerary, Hardikar would recall being asked by a Japanese on the ship taking him to America what the Indian flag looked like, and his incapacity to reply.[20] While in America he had been struck by the vibrant flag culture encouraged by social reformers and veteran organizations. They were promoting flag rituals as a means of instilling a patriotic spirit among the newly arrived immigrants and better integrating them into American society. Certainly, America was the first country to adopt the ritual of Flag Day with a civic worship of the flag centred on a patriotic salute that had been designed in 1891 for express use in school patriotic ceremonies. American educators saw flag rituals and flag veneration as fostering a spirit of unity and loyalty among future citizens, regardless of the many racial stocks from which the children may have sprung.[21] The First World War gave a fresh impetus to this movement,[22] inaugurating a veritable Americanization campaign in schools and universities to instil citizenship in the hearts of 'hyphenated Americans', like German-Americans.[23] President Wilson's description of the flag, as 'the emblem of our unity, our power, our thought and purpose as a nation',[24] could well have summed up Indian nationalist aspirations in the 1920s.

[20] N.S. Hardikar recalled these facts in the introduction of a small booklet, *The National Flag*, with a foreword by Nehru. I have used a typed manuscript, written in English, in NMML, AICC Papers, file no. 61. This version is dated September 1937. On its cover it carries a map of India with the flag. Hardikar indicates that the first version was published in Marathi on 26 January 1931, then translated and published in Hindi, Gujarati, Kannada, and English. To date, I have not found any copy of these different editions.

[21] Scot M. Guenter, *The American Flag 1777–1924. Cultural Shifts from Creation to Codification* (Cranbury, NJ, Associated University Presses, 1990), pp. 114–32.

[22] A special number in *National Geographic Magazine* was dedicated to the flag in October 1917 with a view to inspiring Americans with an understanding and appreciation of the motives, traditions, and sentiments that gave birth to this symbol of sovereignty.

[23] Desmond King, *Making Americans. Immigration, Race and the Origins of the Diverse Democracy* (Cambridge, Mass., Harvard University Press, 2002), pp. 90–103.

[24] President Wilson's speech on the American Flag Day, *The Great Faith* (London, 1914), p. 3.

Hardikar's involvement in the Nagpur flag satyagraha and his one-year rigorous imprisonment during the course of the struggle gave him a public notoriety and a convincing argument to elaborate something like a political strategy around the flag.[25] His American experience had convinced him that the Indian nationalist movement not only needed a flag ritual but equally a voluntary organization dedicated to explaining its meaning and use. In short, the Indian public was to be educated in national construction.[26] Hardikar emphasized the ritual's immediate political utility in instituting an alternative circuit for the diffusion of a national imagery, and its long-term effects of rendering the nation a familiar, accessible idea. The fact that Egypt, Japan, America, England, South Africa, and Tanganyika all observed a Flag Day was particularly appreciated by Jawaharlal Nehru, whom Hardikar had been pressurizing to adopt Flag Day as a festival for the nation. His thoughts also coincided with the Gandhian belief in the centrality of the flag for showing the consensus and unity of Indians on the field. He took advantage of the presence of other nationalists at Nagpur, especially Nehru, to press this point home.[27]

On 25 May 1923, in the AICC meeting at Bombay, at the height of the Nagpur satyagraha, Congress decided to institute a Flag Day in India for the display and veneration of the national flag. It was to be celebrated at 8.00 a.m., on the last Sunday of every month.[28] C.R. Rajagopalachari, one of the principal theoreticians of the cult of the flag, announced the contours of this national celebration: 'Throughout the country in every centre, big and small, processions should be organized to march with the National Flag early in the morning. The Flag should be displayed everywhere throughout the day. Khaddar is the proper fabric for making the Flag, but if Khaddar is too expensive for extensive and temporary display, paper must be used.'[29] *Young India*

[25] *Bombay Chronicle*, 23 June 1923.

[26] Scot M. Guenter draws attention to the decisive role of veteran associations and patriotic societies in propagating what he calls an 'American political culture', *American Flag*, op. cit., pp. 103–9.

[27] N.S. Hardikar, *The National Flag*, op. cit., ch. 1.

[28] B. Pattabhi Sitaramayya, *History of the Indian National Congress, 1885–1935* (Madras, 1935; Bombay, Padma Publications, 1946), vol. 1, p. 257.

[29] C.R. Rajagopalachari, 'The Flag Calls You', *Young India*, 5 July 1923, p. 225.

too carried a similar message: flags, it announced, should become a ubiquitous feature in the lives of Indians. Its presence in all spheres, private or public, would ultimately reconcile officials and Europeans as well to the Indian tricolour.[30] This decision was a turning point in instituting a national, secular ceremony to celebrate the nation. It relegated traditional festivals propagating the cults of heroes or mythical gods and goddesses to the sphere of religious or socio-cultural practices, be they local or private.

The first celebration of Flag Day in July 1923 took place when the flag satyagraha was in full swing. All Congress committees were directed to organize flag processions and public displays of the tricolour.[31] In Bihar, for example, Congress volunteers were called to observe the day at Muzaffarpur, Patna, Bhagalpur, Monghyr, and Gaya. Both Hindus and Muslims participated.[32] In Nagpur and other provinces of British India, public hoistings, salutations, songs, and fiery speeches marked the occasion and the event was reported to have attracted large crowds of participants and observers, including women and children. In 1923 and the following years, the organization of Flag Day met with little resistance from within the ranks of the Congress party, even from those like C.R. Das or Motilal Nehru, who had initially been sceptical of its utility.

We do not have a precise description of these first ceremonies. Their codification seems to have taken place progressively, to be fixed finally in 1931 under Hardikar's inspiration. Hardikar's efforts towards an organization of Flag Day aimed, like the American patriotic societies he had observed, at instilling a patriotic sentiment within a synchronized and stabilized political behaviour. Like its Western counterparts of Flag Day or Empire Day, the Indian Flag Day focused on two key elements, hoisting and saluting the national flag and singing the national anthem. Around these, Hardikar elaborated the details of a ceremony

[30] Harilal Maneklal Desai, 'The Flag Day', *Young India*, 26 July 1923, p. 245.

[31] Narayan Iqbal Singh, *The Indian National Congress. A Reconstruction, 1919–23* (Delhi, Manohar, 1988), vol. 2, p. 465.

[32] P.N. Ojha (ed.), *History of Indian National Congress in Bihar 1885–1985*, Historical Research Series, no. 21 (Patna, K.P. Jayaswal Research Institute, 1985), p. 248; Mohammad Muzaffar Imam, *Role of Muslims in the National Movement 1912–30. A Study of Bihar* (Delhi, Mittal Publications, 1987), p. 153.

where the preoccupation with uniformity was extended to all aspects of the flag, from the material to the symbolic, including all the different stages of the ceremony (dimensions of the flag, its texture and positions, the dresses of participants and their attitude, etc.). He compiled these instructions and norms in a small illustrated booklet in Marathi, entitled *The National Flag*, published on the very day of the declaration of independence, 26 January 1931. Eager to broadcast these practices through the entire country, he published the book in Hindi, Gujarati, and Kannada in the months following. He even added further detailed instructions in the Hindi pamphlet, published by the Hubli central office of the Seva Dal. The local branch offices were put in charge of diffusing this information.[33]

Explaining his strategy of action, Hardikar said he had noted the absence of discipline, method, and organization at the first national flag hoisting at the Cocanada Congress in December 1923, although the next session at Belgaum in 1924 had been a little better. As the idea of the flag itself was new, they could not perhaps expect the formalities of flag hoisting to be rigorously observed. For the moment, there were even so many different words for flag: 'Gudi, Nishan, Bauta or Zenda'.[34] They should strive to replace this multiplicity with a unique word. In a similar vein, the president of the Tamil Nadu Seva Dal, E. Krishna Aiyar, emphasized the need to regularize the ceremony in light of 'the growing importance of the national flag and its salutation in our national life of late', for 'instances were not wanting when the effect of the patriotic ceremony was marred by many irregularities'. In fact, Krishna Aiyar explained, the proper performance of the ritual was a kind of discipline in itself. The main purpose of the function was the expression of intense patriotic feeling in a simple and prayerful mood and form,[35] whether it was held on a big public beach or in a private garden, whether attended by a large number of people or a small, limited gathering. The London Indian National Congress Association too warned against any archaic utilization of the flag, urging the adoption of precise, fixed rules, laying down its form and size. It even issued a manifesto specifying its dimensions: the cloth of the national flag must

[33] *The Hindu*, 24 July 1931.

[34] N.S. Hardikar, *The National Flag*, op. cit., esp. glossary.

[35] *The Hindu*, 24 July 1931.

be square, its length should be one and a half times its breadth. There would be three equal pieces of cloth, one over the other, white at the top, green in the middle, and red at the bottom. The spinning wheel, one-fourth of its breadth in the centre, could be printed or stitched, taking care to leave an equal portion of cloth round the wheel. When carried, the proper position of the flag was always on the left side and the red of the hand flag was to be kept erect.[36]

The formal ceremony itself, designed by Hardikar, and called Dhvaja Vandan (prayer to the flag) would take place later in the morning in an open, broad and level plot of land. The flagstaff was to be a straight white` pole, 24′ to 40′ in height; the flag of khaddar was 6′ x 4′. A strong white rope, a little more than double the length of the post, tied in three successive rings to the staff, was to be used for the hoisting. Volunteers stood in a file around the flagstaff in a horseshoe formation. An attitude of reverence and solemnity (*shradha* and *vratabandhan*), a demeanour earlier recommended by Bipin Chandra Pal for Rakhi Day, was to be observed. All participants, drawn from the different creeds and communities, were to engage in the ceremony with the intense patriotic feeling of being prepared to give up all to defend the honour of their country. They would sing *Bande Mataram* in Hindi, the flag would then be hoisted by the person presiding over the ceremony, the volunteers would do *namaste*, then sing the Hindi flag song, *Vijayee viswathi ranga piyara, Jhanda uncha rahe hamara* (The world triumphant tricolour, Let our tricolour fly high), sung by the Congress Seva Dal for the first time that very year at the Kanpur session of the Congress.[37] In the south, the patriotic poet Bharati's '*enthamil nadu*' (the land of the Tamils) could be sung. Naturally, there would be a speech by an invited personality. The ceremony would culminate with cries of *Bharat mata ki jai* (Long live Mother India) and *Bande Mataram.* Hardikar explained that prominence should be given to *jais* (hurrahs) in the ceremony. He believed they created enthusiasm, arousing proper national feeling and desire for national service.[38]

[36] Kusoom Vadgama, *India. British-Indian Campaigns in Britain for Indian Reforms, Justice and Freedom 1831–1947* (London, Banyan Tree, 1997), p. 174.

[37] K.V. Singh, *Our National Flag* (New Delhi, Publications Division, Ministry of Information & Broadcasting, Govt. of India, 1991), p. 102.

[38] These programmes were detailed in N.S. Hardikar, *The National Flag*, op. cit., pt 2.

Many of the rules Hardikar conceived as fundamental to this demonstration were hardly original: for example, that flag hoistings be held early in the morning and at sunset and that they be ideally conducted in the presence of a guest of honour, a prominent nationalist worker or personality. Among the more distinctive features of the Indian ritual was the early morning *prabhat pheris* (circumambulation at dawn), accompanied by devotional songs.[39] This practice was adapted from the religious ritual of circumambulation that marked the king's accession to the throne. As the monarch left his palace and circled the city in a triumphal procession accompanied by his entourage, he was figuratively taking control of his capital, and indirectly of his entire kingdom, since the metropolis was the symbolic, microcosmic centre of his kingdom.[40] Similarly, when on Flag Day a group of men and women assembled and then went round a specific neighbourhood with the flag, the ritual could serve to signify their proclaimed control over their locality and by extension over the entire nation through the flag. This custom of *prabhat pheris*, originating in Congress singing parties sent out over various neighbourhoods of Bombay a few days before the inauguration of 'boycott week', was taken over by people and conducted independently.[41] Some of the songs were about the charkha: *Charkha chala chalake lenge swaraj* (We will win swaraj by turning the charkha), *Azadi Tamanna* (Ode to Freedom), *Sar faroshi ki tamanna* (In praise of independence), *Todi pado sarkari zulmi kaidea re* (Break all the oppressive laws of the government) and *Nahin jhukenge ham* (Never shall we be defeated).[42]

Concerned about enclosing the ritual within a strong orderly framework, Hardikar considered it equally important to preserve its secular, civic character and prevent it from being transformed into yet another religious ceremony. He included a strict injunction in his booklet against the temptation of waving a tray of *arati* before the

[39] OIOC, R/1/1/1971/(1), Residents report of events in Indian states for fortnight ending on 15 August 1930, Ichalkaranji Jagir, Kashmir.

[40] Ronald Inden, 'Ritual, Authority and Cyclic Time in Hindu Kingship', in J.F. Richards (ed.), *Kingship and Authority in South Asia* (Delhi, Oxford University Press, 1998), p. 76.

[41] *The Times of India*, 11 July 1930, p. 11.

[42] *The Times of India*, 11 August 1930, p. 6.

flag, smearing the pole with sandalwood and *kumkum* (red vermilion powder), or breaking a coconut. Of course, despite the emphasis on the civic, secular aspect of these ceremonies, meanings imbued with a religious ethos could still be freely attritubted. M.R. Jayakar felt that though such occasions were a moment to 'feed the currents of the national sentiment', they could nonetheless be infused with a religious sentiment. He admitted his own inability to leave aside his religious outlook and beliefs. Notions like *shradha* (mourning)—a ritual carried out in memory of ancestors; or *vratabandha* (renewing a vow)—undertaking a fast and committing oneself single-mindedly to a fixed goal—coloured his sentiments whilst engaged in this civic ceremony. The former was relevant because it revived the memory of those Indians who were 'sacrificed at the altar of barbarism in 1919', irrespective of caste, creed, or religion. The latter because it required one to observe the solemn obligation of taking and maintaining a national vow of 'consecrating one's life to the pursuit of a patriotic endeavour to alter the system of rule in their country.'[43] Jayakar's interpretation of these notions indicated the dangers of religious practices and codes pervading flag rituals. For Hardikar also, such religious components threatened to weaken the construction of a unified political culture by introducing elements that were not common to all Indians and could even alienate some of them.

A similar diagnosis led other political figures to emphasize the universal political values that must be attached to the flag. Imposing such an understanding demanded not only repetition of the ritual but a constant reminder of the political sense and meaning they wished the flag to incarnate. This was most probably the goal desired by Nehru when, three years later, on the eve of Flag Day, he detailed the meaning of the ceremony for all Indians in this lengthy press statement:

> The great campaign for freedom of the past year has brought honour to our flag and made it very dear to us. Under its shelter men and women have performed deeds of heroism and it has become a source of inspiration for us, a symbol of the yearning for freedom in our hearts. I hope therefore that Sunday April 26 [1931] will be duly celebrated all over the country and our brave tri-colour will be everywhere in

[43] M.R. Jayakar, *The Story of My Life*, op. cit.

> evidence, floating gallantly against the blue Indian sky, and as we salute it and carry it in procession we shall remember that though much has been done, much still remains and the freedom for which it stands is still to be. Under it and through it, we shall salute those who have died for our country and those who have suffered and sacrificed for her freedom. And we shall resolve to carry on their great work till India is completely free and independent. Let us meet at 8 a.m on April 26, hoist the flag, salute it, sing national songs and pray to God to give us strength to follow in the footsteps of those that have suffered and sacrificed in the cause of the flag.[44]

Far from being a simple religious act of worship, Nehru highlighted the political commitment which must be the basis of a future India, grounded in common civic values, sacrifice, honour, and unity. Flag hoistings provided the occasions to exhibit these values by a simultaneous organization of khadi sales or charkha competitions.[45]

The regularity of this celebration led to its official adoption in December 1928 at Calcutta during the annual Congress session.[46] The flag's hoisting, carried out by Motilal Nehru, provided a 'spectacle designed to make a direct appeal to the patriotic nationalism of the people', according to a Western observer. The sight of a tall 'Asoka pillar', or flagstaff, sixty feet in height, erected in the pandal and the flag draped upon it was 'unprecedented in the annals of India', as both friends and foes of the Congress admitted, the former to acclaim it as full of personal inspiration and national significance and the latter to ridicule it.[47] In 1929 Congress directed that flags, big and small, made of khaddar or paper be hoisted on offices, houses, and places of amusement in order to make it ever-present in the lives of Indians.[48] Henceforth, Flag Day was to be celebrated on the first Sunday of every month. Subsequently, this was shifted before the summer of 1930 to the last Sunday, and officially confirmed at the moment of the flag's formal adoption in August 1931.[49]

44 *Hindustan Times*, 24 April 1931.

45 OIOC, L/I/1/874, file no. 462/38.

46 NMML, AICC Papers, file no. 70, Annual Report for 1929.

47 William Isaac Hull, *India's Political Crisis* (Baltimore, London, 1930), pp. 11–12.

48 NMML, AICC Papers, file no. 70, Annual Report for 1929.

49 NMML, AICC Papers, file no. 70, Resolution III, 6–8 August 1931.

Nationalizing Flag Rituals

From 1930 onwards Flag Day was widely observed all over British India and even princely India.[50] Sources present it generally under local miscellaneous items, which should in fact be considered as elements of a larger, progressive movement that does not seem to have spared any province of India.[51] The regular accounts of local events compiled by provincial British administrators and sent every fortnight to the British government mention these flag hoistings, processions, and community celebrations all through the decade: they were taking place in all the big Indian cities: Rawalpindi, Lyallpur, Peshawar, Multan, Hyderabad, Bombay, Ahmedabad, Delhi, Patna, Dacca, Mymensingh, Nellore, Cuttack, Madras.[52] Moreover, this was not only an urban phenomenon. Within small remote villages of central India, for example, which could be considered as cut off from the main political debates and mobilization, it was happening too.[53] On the frontiers, too, in tribal areas, the ceremony was equally integrated. Touring the North West Frontier Provinces in January 1939, Nehru gave evidence

[50] *The Hindu, Pioneer Mail, Indian Weekly News*, and *Madras Weekly Mail* reported the large number of flag-hoisting ceremonies in the country, the speeches delivered, and the public response, particularly from women and children. British governors' fortnightly reports from 1929 onwards list the areas and sites of flag hoistings, salutations, and processions: cf. OIOC, in the Punjab, L/P&J/12/10, 21, 55, 56, 66; in Bengal, L/P&J/12/2, 47; in Bombay, L/P&J/12/27, 33, 38, 49, 60; in Delhi, L/P&J/12/18, 30; in Madras, L/P&J/12/19, 31, 53, 64; in the United Provinces, L/P&J/12/11, 22; in the Central Provinces and Berar, L/P&J/12/6, 17, 29, 40.

[51] The sources I have consulted give evidence of flag hoistings on public buildings all over British India: in the Central and United Provinces, and the Madras and Bombay presidencies. It is not possible here to list the variety and number of sources consisting of newspaper reports and administrative notes detailing these events. They merit a deeper analysis of the actors and networks involved. Despite their widespread diffusion and political impact, they have been neglected in favour of studies of more visible events like the civil disobedience movement 1931–4, the Quit India movement of 1942, and the mass contact programme of 1944.

[52] *The Madras Weekly Mail*, 10 April 1930; *Pioneer Mail & Indian Weekly News*, 11 April 1931; *The Hindu*, 4, 25 May, 1–6 June 1931; *The Tribune*, 2 September 1931.

[53] *Searchlight*, 6 October 1931.

of the power of this 'solemn and significant ceremony' in such remote areas as Bannu. He realized, he wrote to his daughter, that to the Pathans who took the independence pledge before the national flag in the local language Pushtu, 'it was no empty ritual, no ceremony without inner meaning, but a vital real thing, symbolizing the long suppressed desire . . . Thus we sealed our bond of brotherhood in the great cause of India's freedom.'[54] Princely states did not remain unaffected either: at Mysore, a special construction was made in 1930 by Congress sympathizers for flag hoistings.[55]

One consequence of this ritual was that it gave consistence and an aura of legitimacy to flag hoistings on public buildings: municipalities, local district boards, and court buildings from the middle of the 1920s. In certain contexts, it permitted Indians to assert their takeover of public institutions at the local level. In the Central Provinces and Berar, the municipal officers of the district council at Amraoti requested the minister for agriculture to visit Amraoti for the purpose of performing a national flag-hoisting ceremony on the district council building. Not surprisingly, the invitation was summarily turned down by the British authorities.[56] During the 1930s other public places were involved: schools, colleges, universities, hospitals, and dispensaries. As early as 1930 the Indian flag was hoisted on Independence Day in the universities of Lucknow and Benares,[57] and on special occasions like the Allahabad University Convocation in 1930.[58] Behind this common act lay different motivations. For local district boards and municipalities,[59] flag hoistings on their premises were a means to display coherence and a power they did not always necessarily possess. When performed in enclosed spaces like houses, shops, public parks (*maidans*), or gardens, political intentions could mingle with the desire to manifest a personal opinion or stand. Extended to large processions, flag hoistings dramatized and integrated local events and places in a broader national

[54] *Important Speeches of Jawaharlal Nehru, 1922–45*, ed. Jagat S. Bright (Lahore, 1945), p. 49.

[55] *The Hindu*, 9 July 1931.

[56] OIOC, L/P&J/12/6, Governor's fortnightly reports from the Central Provinces and Berar for the first half of March 1930.

[57] *The Times*, 6 September 1930.

[58] *The Times*, 1 December 1930.

[59] *The Times*, 21 January 1932; 22 February 1932.

current. Vijaya Lakshmi Pandit's description of a flag hoisting on the Tilak Library at Mussoorie in September 1931, in a private letter to her brother Jawaharlal Nehru, emphasized their concern to publicize the event in the press.[60]

The ritual could lend itself to a more improvised, playful treatment in the private sphere. When Nehru joined his family in Mussoorie in October 1930 after being released from prison, he evoked how this new ritual was assimilated by his nieces in their games: 'I would play with the children and sometimes we would march bravely round the house in a stately procession, led, flag in hand, by the youngest, aged three or four, singing *Jhanda uncha rahe hamara*, our flag song .'[61] No doubt this account, coming from a well-known figure whose private life at all times was equally under public gaze, could not be ideally considered as a typical example of the private behaviour of Indians. Nevertheless, it revealed the possibilities of the ritual and its adaptability to different kinds of contexts and situations.

The rite was also adopted and propagated outside political parties. The president of the provincial committee of the Punjab Students' Union made a special appeal to all students of the province to hoist the new national flag on 30 August and observe the national Flag Day.[62] Even political prisoners, kept at a distance from public ceremonies, succeeded in organizing it and manifesting a form of flag exhibitionism. In Alipur jail, for example, prisoners smuggled in a national flag and celebrated Independence Day.[63] Some flag ceremonies were also held in temples, as in Poona at the Shivaji Mandir, with flowers being showered over the national flag,[64] and in the Parthasarthy temple at Triplicane, near Madras.[65] Others took place in spaces restricted to specific professional activities, like the Bombay Cotton Exchange: a large number of Bombay cotton merchants—who had supported the

[60] In Nayanṭara Sahgal (ed.), *Before Freedom: Nehru's Letters to His Sister* (New Delhi, HarperCollins Publishers, 2000), pp. 110–11.

[61] Jawaharlal Nehru, *An Autobiography* (London, John Lane The Bodley Head, 1936, 9th edn, 1995), p. 233.

[62] *The Tribune*, 23 August 1931.

[63] Ibid.

[64] *The Tribune*, 16 January, 26 January 1930; *The Hindu Illustrated Weekly*, 16 February 1930, p. 14.

[65] *Amrita Bazar Patrika*, 26 January 1931.

first phase of civil disobedience from 1930 to 1931 in the hope that the British government would be forced to change its financial and monetary policy[66]—invited twelve Japanese cotton merchants to attend a flag-hoisting ceremony in August 1931.[67] Japanese, more than British, competition was a threat to the Bombay textile industry, and the act could be interpreted as the cotton merchants' desire to show their rivals the political configurations that would be determining Indian economic policies.

Once launched, the ritual of Flag Day cultivated a patriotism that could touch large sections of the public. Announced well in advance, it allowed public enthusiasm and expectancy to build up. The new civic festival was presented as a public occasion, a celebratory moment in the community, open to all, political militants as well as ordinary citizens. Women in particular, from young girls to elderly *desh sevikas* (servers of the nation), participated in these salutations.[68] They were considered to naturally epitomize and transmit their customary devotional virtues of religious worship to this civic ritual, 'to preserve the honour of the flag at all costs'.[69] Thus, a thousand women participated in the National Flag Day procession at Lahore on 26 August 1930,[70] and lady volunteers hawked miniature tricolour flags in Bombay.[71] Children became equally involved in the ceremony. A freedom fighter from Gujarat, Jayanti Pranlal Thakore, remembered having formed a children's brigade, *vanarsena* (literally, army of monkeys), and teaching them the flag salutation.[72] Among families implicated in the nationalist struggle, the ritual became part of an established routine. Vijaya

[66] On the political response of the Indian business comunity, see Claude Markovits, *Indian Business and Nationalist Politics 1931–1939. The Indigenous Capitalist Class and the Rise of the Congress Party* (Cambridge, Cambridge University Press, 1985).

[67] *Bombay Chronicle*, 31 August 1931.

[68] *The Madras Weekly Mail*, 10 April 1930, p. 412.

[69] A special appeal by Lajpat Rai's daughter to women, *The Tribune*, 28 August 1930.

[70] *The Tribune*, 28 August 1930.

[71] *Searchlight*, 1 September 1930.

[72] Naveen Joshi, *Freedom Fighters Remember* (Delhi, Publications Division, Ministry of Information & Broadcasting, Govt. of India, 1997), pp. 29–30.

Lakshmi Pandit dwelt on the psychological succour it brought into their sometimes lonely struggles for freedom. After 26 January was declared Independence Day, on that morning and every year thereafter, they foregathered on the upstairs terrace of Anand Bhawan, the family home in Allahabad, to read the independence pledge, hoist the Congress flag, and sing the national song. In this ceremony, every member of the family, including the servants, was associated, and generally the youngest member hoisted the flag. This continued even when the elders were in jail. There was a time, she noted, when only her two elder daughters hoisted the flag on their own, the entire family being in prison.[73]

Behind this rapid and successful diffusion, partly, lay the efficiency and reach of a political party. At the same time, Hardikar's role as the principal author of these ceremonies was far from negligible. He was eager to establish a nationwide ritual that was distinguished by its uniformity and standardization. In his eyes, publicizing and teaching a flag culture required rules and regulations. If the ceremony were to inculcate national criteria of behaviour, it could not be left to the whims and fancies of the crowd or even in the hands of local organizers, without any fixed features. It was with this intention that in 1923 he founded a voluntary organization, the Hindustani Seva Dal ('team in the service of Hindustan'). Determined to generate and develop a patriotic spirit, recruit and mobilize people to participate in the national struggle, this body, distinct yet subordinate to the Congress, was founded to oversee the material aspects of this civic, national function.[74] On the occasion of Flag Day, the Hindustani Seva Dal and

[73] Vijaya Lakshmi Pandit, *The Scope of Happiness. A Personal Memoir* (London, Weidenfeld and Nicolson, 1979), p. 93.

[74] The Hindustan Seva Dal was set up in 1923 at Cocanada under the presidentship of Jawaharlal Nehru; Dr Hardikar was responsible for the nucleus of an All India Volunteer Organization: *Janmabhumi*, January 1926, p. 7. In July 1931 the Congress Working Committee would recognize the Dal as the central volunteer organization of the Congress working directly under its authority. It was apprehensive about unauthorized volunteer organizations working in various corners of the country in the name of the Congress. Cf. *Indian Annual Register*, July–December 1931, vol. 2, p. 65. No detailed study has been made of this key organization.

the Servants of the People Society ensured the supply of national flags, in cloth or in paper, to the civil population. In Bombay the local office of the Seva Dal sold lockets of the national flag with a design of the map of India and the words 'Swatantra Bharat' (Independent India), for one anna.[75] The ladies' branch of the Hindustan Seva Dal (the Desh Sevika Sangh), along with the Rashtriya Mahila Mandal (National Women's Group) contributed to organizing the ritual, explaining the full significance of the flag, the manner in which the function should be performed, how they should design the horseshoe formation on the ground around the flagstaff, which songs they could sing, and the discipline to be observed on the occasion.[76]

Hardikar's concern to discourage the intrusion of deviations and local fantasy from overtaking the ritual corresponded to the Congress objective of publicly exhibiting the Indian consensus. Gandhi for his part perceived the Seva Dal's role as exceeding the specific control and direction of the national symbol. He glimpsed its larger potential to lead and direct the movement of non-violence. 'There can be no provincial organization without an officer certified by the Seva Dal office', he declared. 'Non-violence is a trust, which has to be zealously guarded by the Seva Dal.' For Hardikar, too, the principal contribution of this organization was to teach, explain, and form Indians from their youngest age in a national mould. Hence, after 1923, Hardikar himself undertook an all-India tour, persuading school headmasters to include a pedagogical civic ritual of songs, lectures, and exercises around the flag in the after-hours school programme in order to develop a national spirit among the children. His arrangement with the headmaster of the National High School in Bangalore was an example of his belief in the flag as a national antidote to sectarian ties and identities.[77]

Other elements, until then subsisting on the periphery of party strategies, like documentaries and even theatrical productions, contributed to the popularization of Flag Day. In the 1930s the first Indian newsreels and documentaries made their appearance.[78] A. Narayanan Srivastava's 'Unfurling of the National Flag' was later shown in

[75] *The Tribune*, 16 January 1930.

[76] *The Hindu*, 26 January 1930.

[77] James Manor, *Political Change in an Indian State. Mysore 1917–55* (New Delhi, Manohar, 1978), pp. 82–3.

[78] *Amrita Bazar Patrika*, 9 August 1931.

Bombay and other provincial towns.[79] They were exploited by a Congress concerned about a national policy of political propaganda. The British government came to view it as a serious propaganda weapon: in 1934 it banned the Bombay Provincial Congress Committee's film on the 'National Flag hoisting and Salutation Ceremony'.[80]

During the 1930s the flag ritual lent itself to all the national commemorations that punctuated all the months of the year: beginning with Independence Day on 26 January, Flag Day on the last Sunday of every month, Gandhi month from 18 February to 18 March, followed by National Week in April, and Tilak Day in August. In some cities of South India, in the summer of 1923, Flag Day replaced Tilak Day.[81] To this list was added Jawahar Day in 1930, at the bequest of Motilal Nehru, who was motivated by a certain degree of parental pride as well as by the political calculation of channelling Jawaharlal's popularity among the masses towards a national end. After 1942 the national calendar was further extended to include a Martyrs Day in August to commemorate the 1942 arrests, Liberty week from 9 to 15 August, and after 1945 a Political Prisoners Day, a Civil Liberties Day, a Student's Demand Day, a Charkha Demonstration Day, a National Unity Day, and an Anti-Untouchability Day.[82] The ritual of Flag Day seemed to have become the central national ceremony, even imposing itself on other celebrations.

The Ambiguities of a Colonial Situation

While the Congress and its Indian allies hailed Flag Day's diffusion all over the country as a triumph in 'touching the hearts of the people' and representing 'the soul of the country',[83] the British administration viewed the nationalist intrusions in this domain of colonial power

[79] *Bombay Chronicle*, 31 August 1931.

[80] *Amrita Bazar Patrika*, 9 August 1931.

[81] CAOM, E-8, Report of the Anglo-Indian Press, July–September 1923, Governor of Pondicherry, 24 October 1923.

[82] Sucheta Mahajan, 'British Policy, Nationalist Strategy and Popular National Upsurge, 1945–6', in A.K. Gupta (ed.), *Myth and Reality: The Struggle for Freedom in India 1945–47* (Delhi, Manohar, 1987), p. 67.

[83] OIOC, L/R/5/59, *Indian Newspaper Reports, United Provinces of Agra and Oudh*, for the week ending 8 February 1930.

with varying degrees of scepticism, caution, and alarm. Viceroys since Curzon had been prone to treat 'rituals of propaganda' like Empire Day as necessary though problematic instruments of rule in an increasingly nationalist Indian climate. They were wary of provoking a battle of symbols that British experience in Ireland had shown to be a difficult terrain to control. The Indian government did not fail to point out Muslim indifference to the rituals or the greater female participation in the ceremonies as proof of its limited reach and feeble impact in important cities.[84] Thus the British-owned *Civil and Military Gazette* of Lahore insisted that attempts to celebrate Independence Day on 26 January in the country had fallen very flat apart from a few arrests in Bombay, Poona, Delhi, and in four or five places in the United Provinces, including Allahabad, Lucknow, and Dehradun.[85] In Madras the government affirmed that the morning flag procession was a damp squib that would have attracted no more than 200 people and only 700 people at a beach gathering with no prominent Congress leaders. Here too, Muslims had remained aloof, even hostile, while in Salem and Calicut they had even led a counter-procession, upholding the Union Jack. Nonetheless, it could not be denied that in Madras some 1500 vernacular translations of the independence resolution in leaflet form were distributed and 500 small flags had been sold in two weeks.[86] And as administrative reports increasingly signalled flag hoistings on official public buildings like schools, municipal bodies, hospitals, courts, universities, youth hostels, and police stations,[87] the government was forced to press local authorities to quell the movement.

Until 1930 the officially declared policy of the Government of India remained that flying a flag not authorized by the government was not in itself an offence as long as the act did not show any hostility to British rule. But it was under increasing pressure from the home government, which demanded a robust strategy of action. Against the

[84] OIOC, L/P&J/12/2, Governor's fortnightly reports for the second half of January 1930, Bengal.

[85] RCSC, Cambridge, *Letters on Political, Constitutional Problems of India, 1933–37*, Extract from the Civil and Military Gazette, no. 2, 1934, p. 21.

[86] OIOC, L/P&J/12/19, Governor's fortnightly reports for the second half of January 1930, Madras.

[87] NAI, Home Political, file no. 14/24-1932, letter from the India Office, 22 April 1932. This letter notes the magnitude of the phenomenon.

background of civil disobedience, these acts had acquired a greater gravity for London. But local authorities found themselves in a quandary before the recurring monthly ritual of Flag Day with its fully developed liturgy representing state power. Provincial authorities responded by removing flags from official sites, and sometimes denying government grants to defiant municipalities for essential services like education, roads, etc,. But the latter was not always easy, as the Central Provinces government pointed out when pressed to take strong action on the lines of the Madras government. If grants were withheld, Congress local leaders were quick to publicize these measures and turn public opinion against the government.[88] Still, 'We must be careful not to give the Secretary of State any impression that we regard this matter too lightly', cautioned H.G. Haig, governor of the Central Provinces.[89]

British concern to show their mastery of the situation was greater because in fact they were quite uncertain about their executive legal powers to intervene in these matters. Sir James Crerar, a home assembly member, estimated that if a municipal body itself had not been declared unlawful, the flying of the flag was 'neither illegal nor seditious'.[90] This view reinforced local governments that were reluctant to tread the ground of confrontation and repression. Even when the AICC and its working committee were declared unlawful by the government on 30 June 1930, the flag's proclaimed national status protected it from being treated as the flag of the party and therefore also illegal.[91] In the absence of a clear guideline, individual officers were thus left free to act on their own guise. In Bijnore district of Uttar Pradesh, for example, the exasperated English district settlement officer, Bait, threw away national flags hoisted on buildings during Independence Day celebrations. In response, the Provincial Congress Committee declared a satyagraha, sending a batch of ten volunteers singing national songs and slogans to follow Bait through all the villages he passed, and hoisting and saluting the flag before the Englishman's tent.

[88] Ibid., H.C. Gowan, Chief Secretary, Central Provinces, 10 June 1932.

[89] Ibid., H.G. Haig, 10 July 1932.

[90] *The Hindu*, 4 February 1932.

[91] Correspondence on this subject is available in NAI, Home Political, file no. 14/27, 1932.

The settlement officer finally cancelled his tour programme and left the neighbourhood.[92]

Despite the government's keenness to prevent what was clearly a celebration of self-government and independence as well as a defiant response to imperial rituals, its punctual interventions and show of force were ineffective. 1937 found the British Resident at Trivandrum protesting against the deliberate omission of the British national anthem on a 'fundamentally British empire function', Armistice Day, on the Bandmaster's feeble pretext that he had not got the music with him.[93] The state minister promised to redress matters,[94] but one year later the situation was very much the same. This time the British officer of the Trivandrum State Force protested that at sports functions 'particular tunes have been played . . .' and '. . . some persons present have stood to attention'. Clearly, the tunes referred to were Indian national songs, for he maintained that people normally must stand to attention only for the Travancore or the British national anthem.[95] An examination of the government files of these years reveals that the British had found no answer to the displays of the flag in public ceremonies and its persistent exhibition on municipal buildings, local bodies, and even private houses. It was precisely what the flag's advocates had hoped for.

A National Success?

Irrespective of the advances and retreats of movements of civil disobedience, the flag rituals survived and spread. As one newspaper put it, the flag was 'a household symbol'.[96] The Congress' official historian, Pattabhi Sitaramayya, termed its success as being beyond their expectations.[97] The impact of Flag Day consisted in showing the British government's impotence in preventing the diffusion of the flag

92 *The Hindu Illustrated Weekly*, 30 March 1930, p. 22.

93 OIOC, R/2/889/231, Resident to Sir C.P. Ramaswami Aiyar, Diwan of Travancore, 13 November 1937.

94 Ibid., C.P. Ramaswami Aiyar to the Resident, 14 November 1937.

95 Ibid., H.L. Dalthus, Trivandrum State Forces Headquarters, to Raja Bhakta A. Nallaperumal Pillai, Sarvadhikarikar Palace, Trivandrum, 27 March 1938.

96 *The People*, 5 April 1931, p. 216.

97 Pattabhi Sitaramayya, *History of the Indian National Congress, 1885–1935*, op. cit., p. 346.

throughout their colony. By creating a protocol for an Indian nation that did not yet exist, it presented a façade of solidarity and unity that masked important divisions and tensions within the Indian political parties. The demonstration of discipline and consensus legitimized Indians before the colonial authorities, their co-citizens, and themselves. The ritual came to play both the role of self-representation as well as self-definition in a situation where, as dominated subjects, Indians were called to show their strength, determination, and confidence.[98] (Illustr. 4.)

In the 1930s monthly flag ceremonies accompanied by national songs were an established element of political language and a mode of nationalist action, giving the impression that, at a local level, Indians were really governing the country. Not only had an equivalent but

Illustr. 4. Police dispersing a crowd demonstrating with a flag, *c.* 1925. (Roger Viollet.)

[98] Similar examples of the legitimizing, representational, or consolidating role of political rituals are observable in other post-colonial contexts. Cf. Sally Falk Moore, 'Political Meetings and the Simulation of Unanimity. Kilminjaro 1973', in Sally F. Moore and Barbara G. Myerhoff (eds), *Secular Rituals* (Assen, Van Gorcum and Co., 1977), p.166; J. Arch Getty, 'Samokritika Rituals in the Stalinist Central Committee, 1933–1938', *Russian Review*, vol. 58, no. 1, January 1999, pp. 49–70.

alternative nationalist ritual with an Indian flag and anthem succeeded in occupying the political landscape and capturing public attention, it had even eclipsed British imperial ceremonies.[99] The ritual retained its relevance in the 1940s despite the sharpening of political differences and the temporary retreat of Congress from public activity. Thus, Subhas Chandra Bose's break with the Congress line of non-violence did not prevent his Indian National Army based in Singapore from hoisting and saluting the national flag every day. Lakshmi Sahgal, the captain of a women's regiment, who found herself at Singapore in 1943 for regular training, narrated that every morning, at 6 a.m., they assembled outside their barracks to hoist the national flag and, at sunset, to lower it.[100]

Be that as it may, estimating the impact of the Flag Day ritual from the perspective of its political institutionalization in the ceremonials of power offers a partial and falsely consensual image. As an Indian response to imperial rituals of sovereignty and propaganda, it certainly marked a moment 'sanctifying and marking off a space and a time of special significance . . . in which meaning is crystallized.'[101] But this visibility cannot be taken as confirmation of what Nicholas B. Dirks terms 'claims to power, sites of resistance and contestation, or social moments of liminality in which all relations of power are up for grabs.'[102] Firstly, it is impossible to know the influence of the ritual on participants and the internal shift if any that it accomplished. Certainly, Gandhi considered them a crucial exercise in expanding the consciousness of the national self and serving to renew commitment to intensive national work and national regeneration. He hoped this growth would follow from a silent and inward participation in the external observance of the ritual.[103] But the glimpses offered by personal accounts and reports into its impact do not allow categorical judgements as to how

[99] Celebrations of Empire Day gradually receded in the 1930s to be finally dropped by 1940. RCSC, Cambridge, *Report on the Empire Day Movement* (London, 1937), pp. 22–3.

[100] Lakshmi Sahgal, *A Revolutionary Life. Memoirs of a Political Activist* (Delhi, Kali for Women, 1997), p. 66.

[101] N. Dirks, 'Ritual and Resistance', op. cit., p. 214.

[102] Ibid., p. 220.

[103] *Young India*, 7 February 1924, p. 51.

it moved its public, transformed them, or on the contrary left them indifferent.

Secondly, the very success of the national flag ritual also risked diminishing its impact and dulling its intensity. It certainly did not remain static and unchanging from its inception until independence, but followed different momentums after the initial peak of public enthusiasm in 1930–1. The slogan 'Up, up with the National Flag, Down, down with the Union Jack', which had built up a movement of popular support and intensity for flag rituals, receded into the background in favour of 'Quit India' when the flag became almost a banal, taken-for-granted feature of the political decor. This dilution of its intensity and reduction to a mechanistic replay, devoid of feeling or any true understanding of its significance was a point raised in 1947 on the eve of independence. Indians, wrote *National Week*, had become conditioned and disciplined to react to these occasions, hearing their leaders' messages, holding meetings in which words like 'honour', 'freedom', and 'sacred' were too often repeated and frequently misused. Words once hallowed, it complained, were today lost in the ritual and their symbolic meaning overlooked. It reminded its readers of the original meaning—how National Week had been initially set aside as a time of prayer and preparation under the Home Rule movement, how it had come to represent the creed of satyagraha as conceived by Gandhi to commemorate Jallianwala Bagh. The historical meaning of this week was particularly important to remember in this period of transition to independence.[104]

It was this very consciousness of the risk of political rituals losing their original intensity and meaning that was highlighted by authors like Saadat Hasan Manto and Bhisham Sahni in their portrayals of the nationalist movement of these years. Manto's story, *The Price of Freedom*, set in the 1930s, described Shahzada Ghulam Ali, a Congress volunteer at Amritsar, falling in love with a Muslim orphan girl called Nigar. Their marriage ceremony, blessed at Jalianwala Bagh, concludes with hoisting the Congress flag. Nigar is in a sari, which bears the three colours of the flag of the Indian National Congress, white, green, and orange. Ghulam Ali is imprisoned after the ceremony and when he

[104] *National Herald*, 12 April 1947.

comes out the world outside has changed. 'Spun cotton, tricolour flags and revolutionary slogans had lost their power.'[105] Similarly, Bhisham Sahni's novel *Tamas* describes the same problem in a small town in the North West Frontier Province, soon to be included in Pakistan. A handful of people assembled for the morning singing party (*prabhat pheri*), take charge of the tricolour (the party flag, notes the author): 'Master Ram Das started singing in his heavy tuneless voice—the same song with which they always started the march, a song that had gone stale with repetition.'[106] The political triumph of a symbol and the re-enactment of these rituals did not necessarily imply a continued emotional connection with the nation.

Finally, participation in the function could not be taken as an absolute indicator of the participant's political beliefs, or of 'an alliance between a political symbol and the unanimity of a society.'[107] Indeed, it was also the rejection of ritual that can be seen as revealing the truth.[108] Though conceived as a means of uniting and gathering passions—a kind of magic potion leading to an ideological unanimity of social groups and political actors—the ritual for the flag was also, as we will see in chapters 7 and 8, susceptible to becoming a source of dissension and political differences.[109]

The importance of instituting a national liturgy characterized by Flag Day, and a national calendar for Indians, cannot be underestimated. A long and impressive track of historical as well as anthropological analysis, extending from medieval times to the contemporary world, has shown that ceremonial pageantry and rituals are not merely colourful

[105] Saadat Hasan Manto, *Kingdom's End and Other Stories* (London, Verso, 1987), pp. 66–7.

[106] Bhisham Sahni, *Tamas* (New Delhi, Penguin, 1974), p. 26. I am grateful to Christopher Mincowski for drawing my attention to this passage.

[107] Jean Duvignaud, 'La fête civique', in Guy Dumur (ed.), *Histoire des spectacles* (Paris, Gallimard, 1965), pp. 248–50.

[108] Jack Goody notes that what was demanded in the Greek city state was compliance in the ritual and not acceptance of belief. The acknowledgement of ritual did not necessarily affect deeper values. 'Against "Ritual": Loosely Structured Thoughts on a Loosely Defined Topic', in Sally F. Moore and Barbara G. Myerhoff (eds), *Secular Ritual*, op. cit., p. 33.

[109] Sri Lanka in the 1960s and Ulster in the 1970s are two examples of the polarizing effects of rituals.

accessories of 'real' power, displayed once the real battle has been fought and won, but decisive occasions when the stakes in power can be confirmed.[110] From this perspective, Flag Day and the elaboration of a national calendar were what Paul Veyne has termed the 'beginning of proof'.[111] The flag was the reality, although what it symbolized remained an illusion. It was enough to display it, hoist it, and hold it up for the nation to be real. Nationalist rituals around the flag were conceived to unite, to present the form, while awaiting the substance of the real state, and to build a fictional, ritual nation, which had in fact no substance yet.[112] In that sense they can be seen as a form of theatre managed by the Indians, a grand trick of illusion inaugurating the first act of a play Indians hoped would end in independence.

[110] The importance of the interplay of various political forces and interests in ceremonial ritual has been amply proved through the works of medievalists like Jacques Le Goff, or Louis Marin. Alain Boureau offers a broad view of the perils of ceremonialist historiography in 'Ritualité politique et modernité monarchique', in Neithard Bulst, Robert Descimon, and Alain Guereau (eds), *L'Etat ou le Roi: Les fondations de la modernité monarchique en France (XIVe–XVIIe siècles)* (Paris, MSH, 1996), pp. 9–23. In a different context but equally relevant is the analysis of the relation between rituals and state politics in Joseph P. McDermott (ed.), *State and Court Ritual in China* (Cambridge, Cambridge University Press, 1999).

[111] Paul Veyne, *Le Pain et le Cirque. Sociologie historique d'un pluralisme politique* (Paris, Seuil, 1976), p. 80.

[112] In a similar way, ritual demonstrations by Hindus in the 1990s sought to produce cultural and religious meanings and give political expression to their desire for an integral India. Cf. Caroline Humphrey and James A. Laidlaw, *The Archetypal Actions of Ritual. A Theory of Ritual Illustrated by the Jain Rites of Worship* (Oxford, Clarendon Press, 1994), pp. 125–7.

6

Feelings for the Nation

A clearly perceptible succession of public debates, party policies and decisions marked the stages in the elaboration of the Indian national flag from 1920 to the 1930s. They accompanied a process of politicization that transformed a mere piece of coloured cloth into a largely recognized political symbol, representative of a nation that did not yet exist as an independent sovereign state. However, the political analysis of the flag as a public object that I have hitherto presented does not suffice to explain its political success. Its triumph was equally based on a more private, intimate sphere of feeling and emotions. It was almost as if the nationalization of the flag implied a kind of depoliticization. On the one hand its widespread recognition and acceptance by a very large number of Indians had meant an outer diffusion of the symbol in public space through demonstrations, satyagrahas, and collective action. But on the other hand it demanded an inner assimilation until 'feeling national' became inseparable from reason, and passion became part of rational logic. In other words, a mere political symbol had come to be a dear and familiar object to a great number of people, a part of their private world, deeply integrated into their domestic space. In the 1930s the Indian flag was visible on houses, shops, and gardens, even on clothes and stationery. Henceforth, linked to individual experiences, it evoked highly subjective reactions, memories, and sentiment. In order to function as a national symbol the flag had to first merge into many different emotional experiences, becoming practically an inner state of being and then gather these disparate sensations to convert them into a common vocabulary and sentiment of Indianness. Its power and singularity in incarnating the nation derived from this capacity to create strong social cohesion out of distinct strands of sensibilities and impressions. In short, its political force lay in its capacity for an 'emotional socialization'.[1]

It was this insight that heightened Gandhi's sensitivity to all that a flag could bring to the Indian national movement. In his opinion its political role lay above all in its emotive capacity to touch the heart and soul of the masses. If he prevaricated until 1921 in approving any of the designs Venkayya had been proposing since 1917, it was because he felt these projects were the product of a theoretical, intellectual construction which, despite their religious and historical roots, failed to arouse an emotional response. None of the symbols proposed in the preceding years had made it to the heart of anti-colonial struggles; they did not therefore refer to resistance movements, heroic exploits, martyrs and sacrifices which permitted the creation of a national emotion. Earlier experiences of elaborating a flag in 1905–7 or 1916–17 had amply proved that without this emotional dimension it remained a purely intellectual construct. Gandhi's understanding that the flag was a quintessential motor of 'emotional socialization' was backed by the parallel conviction that a particular political language was required to achieve this. The question was not simply of tapping into an unlimited source of human feelings but of harnessing them into an ordered, disciplined struggle, an 'emotional regime'.[2] This would combine a well-established and recognized symbol of national sovereignty—the flag—with a very particularistic Indian language of political battle.

[1] The discipline which first used socialization as an analytic tool was cultural anthropology, itself heavily influenced by psychoanalytic studies. My own use of this concept is from Pearl Katz, 'Emotional Metaphors, Socialization, and Roles of Drill Sergeants', *Ethos*, vol. 18, no. 4, 1990, pp. 457–80. He uses the observations of Basil Bernstein and Sulamith Heins Potter which suggest that, in many hierarchical cultures, emotional socialization encourages action and strict conformity to highly specified role behaviour. In his study of drill sergeants he found that as they believed action and feelings are inexorably linked, the only way to control behaviour is to control emotions (by not acknowledging that they are feeling) and that the only way to constrain emotions is by controlling behaviour (p. 468).

[2] The term is used by William Reddy, *Navigation of Feeling: A Framework of the History of Emotions* (Cambridge, Cambridge University Press, 2001).

An Emotional Approach to India

'In looking for the roots of Indian nationalism we can begin with an emotion . . . The emotion was dislike of the foreigner.'[3] Evoking the link between a national spirit and a sentiment, the British historian Percival Spear hinted at an approach to the understanding of national construction that broke with the well-trodden paths of party strategies, mass mobilization, political programmes, institutions, and associations.[4] Identifying emotions as the source of a national spirit reinstates them as one of the elementary forms of struggle itself.[5] Indeed, the simplest and most widespread expression of patriotism can be seen as born from dislike, anger, inequality, and ill treatment in the colonial state. Dr Aziz in *A Passage to India* observes this metamorphosis taking place in him as his earlier friendship for the British schoolteacher Fielding fades away in a genuine hatred of the English. At that moment he realizes: 'I am an Indian at last.'[6] Having noted this shift, Dr Aziz then simply leaves British India for a princely state to live his newly

[3] Percival Spear, *A History of India* (Oxford, Oxford University Press, 1965), vol. 2, pp. 158–9.

[4] A glossary of the key terms of nationalism today includes 'passions', 'sentiment', 'emotional bonding'. Cf. *Nations and Nationalism*, vol. 10, January–April 2004 in particular, Montserrat Guibernau and Anthony D. Smith, 'Nations and National Identity: A Critical Assessment', pp. 125–42; Mary Kaldor, 'Nationalism and Globalization', pp. 161–78; Walker Connor, 'The Timelessness of Nations', pp. 35–48. Mary Kaldor quotes the reaction of a friend from Nagorno Karabakh, witnessing the crowds' orderly flag-waving welcome of Queen Elizabeth during the last jubilee celebrations at London: 'That's not nationalism. That was a Soviet crowd. Nationalism is about passion.'

[5] Craig Calhoun, 'Putting Emotions in their Place', in Jeff Goodwin, James M. Jasper, and Francesca Polletta (eds), *Passionate Politics. Emotions and Social Movements* (Chicago and London, Chicago University Press, 2001), esp. p. 55. The case for a history of political emotions is made by Christophe Prochasson, 'Emotions et Politique: Premières approches', in S. Audoin-Rouzeau *et al.* (eds), *La Politique et la guerre. Pour comprendre le XXe siècle européen. Hommage à Jean-Jacques Becker* (Paris, A. Vienot-Noesis, 2002), pp. 431–9. For a recapitulation of the historical treatment of emotions, see Barbara H. Rosenwein, 'Worrying about Emotions in History', *American Historical Review*, vol. 107, no. 3, June 2002.

[6] E.M. Forster, *A Passage to India* (London, Penguin, 1st edn, 1924; 5th edn, 1989), p. 290.

discovered identity undisturbed by the invasive presence of colonial foreigners. But princely India, seemingly immersed in its own traditions, was also under British rule. Thus, Forster's description of the process of becoming Indian was left incomplete, for this demanded more than emotional rupture and retreat into a private world. It called for a replacement of anger and disgust with an opposite sentiment of love and longing for the nation, a positive identification with other Indians as well as engagement in a path of collective action. It was necessary to give these feelings suitable political form. No doubt an aversion to the colonial government was, as one British commentator analysed, slowly 'indistinguishable . . . from patriotism, a feeling compounded of national pride, national exclusiveness and desire for national independence.'[7] Yet bringing these sentiments together in a collective surge, capable of unseating colonial authority was a more complicated process. Tagore outlined the problem in his novel *Gora*. One of the figures in his story, Binoy, questioned: 'Where is that India you speak of?' Placing his hand on his breast, Gora said: 'There—where the compass within points to, night and day. Not in your Mr Marshman's *History of India*.'[8] Certainly, this power of the heart was to be felt, it could not be learnt or found in books, knowledge, dates, and facts. Nonetheless it needed to be articulated more clearly in words, actions, and symbols, even if 'translating this feeling for *Bharat* was, as a contemporary Indian poet has observed, not a very straightforward process' (*Bharat ek bhavna hai aur uska shabdo mein anuvada karna ek bahut teda kaam hai*).[9]

Certainly, at least since the beginning of the twentieth century, many Indians recognized the idea that emotions were the force guiding resistance. During the surge of anti-partition demonstrations in Bengal in 1905–8, the idea that nationality had to be desired withheld

[7] Meredith White Townsend, *Asia and Europe. Studies Presenting the Conclusions Formed by the Author in a Long Life Devoted to the Subject of the Relations between Asia and Europe* (New York, G.P. Putnam's Sons, 1901; London, 2nd edn, Archibald Constable & Co., 1903), p. 314.

[8] Rabindranath Tagore, *Gora* (London, Macmillan, 1924), p. 67. Published in 1867–9, John Clark Marshman's *History of India: From the Earliest Period to the Close of Lord Dalhousie's Administration* (London, Longmans, Green, Reader & Dyer), was a classically colonial vision of Indian history.

[9] The lines are of Ashok Chakradhar, Hindi poet and satirist.

the attention of orators and spokesmen. Aurobindo Ghosh summed up the importance of capturing this force. He insisted that the struggle Indians had undertaken was too gigantic and stupendous to be understood and seized by mere intellect, logic, and reasoning. These qualities could only highlight the paucity of material weapons Indians had at their disposal and the high probability of losing the battle. The intellectual process, as they had already observed, led to apathy, despair, and death. It was only, he underlined, when the intellect ceased to work and the heart was opened to inspiration that the whole nation arose with new-found strength and rushed forward to bear down all obstacles. The need of the hour, Aurobindo now urged his audience, was to turn within. The power of the heart, he exhorted, was invincible, almighty, and irresistible, nourishing faith, selflessness, and courage.[10] Aurobindo's passionate plea to Indians to rise above mental constructs and engage their hearts in the nationalist struggle beckoned them on a path of tempestuous action. One example of this was provided by the surge of emotional unity against the partition in his native Bengal. He wished to see sentiments of humiliation mingled with pride in their own traditions that had led many to a state of what he termed national 'madness' metamorphosed into weapons to fight 'the superior force of the British'. Ironically, Aurobindo's own retirement from political action to a spiritual path of meditation in French Pondicherry hardly offered a model.

Aurobindo was not the only one to grasp the unifying power of their feelings of 'humiliation' or 'pride' and realize the potential of converging these into 'national madness'. Bipin Chandra Pal, labelled a radical by the British government for his views during the Bengal partition, also insisted at the same moment on the urgency of converting hatred of the British into love for the motherland. Negative emotions, he proclaimed, would simply divert energies to fighting their rulers; the immediate task was to cultivate and organize strength. Of course, they could not be expected to love the British, for that would be fatal to

[10] Aurobindo Ghosh, 'The Present Situation', speech delivered at Mahajan Wadi, Bombay on 19 January 1908, in Sri Aurobindo, *On Nationalism. Selected Writings and Speeches* (Pondicherry, Sri Aurobindo National Trust,1996), pp. 251–65.

Indian national life—it had already killed the spirit of nationality in many an English-educated Indian. But Indians must, he wrote, develop the longing for salvation. This emotion demanded a strict management in order to be politically effective: in short, restriction, renunciation, training, and discipline.[11] Surendranath Bannerjee too began his address to students on the subject of Indian unity by placing 'this question upon the exalted basis of the human emotions'.[12] The idea that the Indian nation was to be forged from emotion thus continued to animate Indians through these years. In Madras, Annie Besant put her finger on the issue when she asked the Hindu College Boarders' Debating Club in 1910: 'How shall the Indian nation be born?', and gave the answer: 'By sentiment.'[13] And in Punjab, Lala Lajpat Rai pointed out that the public 'could be reached and made to think by an appeal to its emotions rather than to its intellect.'[14]

At least since the second half of the nineteenth century, a sensibility born of anger and humiliation was expressed through the familiar medium of poetry and songs.[15] The role and limits of this exuberant, continuous production in forging a community of feeling remains to be explored.[16] Yet the first manifestations of solidarity and affirmation of the unity of Indian geography came through in this familiar

[11] Bipin Chandra Pal, 'Love and Politics', published in *New Spirit* in 1907, reprinted in *Swadeshi and Swaraj*, op. cit., p. 67.

[12] *Speeches and Writings of Surendranath Bannerjee*, op. cit., p. 227.

[13] Annie Besant, *The Birth of New India. A Collection of Writings and Speeches on Indian Affairs* (Madras, Theosophical Publishing House, 1917), p. 32.

[14] Printed in *Modern Review*, December 1919; reprinted in Shri Ram Bakshi (ed.), *Lajpat Rai. Swaraj and Social Change* (New Delhi, H.K. Publishers and Distributors, 1990), vol. 2, *The Teaching of Patriotism 1919–1922*, pp. 650–5.

[15] A bibliographic presentation of nationalist poems printed during this period can be found in N. Gerald Barrier, *Banned Controversial Literature and Political Control in British India 1907–1947* (Delhi, Manohar, 1974).

[16] Suvir Kaul makes an examination of the rhetorical effort required in England towards building a collectivity in the language of poetry, *Poems of Nation. Anthems of Empire. English Verse in the Long 18th Century* (Charlottesville: University of Virginia Press, 2000); Jeffrey Richards, *Imperialism and Music: Britain 1876–1953* (Manchester University Press, 2001). Bernard Porter in his critique of Richards' questions whether the quantity of imperial music produced in this period was proof of the even spread of an imperial spirit in Britain, and not

medium of traditional oral culture. Following the pattern of hymns and prayers, they transposed the poetical modes onto a new subject—the country or motherland—and celebrated bonds of affection with a familiar landscape and physical geography. The emotion that gripped the country, Bipin Chandra Pal pointed out on the eve of the Bengal partition, infused a new strength into these songs. They were transported by a flow of powerful energy that was quite different from the 'airy, fairy sentiment . . . too abstract' approach that had characterized older patriotism. While earlier they had sung of their loss of freedom, he analysed, they had simply revelled in a strange and weird fancy, imitating sentiments that found but a feeble echo in the actual experiences of their daily life. And when, he pursued, they sang '*Gao bharater jay, jay Bharater jay, gao Bharater jay*' (Sing long live Bharat . . .), they simply indulged in a noble fancy. This old patriotism had involved few risks; references to ancient heroes were also unreal and therefore the songs and music failed to strike their hearts. But for Bipin Chandra Pal the hymnology of the new patriotism of 1905, like the sentiment that had called it forth, was intensely real. It hit a chord that had never been touched before.[17]

The new patriotism Pal referred to was born in and fed by public meetings and processions. In this context, patriotic poems and songs carried the leaders and participants of the struggle against the Bengal partition along in a wave of excitement and invisible yet palpable sentiment of communion. It was these, wrote Surendranath Bannerjee, that led many to form and follow the crowd, swept them along, engulfed by a collective emotion that communicated itself to the whole community, inspiring it with a new momentum, above all capturing the hearts of womenfolk. 'Reason halts; judgment is held in suspense; it is one mighty impulse that moves the heart of the community and

---

simply at times an easy 'veneer'. Cf. Bernard Porter, 'Edward Elgar and Empire', *The Journal of Imperial and Commonwealth History*, vol. 29, no. 1, January 2001, pp. 1–34. Studies on the literary and poetical expression of the emotional unity of the Indian nation in Hindi and Urdu include Vasudha Dalmia, *The Nationalization of Hindu Traditions. Bharatendu Harischandra and Nineteenth-Century Banaras* (Delhi, Oxford University Press, 1997).

[17] Bipin Chandra Pal, 'On National Songs', 19 March 1903, *New India*, reprinted in *Swadeshi and Swaraj*, op. cit., pp. 98–9.

carries everything before it.'[18] One newspaper invited its readers to compose a national song fit to be sung by Indians. It published five such compositions calling for the emancipation of Bharat from the hell of slavery and alien rule and evoked the Marathi heroic tradition as a source of inspiration for their current struggle.[19]

Before the popularity of this literary idiom, the flag provoked little reaction. It was an element of decoration, secondary to the slogans and songs that dominated the crowd in 1905. Meanwhile, songs became part of the cultural and emotional baggage of both children and adults, inserted into a national community irrespective of their political involvement. They were at the crossroads of prayers and political exhortations, merging the familiar forms of religious devotion with new political practices. They required little explanation or publicity—unlike the flag, which initially demanded a real exercise of interpretation, simplification, and absorption.

Hence, a song like *Bande Mataram*, which Rabindranath Tagore called the '*Swadeshi Atma*', that is to say, the 'indigenous soul',[20] though in Sanskrit and quite incomprehensible to many of its auditors and singers, became popular almost effortlessly. Gandhi's explanation of the power exercised by the song on him is a good illustration of this: 'As a lad, when I knew nothing of *Ananda Math* or even Bankim, its immortal author, *Bande Mataram* had gripped me and when I first heard it sung it had enthralled me. I associated the purest national spirit with it . . . It stirs to its depth the patriotism of millions in and

[18] Surendranath Bannerjee, *A Nation in Making. Being the Reminiscences of Fifty Years of Public Life* (London, Humphrey Milford, 1925), p. 182.

[19] OIOC, L/R/5/162, N.N.R., Bombay 1907.

[20] The song, though composed in 1885 by Bankim Chandra Chatterji, had remained obscure. A few lines of the song did find a place in Hem Chandra Bannerjee's Bengali poem 'Rakhi Bandhan' composed in 1886 for the second Congress annual session in Calcutta. In 1896 Tagore set a tune and sang it again at the Congress session. It was only in 1905 that its metamorphosis from a song to a nationalist cry was achieved. Haridas Mukherjee and Uma Mukherjee, *Bande Mataram and Indian Nationalism, 1906–1908* (Calcutta, K.L. Mukhopadhyay, 1957), p. 11; Haridas Mukherjee (ed.), *Sri Aurobindo and the New Thought in Indian Politics. Being a Study in the Ideas of Indian Nationalism, Based on the Rare Writings of Sri Aurobindo in the Daily Bande Mataram during the years 1906–1908* (Calcutta, K.L. Mukhopadhyay, 1964), p. xx.

outside Bengal.'[21] Acknowledging the power of this literary form and the sentiment it evoked in their young hearts, Nirad C. Chaudhuri recalled that, as a eight-year-old in Kishorganj, Bengal in the 1900s, though too young to have an understanding of the intellectual content of the new nationalism, he, like his friends, was swept along by its emotional fervour, which consisted of an almost religious hopefulness, a faith in the reality of India and her greatness. This faith, he was to analyse later, was fixed by a large number of patriotic songs, without which, he confessed, all their patriotic fervour would have soon vanished.[22]

In these years Tagore's Bengali poems were slowly being translated into English. Known as *Rabindra Sangeet* (the music of Tagore), they were filled with lyrical love for the country. Expressing almost a longing of the soul, they gave poignant reality to the nation through a constant evocation of its fields and rivers, its seasons and fragrances, its mountains and oceans.[23] The words and melodies sought to establish a sense of unity between the individual and the landscape, effacing all sense of time and movement, and giving the feeling of an eternal union. Tagore's *Sonar Bangla*, first sung at the New India Lecture in the Calcutta Town Hall in September 1905, had, maintained Bipin Chandra Pal, percolated down to the most illiterate classes of the community within less than six weeks.[24] Nirad C. Chaudhuri even years later, as an adult, could not read these songs without instantly recalling all the sounds and sights which evoked for him the idea of Bengal. However, as the nationalist movement took a more extremist turn in Bengal, he said, they began to find these very Tagore songs tame and uninspiring, pronouncing namby pamby sentiments. They then took to new songs and slogans that were more belligerent and also more Hindu in tone, as the widely adopted Maratha war-cry 'Hara,

[21] *Harijan*, 1 July 1939, p. 20.

[22] Nirad C. Chaudhuri, *The Autobiography of an Unknown Indian* (London, Macmillan, 1951, 11th edn, Delhi, Jaico Publishing House,1994), pp. 260–6.

[23] Tagore's reconciliation of the 'romantic' idealization of the nation with a critical analysis of society's abusive practices is analysed by Dipesh Chakrabarty, *Provincializing Europe. Postcolonial Thought and Historical Difference* (Princeton, Princeton University Press, 2000), ch. 6.

[24] Bipin Chandra Pal, *Swadeshi and Swaraj*, op. cit., p. 101.

Hara, Mahadev' (Hail Lord Shiva), or the song 'If I should die, By our Mother, let me die, Fighting for my land . . . The more our blood shall flow, The stronger should we grow . . .'[25] In contrast to Tagore's poems, these more militant calls to combat held greater appeal for the young.

The easy and rapid success of these songs could be partially explained by the fact that they were still close to the pattern of religious hymns. Traditional *kirtans* (group singing) gave way to nationalist *harikirtans* in which bhakti for God was adapted to love for the motherland.[26] It was gathered into a common pool of shared geographical, ethnographic, and epic associations. The shift from chants praising the lord to invocations of the mother-image of India, with her 'hurrying streams and rich green fields' (so ran a line of *Bande Mataram*), merging an aesthetic spirit with nationalism did not involve a significant rupture in styles and habits of expression and remained accessible to children and adults alike. This religious–political duality was brought out in the future national anthem *Jana gana mana adhinayaka jai hai* (Thou art the ruler of the minds of all people, dispenser of India's destiny) composed by Rabindranath Tagore and first sung at the Indian National Congress on 27 December 1911. It was welcomed both as an exaltation of the land Bharat (India), and as a hymn in praise of the lord of the universe. Thus, a few months after its composition, it was used as a devotional song at a religious ceremony, the Maghotsav, an annual spring festival of the Brahmos.[27]

As one journal put it, the patriotic songs of the 1900s 'make the heart beat thick and fast, and the blood tingle and leap and course in our veins.'[28] They were immediately integrated into annual Indian National Congress sessions which began with a national song set in different ragas, or prayers: 'Orissa, Bihar, Bengal, Oudh, Nepal,

[25] Nirad C. Chaudhuri, *Autobiography*, op. cit.

[26] Ellen E. McDonald, 'The Growth of Regional Consciousness in Maharashtra', *The Indian Economic and Social History Review*, no. 3, 1968, pp. 223–43.

[27] It was published under the title *Bharata Vidhata* in the *Tattvabodhini Patrika* (the official organ of the Adi Brahmo Samaj) of which Rabindranath was the editor. Cf. *Our National Anthem* (Delhi, Faculty of Arts, 1967), pp. 19–20.

[28] *Modern Review*, February 1912, p. 229.

Madras, Bombay and Rajputan! Hindu, Parsee and Jain, Sikh, Christian, Mussalman! Let every voice in concord ring, in every tongue the burden sing, all hail to Hindustan!' (Calcutta session, 1901).[29] Rabindranath Tagore's niece, Sarla Chaudhuri, had composed songs on the unity of India which were sung at the Indian National Congress of 1905 at Benares. Hymns from the Rig Veda were also adaptable to the new political ambitions. One of these '*Namo Namo Jagdish Essh Bhuvneshwar data, Namo Namo man Prannath Jag ke pitamata*' (Hail, hail Lord of the world, hail hail father and mother of the human race) opened the Congress session of 1912. Nivedita's impressions of the combined effect of the music and words, when sung by the entire assembly of Congress members in 1905, at Benaras, confirmed the political force of this medium when directed to the cause of the nation. She recorded that when it was sung the whole audience was thrown into a state of wild but dignified excitement.[30] Asaf Ali's experience of the Congress session of 1917 at Calcutta was similar; as was the custom, the opening notes of *Bande Mataram* inaugurated the annual meeting, inciting the entire audience to rise in a hush of almost devotional silence: 'the strains of the chorus and the band rose and filled the air. It was a moment of soul stirring solemnity. My eyes filled with tears. Insignificant and of no account individually, I was also a note in this grand orchestration of human aspiration.'[31]

Patriotic songs continued to inspire a strong following even after other modes of political action captured public attention. *Bande Mataram's* spectacular propagation has overshadowed an equally prolific and vigorous output of vernacular national songs that occupied political space from the 1900s, particularly in Marathi, Konkani, Hindi, Gujarati, and Tamil.[32] Like other national hymns and patriotic songs of their ilk all over the world, they turned around themes of

[29] K. Iswara Dutt, *Congress Cyclopaedia. The Indian National Congress: 1885–1920* (New Delhi, The Author, 1967), vol. 1, pp. 198–9.

[30] Moni Bagchee, *Bande Mataram* (Bombay, Bharatiya Vidya Bhavan, 1977), p. 16.

[31] M. Asaf Ali's memoirs, *The Emergence of Modern India* (Delhi, Ajanta, 1994), p. 130.

[32] NMML, Indian National Congress Report, 1920 (microfilm).

sacrifice, unity, and glory.[33] One Marathi song representative of this genre declared: 'Let us sing a victory song to the revolution, and for so doing, we shall take blows of thunderbolt on our chests. Let these heavy iron chains clatter in our legs and wrists. What do we care for them while we are at the threshold of death.'[34] They evoked the glories of their land, called for sacrifice, and recalled India's intrinsic unity and inevitable freedom. Their words, associations, and melodies were designed to touch hearts, and appeal to a source beyond regional boundaries, social origins, groups, and religious faiths. Even for sympathetic Britishers like C.F. Andrews or Annie Besant the images they proposed of the 'Mother' were equally accessible and appealing. Thus, Andrews made it the focus of his poem 'The Motherland', and so did Besant in 'Wake up India'. 'Arise! Ye sons of India! Be just and fear naught.'[35]

In the course of a decade the output of nationalist songs and poems in the North and South continued to cultivate the sensations of freedom in modes varying from the prayerful and spiritual to the revolutionary. Sarla Chaudhari's poems were succeeded by Anantarao Krishnaji Tekade's song in Marathi, at the 1920 Congress session '*Jai Hind Devichi bola, har har mahadev bola, gela gela rashtra dhurandhar, hrinuni sakal vadati.*'[36] The poet Bharati's songs on the cause of independence were published in Madras in 1922 in two volumes.[37] And

[33] Anne-Marie Losonczy, 'Dire, chanter et faire. La construction de la 'patrie' par l'hymne national hongrois et l'Exhortation', *Terrain*, no. 29, 1997, pp. 97–112; Christopher Kelen, 'Anthems of Australia: Singing Complicity', *National Identities*, vol. 5, no. 2, 2003, pp. 161–77; Serhy Yekelchyk, 'When Stalin's Nations Sang: Writing the Soviet Ukrainian Anthem 1944–1949', *Nationalities Papers*, vol. 31, no. 3, 2003, pp. 309–26; Chang-Tai Hung, 'The Politics of Songs: Myths and Symbols in the Chinese Communist War Music, 1937–1949', *Modern Asian Studies*, vol. 30, no. 4, 1996, pp. 901–29.

[34] Lt. Col. Gautam Sharma and R.K. Murthi, *Indian National Songs* (New Delhi, Reliance Publishing House, 1998), pp. 62–5, 90–3.

[35] R.K. Prabhu, *Indian National Songs* (Bombay, Popular Prakashan, 1966), pp. 6–7.

[36] NMML, Indian National Congress Report, 1920 (microfilm).

[37] Fifty-four of these songs compiled in *Swadesa Geethangal*, published from Madras, were proscribed by the governments of Madras and Burma in

Iqbal's *Sare Jahan se acha Hindustan Hamara, Ham bulbule hai iske, ye gulsitan hamara* (Our Hindustan is the best in the world, we are its innocent children, it is our garden) became an unofficial national anthem. Written in 1903 on the occasion of the anniversary of the Youngmen's Indian Association of Lahore,[38] it was instituted by Nehru in the school curriculum when he was chairman of the Allahabad Municipal Council in 1923 and was to become Indian television Doordarshan's signature tune in post-independent India: these lines were quoted by the first Indian astronaut on board a Soviet spaceship when asked by Prime Minister Indira Gandhi how India looked from space.[39]

Such songs were to capture the hearts and minds of more than one generation, rooting the sentiment of a united Indian people. Emotional renderings of *Swadeshi, Bande Mataram* and the Mother were made by women poets like Cuddalore Asalambigai Ammal and Chidambaram Agilandammal,[40] by Shanmugam Pillai of Madurai and by Subramania Bharati.[41] The future poet Harivansh Rai Bachchan's first efforts at composition in Hindi consisted of writing nationalist songs to be sung in processions after the salt satyagraha. One dramatic song, which proclaimed '*Sar jae to jae par Hind azadi pai*' (Our heads may fall but Hind will win freedom), was particularly successful.[42] The writer Shashi Deshpande remembered accompanying her parents to functions

---

1928. Cf. V. Venkat Raman, 'Subramania Bharathi and Colonial Proscription: 1928–1929', *Proceedings of the Indian History Congress, Kolkatta 2000–2001*, pp. 704–5.

[38] Iqbal was asked by the patriot and revolutionary Har Dayal to compose a poem for this celebration. Cf. Hira Lall Chopra, 'Iqbal and India', in Mohammad Haneef Shahid (ed.), *Tributes to Iqbal* (Lahore, Sangemeel Publications, 1977), pp. 219–9, esp. p. 220.

[39] Lt. Col. Gautam Sharma and R.K. Murthi, *Indian National Songs*, op. cit., p. 51.

[40] N. Rajendran, *National Movement in Tamil Nadu, 1905–14* (Madras, Oxford University Press, 1994), pp. 53–4.

[41] His song *Bande Mataram* was published in 1907 as a booklet by a moderate, V. Krishnaswamy Iyer, in Prema Nandakumar (ed.), *Poems of Subramania Bharati: A Selection in an English Verse* (New Delhi, Sahitya Akademi, 1977), p. 20.

[42] Harivansh Rai Bachchan, *In the Afternoon of Time. An Autobiography* (Delhi and London, Viking, 1998), p. 136.

of Independence Day after 1931 where girls, dressed simply in white saris with narrow borders, sang invocatory songs in praise of Bharat Mata.[43] The Indian National Army formed by Subhas Chandra Bose had a marching song that remained popular after independence, and it was only one example of a number of melodies that continued to resound and be mobilized through radio and films after 1947, particularly during the wars with Pakistan: *Kadam kadam badaye ja, tu khushi ke geet gaye ja, yeh zindagi hai kaum ki, tu kaum pe lutaye ja* (March forward step by step, singing songs of joy, this life is for the country, sacrifice it to the country).

Admittedly, national songs and poems fed a strong emotional current, targeting it towards a political idea of the nation. An aesthetically appealing political vehicle, these nurtured a shared sense of national belonging. As studies of Hungarian, Australian, Chinese patriotic songs and hymns also show, they were a classic medium for glorifying an attachment and loyalty to a territorial whole, to the soil, to ancestral heroes, myths, legends, and martyrs. In this sense they were a step forward from the basic emotion of humiliation and anger at colonial subjection. The idea and spirit of patriotism they promoted might well have been found in earlier times, but it was now being articulated more aggressively around demands for freedom and the denunciation of colonialism. Underlying this musical celebration, an education of sentiment in the cause of the nation through art was at work.

Notwithstanding their popularity and capacity to propagate an attachment to the motherland, they proved difficult to nationalize. Many of the vernacular songs remained unknown outside their regional frontiers. The few that did attain national popularity became almost immediately equally controversial. The most popular song of all, *Bande Mataram*, provoked a strong response of rejection from Muslims who considered it a sign of militant Hindu patriotism.[44]

[43] Shashi Deshpande, 'Them and Us', in Shirley Chew and Anna Rutherford (eds), *Unbecoming Daughters of the Empire* (Sydney, Dungaroo Press, 1993), pp. 101–6.

[44] While its first two stanzas began with acclaiming the motherland and its natural beauties, it went on to include graphic references to Hindu gods and goddesses: 'Mother I bow to thee, rich with thy hurrying stream, bright with thy orchard gleams, cool with thy winds of delight, dark fields waving, mother

Their hostility, already expressed in 1905, strengthened through the years, down to the Muslim League making the song's suppression a *sine qua non* of its co-operation with the Congress, and thence to Jinnah singling it out as proof of Hindu hostility and disrespect of Muslim sentiments.[45] It would need a constitutional measure in 1947 to finally oust this song from its position of a popularly acclaimed 'national' song. Furthermore, this poetic strain of national self-consciousness and self-perception lacked the insistence on political rights and duties that define citizenship.[46] In 1920, when the flag emerged at the centre of the political struggle, it would draw this emotional energy, crystallizing and unifying these sentiments, gathering and concentrating them into its fold.

Private Sentiment and Emotional Socialization

The conversion of the flag from a political abstraction to an object charged with individual and collective emotions was the result of a complex interaction between some philosophical ideas of Gandhi and different strands of emotions generated within the colonial frame. Its widespread presence and circulation through protest movements and beyond from the 1920s onwards made it a depository of a variety of primary and short-term reactions of anger, sadness, outrage, and longing. The particularity of this symbol and its political value lay in

---

of night, mother free. . . . Thou art Durga, Lady and Queen, with her hands that strike and her swords of sheen, thou art Lakshmi lotus-throned, and the muse a hundred toned, pure and perfect without peer, mother, lend thine ear' (Translation of Aurobindo Ghosh), in NMML, AICC Papers, file no. II/35, AICC Newsletter, Allahabad, 28 February 1935.

[45] The high points of this controversy can be traced in Nehru's correspondence with Subhas Chandra Bose in October 1937, in P.N. Chopra (ed.), *Towards Freedom, 1937–47*, vol. 1, *Experiment with Provincial Autonomy, 1 January–31 December 1937* (New Delhi, Indian Council of Historical Research, 1985), p. 1044, 1053. The Congress Working Committee's ruling on 28 October 1937 retained only the first two stanzas of the song and appointed a sub-committee to review national songs in order to choose one: pp. 1090–1.

[46] Edward Shils, *Tradition* (Chicago, University of Chicago Press, 1981).

transforming these temporary, short-lived responses to events and information into more permanent, shared feelings of loyalty to the nation. It socialized individual sensations into national patterns of political behaviour.

Presenting the Swaraj flag to the readers of his journal *Young India* in 1921, Gandhi began by declaring: 'A flag is a necessity for all nations. Millions have died for it. It is no doubt a kind of idolatry, which it would be a sin to destroy. For a flag represents an ideal . . . It will be necessary for us Indians-Hindus, Mahomedans, Christians, Jews, Parsis, and all others to whom India is their home—to recognize a common flag to live and to die for.'[47] Although vigorously opposed to any mimesis of the West, Gandhi was convinced that the flag would permit the development of an emotional attachment to the nation and identification with other Indians. Committed since his South African years to the idea of non-violent political action arising from a love free of hatred or anger for all human beings, Gandhi saw the flag as a perfect instrument for their struggle. The idea of individuals merging into a larger entity, which was itself integrated into a largely international reality, namely humanity, had also been enunciated by Bengali thinkers and nationalists like Aurobindo, Pal, and Tagore in a frame of 'spiritual nationalism'.[48] They rejected a material and historical framework of national movements as Western and foreign to the Indian situation. But they did not go as far as giving a material form to this idea—as Gandhi did.

In his philosophy the flag, incarnating the nation, was to be the source of an emotional community that would unite all Indians in a shared battle. Reminding them of their ultimate goal, it would draw them into a net of solidarity, concentrating their passions and energy for the motherland. Gandhi's total opposition to the methods of both extremists and moderates—both ultimately relying on violence—was enunciated as early as 1909.[49] Expressed in his words as love conquering

[47] M.K. Gandhi, 'The National Flag', *Young India*, 13 April 1921, p. 116.

[48] On this proposition, see Arundhati Virmani, 'The Burden of the Past. L'uso politico della storia nell'India coloniale del ventesimo secolo', *Storica*, no. 22, 2002, pp. 103–33.

[49] M.K. Gandhi, *Hind Swaraj and Other Writings* (ed.), Anthony J. Parel (Cambridge, Cambridge University Press, 1997), p. 135.

hatred, or a universal love for all human beings (even the adversary), these ideas were not easily acceptable or even accessible as a political strategy. They had already proved their power to irritate, antagonize and even repel some people since the first experiments in South Africa. Sceptics considered them 'pernicious', 'utterly disastrous to the public welfare', 'mere anarchy', in short, an idea that was clearly fatal for Western nations and South Africa.[50] Gandhi, though resolutely placing himself outside political customs and norms, nevertheless realized that the inner shift from rampant, unrestrained emotions to love, or what he called self-realization, had to be clothed in a political language that was accessible to the people. His idea that only those Indians who were imbued with real love would be able to speak to the English without being frightened, needed more than personal conviction to touch the masses.[51] In 1920 his wanderings in India made him realize that his compatriots had not yet reached a conscious recognition of their national state. He hoped that the flag would awaken in them this principle of love through self-suffering and peace. For, he maintained, '*satyagraha* admits of no violence, no pillage, no incendiarism'.[52] The flag would enable them to apply these principles indiscriminately to the British, to Muslims, to Harijans. It would lead to the development of a community of feeling.

Gandhi developed a historical and comparative reflection on the flag, giving examples of the flag's sacralization in Western countries, its role in inspiring sacrifice for the honour of those nations, arousing love, courage, enthusiasm, and devotion, and evoking common memories.[53] Every strong nation or community provided an example of the emotional bonding generated and sustained by the flag. He drew attention to the British, American, and Muslim relationship with their country's banner: 'The unfurling of the Union Jack evokes in the

[50] This was the judgement of W.J. Wybergh, theosophist, member of the Transvaal legislature and commissioner of mines. Cf. M.K. Gandhi, *Hind Swaraj*, op. cit., p. 143.

[51] M.K. Gandhi, *Hind Swaraj*, op. cit., p. 116.

[52] *Speeches and Writings of Mahatma Gandhi*, p. 474, quoted in M.K. Gandhi, *India of My Dreams* (Ahmedabad, 1st edn, 1947, 7th edn, 1999), p. 86.

[53] His principal ideas were developed in an article published in *Young India*, 13 April 1921, analysed in the following paragraphs.

English breast, sentiments whose strength it is difficult to measure. The Stars and Stripes mean a world to the Americans. The Star and the Crescent will call forth the best bravery in Islam.'[54] This very awareness made the adoption of a national flag such a difficult task for Gandhi. He explained:

> Mr P. Venkayya of the National College, Masulipatam has for some years placed before the public a suggestive booklet describing the flags of the other nations and offering designs for an Indian National Flag. But, whilst I have always admired the persistent zeal with which Mr. Venkayya has pursued the cause of a national flag at every session of the Congress for the past four years, he was never able to enthuse me; and in his designs, I saw nothing to stir the nation to its depths.

The words mirrored Gandhi's political predicament. He was convinced that the flag was an essential element of their political battle because it had the power to unite Indians against the British and among themselves. And yet the flag must contain something that could attract people, stir them into action, bind them together and make them forget their different origins, faiths, customs. This ingredient had to be identified and present in the flag, and Gandhi did not find it in the numerous designs composed by Venkayya, ranging from the Indian deities, flora and fauna, historical legends, and myths. His first task therefore consisted of assembling the elements that were capable of speaking to the people, touching their hearts, igniting the first spark of interest.

'I personally feel that the spinning-wheel and *khadi* are the very soul of our flag; and a national flag which is printed on uncertified *khadi* and without the spinning-wheel mark on it, or a paper flag cannot be a national flag', wrote one correspondent to Gandhi in the spring of 1940.[55] This testimony, given twenty years later, clearly

[54] This political argument was developed in the following years, notably by C.R. Rajagopalachari ('The Flag Calls You', *Young India*, 22 March 1923, p. 91), and echoed by some editorials ('Honour the Flag', *The Hindu*, 27 June 1923, p. 3), until its lengthy treatment by Suniti Kumar Chatterji ('The National Flag', *Modern Review*, June 1931; reprinted in *The National Flag. A Selection of Papers, Cultural and Historical* (Calcutta, Mitra & Ghosh, 1944), pp. 1–12.

[55] Ibid.

confirms that Gandhi's decision to put the charkha on a piece of indigenous handspun cloth called khadi was a key factor in the emotional success of the flag. Khadi referred to the swadeshi agitation of 1905, the first tentative to infuse national pride by urging the use of Indian goods.[56] Gandhi's campaign from 1920 to popularize the spinning wheel had sprung from the conviction that it was 'the most important, common factor of national life'. This movement was amplified by the creation of the All India Spinners' Association (AISA) in 1925, which organized competitions, demonstrations and tours all over the country, especially in 1926–8.[57] The rediscovered practice of spinning by each individual made it possible for Indians to appropriate it exclusively. Love for the nation was thus not a mere abstract notion or idea articulated by intellectuals or political leaders, nor an artificial, moral maxim borrowed from other political traditions. Instead, it was the outcome of each Indian's investment in shared and dignified manual labour. As khadi was transformed through the flag into the symbol of the Indian nation, every individual who spun cotton thread and wove cotton could feel himself to be a 'producer' of the nation, which could then be considered an extension of the self. In fact, as Gandhi would insist later, 'any rag could not be used as a flag'.[58]

In spite of differences over political strategies and goals that continued to plague and divide Indians in the 1920s, the nationalization of the flag progressed through these years. For political activists and leaders broadly agreed that the fight for the nation's liberty implied building up national emotion at different levels. Lala Lajpat Rai had already pointed to the American use of flags and banners in parades to appeal to the emotions. His observations of the American political system led him to conclude: 'Moulding opinion was purely a matter

[56] C.A. Bayly, 'The Origins of *Swadeshi* (home industry): Cloth and Indian Society, 1700–1930', in Arjun Appadurai (ed.), *The Social Life of Things. Commodities in Cultural Perspective* (Cambridge, Cambridge University Press, 1990), pp. 285–321.

[57] Lisa N. Trivedi, 'Visually Mapping the "Nation": *Swadeshi* Politics in Nationalist India, 1920–1930', *Journal of Asian Studies*, LXII, 2003, pp. 11–41.

[58] 22 April 1940, Sevagram, *CWMG*, LXXII, *16 April–11 September 1940* (Government of India, Ministry of Information & Broadcasting, 1980), p. 14.

of psychology.'[59] The Maharashtrian lawyer M.R. Jayakar stressed the importance of including this factor in their electoral battles to C.R. Das, his Bengali counterpart and spokesman in 1923. He pointed out its value in organizing civil resistance to British rule in the country, reminding Das that civil disobedience on abstract principles was a lost cause. Jayakar was not alone in his conviction that in the struggle against colonial rule 'it was useless to talk of satyagraha until and unless that spirit and desire was created amongst the people which would prompt them to think that they should either get *Swaraj* or die for it.'[60] Motilal Nehru too affirmed that if they were to reach across districts and provinces, across British India to princely India, it could not be exclusively through the force of a reasoned, rational demonstration of the ills of colonialism and of British rule in India, or uniquely through means of a well-organized political body like the Indian National Congress. Dissensions and apathy could only be overtaken by a feeling of unity created by the power of a national emotion.[61]

Yet, it was one thing to reiterate that the flag could inspire love, devotion, heroism, and sacrifice, and quite another to translate these words into a widespread gut reaction that would continue beyond particular events like those of Jubbulpore or Nagpur in 1923, for example, and also reach out to all Indians—even those who were not particularly involved in resistance, or convinced by Gandhi's calls to fast, purify, and recover national dignity and liberty. For these passive observers and spectators, all those who remained on the margins of the struggle, other paths of assimilation into a nationalist ethos were required if the flag was to become anything other than simply a symbol of a 'political fight between rulers and ruled in British territory'.[62] This extension of the flag from cloth to emotion was not, could not, entirely

[59] He wrote the 'Teaching of Patriotism' in the *Modern Review* in 1919; reprinted in Shri Ram Bakshi (ed.), *Lajpat Rai. Swaraj and Social Change* (New Delhi, H.K. Publishers and Distributors, 1990), vol. 2, *The Teaching of Patriotism 1919–1922*, pp. 650–5.

[60] M.R. Jayakar, *The Story of My Life, 1922–25* (London, Asia Publishing House, 1959), vol. 2, pp. 105–6.

[61] Ibid.

[62] *The Hindu*, 16 July 1931.

be an imposition from above. In the colonial context, acts like hoisting and saluting the flag implied a personal, voluntary, sometimes risky adherence. This attachment could not be forced, it could be suggested. It was necessarily an option available among others to people. They could as well continue to proffer loyalty to the Union Jack or to other symbols that were being proposed by political parties.

In the various protest actions through the 1920s and 1930s—satyagrahas, processions, public speeches, gatherings, salt-making, Flag Day or Independence Day rituals in cities and in the countryside—the flag's invariable presence made it the repository of a range of sentiments. As Nehru would remind his compatriots in 1947, in the ups and downs of their struggle for the nation 'we looked up to this Flag not only with pride and enthusiasm, but a tingling in our veins . . . when we were sometimes down and out, the sight of this Flag gave us courage to go on.'[63] Indians were gradually drawn into the flag's orbit. The growing list of martyrs for the flag, both men and women all over British India, from Nagpur to Madras, Calcutta to Karachi, in Bihar, Punjab, and even Mysore in princely India, reinforced its political image and national status.

Displaying it on tongas, scooters and cars, schools and colleges, on badges, walking sticks, clothes, stationary, in religious ceremonies and rituals of ear piercing,[64] all made it an omnipresent sign, both on scenes of action and in more commonplace situations. Flag songs authored by enthusiastic amateur poets expanded its reach. Produced independently of any guidelines from above, they brought the values of public national interest into private, intimate space. '*Jhanda vandan*' (Flag prayer), in the pattern of traditional hymnology, described the flag as wanting the good of everyone, not as a banner of war or conflict, bringing home to all the love for truth and non-violence.[65] '*Jai tiranga dhvaja*' (Long live the tricolour banner), '*Jhanda gayan*' (Flag song) spoke of the love and harmony bestowed by the flag, '*Sankalp*' (resolution), '*Lahar tirange*' (Fly tricolour), and '*Jai rashtriya nishan*'

[63] Address to the Constituent Assembly, 22 July 1947, in *Our Flag*, op. cit., p. 8.

[64] *Young India*, 3 April 1923, p. 17.

[65] '*Sabka suhit, sumangal subka, nahin vair vidhesh; lahar uthe jan jan ke man me satya ahimsa pyar*', '*Jhanda vandan*' (Flag prayer), ibid., p. 15.

(Long life to the symbol of the nation) popularized the national idea through melodies and stirring music.[66] Processions in the Nagpur flag satyagraha started with songs like 'The flag of *Bharat Bhumi* (the land of Bharat) shall never bend.'[67] Their dramatization of exploits related to the flag in a set vocabulary laid down a clearly identifiable pattern of political behaviour and national loyalties. One of the prominent converts to the central place of a national flag in their struggle, we have seen, was Motilal Nehru. In 1923 he had criticized the organization of a satyagraha for the flag, as a distraction,[68] incapable of instilling a high consciousness of patriotism among the masses.[69] But by 1925 he too had included the flag in his political vocabulary, pointing to the symbol's capacity to unite in his speeches.[70]

By directing love for the nation to the flag, Gandhi hoped to transfer what Bengali orators had seen only as a 'robust religious emotion' for the motherland in 1905, into a quintessential non-religious object. In the process he expanded its limits to include even broader currents of feeling: of oneness with fellow countrymen, tolerance, acceptance, and identification. 'Salutation of the national flag is in my opinion unobjectionable', Gandhi explained to C.F. Andrews in 1925. 'I see nothing inherently wrong about it. A national spirit is necessary for national existence. The flag is a material aid to the development of such a spirit.'[71] It was the symbol of a political culture based on love that Gandhi was trying to elaborate. Nehru realized this when he wrote that Gandhi 'spoke to the heart of India . . . and the heart of India responded. In a sudden movement her fetters began to be loosened, and the pathway of freedom was opened.'[72]

[66] A number of compilations of national songs can be found, but none trouble to date these compositions. For example, R.K. Prabhu's op. cit., or Omdat Sharma, *Hamare Rashtriya Geet* (Delhi, Vikas Paperbacks, 1999).

[67] *The Hindu*, 16 June 1923.

[68] See ch. 3.

[69] M.R. Jayakar, *The Story of My Life*, op. cit., p. 106.

[70] *Hindustan Times*, 28 October 1925; *The Pioneer*, 30 December 1928.

[71] Gandhi to C.F. Andrews, 25 April 1925, *CWMG*, XXVI, January–April 1925 (Ahmedabad, 1967), p. 544.

[72] Jawaharlal Nehru, *An Autobiography* (London, Oxford University Press, 1936, 9th edn, 1995), p. 67.

It was precisely because the flag could lend itself to the everyday, ordinary, even discrete forms of nationalist affirmation, from envelopes to clothes, and absorb and mirror a variety of commonplace sentiments, that it could be both a symbol of a free nation as well as an emotional, political statement.[73] When, for example, Santha Rama Rao returned to India in 1939 after her education abroad, she was struck by the ubiquity of the flag's colours. During a lecture to girl students of Lady Irwin College, Delhi, she observed that all the students usually wore white cotton saris with the flag colours on the borders.[74] Nation-building was no longer only a matter of institutional affiliation, street action or politics. It had, thanks to the flag, also permeated individual tastes, moods, and styles of dress.

A similar conclusion can be obtained from the recollections of a young schoolgirl at Patna in the 1940s. Meenakshi Mukherjee, compelled by her age and protective milieu to be on the margins of the nationalist movement, but in search of ways to express her 'sentimental patriotism', found a satisfactory outlet in sketching the flag. Diligently, she and her friends at Bankipore Girls' High School drew and coloured the flag wherever they could, even on textbook covers, greeting cards, and letters. They meticulously numbered the twenty-two spokes of the blue wheel of dharma on the white section that separates the saffron and the green of the tricolour, passionately inscribing it with slogans like *Jai Hind* and *Bande Mataram*. A friend embroidered the flag on a handkerchief; another girl wore a sari with a flag border. They displayed tricolour badges as they did gymnastics in the school playground by the Ganges and vigorously sang Hindi and Bengali songs about national solidarity. As they inscribed the flag on their stationery and belongings, the notion of dharma was foremost in their minds. It showed the extent to which these principles had permeated the flag and political culture.[75] A multiplicity of meanings—sacrifice, discipline,

[73] A stamped envelope addressed to Rajendra Prasad carried the flag with the words *Hindustan ka jhanda* (the flag of India), NMML, AICC Papers, file no. III/35.

[74] Santha Rama Rao, *Home to India* (New York, Harper and Brothers, 1944), p. 94.

[75] Meenakshi Mukherjee, 'Growing Up by the Ganga', in Shirley Chew and Anna Rutherford (eds), *Unbecoming Daughters*, op. cit., p. 111.

self-control, non-violence—and sentiments like reverence, devotion, and fearlessness were bound to the flag from the political battles it was linked to, from rituals and celebrations, songs, films, and dramas. These meanings jostled with each other, fusing to form a monolithic whole, sometimes striking one particular chord or another in the observer. All these emotions rooted in everyday life were now bound to a symbol of national sovereignty that three decades ago was quite unknown. More than that, they were legitimized as politically relevant forms of behaviour.

In 1923 the claim of 'the hold of the tri-coloured *khadi* on the nation's mind'[76] had appeared a nationalist boast. But the following years were to reinforce this idea. Hitherto distant spectators admitted it was the flag that proved the decisive turning point in the directions of their lives and their activities. For Vejubhai Shah of Gujarat, for example, who went to Lahore in December 1929 simply to attend the annual Congress session the sight of the flag was a revelation which transformed him, he said, into 'a changed person'.[77] His nationalism was not a reasoned, political decision, arrived at after long reflection, reading and analysis. It was an unmeditated, sudden emotive response, yet profound enough to determine his subsequent choices. In a similar vein, Dr D.N. Pai, future director of family planning in the Bombay Municipal Corporation after Independence, recounted how he suddenly became a nationalist at fifteen, when he witnessed the unfurling of the Indian national flag and the lathi charge at Gwalior Tank, Bombay in 1942.[78] For Indians like these, expressions such as the 'object of worship round which gather devotees',[79] 'an emblem of unity and peace . . . a sign of love and good-will',[80] 'the emblem of liberty',[81] were not simply words, but feelings that 'spring up spontaneously, self prompted by the first glance at the waving scarf, the first grip of the hand upon its staff'.[82] The flag could now evoke the qualities promised by its

[76] *The Hindu*, 27 June 1923.
[77] CSAS, tape recording of Vejubhai Shah.
[78] CSAS, tape recording of Dr D.N. Pai.
[79] *Janmabhumi*, 5 July 1923.
[80] *The Hitavada*, 30 May 1923, p. 5.
[81] *The Hindu*, 7 July 1923.
[82] *The Hindu*, 27 June 1923.

proponents in 1917 or 1923: a spirit of enthusiasm, a 'madness of devotion',[83] 'calling up a passion that none outside could understand'[84] 'the representation of our dream', or 'a concrete and static embodiment of a spiritual and dynamic idea', 'a fountain of power' and 'inspiration'.[85] For many Indians its importance was a reminder of the roles it had played in the past; of royal standard, military banner, religious symbol . . . the flag too had its lineage.[86] The use of the tricolour on Motilal Nehru's death in 1931 to cover his body conveyed its new status.[87] It had become the ultimate sign of acknowledgement of national service and public respect.

Even when initial reactions had been forgotten or replaced by more pragmatic behaviour, a sudden sight of the flag could revive memories buried somewhere in the unconscious, establishing a continuity of national emotion that went back and forth from earlier movements of anticolonial protest to the present. Such was the experience of the hero of the novel *So Many Hungers*. Rahul, an 'England returned' astrophysicist in Calcutta University, has long forgotten his youthful emotional response to the civil disobedience movement. And yet, when, from his laboratory window in 1942, he watches huge demonstrations of thousands carrying the tricolour, armed with nothing but non-violence and sees the police charge and fire upon people ready to carry out Gandhi's command of 'Do or die', he is lost: 'emotion flooded up in him and he bounced down to the street, possessed with only one thought: Hold up the flag.'[88]

Besides serving as a factor of social action, the flag's association with groups like women and children communicated an additional emotive

[83] P.A. Venkayya, op. cit., p. 60.

[84] Ibid., p. 54.

[85] *New India*, 31 August 1917, p. 6.

[86] *The Hindu*, 10 July 1923.

[87] His daughter described the moment: 'Father's body covered with our orange, green and white national flag, was put in an automobile. A huge Indian flag flew from the car'; 'We came through the iron gates of Anand Bhavan. I looked up to see the tall flagpole on the roof from which our national flag always flew defiantly high; it was at half-mast.' Krishna Nehru Hutheesing, *We Nehrus* (Bombay, Pearl Books, 1968), pp. 100–1.

[88] Bhabani Bhattacharya, *So Many Hungers* (London, Left Book Club, Victor Gollancz, 1947), p. 66.

Illustr. 5. Women demonstrating with the flag on the Maidan, Bombay, July 1930. (Roger Viollet.)

power to the symbol. The first photographs published in foreign magazines at the beginning of the 1930s were of women saluting the flag, carrying it in processions, and being lathi-charged by the police. (Illustr. 5.) From the first appearance of the flag in the hands of Bhikaji Cama in 1907 at Stuttgart—highly remarked by the foreign press—to the 1930s, the relationship of women with the flag, from the act of production to its physical absorption in their clothes, created an intensity of emotion that made the flag like their personal possession. On the one hand, women presented a specifically intimate way of relating to the flag; on the other, they placed feminine patterns of feeling squarely at the heart of a political process. Gandhi considered their silence as a specific contribution to the success of demonstrations and exhibitions. Women, urged Gandhi, should refuse to be swept off their feet and imitate men's language.[89] It was no coincidence that it was a woman, Sarojini Naidu, who recapitulated the flag's growth in such

[89] *Harijan*, 13 July 1940, reprinted in *CWMG*, vol. LXXII, op. cit., p. 207.

personal terms of 'tears', 'anguish', and 'desire' in the Constituent Assembly in 1947. As after 1921, stories in the press related how women were displaying the flag's colours on their saris, tearing them up to make a flag, suffering police violence and imprisonment to vindicate its 'honour': they were integrating womanly intuition or feeling into a national political culture. What had been until then 'feminine' stereotypes—honour, sacrifice, suffering, effacement in favour of the family—idealized in the form of an eternal 'Mother' and a source of inspiration for a 'masculine' nationalism—were assimilated into the flag as emotional patterns common to all. The flag provided a means to translate a certain kind of femininity into an active, explicitly dynamic political culture, effacing to some extent the boundaries between passive, romantic 'sentimentalism', and 'political sentiment'.

The role given to children in public processions and demonstrations further helped project images of confidence, bravery, and pride onto the symbol and largely contributed to develop national feelings in the family sphere by becoming a part of games or private behaviour. Children magnified the emotional attitudes they observed in public space. In 1923 it was young ten-year-olds who were hoisting the flag in the town hall of Nagpur, singing flag songs and displaying it in the court premises.[90] Vijaya Lakshmi Pandit recalled how for her children the flag had become a kind of charm to ward off evil. When in 1932 she and her husband were arrested, she told her daughter who was clutching a large national flag: 'Don't carry that flag, darling.' But the little girl refused to give it up, insisting, 'It is to frighten the police with'.[91] The response was almost identical to the sentiment expressed by bands of satyagrahis who faced the police armed with nothing but the flag when they broke the salt laws, or marched peacefully in the streets.

Newspapers printed letters and statements on readers' relationship with the flag. One of the most frequently used expressions was 'sacred emblem of suffering and sacrifice'. They described their own perceptions: 'stuck to the nation', 'difficult for the people to tear themselves away from it', and able to infuse 'enthusiasm and courage even

[90] *The Hindu*, 1 June 1923.

[91] Vijaya Lakshmi Pandit, *The Scope of Happiness*, op. cit., p. 165.

amongst children'.[92] These illustrate what the flag meant to many Indians: 'not a mere rag of coloured cloth' but a 'perpetual reminder of nationhood',[93] 'welcomed, adorned and worshipped',[94] building up a narrative of its power to transform. Accompanying political clashes deepened the flag's national meanings, contributing to the development of the 'shared feeling' considered to hold nations together. Apa Pant, heir to the small principality of Aundh, confessed that to his mind being a socialist revolutionary committed to the freedom struggle included 'the waving of flags, emotional speeches, thunderous applause . . .'[95] For those who were reluctant and unwilling to venture into anything more daring, flag waving was a sufficiently meaningful gesture of adherence to the nation and to a national community. For the many others more deeply involved in the nationalist movement, the description of these years of marches and propaganda work, imprisonment and protest, often turned around the flag.

The culmination of this outpouring of emotion for the flag came in 1947, a month before independence. On the publication of a flag supplement in the nationalist English daily *Hindustan Times*, on 28 July 1947, readers shared their 'great joy', 'thrill', 'pride', the 'tears of emotion' on receiving the 'sacred gift' of the national flag, which was 'rooted in the heart of millions' and now in their homes. Others described the 'surging emotions and sentiments' at the sight of the flag that reminded them 'of the tremendous hardships' through which their country had lived.[96] In 1931, a campaign, had invited readers to share their views and opinions about the flag in order to help the Indian National Congress devise a symbol that corresponded to a widespread public sentiment. Now, on the eve of independence, a similar process gathered the positive emotions of approval, pride, satisfaction, gratitude, solidarity, and hope around the flag and transferred them to the

[92] OIOC, L/R/5/99, *Indian Newspaper Reports, United Provinces of Agra and Oudh*, for the week ending 2 August 1930.

[93] *The Mahratta*, 25 July 1931, Nayan H. Pandia, Bombay.

[94] *The Hindu*, 30 July 1931, T. Prakasam, Mysore.

[95] Apa Pant, *An Unusual Raja. Mahatma Gandhi and the Aundh Experiment* (Hyderabad, Sarigam Books, 1989), p. 44.

[96] *Hindustan Times*, 5, 6, 8 August 1947.

nation. Expressed in simple language, dissociated from party politics or positions, the very repetitiveness and simplicity of these communications strengthened some basic points about being part of a national community.[97]

A small corpus of a hundred-odd letters to the editor in 1947 provides an insight into the flag's passage from a political symbol in public space to an almost personal possession or feeling, alongside poems, songs, music, rituals, and collective action. Its significance was explained not in terms of an object people thought about or understood but in terms of how they related to it, or the effect it had on them. In itself this was unremarkable—as Robert Bonner shows, the same expressions and associations could be found two centuries earlier in a different continent in the pens of southerners defending the Confederate flag in the 1860s.[98] Even if the views expressed in 1947 are but a partial representation by the newspapers, the persistent reproduction of this kind of epistolary communication, projecting sentiment outside the boundaries of the intimate, confidential realm, made it a shared public reality. A huge emotional crucible was created in which it was possible to find a ready-made national sentiment and make it one's own.[99]

It would be too simple to consider these accounts merely as part of personal, private memories, family histories, or anecdotes, fascinating and moving to read but of little explanatory value in understanding the course of social and political movements. It is equally unwise to dismiss them as retrospective intellectual reconstructions of personal itineraries around an object that had become a sacralized, legitimate symbol of nationhood. On the contrary, emotions were crucial, at times decisive in determining individual choices, political action, and

[97] Not all daily newspapers printed such letters. Notable among the English dailies that contain nothing in these years are *The Statesman* and *The Times of India*. The Hindi newspaper *Aaj*, apart from a few snippets of information, did not dwell on the subject. On the contrary, *The Hindu*, *The Mahratta*, *Hitavada*, *Bombay Chronicle*, and *Janmabhumi* were at the forefront in communicating views and opinions on this issue. In 1947 the flag was a prominent item of news and discussion in *The Hindustan Times*.

[98] Robert E. Bonner, *Colors and Blood. Flag Passions of the Confederate South* (Princeton, Princeton University Press, 2002).

[99] *The Hindu*, 6 August 1931, Letter to the Editor, K.S. Gopalakrishnan, Madras.

behaviour. Even in the 1930s and 1940s, these feelings could influence people's actions and behaviour and determine public postures. Indeed, it was the shift in the emotional mood of these years that constituted the deep 'psychological change' many held to be necessary for the emergence of the Indian nation. In his analysis of these years of struggle, the imprisoned Nehru recognized the importance of this 'vital upheaval from within . . . the soul of India itself', which C.F. Andrews had analysed as the essential, primordial need of Indian nationalism. The passionate intensity built up around the flag had succeeded in gathering the 'confused desires of the people' and giving form to this upheaval.[100]

A Gandhian Emotional Regime

On the one hand the flag was permitting the interiorization of national sentiment. On the other it was serving as a factor of an 'emotional socialization' that gathered these feelings in a common political vocabulary and practices. But the particularity of Gandhi's 'emotional regime' constructed around the Indian flag was to canalize this national emotion in 'the requisite discipline, spirit of self-sacrifice, humility and resoluteness of will'.[101] The distinctive feature of the flag as a tool in their anti-colonial struggle was its pacific nature. It was not linked with killing and bloodshed—the more classic, militaristic, aggressive sentiment that had characterized the Confederate struggle in America or the French anti-German sentiment.[102] Rather, Gandhi saw it as an instrument of civilizing the passions of Indians, not by dulling them into a sentimental state of euphoric well being but by strengthening them through a form of action that called for mastery over passions. This control also imposed a similar restraint on the British authorities, obliging them to respond with moderation and

[100] Jawaharlal Nehru, *An Autobiography*, op. cit., p. 67. Urvashi Butalia suggests, in the context of Partition stories, that emotions crucially determined political action. See her *The Other Side of Silence: Voices from the Partition of India* (London, C. Hurst, 2000).

[101] 'The Satyagraha Week', *Young India*, 31 March 1920, p. 3.

[102] This aspect is examined at length by Robert E. Bonner, *Colors and Blood*, op. cit., pp. 67–96.

consideration. It troubled the conventional lines and norms of political confrontation.

Gandhi wished to see this shared emotion move individuals and crowds to a behaviour that was disciplined and orderly, 'There should be no trace of bitterness, no violence of language, but absolute fearlessness and firmness', he had announced in 1920.[103] His long combat to command his own emotions, whether desire, fear or dislike, anger and hate of the opponent, led him to see this self-control as a necessary code of political conduct for the crowd. Hence, instead of being satisfied with the flag producing enthusiasm, Gandhi wished it to pacify and restrain. While he encouraged mass involvement in politics he was also equally fanatical about the need to master collective emotions.

Nonetheless, many of his contemporaries remained wary of mixing up passions in politics. Tagore, for example, who had given much thought to the gulf separating Western and Indian civilization in their understanding and uses of 'collective feeling and ideas', decried the force of passion when it was at the helm of social and political movements. He considered that it was the generalized passion for power and wealth that had inevitably nurtured the principle of separation and conflict in the West. Sceptical of the constructive power of passions in the course of humanity, Tagore, on the contrary, believed in the passion for ideals. Although it appeared evident to him that 'red tape can never be a common human bond', or that 'official sealing-wax can never provide means of mutual attachment',[104] this belief did not propel him to approve the upsurge of passion that animated students in the Swadeshi movement in 1905, leading them to confuse renunciation of education in British institutions with national feeling and action. By 1921 Tagore was frankly expressing his dismay at what he termed the 'fanaticism of the crowds'. He disapproved of the turn the nationalist movement had taken, with non-cooperation gaining ground, and the boycott of schools and colleges. In his eyes this presented a source of danger rather than fulfilment. Nehru too, though convinced of the necessity of the Gandhian method to reach the pulse of the masses and

[103] 'The 6th of April and the 13th', *Young India*, 10 March 1920, p. 3.

[104] Krishna Dutta and Andrew Robinson (eds), *Rabindranath Tagore. An Anthology* (London, Picador, 1997), p. 212.

admiring the moral and ethical side of satyagraha, was sometimes driven to doubt its capacity to control the emotional surge that tended to spill over into violence. From 1932 to 1933 Nehru, watching the emotional upheaval of the country, Gandhi's fasts, and the suspension of civil disobedience 'wondered more and more if this was the right method in politics'. For Gandhi 'did not encourage others to think; his insistence was only on purity and sacrifice.'[105] Nehru also held this mass involvement and fervour, this 'mob-hysteria', to be one of the reasons for Jinnah's estrangement from the Congress.[106]

Seen from a distance the Indian national movement thus seemed to contain two distinct, even incompatible, strains. To the French writer Romain Rolland, for example, these two currents were epitomized by the two greatest leaders of the Orient, Gandhi and Tagore. The first embodied the emotion and élan indispensable to a national movement; the second represented the tradition of studies and reflection.[107] This distinction between a sphere of mass action, led by the sway of unreliable and dangerous passions, and a sphere of rational commitment to justice or freedom could have been the reflection of a Western mind fashioned by the tradition of the Enlightenment. Tagore also rearticulated a similar dichotomy. In his opinion, Gandhi's political strategies of boycott and non-cooperation invited the abandon of discipline and control, and the poet had little confidence in Gandhi's advocacy of the methods of fasting and self-imposed values of truth. He shared his misgivings with Andrews, admitting that they remained, despite 'striving with all my power to tune my mood of mind to be in accord with the great feeling of excitement sweeping across my country'. Non-cooperation, wrote Tagore, drew attention to the negative aspect, a 'joy of annihilation' that 'in its active moral form is violence.'[108] But while Tagore stressed the path of analysis, contemplation, and studied action, Gandhi upheld the validity of emotions as a force to be captured and directed, not necessarily relegated to the realm of superstition,

105 J. Nehru, *An Autobiography*, op. cit., p. 373.

106 Ibid., p. 68.

107 Romain Rolland, *Mahatma Gandhi* (Paris, Stock, 1924), p. 125.

108 Rabindranath Tagore to Charles Freer Andrews, Chicago, 5 March 1921, in Krishna Dutta and Andrew Robinson (ed.), *Rabindranath Tagore*, op. cit., pp.168–73.

religion, and the substratum of political life. Finally Tagore too, though critical of these unknown, unpredictable, and risky paths of political action that Gandhi advocated, could not reject the emotional appeal of the flag. It was sufficiently modern to reassure those who feared a resurgence of religious passions, and satisfy others who desired a strong object of national veneration.

In 1920 Gandhi reminded Indians that National Week (6–13 April) was designed towards the end of purification, self-examination, sacrifice, and exact discipline.[109] Every national commemoration if approached with this intention would lead inevitably to the qualities that formed the basis of swaraj, mainly humility, a renewed dedication to truth, love, and non-injury. 'There can be no room for selfishness, anger, lack of faith, or impatience in a pure fast . . . Infinite patience, firm resolve, single-mindedness of purpose, perfect calm, and no anger must of necessity be there.'[110] Forming a coherent whole, these two facets—love and self-discipline—were to be fed by the flag.

This 'emotional regime' was considered by Gandhi to be the basis of the political culture required by the freedom struggle. At the apex of his system stood the flag, epitomizing a source of national feeling that was being fashioned by his system of controlled collective force. When Gandhi voiced these tenets in a book, *Self Restraint vs. Self-Indulgence*, published in 1927, the first edition sold out in a week and solicited a large correspondence from its readers.[111] Young Indians like Nehru were particularly impressed by the success of this approach, combining an appeal to the crowd's emotions and its management towards the end of colonial subjection.

After the massacre of policemen by the crowds at Chauri Chaura in 1922,[112] mob violence had led Gandhi to suspend non-coopera-tion and raised doubts about the effectiveness and practicability of

[109] *Young India*, 10 March 1920, p. 3. He developed these ideas in his articles on satyagraha week or national week in his journals, *Harijan*, 18 March 1939 and *Young India*, 31 March 1920, p. 3.

[110] *Young India,* ibid.

[111] Joseph S. Alter, *Gandhi's Body, Sex, Diet and the Politics of Nationalism* (Philadelphia, University of Pennsylvania Press, 2000), pp. 8–9.

[112] On this crucial event, cf. Shahid Amin, *Event, Metaphor, Memory*, op. cit.

non-violence as a strategy of resistance. In striking contrast, in the summer of 1923 at Nagpur, the flag was hailed as having succeeded in enthusing, containing, and structuring the crowds. One newspaper editorial acclaimed its power to incite both love for the motherland and exemplify a set of civic virtues linking the individual to the collective. Entitled 'National Flag for India. An emotional appeal', it analysed this element as the crucial yet missing feature of the colonial relationship.[113] The British would have overlooked the importance of an emotional investment in their relationship with Indians. Now that this aspect was clearly recognized and developed, the author predicted the momentous consequences of the flag not only in the sphere of politics but also in unexpected ways. These included not only a willingness to sacrifice, but gave a sharper meaning to 'feeling nationally'. The political status of a country, it argued, was not a matter of reasoning or logic but sentiment. At the height of this satyagraha, Sarojini Naidu presented this emotional dimension as well as its capacity of restraint in a movement that could have become a 'hysterical, evanescent and torrential flow'.[114] Thus, by leading a large crowd stirred by a strong emotion, within the parameters of discipline and consensus, the flag had achieved the delicate balance between collective enthusiasm and controlled display in a crowd. After the trauma of Chauri-Chaura, wrote one observer, hard and cold-blooded discipline was necessary to prevent the disintegration and degeneration of popular action into violence.[115]

At the end of the satyagraha in August 1923, Patel hailed the special triumph of their flag 'as a victory of truth, non-violence and penance'.[116] Rajagopalachari too emphasized this dimension that set it apart from other flags: 'There is however a great difference between other national flags and ours. The flags of other nations are yet emblems of war and aggression. Ours is from the inception an emblem of peace. Our flag

[113] *The Hindu*, 14 July 1923.

[114] Sarojini Naidu's speech at the AICC meeting in Nagpur, reported in *The Hindu*, 12 July 1923.

[115] *The Hindu*, 12 June 1923.

[116] P.N. Chopra (ed.), *Collected Works of Sardar Vallabhbhai Patel*, op. cit., p. 200.

is not at war with any other standard. It bears the message of peace to everyone on earth . . . it does not thirst for others blood . . . does not symbolise a bloody revolution . . .'[117] He repeated this subsequently and frequently when he insisted that the charkha on the flag 'symbolises non-violence, self-reliance and industry, says peace not war, love not hatred'.[118] *Young India* clarioned the message: the flag 'stands for awakened India giving the message of peace, goodwill, industry to a distracted world';[119] Nagpur was 'a triumph of non-violence'.[120] In the absence of a system of formalized rules and rituals that characterize democratic traditions, the flag proposed an alternative: it was a Gandhian signal of orderly, disciplined, peaceful resistance.

The slogan 'Up, up with the National Flag, Down, down with the Union Jack' that inaugurated and accompanied the civil disobedience movement in 1930, besides proclaiming the intention to win sovereignty, also affirmed the difference between the dominating, repressive flag of empire and the flag of independent India, upholding peace and fearlessness.[121] It was affirmed to stand for 'truce and abandonment of war as an instrument of national policy'.[122] The point would be reiterated by Nehru in his speech before the Constituent Assembly on the formal presentation of the flag: 'This Flag is not a Flag of Empire, imperialism, of domination over anybody . . .'[123]

In 1931 the flag's success in concentrating and assembling emotions, then ordering and unifying them in a national movement of resistance, was evident. But this very triumph brought in its wake dissensions and differences. As it grew in importance and occupied the sites of state power or intruded into civilian space, its omnipresence invited reactions of disagreement and dispute. The motor of pacific socialization of emotions that Gandhi had envisaged thus also carried in itself the seeds

[117] *Young India*, 22 March 1923, p. 91.
[118] *Young India*, 24 May 1923, pp. 171–2.
[119] *Young India*, 5 July 1923, p. 225.
[120] *Young India*, 23 August 1923, p. 281.
[121] *Harijan*, 24 November 1933.
[122] *The Mahratta*, 14 June 1931.
[123] *Constituent Assembly Debates* (New Delhi, Lok Sabha Secretariat, 1950), vol. 5, 22 July 1947, p. 741.

of violence. Instead of producing order, it led to disorder, making Gandhi despair that 'still in the name of satyagraha we have burnt buildings, forcibly captured weapons, extorted money, stopped trains, cut off telegraph wires, killed innocent people and plundered shops and private houses.'[124]

It invited counter-responses from Muslims and Hindus who did not agree with Gandhian politics or believe in the effectiveness of truth and peace as tools of decolonization. The old battle between the National Flag and the Union Jack was replaced by a new conflict between the Muslim League flag for Pakistan, and the National Flag. As the following chapters will show, growing numbers rejected the tricolour with equal vigour, turning their backs to its call for national unity and solidarity in favour of communitarian symbols celebrating narrow cultural traditions and identities. These competing allegiances were not articulated within the larger system of philosophical maxims—non-violence, self-control, and truth. They were conceived as political flags, to mobilize and rally, but within sectarian limits and for specific political targets. Their forms of 'emotional socialization' encouraged action conducive to group interests, and recognized the need for aggression, even legitimized violence. Thus, though Ambedkar admitted that nationality was a 'feeling of a corporate sentiment of oneness', he also qualified that it was a 'double edged feeling': of fellowship for one's own kith and kin and an anti-fellowship feeling for those who were not one's own kith and kin.[125] Gandhi had taken note that, by the end of the thirties, the flag instead of being a symbol of simplicity, purity, unity, and through these a determined revolt against moral, material, and political exploitation, had become a symbol of conflict. Even Congressmen, he complained, sometimes preferred the red flag and did not hesitate to run down the tricolour.[126] For him, the flag had not been designed to be called the tyranny of one person, but conceived to

124 *Speeches and Writings of Mahatma Gandhi*, p. 474, quoted in M.K. Gandhi, *India of My Dreams*, op. cit., p. 86.

125 Vasant Moon (ed.), *Dr Babasaheb Ambedkar. Writings and Speeches* (Government of Maharashtra, 1990), vol. 8, p. 31.

126 *CWMG*, vol. LXIX, March 1939–July 15 1939 (Ahmedabad, 1977), p. 380.

represent non-violence through real communal unity and manual labour which poor and rich alike could undertake. It had to be withdrawn.[127]

The outbreaks of communal violence as well as the turn taken by the nationalist struggle with the Quit India movement in 1942 in favour of sabotage, bomb explosions, and attacks, demonstrated the power of alternative emotional systems. The highpoint of these breakdowns was of course the violence that preceded and accompanied the independence of India and Pakistan. Aruna Asaf Ali's account of her own full participation in these protests in 1942 shows how one idealized pattern of political behaviour could suddenly give way to another, completely opposed. On 9 August 1942, following the arrest of all Congress leaders, she proceeded to the Gwalior Tank maidan in Bombay where Maulana Azad was to have performed a flag-hoisting ceremony. The ritual was accomplished nonetheless and the police intervened to disperse the crowd. In her autobiography she identified this act as a decisive moment: the sight of a 'white sergeant trampling over the flag I had unfurled ten minutes ago' led her to 'vow that I would help to tear up the British rule.'[128] Her subsequent engagement in acts of violence, so contrary to the pacific philosophy espoused by Gandhi (and more significant in the wife of a prominent Congress party member), gives this statement a deeper meaning. It shows that the flag had ceased to function as a means of control. It had been appropriated for ends quite opposed to Gandhi's project. More dramatically, Gandhi's system of emotions with the flag at its centre was swept aside by the force of reactive emotions that were to find such tragic expression during Partition.

[127] *Harijan*, 5 November 1938.

[128] Aruna Asaf Ali, *Fragments from the Past. Selected Writings and Speeches of Aruna Asaf Ali* (New Delhi, 1989), p.12.

7

A Flag for Pakistan

From the second half of the 1920s to the1940s the League's reactions to the tricolour ranged from initial acceptance of a national symbol for India, to resentment at Congress manipulation, to outright hostility. In 1937 the Muslim League began to use the green flag in its demonstrations. Until then, expressions of the place and rights of Indian Muslims or the political contours this called for, had principally taken the form of historical arguments or cultural logic. That year, the party's debacle in the assembly elections raised a new question, mainly that of the symbolic representation of Muslims. Just as the imperative of exhibiting their identity through the tricolour in answer to the Union Jack had become apparent to Indian nationalists, so too the Muslim League was led to reject the tricolour and uphold its own flag. New lines of antagonism were henceforth drawn within the Indian world, as if the Union Jack had in a way been expelled from the political arena. In the following years, a war of symbols developed from the impossibility of having twin loyalties to the tricolour and the green flag.

During this battle of symbols, the League was transformed from a party with a small base, a weak organizational structure, and a divided leadership, into the principal mouthpiece of a separate Muslim nation, carried along by the triumphant wave of Muslim sentiment in its favour.[1] After 1937 the green flag was one of the resources that permitted the Muslim League to mobilize Muslim sentiment with

[1] In his historiographical overview of the growth and emergence of the Pakistan 'movement', Mushirul Hasan concludes that 'the critical and unresolved issue is how Jinnah and the League were able to secure the support of so many Muslims in so short a time': Mushirul Hasan, *India's Partition. Process, Strategy*

surprising rapidity. The power of the symbol no doubt greatly facilitated popularization of the idea of Pakistan, which grew from a paper project to a constitutional argument and then a political reality.[2] The League's employment of this visual medium as a social, cultural, and political shorthand after 1937 projected a common, even if illusionary Muslim experience and identity distinct from other communities and groups. In front of the tricolour, which was thought of and used as an inclusive symbol, the green flag stood as an exclusive symbol, a unique representation of Indian Muslims who became in fact separated by their religious practices, beliefs, and rituals.

1937: A Political Symbol for Muslims in India

We have seen that, until 1923, Muslim reactions manifested little organized opposition to the tricolour destined by Gandhi to be the national flag. Although the Muslim League seems to have used the

---

and Mobilization (Delhi, Oxford University Press, 1993), p. 42. Mukul Kesavan's work on Muslim politics in the 1930s and 1940s raises the same question but examines it from the perspective of Congress policies and positions in 1937: '1937 as a Landmark in the Course of Communal Politics in the U.P.', Occasional Papers on History and Society, Second Series, NMML; 1988.

[2] Studies now abound analysing the development of Muslim politics and strategies, religious leadership and mobilization, Congress–League–British relations, the colonial government's policies or Hindu-Muslim relations. The genesis of Pakistan remains a central question for historians. On this growing literature, some notable contributions are Ayesha Jalal, *The Sole Spokesman: Jinnah, the Muslim League and the Demand for Pakistan* (Cambridge, Cambridge University Press, 1990); Asim Roy, 'The High Politics of India's Partition: The Revisionist Perspective', *Modern Asian Studies*, vol. 24, no. 2, 1990, pp. 385–408; Joya Chatterji, *Communal Politics and the Partition of Bengal 1932–1947* (Cambridge, University of Cambridge, 1991). For a succinct review of this subject see Mushirul Hasan, *India's Partition. Process, Strategy and Mobilization*, op. cit. However, the treatment of symbols in the growth of the Pakistan 'movement' remains an unexplored terrain. Despite the persistence of this theme since G. Minault's *The Khilafat Movement. Religious Symbolism and Political Mobilization in India* (New York, Columbia University Press, 1982), or Paul Brass's *Language, Religion and Politics in North India* (Cambridge, Cambridge University Press, 1974), the subject remains marginal to the understanding of the construction of community and nation.

crescent and star flag in its sessions since its foundation in 1906,[3] this flag was not projected in public space as the symbol of a distinct political programme. On the contrary there is evidence to show that many Muslims could sympathize and identify with a symbol representing the whole of India and not simply one or other community or religious tradition. Already, in 1917, the mother of the Muslim journalist and Khilafat leader Mohamed Ali provided an example of such Muslim responses. Reacting to the Madras government's prohibition of the Home Rule flag and its leader Annie Besant's internment, she declared her intention of putting the Home Rule flag colours on her white burqa, although she admitted to never having worn colours throughout her widowhood.[4] In 1923 Muslims rallied to Gandhi's 'Swaraj flag' when it was being defended in the Nagpur flag satyagraha as the symbol of Indian identity and nationhood. Mohamed Ali acclaimed it as 'the flag of the nation' at the AICC meeting of 28 December 1923. 'This flag is nothing if it is not the flag of freedom . . . but it cannot be the flag of our freedom unless it is also the flag of our national unity.'[5] At the same moment the All India Khilafat Conference, at its tenth session at Cocanada, was paying homage to the green flag presented by the Khalifat-ul-Mausalmia to Indian Muslims.[6] Acclaiming the Muslim flag with cries of 'Allah-o-Akbar' on the one hand and saluting the symbol of national unity on the other posed no contradictions yet for Indian Muslims.

In the aftermath of 1923 the Muslim League's relationship with the Swaraj Flag evolved from one of acceptance to a certain wariness, then to a more systematic opposition in the early 1930s, and finally to a massive rallying behind its own flag after 1937. Already in 1924 British

[3] A brief evocation is found in Pierre C. Lux-Wurm, *Les Drapeaux de l'Islam*, op. cit., p. 67.

[4] Abadi Bano Abdul Ali Begum to Sir Subramanyam, President of the Madras Home Rule League, Chindwara, Central Provinces, 4 September 1917, in Shan Muhammad (ed.), *Unpublished Letters of the Ali Brothers* (Delhi, Idarah-i Adabiyat-i Delli, 1979), p. 108.

[5] Mushirul Hasan, *Mohamed Ali in Indian Politics: Select Writings 1920–23* (New Delhi, Atlantic, 1986), vol. 3, p. 320.

[6] A.M. Zaidi, *Evolution of Muslim Political Thought in India, Sectarian Nationalism and Khilafat* (New Delhi, Indian Institute of Applied Political Research, 1975), vol. 2, p. 578.

administrators were reporting Muslims' lack of interest in the Congress national Flag Day processions.[7] Such commentaries could of course have been advanced with the idea of dismissing Congress claims of the flag as a national symbol. But on the other hand as this trend strengthened during the 1920s it cannot be denied that they reflected the beginnings of a real and strong rejection of the symbol devised by Gandhi. The more the national flag was used and recognized, and the more its emotional unity was celebrated around the Gandhian principles of peace and satyagraha, the more it opened itself to charges of political hegemony and suppression of other identities and traditions. It became in its turn a flag to rebel against as well as a model of emulation. Consequently, when the Indian National Congress began its vigorous promotion of flag-hoisting ceremonies and processions during the 1930s, many Muslims conveyed their discontent by hoisting the Islamic flag. Instances of sporadic battles between the two flags can be found. At Karachi, a procession and meeting with the tricolour flying at half-mast was interrupted and the flag torn and replaced with the Islamic flag.[8] According to the secretary of the All India Khilafat Committee, at the height of the civil disobedience movement the 50,000 Muslims assembled in the Esplanade Maidan of Bombay in 1931 to honour the Muslim flag mirrored this new political mood.[9]

Such punctual incidents acquired greater coherence and unity when in 1933 Choudhary Rahmat Ali, a Muslim student at Cambridge, coined the word 'Pakistan' and designed a flag for it. Though different, it was not yet noticeably dissimilar from the Islamic banner in use in India. A book by him published in 1935 detailed the ancient geographical and historical roots of Pakistan in the Indian subcontinent and devoted an entire chapter to the national symbols of the 'Paks', quite different, he claimed from those of 'caste Hindoos'. He presented Pakistan's national flag as a green oblong with a white crescent and five stars in the centre. The colour and the design were justified as the traditional colour and the historic symbol of Islam. Both were seen to express the idea of Muslim fraternity. He explained it as a manifestation

[7] *A Review of the Administration of the Presidency of Bombay 1923–24* (Bombay, Government Press, 1925), p. iv.

[8] *Madras Mail*, 8 January 1931.

[9] *The Hindu*, 3 June 1931.

of the trilogy of faith, fraternity, and fatherland, drawing its meaning and message from the ancient flag which had flown over Ghazni and Kabul, Agra and Delhi since the Mughal conquests.[10]

Yet the symbol Rahmat Ali claimed as the 'mind and soul of the nation' was not officially acknowledged by the League, although the party had by now become categorical in its hostility to the 'Congress flag', labelling the latter a party flag and not at all national. To begin with, the Muslim Mass Contact Programme, launched by Congress in 1937, simply provoked demands from the League that neither the tricolour nor *Bande Mataram* be imposed in schools or public ceremonies as national icons. Saluting the Congress flag and singing *Bande Mataram* featured high in the list of complaints drawn up in the Pirpur report of 1938; it was the result of an enquiry committee set up by the All India Muslim League to look into Muslim grievances in the six provinces where the Congress had recently won power and constituted the government (United Provinces, Bihar, Orissa, Central Provinces, Madras, Bombay); its author, chief secretary of the Punjab Unionist Party, Khan Daultana, pointed out that the ceremony around the Congress flag contained rituals many Muslims would hesitate to perform. If Congress destined the ceremony of salutation for its party members, that was quite acceptable, although political organizations normally did not have distinctive flags and they could not expect everyone to salute what could be called their house flag. For this flag to be anything more, Congress still had to prove beyond a shadow of doubt that it was recognized by the whole of India as the national emblem. Carrying a flag in green with a crescent and star in grey on its cover, the report concluded, 'a national flag cannot be forced upon unwilling people any more than a national anthem.'[11] The committee thus sent a strong signal to Muslims, inviting them to take a clear stand on the flag.

Khan Daultana's assessment was corroborated by other sources. The *Civil and Military Gazette* of Lahore, for example, declared: 'We have reason to believe—and Khan Daultana [. . .] supports our

[10] Choudhary Rahmat Ali, *Pakistan* (Cambridge, Pakistan National Liberation Movement, 1935, 3rd edn, 1947), pp. 154–6.

[11] OIOC, L/I/1/628, Report of the Inquiry Committee into Muslim Grievances, 1938, pp. 19–20.

belief—that a large number of Muslims do not recognize the Congress flag as the flag of India. Besides Muslims, there are other communities in India who would hotly resent the substitution of the Congress flag for the flag which India itself and the world recognises as the flag of India.'[12] In 1939, one Jamil-ud-din Ahmad protested in a strongly argued booklet entitled *Is India One Nation*: 'the tri-colour flag is forcibly hoisted on public buildings and schools and colleges, though the Muslims refuse to acknowledge it as the national flag.'[13]

In these altercations between Congress and Muslim Leaguers, Muslims were confronted with a simple choice: accept the Congress project or refuse it, either by paradoxically adhering to the symbols of empire, or by unfurling their own flag as the national one. When the municipality of Jagadhri (Punjab) for example, emphatically denied the use of one of its grounds for the celebration of Independence Day, it justified this stance by affirming loyalty to the Union Jack.[14] And when the Allahabad Municipal Board wanted to hoist the tricolour on the clock tower, one Muslim member, Abdul Qayum Khan, pointed out the risk of communal conflicts, as a recent example in Lucknow had shown.[15] Similarly, in Karachi, in August 1931, Muslims, backed by Sikh and Christian members of the municipality joined the British in opposing a proposition for hoisting the national flag besides the Union Jack on municipal buildings, on the principle that the flag was not accepted by minority communities; the measure passed by barely one vote (13 to 12).[16]

Such confrontations between Congress and League militants, even if localized, were already perceived by some Indians as early as the beginning of the 1930s as a sign of the division of the country into two opposed religious blocks, Hindu and Muslim. On a visit to Bangalore

[12] 'The Congress and its Flag', *The Civil and Military Gazette*, Lahore, 7 August 1937, in K.K. Aziz (ed.), *Muslims under Congress Rule, 1937–39: A Documentary Record* (Islamabad, National Commission on Historical and Cultural Research, 1979), vol. 2, pp. 3–4.

[13] Jamil-ud-din Ahmad, *Is India One Nation*? (Muslim University Muslim League Publications, 1939), in OIOC, L/I/1/628.

[14] *The Tribune*, 25 January 1930.

[15] *The Pioneer Mail*, 27 June 1930, p. 11.

[16] *Amrita Bazar Patrika*, 12 August 1931.

in July 1931, an Indian journalist, Nihal Singh, was dismayed by the symbolic manifestation of religious divisions, opposing 'tricolour of coarse homespun with the emblem of the charkha proudly held above the heads of Congress volunteers the star and crescent waving above the Muslims.'[17]

Indeed, during the course of 1937 the League began to use a rectangular green flag with the crescent, in its meetings and rallies. This practice does not seem to have been the result of a party decision. Nor did it follow from a discussion within the party or in the newspapers. Nehru's remarks in March 1937 that the Congress and the Raj were the only two political actors in India provoked Jinnah to respond that the Muslim League was a third, a rightful and equal partner of the Congress. This sharpened the urgency for Muslim League leaders and sympathizers to transform the League into a broad-based mass organization and political party at par with the Congress. The Raja of Mahmudabad's analysis of the Muslim situation in the aftermath of 1937 summarized the change in their approach. When he had joined the Muslim League he thought the two parties (Congress and the League) were 'like two parts of the same army fighting a common enemy on two fronts'. But gradually he and other Muslims reacted against what they perceived as a form of contempt for the League and Jinnah. Congress success in the 1937 elections—the Muslim League won only 109 out of the 482 seats allotted to Muslims under separate electorates, securing only 4.8 per cent of the total Muslim votes—held out, he wrote, a lesson for them. They realized that for a similar success, at least in the Muslim-majority provinces, 'two things were essential: a closing of their ranks and a reorganization of the Muslim League.'[18]

It was not a coincidence that this was the moment when Jinnah adopted a changed headgear—his 'samur' cap, which Muslims embraced as a distinctive sign.[19] It also inaugurated a more aggressive political

[17] Nihal Singh, 'Mysore's Ban on Volunteers', *The Hindu*, 25 July 1931, p. 10.

[18] Raja of Mahmudabad, 'Some Memories', in M. Hasan (ed.), *India's Partition*, pp. 414–15.

[19] According to M.A.H. Ispahani's account, Jinnah was staying with the Raja of Mahmudabad on the eve of the Muslim League session at Lucknow on 15–18 October 1937. Trying out Nawab Ismail Khan's cap, he was urged to keep it on while addressing the session. It was to become, in a way, a 'national headgear'

campaigning and publicity for the Islamic flag as the symbol of party and community. Now modelling their tactics on the Congress Party's use of the national flag in the election campaign, the Muslim League's appeal in its public meetings to Muslims focused prominently on the League flag. Henceforth, displaying the Islamic flag on their houses became, for a certain number of Muslims, a way of manifesting their political opinions.[20]

Congress's Muslim mass contact programme after the 1937 elections irked the League, Jinnah viewing it as a strategy to deepen splits within the Muslim community. Hereafter, the League accelerated its own drive to win over Muslims.[21] An article, 'Through Muslim Eyes', published in the newspaper *Ain-et Mulk* (Mirror of the Nation) in 1938 presented the terms of the confrontation: 'any acceptable formula or pact (between Congress and League) would . . . involve the acquiescence of the Congress in redesigning of the tricolour flag or at least agreeing to give the flag of the League an equal importance.'[22] In 1938, for the first time, a Muslim leader, Nawab Mohammad Ismail Khan, laid down the political issue in a letter sent to Nehru: 'I am not aware that any Muslim organisation has recognised the tricolour flag as the national flag. I have always understood it to be the Congress flag.' In a lengthy reply, Nehru defended the Congress position, arguing that the tricolour, which did not belong to any single community, was not imposed on minorities. It was produced by a seventeen-year-long democratic process in which the Muslims had also participated; furthermore, the Congress had taken Muslim protests into consideration

---

of his co-religionists; Mirza Abol Hassan Ispahani, *Qaid-e-Azam Jinnah as I Knew Him* (Karachi, Royal Books Co., 3rd edn, 1976), p. 37.

[20] *Rajendra Prasad Correspondence and Select Documents*, ed. Valmiki Choudhary, *January–July 1939* (Delhi, Allied Publishers, 1984), vol. 3, pp. 339–40.

[21] Vapal Pangunni Menon, a civil servant and subsequently political advisor to the viceroy of India, Louis Mountbatten, emphasized this point in his analysis of these years in *The Transfer of Power in Inda* (New Delhi, Orient Longman, 1968, 1st edn, 1957), p. 55.

[22] In Basudev Chatterji (ed.), *Towards Freedom. Documents on the Movement for Independence in India, 1938* (Delhi, Indian Council of Historical Research, Oxford University Press, 1999), Part 1, p. 192.

before officially endorsing the flag in August 1931: 'We did try later not to lay stress on the communal reason for the colours as we wanted it to be considered the common national flag of all . . . It is obvious that India must have a national flag, a flag which all can call their own. A communal flag can't possibly take its place and it is hardly proper to put up any communal flag on public buildings used by people of all communities.'[23] This argument would be developed in his subsequent exchanges with Jinnah. Nehru would continue to point out that this historical process could neither be interrupted nor reversed. In this conflict, the two symbols did not reflect similar comparable realities. Communal flags, Nehru stressed, could be used for religious functions but they had no place at any national function or over any public building meant for diverse communities. Recalling the fact that during the past few months the national flag had been insulted by some Muslim Leaguers, he underlined the Congress intention to avoid interference with the Muslim League flag, a source of conflict and communal bitterness.[24] But Nehru's logic did not convince Muslims, nor did it quieten their opposition.

From the end of 1937 escalation of conflicts around the flag was reported in the Punjab and the United Provinces. In Lahore the British noted that the promotion of the tricolour was increasing Muslim apprehensions.[25] The British governor Haig drew the government's attention to the new political duel Congress and the League were engaged in. This game of symbolic seesaw involved the Muslim League's 'counter-exhibition of the star and crescent emblem' and the subsequent toning down of the Congress campaign of hoisting flags.[26] Relations between the two parties were dominated by this new form of repartee, particularly virulent at the municipal and district board level. It spread

[23] A.M. Zaidi, *Congress and the Minorities. Preserving National Cohesion* (New Delhi, Publication Dept., Indian Institute of Applied Political Research, 1984), Nawb Mohd. Ismail Khan to Pandit Nehru, 16 January 1938, p. 148.

[24] Ibid., Nehru to Jinnah, 6 April 1938, p. 164.

[25] Emerson to Linlithgow, Lahore, 21 October 1937, in Lionel Carter (ed.), *Punjab Politics, 1936–39. The Start of Provincial Autonomy. Governors' Fortnightly Reports and Other Key Documents* (Delhi, Manohar, 2004), p. 143.

[26] Haig to Linlithgow, 9 March 1938, Linlithgow to Zetland, 15 March 1938, Linlithgow Papers, in Basudev Chatterji (ed.), op. cit., pp. 984–6.

rapidly among university students, becoming, as we shall see, an easy means of expressing political opinion and identity. The persistence of this theme through the 1940s and the passion it evoked suggests the significant role of the flag in the development of a separate national loyalty, sometimes described as 'sub-nationalism' or 'exclusionary nationalism'.[27] Frequently quoted by Muslims as proof of Congress's Hindu leanings, it continued to smoulder, inciting tensions and embittering Hindu-Muslim relations. The Gaya communal riots in Bihar in 1939 were among those attributed by the Muslim League to the hoisting of the 'Congress flag' on the city school on Independence Day and the singing of *Bande Mataram* in the *zila* school.

For many Muslims it could provide a convincing justification for breaking links with Congress, or clearly opting for what was still a mythical Pakistan. Begum Ikramullah, the wife of a Muslim Indian civil servant, wrote: 'they were wrong' to force Muslims 'to salute the Congress flag, to sing the *Bande Mataram* . . . It also resulted in great bitterness.'[28] Certainly, it confirmed her drift away from Congress, as also her ardent championship of League work. This theme would find a place in the novels based on this period. For the characters in Qurratulain Hyder's *River of Fire*, this was a factor creating a sense of alienation among Muslims. As Champa, a young university student in Calcutta, put it: 'I used to sing *Jana Gana Mana* under the tricolour at Basant College and I often felt that I was considered an outsider under the flag.'[29] The unambiguous promotion of the Muslim League flag whetted such sentiments of resentment or exclusion and directed them towards a visible alternative.

Thus, after 1937, in response to the Congress strategy of mobilization around the trinity of 'flag, nation and Congress', Jinnah developed a

[27] The term is used by J. Breuilly, *Nationalism and the State* (Manchester, Manchester University Press, 1982); also see David E.F. Henley, 'Ethnographic Integration and Exclusion in Anticolonial Nationalism: Indonesia and Indochina', *Comparative Studies in Society and History*, 1995, pp. 286–321.

[28] Shaista Suhrawardy Ikramullah, *From Purdah to Parliament* (Karachi, Oxford University Press, 1998), p. 84.

[29] Qurratulain Hyder, *River of Fire* (1st edn, 1927, New Delhi, Kali for Women, 1998), pp. 252–3.

determined opposition to the tricolour and *Bande Mataram*,[30] on which he would henceforth refuse all negotiation.[31]

The position became clearer in 1940, at the Lucknow Muslim League session, when Jinnah decreed the green flag with a crescent and star to be the 'national flag of Muslim India.'[32] The act had several implications. It marked a change in Hindu–Muslim relations and the end of a period of cultural and religious pluralism that had characterized medieval India. In its place, it proposed a single 'Muslim' identity over and above the deep-seated religious, regional, and doctrinal differences among the community. It was on these grounds that the community could be represented as a nation.

Jinnah would later announce: 'We have established a remarkable platform which displays and demonstrates a complete unity of the entire solid body of Muslim India.'[33] This 'ethnic-genealogical' approach, to use Anthony Smith's concept (which emphasizes the ties of blood and tradition), could be contrasted to the more 'civic territorial' model of the nation advanced by the tricolour.[34] The Muslim League now called upon its volunteers to integrate the symbol in the party's political decor, visually or rhetorically, in public meetings, processions, and monthly flag-salutation ceremonies. Thus, when the women's section of the All India Muslim League held its annual session at the

[30] Syed Sharifuddin Pirzada (ed.), *Quaid-e-Azam Jinnah's Correspondence* (Karachi, Guild Publishing House, 1966), pp. 441, 443.

[31] When, in an effort at reconciliation, Jinnah promised his accord to the Congress during the duration of the war, it was on the grounds that the latter concede on certain points such as agreeing not to fly the Congress flag over public institutions. Cf. Ishtiaq Husain Qureshi, *The Struggle for Pakistan* (Karachi, University of Karachi, 1969), p. 126.

[32] Syed Sharifuddin Pirzada (ed)., *Foundations of Pakistan. All India Muslim League Documents 1906–1947, vol. 2, 1924–47* (Karachi-Dacca, National Publishing House, 1970), pp. 325–6.

[33] *The Dawn*, 7 December 1941; Ian Talbot, *Freedom's Cry. The Popular Dimension in the Pakistan Movement and Partition Experience in North-West India* (Karachi, Oxford University Press, 1996), p. 72.

[34] The distinction is drawn by Anthony D. Smith in 'Nations and Their Pasts. The Nation, Real or Imagined', *Nations & Nationalism*, vol. 2, November 1996, pp. 358–65, esp. p. 363.

Islamia College for girls at Lahore on 23 March 1940, its organizer Begum Hafeezuddin called upon the nine million Muslims of the Indian subcontinent to 'unite under the flag' of the Muslim League. The refrain 'the flag of the Prophet of Islam' was taken up by the local pirs in Sind in 1940.[35] Pakistan Day, Jinnah Day, and Iqbal Day was the Muslim League's answer to the institution of Tilak Day, Gandhi Day, Flag Day, and Independence Day rather than an imitation of British ceremonial, as Ian Talbot sees it.[36] They provided a new ritualized framework for displaying the symbol of their separate nationhood.

The League's ethnic-genealogical definition of their flag brought in its wake some specific elements that distinguished it from the tricolour. Primarily, this ethnic consensus appeared to exclude any public debate within or outside the party. It was unequivocally imposed from above, almost as if there could be no two opinions about a united Muslim identity. No traces of discussion or reflection on the matter can be found in the accounts of the leading political actors of the period. Although there was a large discussion among Muslims on the political necessity of obtaining an equal status between the League's and the Congress flags—the latter being castigated as a flag of domination, the former hailed as the symbol of the very survival and continuity of the Muslim community of India—there was no discussion within Muslims circles about the shape, design or colours to be given to an Indian Muslim flag.

The reasons for such absence of debate are surely complex. For the present, a few central elements must be retained. Contrary to the tricolour, which was the product of a succession of broad debates, at different levels and sites, the green flag was presented as the logical outcome of a closed process, entirely controlled and decided by political elites. Secondly, no theoretical elaboration of rules and procedures of the ritual seems to have been made by the Muslim League or any other auxiliary body: it was not the object of a broader pedagogical reflection, but immediately centred around para-military demonstrations. Thirdly, unlike the Congress, which did not cease to proclaim its aim of uniting all the diverse ethnic groups and religious faiths into

[35] On the involvement of *pirs* in the Muslim League activities, see Sarah F.D. Ansari, *Sufi Saints and State Power. The Pirs of Sind, 1843–1947* (Cambridge, Cambridge University Press, 1992), esp. p. 120.

[36] Ian Talbot, *Freedom's Cry*, op. cit.

a single Indian nation upon the principle of unity in diversity, the Muslim League emphasized its flag as the symbol of one distinctive Muslim material culture, beliefs, and practices.

In 1933 Rahmat Ali's 'Pakistan scheme' and the flag designed by him had seemed more a flight of fancy—an exaggerated, impractical idea and a superfluous, peripheral symbol. Barely six years later, true to the precept that 'there is no power except that which is staged',[37] the flag had become the means of enacting the nation in the street, giving it visibility and legitimizing its demand. From a paper project it became the hub of party ceremonials, giving continuity to different manifestations and public meetings and marking out an autonomous political space for the Muslims. The Muslim National Guards, a group whose ground rules had been drafted by the Raja of Mahmudabad in 1937, formalized the protocol of the ritual to resemble a veritable state ceremony. The presence of guards structured the ceremony, investing it with an official, strict character, designed to impress observers and serve to lend a solemnity to the League's demand. The flag-hoisting ceremony performed by Jinnah at the League session in Patna in 1938 was accompanied by inspection of the guard of honour formed by the national guard representing different provinces and districts. Verses from the Holy Koran, Iqbal's '*Chin-o-Arab Hamara*' or '*Purcham Rahey Buland Hamara*' (May our flag fly high) were included. This military salute to the flag remained central until the formation of Pakistan.[38]

Rallying Muslims to the Green Flag

Jinnah's addresses invariably included a communitarian appeal, celebrating the flag of the Muslim League, the Muslim community, and Islam all in one.[39] The reference to Islam canalized the pan-Islamic sentiment that had until then served to express various strains of Muslim dissent and directed this to a political goal. From 1940 to 1947

[37] G. Balandier, *Le Pouvoir sur scènes* (Paris, Balland, 1980).

[38] Ian Talbot, *Freedom's Cry*, op. cit., pp. 63–72.

[39] *Qaid-i-Azam M.A. Jinnah, The Nation's Voice: Towards Consolidation. Speeches and Statements, March 1935 to March 1940.* ed. Waheed Ahmad (Karachi, Quaid-i-Azam Academy, 1992–3), p. 321; *The Dawn*, 26 October 1941, p. 4.

Jinnah stressed the two dimensions, which placed the crescent and star banner in a long, uninterrupted historical tradition as reconstructed by Rahmat Ali in 1933 and, at the same time, gave it the aspect of a recent invention. Thus, at a flag-hoisting ceremony in Bombay in 1938 when the Punjab premier, Sikander Hyat Khan, described the Muslim League flag as similar to any ordinary army regiment's colours, Jinnah was quick to refute this statement publicly. Unlike other party flags, he insisted, the Muslim emblem was distinctive because it was both 'new' and deep-rooted. It went back to an ancient Islamic tradition, having been given to them by the Prophet. In its most recent form, it depicted the awakening of a new Muslim consciousness, demonstrating to the world the unity of Indian Muslims.[40] Finally, it was of course the flag of the League, representative of this group and its unity.[41]

In effect, Indian Muslims, who presented a picture of conflicting interests between the political elites of the United Provinces, the Muslim populations of the Punjab and the north-west, and Bengal, could all be embraced in its fold.[42] This new convergence also glossed over the Shia, Sunni, and Sufi differences as well as those between other religious schools of thought and regions within the Islamic fold, in favour of a real political community. Muslim leaders echoed this refrain. At the Aligarh League Conference in 1941 Sir Currimbhoy Ibrahim of Bombay proclaimed it to be a most powerful flag revered by Musulmans.[43] Simultaneously, at the fifth annual session of the Muslim Students' Federation in December 1941, the Raja of Mahmudabad, addressing 40,000 Muslims, described it as the flag that had served to

[40] W. Ahmad, *Nation's Voice*, op. cit., p. 261.

[41] *The Dawn*, 26 October 1941, p. 4.

[42] The depth of these differences cannot be underestimated, as Mushirul Hasan notes, although they have only now begun to be studied: 'Memories of a Fragmented Nation', in S. Settar and Indira Baptista Gupta (eds), *Pangs of Partition, The Human Dimension* (New Delhi, Manohar, 2002), vol. II, pp. 171–90, esp. p. 181 and fn. 36; the complexities of strains within Islam are discussed in Mushirul Hasan (ed.), *Islam. Communities and the Nation. Muslim Identities in South Asia and Beyond* (Delhi, Manohar, 1998). See in particular, the contributions of Marc Gaborieau, Joya Chatterji, and Shail Mayaram.

[43] *The Dawn*, 9 November 1941.

rally a hundred million Muslims of India under one organization and roused their political consciousness.[44] And in his presidential address to the All-India Muslim Students' Federation at Nagpur on 26 December 1942, Jinnah glorified its revolutionary dimension and potential, analysing the transformation in the political consciousness of Muslims from their 'wretched position . . . three years ago' as due partly to the League's equipping itself with a national flag.[45]

After 1940 the flag became central to the League's political strategy. Without expressing the details of an alternative programme, the League affirmed itself as an equal opponent of the Congress. In his analysis of the 'road to Pakistan', the journalist Kalim Siddiqui recalled the impact of the Muslim League flag on little children when League volunteers carried the party's message into the villages in the 1940s.[46] To village children, he wrote, the flag, accompanied by the slogan 'Pakistan' appeared as a new element of play. In their innocent search of novelty in their games, such children were ideal vehicles of political propaganda. In fact one of his earliest memories of his ancestral village in northern India centred around the arrival of three young male students from Aligarh University with the Muslim League flag—the Islamic crescent and star on a deep green background. They planted the flag in the village square and a group of little boys followed by a big crowd soon gathered. The students shouted 'Allah-o-Akbar' (God is Great) and 'Pakistan Zindabad' (Long live Pakistan) and showed the boys how to salute the flag. After visiting a few houses and carrying the flag round the village, they left for the next village. The author narrated how his little village was completely transformed by this visit. 'Every piece of green material our mothers could find was made into a Muslim League flag. We boys who were otherwise bored had found a new game.'[47]

[44] *The Dawn*,18 January 1942.

[45] *The Dawn*, 4 January 1942.

[46] Kalim Siddiqui, having opted for Pakistan in 1948, then left for England in the early 1950s, after being thrown out of the Pakistan Army cadet school for not being, he wrote, 'officer material'. He worked as a journalist for *The Guardian*.

[47] Kalim Siddiqui, *Conflict, Crisis and War in Pakistan* (London, Macmillan, 1972), pp. 50–1.

This was not the only account emphasizing the aspect of amusement in apprehending the nation and installing it in a child's imagination through slogans and songs on the flag. Begum Ikramullah noted that unable to participate in the key ceremonial events at the time of Pakistan's birth on 14 August 1947, her daughters celebrated by making little green flags and marching around with them.[48] Lending itself both to playful handling as well as solemn ritual, the Muslim League flag too was both legitimized by political use and individual appropriation by Muslims. Fictional portrayals of the period invariably evoke its omnipresence. Akhtar Jamal's novel *Samjhota Express,* for example, portrayed the principal character, Bi Apa, as a dedicated Muslim League worker who even dressed so that from a distance she looked like a Muslim League banner.[49]

A second channel that showed itself particularly suited to publicizing the League flag was the small but powerful university circles. In schools, colleges, universities, it was adopted quickly by youngsters, ardent in its defence. In 1941 a flag hoisting during the Gandhi Jayanti celebration week in the R.D. Tata High School compound in Bombay degenerated into a brawl when Muslim students snatched away the flag and burnt it.[50] Muslim students of Allahabad University announced their intention to hoist the Muslim League flag on the Senate Hall in 1942. When refused authorization by the vice chancellor, they sought support from their own leaders. Chaudhury Khaliq-uz-Zaman and the Raja of Mahmudabad intervened on their behalf. The matter was then referred to the executive council, which on the contrary recommended refusing any party displays, whether Congress or Muslim League.[51] In a similar vein, in April 1942, the Congress body of students of Allahabad University announced that Acharya Kripalani, general secretary of the AICC, would hoist the Congress flag on the Senate House. Muslim students objected to this on the grounds that an educational institution included students of diverse political opinions. If, however, Congress students insisted on hoisting their

[48] S.S. Ikramullah, *From Purdah to Parliament*, op. cit., p. 153.
[49] Quoted in Ian Talbot, op. cit., p. 139.
[50] *Searchlight*, 4 November 1946.
[51] *Hindustan Times*, 6 April 1942.

flag, Muslim students should also be allowed to hoist the Muslim League flag. On the morning of the Congress-instituted Flag Day, Muslim students gathered and protested when Acharya Kripalani rose to make a speech before hoisting the tricolour. In its turn, the Punjab Muslim Students' Federation gave instructions that the League flag be hoisted on Pakistan Day on 23 March 1943 and flags distributed among students and the people.[52] When Congress girl students decided to hoist the Congress flag on the hostel building of the university girls' hostel, Muslim girls were quick to react by raising the League flag on the roof.[53]

Anxious about the spreading communal tendency among the youth, Gandhi ultimately remonstrated students, both Hindus and Muslims, against taking such initiatives. Schools and colleges, he said, were meant to heal communal breaches, not reinforce them. Political differences were best left to professional parties and authorities.[54] However, none of the parties took any measures to discourage the politicization of these establishments: Congress leaders accepted invitations to flag-hoisting ceremonies and Muslim leaders intervened to defend their students. Jinnah's position did nothing to tone down the temper of Muslim students. In his presidential address at the All India Muslim League session in 1946 he complained: 'Admittedly it [the Congress flag] is not the national flag of India, yet that flag must be respected by everyone and hoisted on every government and public building. It does not matter if the Muslims object to it, the Congress flag must be paraded as the national flag of India and thrust upon the Muslims.'[55] Consequently, each academic institution or local authority was left to decide for itself, leaving the ground open to rivalries and opportunist alliances, and embittering Hindu–Muslim relations considerably. Lucknow University became the seat of a controversy

[52] Sarfaraz Hussain Mirza, *The Punjab Muslim Students Federation, 1937–1947* (Lahore, Research Society of Pakistan, 1978; Islamabad, 1991), p. 231.

[53] Mukhtar Zaman, *Students' Role in the Pakistan Movement* (Karachi, Qaid-i-Azam Academy, 1978), p. 130.

[54] *Harijan*, 17 February 1946.

[55] K.K. Aziz (ed.), *Muslims under Congress Rule 1937–39. A Documentary Record* (Islamabad, National Commission on Historical and Cultural Research, 1978), vol. 1, p. 170.

between Hindu and Muslim students. The latter demanded the right to hoist their flag if Hindu students hoisted the tricolour.[56]

As the League embarked on a programme of reconstruction at the provincial level, in the Sind countryside, in Punjab, Bengal, and Gujarat, symbolic displays of the flag over municipalities, district courts, and jails intensified. In a move strongly reminiscent of Congress tactics in the 1930s, the League launched itself in the symbolic conquest of structures of government authority.[57] Muslim members of the Multan municipal committee passed a resolution to install the Muslim League flag on the town hall. The decision to hold central and provincial elections in Punjab was the final incentive. Over a thousand students from all over the province, for example, campaigned in the countryside in these elections with the League flag.[58] Discipline marches of the Muslim National Guards in Delhi at the Muslim League session in April 1943 consisted of volunteers simply walking along more or less in step, carrying flags on sticks.[59]

Increasing tentatives to hoist the Muslim League flag on district courts and post offices demonstrated the legitimacy of political arguments advanced by Jinnah and the League at a provincial level.[60] The struggle for the nation was also being waged in the cadre of the regions. For example, the Muslim League flag was put in place on one high court building, and on another occasion a girl climbed the Punjab

[56] *The Eastern Times*, 6 February 1947.

[57] The importance of symbolically occupying the seats of government authority before any real seizure of power can be found in other situations of conflict, as for example, the United Irishmen's attacks in 1792 on the post offices or nocturnal planting of liberty trees in the army camp. Cf. Nancy J. Curtin, 'Symbols and rituals of United Irishmen Mobilisation', in U. Gough & David Dickson (eds), *Ireland and the French Revolution* (Dublin, Irish Academic Press, 1990), pp. 68–82.

[58] Mukhtar Zaman, *Student's role in the Pakistan Movement*, op. cit., pp. 129, 153.

[59] Commissioner of Delhi to Secretary, Home Dept, in P.S. Gupta (ed.), *Towards Freedom, 1943–1944*, pt 3 (Delhi, ICHR, 1997), pp. 2916–17.

[60] Reports of flag hoistings on *thanas* (jails), courts, treasury, and post offices, can be found in the Muslim press: Z.H. Zaidi, *Quaid-i-Azam Mohammad Ali Jinnah Papers. Prelude to Pakistan, 20 February–2 June 1947* (National Archives of Pakistan, 1993), First Series, vol. 1, pt II, pp. 207, 219, 229, 249.

Secretariat building and hoisted it.[61] On the celebration of Pakistan Day on 23 March 1947, League flags were unfurled on all the district offices of the Provincial Muslim League, and in Calcutta, where the day was observed with special enthusiasm, flag-hoisting ceremonies took place. A number of Muslim shopkeepers were reported to have flown green crescent flags over their shops and houses.[62] In April, at Peshawar, Muslim League women demonstrators in veils entered the radio station and hoisted the Muslim League flag.[63] If formally these displays resembled the Congress campaign of the early 1930s, their political significance was quite different: whereas the Congress aimed to assert its programme of reappropriating powers of all kinds at all levels by Indians, the League did not aspire so much to mark its own territory as to demonstrate the existence and power of Muslims in India. In the process, the dissemination of the flag, by proposing a unique political symbol for diverse and scattered groups, helped unify Muslims in a single community.

The demand for Pakistan manifested itself through these displays and hoistings of the crescent and star, but also by making the Congress rival flag the target of demonstrations. The incompatibility of the two flags grew, except on very rare occasions when common opposition to the British government brought the various flags, Muslim League, Congress, and Red flag, together. Expressing astonishment at the attempt to juxtapose the Congress and League flags, an article in *The Mahratta* asked whether anywhere in the world there was a country with two national flags.[64] In June 1947, at a meeting of the Muslim League in Peshawar on the eve of the ballot, the prominent contingent of the Muslim National Guards tore up the Congress flag. The Union Jack was not spared either. Punjab in particular was the scene of the

[61] Dushka Saiyid, *Muslim Women of the British Punjab. From Seclusion to Politics* (Basingstoke, Macmillan Press, 1998), pp. 89–101.

[62] *The Eastern Times*, 26 March 1947; NAI, Extracts from fortnightly report from Bengal for the second half of March 1944, file no. 18/3/44-Home Political I, in P.S. Gupta (ed.), *Towards Freedom*, op. cit., p. 3139.

[63] *The Eastern Times*, 7 March, 24 April 1947.

[64] *The Mahratta*, 8 March 1946, C.L.R. Sastri, 'Gentlemen's Agreement between Congress and Government? Deep Intrigue for New Approach to Communal Problem'.

Union Jack being removed by crowds. Meanwhile, Congress leaders and volunteers were no less conspicuous displaying their colours. April Darling, the daughter of the retired Punjab civil servant Sir Malcolm Darling, when in Delhi for the Asian Conference, noted in her journal that 'Mrs Naidu who was presiding, wore a homespun sari, saffron with green border, the colours of the Congress and she was raised above us on an orange platform.'[65]

When the Muslim League celebrated 'Victory Day' on 11 January 1946 after winning all the Muslim seats to the central assembly, the Muslim League flag was flown from houses, cars, and tongas in Punjab. Mehboob Ludhianvi's Urdu poem written in 1945–6 was an appeal to Muslims to rally, as well as a warning against taking the symbol too lightly or underestimating its power: 'There is only one God, one flag, all else is fraud; The flag of the League is our flag; That flag of the other will throttle you; If you want power, join the League; The League puts us straight on the righteous path; Whoever has deserted the flag of the League has been trapped.'[66]

From formal state-like ceremonies, the flag had moved into mosques and religious gatherings, to university campuses, schools, municipal buildings, houses, parks, and villages. Jinnah's appeal to Muslims at the Muslim Conference in Srinagar in May 1944 to recognize their unity, which the flag represented, carried this reminder: 'We have one God, one Quran, one Ka'aba and one Prophet. Let us have one organization, one platform, one flag and one leader.'[67]

No National Flag Without a Nation

Flag displays lent a new visible political force to Muslim separatism. This factor is essential to understanding the conversion in the League's status and its project in this short period. Yet, as the prospect of Pakistan appeared certain and the constitutional adoption of the flag imposed itself, Muslim leaders were faced with a political alternative:

[65] CSAS, Papers of Sir Malcolm Darling, box LIX, 31 October 1946.

[66] Mushirul Hasan (ed.), *India Partitioned. The Other Face of Freedom* (Delhi, Roli Books, 1995), vol. I, pp. 43–4.

[67] Khalid Hasan Khurshid, *Memories of Jinnah* (Karachi, Oxford University Press, 1990), p. 6.

they could continue the emphasis on Muslim natural bonds of kinship, language, religion, and social practices, or they could promote a civic contract between citizens and the state. The attitude of the Muslim League at this moment was decisive in determining the form of their future state and its political culture.

Earlier, even detailed territorial proposals of a separate unified Muslim state in the north-west as part of new federal India had evoked limited appeal—until the entry of the flag in the political debate. The poet philosopher Iqbal's scheme, presented at the Muslim League session at Allahabad on 29 December 1930, had thus remained a paper project. Only the League's association of 'one community, one party, one flag' in 1940 provided the momentum and began rallying many Muslims to the party and to Pakistan. It would not be excessive to affirm that this symbol was central in confirming the Muslim metamorphosis from 'community' to 'nation'. One explanation for its spectacular success is of course the fact that its appeal was directed uniquely to Muslims and not to other communities or faiths. As such, the problem of making it equally 'representative' of others did not arise. A further element contributed to its success—mainly, that no other Muslim state dynastic flag, even from important states like Mysore, Bhopal, and Hyderabad, was advanced as an alternative pole for Muslim loyalties. Nor was any effort made to resurrect the flags of the Mughal emperors in India. The exclusive glorification of the Muslim League banner, without any rivalry from other Muslim symbols, made its political victory a less problematic process.

Muslim leaders insisted on the international conventions of a flag representing a nation. 'Every nation has its national flag', declared Jinnah at Quetta in July 1943, as he performed the flag-hoisting ceremony at the Provincial League Conference. Muslims must 'stand united', uphold 'the dignity of this flag' and 'make your sacrifices for the achievement of your final goal . . . Just like other nations have their own flag in their own territory we shall have our own in Pakistan when we get it.'[68] The vocabulary was scarcely unlike that used in relation to the tricolour since 1920. Nor were the sentiments very dissimilar. Jinnah's speeches were infused with the same references to 'dignity', the

[68] *The Dawn*, 4 July 1943.

need for 'sacrifices under this flag', 'a symbol of the achievement of your final goal'. What was new was the emphasis on the territory for this flag. The Indian National Congress demand had focused on a flag for an Indian nation. The Muslim demand was couched in terms of a national territory for a flag.

In the 1930s the persistent reference to Islam focused on the genealogical continuity of Muslims in India without any precise details. From 1937 the flag, referring to the primordial nature of the Muslim ethnic community was above all a tool to mobilize votes in elections. It was a reminder of intrinsic bonds of kinship, language, religion, and social practices. Around this core culture the idea of a nation for their community could be elaborated. 'We have got millions and millions of Musalmans behind us; we have got our flag and our platform, and what is more, our definite goal of Pakistan.'[69] The logic was simple, clear-cut and final—one community, one party, one flag, and therefore one nation.

The impact of this message did not go unnoticed by Jinnah's political opponents in states where the struggle for power was crucial—in Muslim-majority provinces like Punjab and Bengal. Nor did the British, who until then were inclined to consider the absence of a clearly articulated Muslim proposition as evidence that Pakistan was not a practical or valid scheme, underestimate it. They now registered the changed configurations of local politics, thanks to the entry of this symbol. The British analysis was that Malik Khizar Hayat Khan Tiwana, premier of Punjab, was not keen to provoke a clash because of the danger of Jinnah's unfurling the green flag of Islam. In fact, in their eyes, one of Khizr's main difficulties was the absence of any convincing battle cry with which to rally his own followers and they doubted whether many Unionist Muslims would be able to resist the pressure of Jinnah's manoeuvre of using the Islamic flag.[70]

[69] Pamphlet published by the *Daily Gazette Press*, Karachi, in Syed Sharifuddin Pirzada (ed.), *Foundations of Pakistan, All India Muslim League Documents 1906–47, 1924–1947* (Karachi-Dacca, National Publishing House, 1970), vol. II, pp. 449–50.

[70] Governor of Punjab to Viceroy, 21 July 1943, in Partha Sarathi Gupta (ed.), *Towards Freedom 1943–44*, Part 3, op. cit., p. 2950.

It can be argued that the logic of survival among other Muslim groups and parties, as well as the Congress, imposed a strategy of ethnic consciousness on the Muslim League, forcing it to define its symbol in such terms. But in 1947, when the decision in favour of Pakistan had already been taken and the official adoption of a flag presented itself before the Muslim Constituent Assembly, the idea of defining their nation in other terms was still not envisaged.

Little was done to invite proposals and suggestions from the public or associations and political groups. After the Mountbatten Declaration of 3 June 1947, a few Muslim League members were called upon to design a national flag for Pakistan. Apart from Liaquat Ali, even their identity remains unknown. He attributed this absence of discussion and disregard of the Constituent Assembly to the shortage of time.[71] However, it appears evident from the very brief commentaries allowed on the subject of the formal adoption of the flag that the party did not conceive of this form of open debate.

The Muslim League and the press gave no special attention to the question of the 'flag design', either defending the existing design or summarily rejecting other propositions. For other suggestions were made, expectedly though unrealistically by Mountbatten himself. The long-drawn-out negotiations between Jinnah and Mountbatten were not made public. They appear to have been conducted as a personal exchange that did not concern the people. Barely a month after the government's declaration in June to form Pakistan, Mountbatten proposed a design in the tradition of the colonial system of flags for the dominions (Illustr. V). It placed the Union Jack in the upper canton, very near the crescent of Islam. Mountbatten's notes and letters reveal that he seriously expected a positive response from the League. But none of his arguments, whether technical or political, carried weight. He even pointed out to Jinnah that the Union Jack would be only one-ninth of the whole area instead of one-fourth, as in the case of the other Dominions, and that Congress was likely to agree to a similar flag. However, a week later Jinnah communicated his refusal on the grounds

[71] M. Rafique Afzal (ed.), *Speeches and Statements of Quaid-i-Millat Liaquat Ali Khan, 1941–1951* (Lahore, Research Society of Pakistan, University of the Punjab, 1967), pp. 115–18.

that his colleagues had at once observed the impossibility of having the cross and crescent on the same flag. All the old hatreds and rivalries would be revived.

Jinnah's response mirrored the League's conception of Pakistan in terms of a single, exclusive community. Jinnah also refused the idea of flying the flag of the governor general, namely a dark blue flag with the letters 'Pakistan' in yellow and a yellow crown above, both on the Government House and his car, a refusal Mountbatten felt to be 'the unkindest cut of all'. Mountbatten insisted that the governor's residence was, 'in a sense, not a personal one'. It was the residence of the king's representative and it seemed only right that the king's emblem should be flown. Jinnah argued that although he personally wouldn't object to flying the Dominion flag, the people might resent it.

> It would be a thousand pities if it were to be flown in the first instance and subsequently had to be changed as the result of agitation in the Pakistan Parliament. I said I entirely disagreed. If Mr Jinnah were to start off by flying his own flag instead of the Dominion flag, public opinion at home would attribute this lack of customary friendly courtesies to Mr Jinnah himself. Whereas, if he were to start off by flying the Dominion flag and it was subsequently changed owing to pressure from his Parliament, public opinion in England would not take it really so badly . . . Finally we got on to the question of the White Ensign. To my great surprise, Mr Jinnah said he thought there must have been some misunderstanding. He was quite determined that the Pakistan navy should fly the White Ensign, which was an emblem of comradeship between all the Dominion Navies. I said 'Thank God' and we left it at that.[72]

Despite the fate of Mountbatten's design, it appears to have solicited the lengthiest negotiation.

Other submissions did not merit even a discussion. Only pro-Congress newspapers like the *Hindustan Times* published a few, indicating what they considered a major problem—the representation of

[72] Mountbatten Papers, Interview between Lord Ismay and Mohammad Ali Jinnah, 24 July 1947, in Nicholas Mansergh and Penderel Moon (eds), *The Transfer of Power. 1942–47, The Mountbatten Viceroyalty. Princes, Partition and Independence 8 July–15 August 1947*, 24 July 1947 (London, H.M.S.O., 1974–82), vol. XII, pp. 322–5.

minorities in the new Pakistan. One design from the Sind Minorities Association suggested interposing the green colour between the white and red bands on the right and left sides of the flag. This design found echoes in similar propositions made during the 1931 debate. The green contained a crescent and star, the red carried the sign 'Om' to represent the Hindu minority, the whole was to be embossed in a full-size balance (another design that had been suggested by the prime minister of Mysore in 1931), signifying justice and fairness.[73] Perhaps it was the combination of 'Om' and the 'crescent and star' that made this design impossible from the League's point of view. The fact that it was not even signalled in the major public platforms indicated that the principal issue was not the foundation of an open, multi-ethnic, tolerant state. Another proposal argued for the inclusion of saffron in the new flag to represent Hindus and Sikhs, maintaining that this symbolic representation of minorities was more important than any official decentralization.[74] The Western Punjab Congress Assembly was reported to demand a non-communal, non-religious flag distinct from the League party flag.[75] A rare article in the Muslim press on 'The Pakistan Flag' repeated the argument in favour of retaining the Muslim League flag as the flag of Pakistan. The article's stand was that non-Muslim minorities be represented by one colour, white, and this could be shown either along the southern border of the flag or at its four ends. The rest of the flag should have a green background with a crescent and five stars painted in white. These stars would represent the five autonomous units of Pakistan, i.e., East Bengal, West Punjab, North West Frontier Provinces, Baluchistan, and Sind.[76]

Ultimately, the flag adopted by the Muslim Constituent Assembly on 11 August 1947 was not very different. It was one-fourth white at the mast end and three-quarters green with a white crescent and star on the green, at an angle of 45 degrees away from the flagstaff.[77] (Illustr. V.) There was some criticism of its strong continuity with the Muslim League flag, suggesting that the new flag was expected to be

[73] *Hindustan Times*, 28 July 1947.
[74] *Hindustan Times*, 1 August 1947.
[75] *Hindustan Times*, 7 August 1947.
[76] *The Eastern Times*, 3 August 1947.
[77] M.A.H. Ispahani, *Quaid-e-Azam Jinnah as I Knew Him*, op. cit., p. 42.

above all a symbol of political sovereignty and self-government and not only a religious marker. Liaquat Ali's rejoinder wasted no time in debating such niceties. He simply declared that the future national flag was not a religious one; therefore, Pakistan's flag was not the same flag as the Muslim League flag. Furthermore, the new national flag gave a prominent place to white, which was present in more than one-fourth of the flag and represented the non-Muslim minorities.[78] This brief response was to be the only reaction to the problem of switching from an overtly religious symbol to a more broadly representative national emblem.

An even more daring proposition to include the motif of the sun by an assembly member, Dhirendra Nath Datta, was summarily rejected as far too obvious an imitation of the Congress tricolour flag.[79] The practice of not making a radical break with the symbolic designs that had marked their nationalist struggles was neither new nor curious, pointed out *The Eastern Times*, referring to the example of the Hindustan Constituent Assembly, which had retained the tricolour flag of the Indian National Congress to represent the new Union of India with only a slight modification of the charkha being replaced by the wheel. The assembly concluded that including white as symbolic of the minorities was quite sufficient guarantee that minorities would be fully protected, as had been the practice in Muslim countries in the past.

Despite the quasi-absence of a public debate, the few suggestions outlined above point to some tension between the possibilities of a tolerant, cosmopolitan Islam and an exclusive vision of Islam that conceded little to non-Muslim minorities. The tension reflected another possible approach to a Muslim-dominated yet pluri-ethnic nation, on the lines of the Mughal empire in India.[80] Finally, the

[78] M. Rafique Afzal (ed.), *Speeches and Statements*, op. cit., pp. 115–18.

[79] *Hindustan Times*, 28 July 1947.

[80] Marc Gaborieau draws attention to this neglected aspect of the heritage of Muslim rule in India, mainly the cultural and religious pluralism that characterized the medieval period, permitting different religious communities to coexist and elaborate a common vocabulary and technical lexique. Cf. 'Le legs de la civilisation musulmane aux formations étatiques du sous-continent indien', in Jean-François Bayart (ed.), *La greffe de l'Etat. Les trajectoires du politique*, 2 (Paris, Karthala, 1996), pp. 114–46.

passage of the League design signalled the defeat of this political possibility. It ceded to the current, which considered that the Pakistan nation could only build itself on Muslim support.

For Muslims who opted for Pakistan, the flag question was thus settled from above and accepted with no contestation. They were asked to offer their loyalty to the flag of Pakistan as citizens of that nation. But for many Muslims who remained in India and who were not indifferent to the green flag that stood for their community, faith, and cultural traditions, this separation presented a problem: on the one hand, as citizens of India, they had to accept the Indian flag as a symbol of their political identity. On the other hand, because of the battle between these two flags, this citizenship now required them to relinquish the crescent and star flag, for it had become the symbol of a rival national identity.

Until 1947, it was not possible for individuals to display the two flags simultaneously. As the Congress member Maulana Abul Kalam Azad declared in 1942: 'Our flag is too firmly planted in our hearts for any other flag to take its place.'[81] After August 1947 displaying the flag of Pakistan in India became even more difficult, although the official line reproduced by newspapers like the *Deccan Times* urged Hindus and Muslims to unite and salute the two flags. Muslims in India could hoist the union national flag as well as the Pakistan flag on 15 August, the former to show their loyalty to the Indian Union, the latter to demonstrate their affiliations with a flag which had a history and tradition common to Muslims. This, it declared, was a moment to turn a chapter and act in the Gandhian spirit. Gandhi had declared that if the Pakistan flag, whatever its design, represented all the inhabitants of that nation equally, irrespective of religion, it would command his salute.

At the state level, this was the official position. Chowdhury Khaliq-uz-Zaman's speech before the Constituent Assembly of India in August 1947 was an appeal to all Indian Muslims to rally behind the Indian national flag. 'I hope that the people of India will forget the bitterness of recent months . . . The flag, although only a piece of cloth, really represents the aims and objects and moral and spiritual

[81] *Hindustan Times*, 1 May 1942.

aspirations of the nation. There is no room for difference of opinion on this matter.' He expressed confidence that every Muslim and Christian who was a citizen of India would take pride in hoisting and honouring the flag. Saadulla, another Muslim member assured the loyalty and allegiance of Muslims to the Indian Union.[82] The president of the Madras Provincial Muslim League, Muhammad Ismail Sahib called upon all Muslims in the province to observe Independence Day on 15 August: 'Musalmans of Hindustan must realise that the new Indian Union Flag is no longer a party flag as it has been accepted as the National Flag of the Indian Union with the consent of all parties in Indian Constituent Assembly . . . it was only right that Muslims living in the Union should henceforth regard it as our flag and respect it.'[83]

With its realistic tone, Gandhi's admonition struck a more sensitive note. In light of the conflicting sentiments evoked by the two flags, particularly at this moment of Partition, and the trauma of deciding future identities, alliances, and loyalties in the backdrop of communitarian violence and hatred, Gandhi felt it more appropriate to underplay national symbols altogether and not exhibit them prominently and triumphantly in public meetings. In his opinion, whereas a widespread presence of the national flag had been desirable in the 1930s as a reminder of their collective goal, their distinct identity and their struggle, the present relations of communal tension could not be healed nor the feeling of uncertainty and insecurity diminished by unrestrained displays of two national symbols. At his Independence Day prayer meeting in Noakhali, Gandhi even opted for not hoisting the Indian national flag in respect of Muslim feelings. The flag belonged to the whole of India but, unfortunately, he explained, his Muslim brothers did not take pride in it, even resented it. He would not flaunt it in their faces.[84] Gandhi's remarks reflected the degree to which the flag's consensual character and its capacity to inspire an exalted patriotism had been overshadowed by sentiments of disavowal, rejection, and communal hatred.

[82] B. Shiva Rao (ed.), *The Framing of India's Constitution*, op. cit., pp. 505–7.

[83] *Deccan Times*, 3 August and 10 August 1947.

[84] *National Herald*, 29 January 1947.

Good feelings and intentions notwithstanding, residues of tensions between double loyalties towards community, faith, and nation were not easy to reconcile or bury. Sentiments and passions for symbols were not obliterated suddenly, nor switched on or off to align with new civic identities. Such dilemmas that were glossed over in post-Independence state politics were identified with perhaps more accuracy in literature. Thus, in a short story by Intizar Husain, the character Pichwa's insistence on continuing to display the Pakistan flag in India, even if 'Pakistan had excluded them from its brotherhood', was the expression of a deep-seated determination that 'no Congress flag is going to fly in Qadirpur.'[85] Even after the adoption in 1947 of a new national flag for India, Muslims could still perceive the old Congress flag in a barely disguised form. Such reactions hinted at the enduring continuity of political sentiment that could not always be altered by state decisions.

Although the League's use of the green flag was initially driven by a political logic of survival and electoral victory, its widespread and persistent display advanced it as visible proof of a nationalist sentiment for Pakistan. When the moment to advance the national dimension of their flag superseded the other strains of religious or party identity, the transition was quickly effected without any hurdles. In the grand effort of the Muslim League to rally public opinion, to attract new recruits to its cause, and thus to convince the British and the Congress that the only solution to the political conundrum was to cede Pakistan, the cult of the flag served to exalt Muslim unity while rendering its coexistence with the Congress impossible. It explained the sentiment of the observer who was struck by the changed atmosphere in Delhi in the course of two years, 1937–9: 'Pakistan was in the air.'

[85] Intizar Husain, *An Unwritten Epic and other Stories* (Lahore, Sang-e-Meel, 1987), p. 32.

8

Symbolic Economy of the New Nation

Up to this point our perspective has focused on the open, public debate on the elaboration of a symbol for the future Indian nation. This, as we have seen, took place in the 1930s around a unique alternative. The Congress project, aimed at constructing a unified, inclusive nation on the basis of diversity, stood in opposition to a counter-project drawn up by the Muslim League, which proposed the community as the mainstay of the nation. But what of the other groups and parties that were increasingly troubled by the emergence of new configurations and their own place? The acceptance of the Congress proposal by a broad spectrum of parties and Indians in return stimulated discussions at different levels. It invited reactions on precise aspects of the national project. Each group could advance its views with greater force by also taking recourse to the political symbolism of flags. To begin with, if the tricolour was the national flag, how could it be accepted in a political space controlled by the Indian princes whose dynasties had become accustomed, since the nineteenth century at least, if not earlier, to displaying their power through a flag? Understandably, the subject vexed the princes.

A second point concerned the conception of the nation, as expressed by the flag: Indians did not receive the ideal of a pacific coexistence of communities within the borders of the nation unanimously. Irked by the propositions of the Muslim League, Hindu nationalists became more eager to advertise their own claims for a Hindu nation and also took recourse to the symbolic language of the flag in order to popularize their project. At the same time, the nascent Communist movement articulated its criticism of narrow nationalism by adopting a language of socialist internationalism and introducing the red flag in the symbolic field. Finally, certain minority communities like the Sikhs, fearing political marginalization, undertook a reflection and negotiation on the elaboration of a political symbol that would be more representative of their traditions, without wanting for all that to make it a political symbol of the Indian nation.

In such a complex mosaic of relations and balance of power, this medley of flags that dotted the political landscape of colonial India cannot be analysed simply as a confrontation whose principal prize would be the definition of a national symbol. Underlying these apparent rivalries lay a deeper process that signalled the emergence of the principal elements that were taking shape in the political field and that would acquire importance in independent India. In the politically charged and uncertain climate of the 1940s, such questions as to who would be the political actors of independent India held particular importance. The parties? The princes? The communities? The profusion of flags at this stage must be read as a sign of a more formal politicization of the country, an indicator that the British could sometimes perceive as a threat or a form of opposition to their domination.

States: A Political Future for Princely Banners?

In the 1930s the projection of a national flag throughout India opened the doors to a political battle with a major political stake for the princes. The project of symbolizing a united, free, and distinct people was considered by many princes as a threat to their own power, rooted in a long dynastic tradition and expressed by their own banners. Henceforth, the coexistence of the two kinds of flags within the princely states became problematic. Could there be compatibility between the existence of a princely power and the institution of a unified Indian nation? Depending on the decisions taken by the princes, the situation could evolve towards a conflict. Were the Indian princes part of the nation or, on the contrary, did their power put their own states and people outside the pale of the nation? From this point of view it is important to note that the princes of Mysore, Kashmir, Hyderabad, and the Rajput states rallied to their own banners, which they defended with greater vigour from the 1930s onwards as the main political symbol of their territorial sovereignty.

From their perspective, the ancient ideal of kingship was the fountainhead of authority portrayed through their state's traditional flags. Many princes hesitated to acknowledge the supremacy of the national flag in their own states, betraying their reluctance to merge into the Indian union and their refusal to renounce power and privileges. The example of the state of Mysore examined below reveals a pattern that pitched the symbols of royal sovereignty and popular will against each other.

In the months following the declaration of 'Purna Swaraj' and the adoption of the celebration of an Independence Day (January 1931),[1] Nehru's visit to Mysore and the hoisting of the national flag in the state unleashed tensions between proponents of the Mysore flag and the national flag.[2] It was the beginning of what *The Hindu* termed the 'Bangalore Flag Strife'.[3] After Nehru's visit the national flag was removed and the police destroyed the flagstaff carrying the tricolour, raised for the occasion. A Mysore government official told the journalist Nihal Singh, on a visit to Bangalore in July that year, that only the Mysore princely flag could fly in the state.[4] In effect, the Mysore government issued instructions to all district officers to prohibit the hoisting of 'what is named as the National Flag'.[5] Its justification: 'propaganda and demonstrations in public places in respect of sectional flags' were to be avoided 'especially in view of the recent communal and political tension in the country.'[6] The dewan of Mysore, Mirza Ismail,

[1] OIOC, R/1/1/2141, R/1/1/2142, Events in Indian States, quarter ending 31 December 1931 refer to the monthly flag hoisting in Bangalore, Mysore.

[2] R.L. Handa, *History of Freedom Struggle in Princely States* (Delhi, Central News Agency, 1963), pp. 109–10, 115.

[3] *The Hindu*, 16 July 1931, p. 7.

[4] Nihal Singh, 'Mysore's Ban on Volunteers', *The Hindu*, 25 July 1931, p. 10.

[5] *The Hindu*, 9 July 1931.

[6] Bjorn Hettne, *The Political Economy of Indirect Rule. Mysore 1881–1947* (London, Curzon Press, Scandinavian Institute of Asian Studies, 1978), pp. 186–7.

made a statement to the press that he opposed the public hoisting of the tricolour although he conceded that he was prepared to accept it on private premises.[7] The civil administration was ordered to implement the measure through the state. In Bangalore the commissioner of the city municipal council ordered its president to demolish the structure built for the national flag within three days.[8] In his turn the district magistrate prohibited its hoisting or display in any public place. Angry reactions to the measures were reported in the nationalist press. The ban was justified on the grounds that its exhibition could be construed by people as derogatory to the sovereignty of the maharajas of Mysore and to the Mysore state flag, an idea that the *Bombay Chronicle* dismissed as 'absolutely silly', given that 'the National flag is in no sense a badge of revolt against any Indian state. It is only a symbol of Indian nationhood and of her determination to be and remain free.'[9]

The prohibition was not a punctual reaction but characterized the decade. Flag demonstrations as well as the celebration of Independence Day were banned on 24 January 1937, and the hoisting of the national flag was prohibited for one year within a seven-mile radius of Mysore city. The Mysore government explained its position on 19 October 1937: it could not allow its display in a spirit of hostility to the Mysore flag or in a manner which could cause annoyance to those who were not members of the Congress party.[10]

During the 1930s hoistings and displays became a means for the local Congress Committee to further the national cause in the state. As early as the summer of 1931 this political line was clearly articulated. The Mysore Congress leader, a Brahmin lawyer K.T. Bhashyam, conveyed to Gandhi the public's anger and desire to keep the national flag hoisted in Mysore despite the prohibition. T. Prakasam, the editor of a nationalist newspaper *Swarajya* (published in Madras), when addressing a big public meeting at Ulsoor, in the neighbourhood of

[7] NMML, AICC Papers, G-145, B.J. Ramaswami Iyengar, President of Bangalore City Congress Committee, to Nehru, 15 July 1931.

[8] *Bombay Chronicle*, 14 July 1931.

[9] *Bombay Chronicle*, 21 July 1931.

[10] Vanaja Rangaswami, *The Story of Integration. A New Interpretation in the Context of the Democratic Movements in the Princely States of Mysore, Travancore and Cochin 1900–1947* (Delhi, Manohar, 1981), pp. 133–42.

Bangalore, on 28 July 1931, criticized the Mysore government, which considered the hoisting of the national flag derogatory to the sovereignty of the prince. He found it ironic that the maharaja should prohibit a symbol already accepted by the British in British India although it was clearly anti-British.[11] Faithful to its broader policy of prudence and non-intervention in the princely states, the national Congress Working Committee took a more nuanced position in order to avoid alienating the prince at this stage. It voiced the hope that 'care will be taken not to do anything that may imply any disrespect to the state flag by the State Congress or to the National flag by the state authorities.'[12] Gandhi himself confirmed this position instructing the Mysore state Congressmen to first hoist the Mysore state flag, i.e. give precedence to the Mysore flag on all ceremonial occasions, as a mark of their loyalty to the ruler and in order to avoid any conflict. Despite the increasing clamour of Congressmen for the total abolition of states as a relic of the middle ages, Congress policy would continue to profess friendliness to the states.[13]

Traces of similar conflicts can be found in some of the Rajput states, such as Ajmer and Bundelkhand, in the princely kingdoms of Baroda and Hyderabad all through the 1930s and 1940s.[14] Local Congress volunteers tried to intensify their mass contact programmes; towards this objective they made increasing use of the flag as an effective political tool. In 1940 Punjab's provincial Congress committee president and members were at the head of satyagrahis who hoisted the Congress flag in Faridkot, capital of a small princely state. In the neighbouring state of Nabha, the president of the Congress mass movement, the Praja Pandal, and other Congress workers were arrested for hoisting the flag. Having accepted the flag proposed by the INC as the national flag, the Travancore state Congress authorized its working committee in its session of 12 December 1945 to remove the ban on the national flag.[15] Other small central Indian states like Indore too witnessed

[11] *The Hindu*, 30 July 1931.

[12] *Harijan*, 21 May 1938.

[13] *The Hindu*, 20 May 1938.

[14] OIOC, R/1/1/2141, Important Events in Indian States.

[15] S.H. Patil, *The Congress Party and Princely States* (Bombay, Himalaya Publishing House, 1981), pp. 64, 75.

public support for the tricolour: in 1944, Independence Day was observed at Holkar College and the tricolour was hoisted and garlanded by students.[16]

Occasional public statements by leading Congressmen, advising people not to hoist Congress flags because the states had their own flags, did not satisfy princely state governments. Certainly, on the terrain, central Congress directions were not always heeded to the letter.[17] As early as 1931 the states were unconvinced by Congress assurances that the tricolour was only intended to drive out the Union Jack and not directed at the state flags, as affirmed by an ex-inspector of Rewa police at a meeting.[18] Nehru, during his presidential address to the eleventh session of the All India States People Conference (AISPC) in December 1945, tried to appease resentments over the flag issue. Hoisting the tricolour in Azad Nagar at Udaipur, he said: 'We respect the Udaipur Flag, but historically and otherwise only the National Flag represents the nation as a whole.'[19] His reassurances left the princes sceptical. Even on the eve of independence, the nizam of Hyderabad refused to let K.M. Munshi—the agent general of India in Hyderabad sent by the interim Indian government formed in 1946—to hoist the tricolour at his official residence. As it was situated on the main road, the nizam did not wish to be compelled to 'let His exalted eyes rest on the National flag flying on the house. It would be an affront.'[20] There were reports of people walking with small tricolours pinned to their coats being attacked in Secunderabad. Police detained the Bombay–Madras Express bearing the tricolour on every wagon in Gulbarga station and the flags were washed off.[21] In this case, the political stakes were more explicit: the political future of Hyderabad was under

[16] Fortnightly reports, in P.S. Gupta (ed.), *Towards Freedom*, op. cit., pt 3, pp. 3329, 3337.

[17] OIOC, R/1/1/2141, Important Events in Indian States, Central India Agency, Indore.

[18] OIOC, R/1/1/2141, Important Events in Indian States, Central India Agency, Rewa.

[19] *Indian Annual Register*, January–June 1946 (Calcutta, The Annual Register Office), vol. 1, p. 353.

[20] Kanaiyalal Maneklal Munshi, *The End of an Era. Hyderabad Memories* (Bombay, Bharatiya Vidya Bhavan, 1957), p. 102.

[21] *Deccan Chronicle*, 17 August 1947.

discussion. As a large Muslim state, would the ruler decide to join Pakistan or could he be persuaded to become a part of the Indian union? Permitting the hoisting of the tricolour in this context carried greater political significance.

These long and uncertain conflicts between different forms of political symbols had at least two consequences. The first concerned the affirmation or the reaffirmation of princely banners as the true emblems of sovereignty during the 1930s and 1940s. Towards this objective, princes attempted to win recognition of their royal banner from the British authorities, just as Indians had done for the national flag in British India. One of the principal stakes was to obtain the right to hoist the state flag on public buildings under British control. In Mysore, for example, the superintendent of the post offices enquired if the British Resident would object to flying the Mysore state flag on the General Post Office building in Mysore, either alone or alongside the British Union Flag on state ceremonial occasions such as the birthday of His Highness or the Dashera procession. He pointed out that when the Resident visited Mysore, the British flag was always flown over his residence building and therefore the acceptance of the Mysore flag would be a reciprocal courtesy.[22] The Government of India accepted this demand with the exception of the days when the postal department rules prescribed the flying of the Union Jack.[23] On the same grounds, the Government of Hyderabad won assurances from the British government that the nizam's flag, with a background sandalwood colour and two green bands each carrying two white stripes, would be hoisted along with the Union Jack on the government buildings in Berar, especially on the income tax offices.[24] This demand continued to be advanced down to the summer of 1947. According to

[22] NAI, Home Pub., file no. 389/1935, Lieutenant Colonel C.T.C. Plowden, Resident in Mysore to Political Secretary to Govt of India, Foreign and Political Dept, Bangalore, 30 October 1935.

[23] NAI, Home Pub., file no. 389/1935, Under Sec. of Govt of India to Resident in Mysore, 17 December 1935.

[24] NAI, Home Pub., file no. 260, 1938, Rai Bahadur Pandit Ram Nath, Second Sec., Central Board of Revenue to Commissioner of Income Tax, Central and United Provinces, Lucknow, 14 February 1938; note of P.C. Hailey, 14 March 1938 and B.J. Glancy, 16 March 1938.

Elizabeth Stewart, the wife of a British civil servant, one of the things the ruler of the north-eastern state of Manipur had been trying to wangle was 'the hoisting of his damned state flag here in the Residency and in the old Palace in the cantonments.' The British refused. At the same time, this did not prevent many processions, mostly by school-children, from going round shouting slogans and waving Congress flags.[25] This political demand was however not advanced as a concerted programme. Each state manoeuvred for itself. Their banners thus more or less receded into oblivion, rendering even the minimal reconstruction of their designs a daunting task for the historian.

The second consequence appeared on the eve of independence, during the final discussions on the national flag in the Constituent Assembly. Some princes then attempted to affirm specific claims concerning the choice of the political symbols for the new nation, in particular by the inclusion of princely state symbols in the new Indian flag. Thus, in July 1947 the maharaja of Bikaner wrote to the chairman of the Constituent Assembly, Dr Rajendra Prasad, suggesting that representatives of Indian states should also be nominated to the Flag Committee they envisaged setting up. Since the states would be integral parts of the Union, it was desirable that they should have some symbol to represent them on the flag.[26] In a long letter to Nehru, the prince confessed 'that the way that it (the tricolour) has been forced upon us, it has certainly not been welcome in the Bikaner State and has been equally resented by my people as well.' He had since 1946 been complaining about such an imposition, arguing that the tricolour was a party flag only claiming to be the Indian national flag; it injured the feelings of loyal state subjects, besides leading to a confrontation between the supporters of the tricolour—shouting anti-state slogans during ceremonial functions—and the state authorities. The Praja Parishad, the committee founded by the Congress to rally the population of the princely states to the Indian Union, had been inciting his people to shift allegiance to the tricolour, claiming that it was superior to the state flag. All this was clearly against the indivisibility and sovereignty

[25] CSAS, G.P. Stewart Papers, Elizabeth Stewart to her parents, 10 and 15 August 1947.

[26] *National Herald*, 21 June 1947.

of the state.[27] Against Nehru's affirmation that no disrespect was intended to the state, its ruler, or its flag, he demanded more convincing proof through specific action: 'in reality and in actual fact, except perhaps a few thousands, all the rest of some fifteen lakhs of my people are neither supporters nor sympathisers of the *Praja Parishad*, much less do they accept the tricolour as their flag. As for the people of Bikaner as a whole it is the Bikaner Flag that they venerate and hold sacred and for which they are prepared to give their lives.'[28] He asked that the Bikaner flag now be popularized by the Praja Parishad in the state as a symbol of their own freedom and individuality as a state.[29] Nehru answered that they wished to avoid conflict over the flag question and hoped that changed circumstances would lead both rulers and the people to mutual adjustment. Furthermore, sentiments could not be thrust upon people.

Finally, the states agreed to hoist the tricolour in their capitals along with the state flag on 15 August 1947. Sadul Singh referred to the controversy in his speech declaring that the national flag did not represent a political party or a section of the people. It could not be appropriated by any group or enclosed within a sectional movement or programme. This was pointing a finger at the Praja Parishad's activities in the states.[30]

Notwithstanding such princely sensitivities, there would be little interest in or defence of princely flags either by the states or by the population in independent India. Kashmir's dynastic red flag with a simple plough in the form of a white silhouette had been the symbol of the state's Hindu maharaja, Hari Singh (1895–1961). But it does not seem to have inspired strong support. On the contrary, as in the

[27] On Bikaner's position on the flag question, see M.S. Jain, 'The Role of Popular Movements in the Integration Process. A Case Study of the Flag Question in Bikaner 1946–48', in Makrand Mehta (ed.), *Regional Roots of Indian Nationalism. Gujarat, Maharashtra and Rajasthan* (Delhi, Criterion Publications, 1990), pp. 245–51.

[28] Speech by Maharaja of Bikaner, 15 July 1947, in *Indian Constitutional Documents. Munshi Papers* (Bombay, Bharatiya Vidya Bhavan, 1967), vol. II, pp. 422–3.

[29] Ibid., pp. 505–12.

[30] *Indian Constitutional Documents. Munshi Papers, Pilgrimage to Freedom, 1902–1950*, op. cit., vol. I, pp. 503–13, esp. p. 508.

1930s, public attention rapidly shifted to other flags, more conspicuously identified with the idea of the nation. In 1931, for example, incidents such as placing a Mohammadan flag before a mosque, or flag hoistings, had been noted.[31] In 1947 this trend was strengthened. An opponent political party like Azad Kashmir (Kashmir independent), led by Sheikh Abdullah, adopted its own green flag with four white stripes with a crescent and star and a red rectangle in the upper left corner. A new state flag, different from the maharaja's flag, was adopted after 1947. It was a variation of the old flag in use since 1846: three vertical bands on the side of the pole, officially representing the Muslims of Kashmir, Hindus of Jammu and Buddhists of Ladakh.[32] The Hindu population of Jammu, the Dogras, demanded the application of the entire constitution of India to Jammu, and 'the same flag as is allowed to other states' and not the flag selected by Sheikh Abdullah', leader of the Kashmir Muslim National Conference. Students of the government college in Jammu also demonstrated against the hoisting of the National Conference flag alongside the Indian Union flag at an official function in the premises of the Gandhi Memorial College where Sheikh Abdullah was to speak.[33] Even in this situation of strong conflicts, the princely flag did not constitute a significant political stake in independent India.

Parties: Political Symbols *vs* National Flag?

If the princely banners were ancient realities, party flags had appeared more recently, at the same time as the parties.[34] We have already seen how the green Islamic flag, used by the Muslim League since its foundation in 1906, evolved during the 1930s into a national flag opposed to the tricolour. Other parties too had their own flags, used during

[31] OIOC, L/P&S/20/F 174, Report on an Inquiry into Disturbances in Kashmir in September 1931 by L. Middleton, ICS.

[32] Pierre C. Lux-Wurm, *Les Drapeaux de l'Islam*, op. cit., pp. 75–6.

[33] Prem Nath Bazaz, *The History of Struggle for Freedom in Kashmir* (New Delhi, Kashmir Pub. Co., 1954), pp. 569, 573.

[34] There are few documentary records noting the precise moment of the birth and adoption of these flags in the institutional histories of these parties or contemporary accounts. For example, no mention is found in *Documents of the Communist Movement in India 1917–1928* (Calcutta, National Book Agency,

demonstrations or electoral campaigns. This practice was not inspired by or derived from British or Western political precedents. Without following the same itinerary as the League and claiming the status of a national symbol, they nonetheless played a double role in the political field. On the one hand, as the race for assembly seats between political parties intensified, they sharpened the lines between political groups by emphasizing their own symbolic distinction. The split in the Congress in 1921 among Gandhians and Swarajists saw the latter designing their own flag—the same white, green, and red tricolour, with the spinning wheel in the middle, but including a leopard and a silver unicorn in one corner.[35] In the same period Hindu parties adopted the saffron flag, while the new Communist Party rallied to the already well-established red banner, as an international socialist symbol. Conversely, these political symbols also contributed to the elaboration of a national flag by introducing important elements in the discussions (colours, designs, symbols). Paradoxically these proposals, perceived as isolated statements or expressions of sectional interests, reinforced the consensual aspect of the tricolour. Thus Motilal Nehru in 1928 explained that while there were political differences between the Swaraj Party and Congress, he 'hoped that the country will not be deceived by the thin disguise but will rally round the national flag held aloft by the Congress.'[36] I will examine two cases here: the flag of the Hindu parties and the use of the red flag. In both instances, the affirmation of a party flag affected the imaginary dimension of national symbols.

1997), vol. 1; C. Kaye, *Communism in India. Unpublished Documents from National Archives of India 1919–1924* (Calcutta, Editions Indian, 1971); Walter K. Anderson & Shridhar D. Damle, *The Brotherhood in Saffron. The Rashtriya Swayamsevak Sangh and Hindu Revivalism* (London, Westview Press, 1987); K. Jayaprasad, *RSS and Hindu Nationalism. Inroads in a Leftist Stronghold* (New Delhi, Deep Publications, 1991); Thomas Blom Hansen, *The Saffron Wave. Democracy and Hindu Nationalism in Modern India* (Princeton, Princeton University Press, 1999).

[35] I have found only one reference to this flag in Archives d'Outre Mer, Aix (CAOM), E-8, Analytic Review of the Anglo Indian press of April–June 1923, Governor of Pondicherry, 25 July 1923.

[36] *Selected Works of Motilal Nehru, vol. 5, 1926–28*, eds Ravinder Kumar and Hari Dev Sharma (New Delhi, Vikas, 1992), p. 702.

Attempts to merge the various Hindu voluntary associations into a national political platform went back at least to the foundation of the All-India Hindu Mahasabha at Hardwar in April 1915. But they focused on propagating the adoption of Hindi and Nagari along with cow protection and Hindu uplift. Little evidence is available of Hindu associations and parties joining hands in the representation of Hindu unity through a flag until the mid 1920s, that is to say four years after Gandhi's proclamation of the national flag. Then, in 1925, the creation of the Rashtriya Svayam Sevak Sangh (RSS) by Dr K.B. Hedgewar at Nagpur was accompanied by the systematic appearance of a triangular saffron flag, considered as the bhagwa dhwaj (sacred banner) in party procedures. Considered an age-old symbol of Hindu culture—the flag of the Hindu god Rama and also of the Maratha ruler Shivaji in the seventeenth century—the saffron flag was now formally adopted as the emblem of the Hindu nation they wished to create.[37] The party's revival of this banner was meant to reinforce its message of the common and ancient past that Hindus shared and which implied more than a territorial bond. RSS branches instituted the practice of saluting and hoisting their bhagwa jhanda in their party functions and gatherings.[38] Despite the militaristic orientation, a Hindu religious tone was evident in the practice of placing an offering of money (*dakshina*) in front of the flag. It was referred to as *gurudakshina*, or an offering to the guru in gratitude of his transmission of learning or skills. This gift was considered to be a return as well as the opening of the disciple to a future transformation. In giving, he created the space to receive more. The integration of this practice in the salutation of the flag served as an effective means of fund collection for RSS activities, and though dakshina was equally part of other religious systems, it was a reminder that the nation was onc with their Hindu religious beliefs. Besides, the RSS developed a different salute for its saffron flag combining elements from a Western salute and the Indian namaste. Everyone kept their right arm folded with their fist touching the heart. A Sanskrit prayer was recited in praise of the motherland and the flag. After the drill, games, or calisthenics, they assembled once again and the flag was taken down with a salute and a prayer. Entry into the RSS

[37] T. Basu *et al.*, *Khaki Shorts*, op. cit., esp. pp. 12–56.

[38] In P.S. Gupta (ed.), *Towards Freedom*, op. cit., pt 3, pp. 2970, 3098.

as a full-fledged member also involved repeating an oath before the flag and saluting it.[39]

Regularly accompanying the activities of party volunteers and members, the flag nevertheless remained circumscribed in such sites. There were few occasions when it was paraded or displayed outside RSS camps. It was thus exclusively destined to a male public until 1936 when the first women's branch (Rashtrasevika Samiti) was set up. There were no confrontations either with the Union Jack or with the Indian tricolour until 1930, when RSS branches were directed to celebrate Independence Day by saluting the saffron flag.[40] The party's espousal of this banner strengthened in the 1930s and 1940s as the Muslim League hardened its advocacy of the green flag. Even if Article 5 of its constitution stated that the duty of every citizen was to be loyal to the state flag, identified as the tricolour, the Sangh saffron flag was still repeatedly proposed as a national flag for a Hindu nation.[41] Thus in 1939 V.D. Savarkar, in his presidential address to the 21st session of the Akhil Bharatiya Hindu Mahasabha held at Calcutta, declared that the 'Kundalini Kripankrit Geraua flag [saffron flag graced by the kundalini energy] shall be the flag of the Hindu nation', with its various constituents. The Muslims, he added, were welcome to have their own religious colours to represent their own community.[42] Over 1930–47 Hindu readers continuously acclaimed the saffron flag in the Hindu press as the fitting colour for the national flag, either on its own or as one of the colours. As we have seen, it was even perceived by the Sikhs as the colour representing their distinctiveness. To many Indians, the saffron flag represented an unbroken link with their past, evoking important episodes of their history.[43] But the development of a civic

[39] Eleanor Zelliot and Maxine Berntsen (eds), *The Experience of Hinduism. Essays on Religion in Maharashtra* (Albany, N.Y., State University of New York Press, 1988), pp. 191–4.

[40] See T. Basu, *et al.*, *Khaki Shorts*, op. cit., pp. 21, 29.

[41] Sundar Lal Poplai, *India 1947–50, Internal Affairs* (Bombay, Oxford University Press, 1959), vol. 1, p. 555.

[42] Vinayak Damodar Savarkar, *Hindu Rashtra Darshan* (Bombay, Laxman Ganesh Khare, 1949), p. 106.

[43] *The Mahratta*, 11 July 1947, R.K. Patankar, 'Glorious Traditions of Our Saffron Flag'.

national culture did not necessarily imply the triumph of a Hindu destiny.

On the whole, despite this almost given popular appeal of saffron and the party's ambitions, as proclaimed by Hedgewar, of reaching out to the 'vast Hindu world outside the Sangh',[44] the saffron flag itself did not become a common rallying point for the different Hindu parties. The ritual remained confined to the RSS and its existence did not lead to an open, violent clash with the tricolour—as the green flag had achieved. In 1947 Savarkar, inaugurating the 28th session of the All India Hindu Mahasabha at Calcutta, could accept the new national flag 'at the same time our Hindu flag. There is that Ashoka Chakra inscribed on it.'[45]

Since its foundation in 1919 the Communist Party upheld the red flag, despite its policy of unity with the Congress and the League. At the Fifth Congress of the Communist International held at Moscow in June and July 1924, the proletarian organizations of Moscow presented a gold embroidered red flag to the Indian working classes as a token of revolutionary unity.[46] When Nehru arrived in Calcutta for the Congress session in 1928, crowds holding aloft the communist flag welcomed him. He acclaimed it, acknowledging the very distinguishable characters of the two flags. Thus, at the outset of Congress's decision to fight for Purna Swaraj on 26 January 1930, he reiterated his position: while they respected the red flag as representing the blood of the people, he would not allow any flag to displace the national flag, or even claim precedence over it.[47] Differences between the communists and the Congress were to sharpen in the 1930s and at times they spilled over onto the flag. During the Civil Disobedience movement Indian communists made clear their independence and their disagreement

[44] Christophe Jaffrelot, *Les Nationalistes Hindous. Idéologie, implantation et mobilisation des années 1920 aux années 1990* (Paris, Presses de la Fondation Nationale des Sciences Politiques, 1993).

[45] P. Bazaz, *The History of Struggle*, op. cit., p. 355.

[46] *The Vanguard. Central Organ Communist Party of India* (Bombay), vol. II, 15 September 1924, quoted in David Petrie, *Communism in India, 1924–27* (Calcutta, Editions Indian, 1972), p. 58.

[47] K.T. Shah, 'The Evolution of the Left Wing Programme in India', *Hindustan Review*, January 1935, p. 450.

with the Congress line by bringing down the national flag on Chowpathy beach in Bombay.[48] Sporadically, communists displayed the red flag during manifestations of protest against some Congress decisions. For instance, when Gandhi agreed to participate in the Round Table Conference (RTC), a Communist Party anti-RTC demonstration in Bombay displayed red flags. On the other side, some altercations with Congress supporters led to red flags being publicly burnt.[49] Later, occasional attacks on the national flag would be condemned. In a meeting organized by the National Congress of French India in April 1947, the Tamil Nadu Congress leader Kamraj decried communist aggression on houses where the national flag had been hoisted, 'tearing it to a thousand pieces. They also attacked persons carrying the insignia of the national flag.'[50] But on the whole there were few such incidents.

On the contrary, during Civil Disobedience, in areas like Malabar district, where the communist movement was strong and the Congress presence weak, the national flag could become the object of fervent defence by communist volunteers even at the risk of police brutality. When a small group of fifty volunteers marched to Calicut beach on 11 May 1930, the future general secretary of the Communist Party in Kerala, P. Krishna Pillai, resisted the police, holding up the national tricolour.[51] Naturally, political priorities could and did change. Nevertheless, in 1936 communist leaders like M.N. Roy reiterated appeals 'to rally in the millions under the flag of the National Congress. Socialism or communism is not the issue of the day, and socialists and communists should realize that the immediate objective is national independence.'[52] During the leftist demonstrations on Protest Day, 15 September 1940, in North Malabar, against government repression

[48] Minocheher Rustom Masani, *The Communist Party of India. A Short Story* (London, D. Verschoyle, 1954), p. 42.

[49] *Bombay Chronicle*, 31 August 1931.

[50] CAOM, H 17, Tracts politiques.

[51] Cited in Robin Jeffrey, 'Matriliny, Marxism, and the Birth of the Communist Party in Kerala, 1930–1940', *Journal of Asian Studies*, vol. XXXVIII, no. 1, November 1978, p. 85

[52] John Patrick Haithcox, 'Left Wing Unity and the Indian Nationalist Movement: M.N. Roy and the Congress Socialist Party', *Modern Asian Studies*, III, 1 (1969), pp. 17–56. Cited on p. 43.

of the Communist Party (the Kerala party leadership had been jailed), the tricolour was flown with the communist flag in Morazha and Mattanur.[53] In Calcutta, communist workers were arrested for demonstrating with the tricolour. According to British intelligence reports, communists were more in the forefront than Congressmen on 'Independence Day'.[54] A British commissioner proposed a pragmatic explanation of this display of unity. At a war meeting, he observed a large Congress flag on a sugar mill. The owner explained it had been hoisted to appease the Congress Bengal government, an excuse that the British treated with some scepticism: 'The flag cannot have been forgotten as . . . it was a landmark for mills around and this incident is possibly merely indicative of the general attitude of many at the present time, who wish to have a foot in both camps.'[55] Their fidelity to the emblem of the working classes never faltered, nor did their commitment to the goal of national independence and social equality.

Communist Party programmes in the 1940s retained the formal hoisting of the red flag with speeches.[56] It continued to be displayed along with the tricolour during the Second World War, in spite of the diverging positions of the communists and the Congress before the war. Workers used the red flag while addressing meetings of farmers in Patiala state in 1943, referring to the day when it would fly over the maharaja of Patiala's residence as well as in Delhi.[57] Both flags appeared side by side in Independence Day celebrations. They were reported in official ceremonies and on shops and housetops as well as on the local CPI office in 1944 in Malda, Bengal.[58] Such simultaneous displays of red and tricolour flags conveyed different messages. For many people

[53] Dilip M. Menon, *Caste, Nationalism and Communism in South India. Malabar 1900–1948* (Cambridge, Cambridge University Press, 1994), pp. 155–6.

[54] NAI, Home Political (I), file no. 7/23/43, Extracts of Official Notings Regarding Communist Propaganda, in P.S. Gupta (ed.), *Towards Freedom*, op. cit., pt 2, p. 1673.

[55] NAI, Home Political (I), file no. 18/2/44, Extracts from fortnightly reports from U.P. for February 1944, in ibid., pt 3, p. 2524.

[56] Secretary Bezwada to President of the All India Kisan Sabha, 28 February 1944, in P.S. Gupta (ed.), *Towards Freedom*, op. cit., pt 2, p. 2155.

[57] Resident's Report, November 1943, ibid., pt 3, pp. 3404–5.

[58] Police Report, 27 January 1944, Malda, ibid., pt 1, p. 189.

they were understood as proof of the peaceful coexistence of multiple political parties fighting against the British in a new political field in construction under colonial domination.

With the 1930s more and more Indians recognized the tricolour as the flag of their nation. Even a dissident political movement headed by Subhas Chandra Bose accepted the logic of a national flag being above all other flags. Bose had designed a separate flag in 1942 for his army based in Burma. Instead of the charkha characterizing the Congress flag, there was the figure of a springing tiger, which had been Tipu Sultan's emblem of revolt against the British in the eighteenth century. Yet it was not perceived as an alternative to the national emblem. In the Singapore headquarters of the Indian National Army (INA) in 1943, the ritual around the tricolour dominated the camp routine, beginning the day and marking its closure at sunset.[59] Subhas Chandra Bose publicly confirmed this position when he called his army to commence its historic march to Delhi. 'This march will end only when the Anglo-Americans are expelled from India and the Indian National Flag is hoisted over the Viceroy's House in New Delhi.'[60] This distinction between the status of the two flags was also clearly perceived by the Congress leaders. Nehru considered the INA flag an important symbol of anti-colonial resistance. Presented with the flag used by the INA on the liberation of Kohima in north-east India, Nehru instructed his daughter to bring it over carefully; though it represented quite a different path from that of the tricolour, it had contributed to the ending of colonial rule.[61]

Instead of considering these tensions as rivalries between different flags contesting a national status together, it is more relevant to see how the recourse to flags of all kinds reinforced the anti-British struggle, especially during the 1940s when parties, acquainting people in the states with the idea of the 'National Task', increasingly used the flag in

[59] Lakshmi Sahgal, *A Revolutionary Life. Memoirs of a Political Activist* (Delhi, Kali for Women, 1997), p. 43, 66.

[60] In P.S. Gupta (ed.), *Towards Freedom*, op. cit., pt 3, p. 2734.

[61] Nehru to Indira Gandhi, Delhi, 2 April 1946, in Sonia Gandhi (ed.), *Two Alone, Two Together. Letters between Indira Gandhi and Jawaharlal Nehru, 1940–1964* (London, Hodder & Stoughton, 1992), p. 528.

hartals, satyagrahas, and on public and private buildings.[62] All of them explicitly referred to Indian symbols and contexts. Over the years the Union Flag, still present during the Home Rule movement, disappeared from these political symbols, affirming that the game was now definitely being played by Indian actors, who with all their differences, cultural, political or religious, were united against the British. This situation, paradoxical in British eyes, is clearly evoked in a literary work like Attia Hosain's *Sunlight on a Broken Column*. The young Anglo-Indian character Joan Davis sums up her Hindu and Muslim friends Nita and Nadira's sentiments about national symbols on the occasion of the viceroy's visit to Lucknow in 1942, which heightens Indian student animosity against the symbols (flag and anthem) of empire. Joan Davis declares: 'I am absolutely against you. To me the whole affair seems childish. This insult to the [British] national anthem was like children making faces and putting out their tongues at one.' If Nadira and Nita quarrelled constantly about flags and anthem, and showed themselves incapable of reaching agreement about a common Indian political symbol, they demonstrated on the contrary that they were united in their strong opposition to British symbols. 'We agree about yours', retorts Nadira.[63] In the 1940s this position was highlighted at moments when, despite profound differences between Congress and League over larger strategies and demands, their flags converged on the terrain to express a common sentiment of opposition to British rule.

Thus in November 1945 at Calcutta, students and workers marched under the joint flags of the Congress, the League and the Communist Party during protest demonstrations and strikes. It marked the high point of solidarity between Congress, Muslim, and Communist ranks during the trial of the three INA officers by the British government. During angry protestations and demonstrations in the city and its suburbs the three flags were tied together and were seen flying on top of every road block: 'Suddenly, we witnessed a big procession of

[62] Fortnightly Reports of Punjab States, March 1944, in P.S. Gupta (ed.), *Towards Freedom*, op. cit., pt 3, p. 3395.

[63] Attia Hosain, *Sunlight on a Broken Column. A Novel* (London, Chatto & Windus, 1961), p. 158.

Muslim students carrying Muslim League flags . . . hundreds of students rushed forward, embraced the Muslim students and tied the Muslim League flags together with the tricolour flags.'[64] In January 1946 naval officers demanded the release of INA men under the collective display of Congress, League, and red flags on their ships. Communist workers hoisted the tricolour along with the red flag during the satyagraha for Hyderabad's accession to India and the introduction of responsible government in the state.[65] At Christian College, Lucknow, the Muslim League flag was tied to the tricolour on Subhas Day celebrations in 1946.[66] In the general strike on 11 February 1946, processionists carried Congress and Muslim League flags side by side as a demonstration of unity.[67] During the revolt of Indian Royal Navy sailors, the three flags—the tricolour, the green flag, and the red flag —were hoisted in a symbolic display of unity in Bombay.[68] A month later, military sepoys paraded all three flags at Jubbulpore on 4 March 1946.[69]

Such incidents, though numerous, do not all need to be cited here. They confirm that the manipulation of these political symbols contributed in creating a new political space. These flags announced a future democratic multi-party field in which the British dimension was completely absent. They demonstrated that a national flag was henceforth the symbolic condition of the existence of a nation in which the role of political parties, made evident by their own flags, was fundamental. The central question remained: which flag could represent the nation? As seen in the preceding chapter, from the late 1930s the real antagonism was focused only on two flags, the tricolour and the Islamic green flag.

The British viewed this multiplication of party flags with the same vigilance that had characterised their reactions to the Swaraj flag since 1921. In their logic this development held the advantage of drawing attention away from the exclusive opposition between the Union Jack

[64] J. Sarkar, A.B. Bardhan, N.E. Balaram, *India's Freedom Struggle. Several Streams* (Delhi, People's Publishing House, 1986), p. 223.

[65] K.M. Munshi, *The End of an Era*, op. cit., p. 90.

[66] OIOC, L/P&J/5/275, Governors Reports for the United Provinces, Lucknow, 5 February 1946.

[67] *Amrita Bazar Patrika*, 17 February 1946.

[68] J. Sarkar, A.B. Bardhan, N.E. Balaram, op. cit., p. 227.

[69] S.L. Poplai, *India 1947–50*, vol. 1, op. cit., pp. 507–8.

and the tricolour. In Allahabad, the British governor, M. Hallet, observed this symbolic expression of political divisions at the height of the Quit India movement: every group hoisted its own banner, the Congress, the League, the Hindu Mahasabha, the Sikhs, the communists. He even quoted a cartoon showing a humorous depiction of a flag carrying the design of a coffee pot and the words 'Drink, mix and be merry' as the motto. For him, in this period of deep political tension between the British and the Indians, 'a little ridicule is often useful': he considered such a visible political division among Indians ultimately favourable to the British.[70] However, in 1946 the British government finally proclaimed that the only recognized official flag of the province was the Union Jack and that flag waving was outside the norms of formal political processes and hence a threat to public order.[71]

Communities: The Symbolic Status of the Sikhs

Among the minority groups that constituted Indian society, the Sikhs were the most committed to distinguishing themselves from the Hindus. Their efforts to reinterpret their doctrines, to assert and codify their religious symbols and rituals in order to strengthen their coherence as a distinct religious community, have been the object of important studies.[72] In the inter-war period, this process acquired a political dimension—a recourse to the use of political symbols. With the opening of the debate on the national flag in the 1920s, the Sikhs too initiated a discussion on the political importance of a Sikh flag, for they wished to be considered as a significant component of the national process.[73]

The fear of being submerged or absorbed in a larger Hindu tradition was a dominant feature of Sikh politics under colonial rule. Their

[70] OIOC, R/3/1/78, Linlithgow Collection, M. Hallett to Lord Linlithgow, 9 November 1942, p. 153.

[71] OIOC, L/P&J/5/275, Press Note, Lucknow, 1 December 1946.

[72] See, in particular Harjot Oberoi, *The Construction of Religious Boundaries. Culture, Identity and Diversity in the Sikh Tradition* (Delhi, Oxford University Press, 1997).

[73] Little attention has been paid to the Sikh flag and its role, except an allusion in J.S. Grewal, *The New Cambridge History of India, The Sikhs of the Punjab* (Cambridge, Cambridge University Press,1990), II, 3, p. 169.

determination not to be confounded with the Hindus but treated as a separate community had been expressed clearly by the end of the nineteenth century through movements of hard-line religious reform, appealing for a return to their sources of religious texts. Provoked partly by the inroads of the Arya Samaj in the Punjab, they continued to reinforce their distinctive traits through the early years of the twentieth century, in literary outpourings in Punjabi and in English on their history, religion, and identity.[74] It was primarily their defiance of the Hindu social system that seems to have been at the root of a widespread use of black and blue on their religious banners in festivals and temples. Taylor's observations had revealed the use of blue by the Sikhs since the seventeenth century.[75]

Their sensitivity to the subject of a national flag and more particularly its colours was thus almost inevitable in the 1920s, when many groups were trying to find a specific place in the process of nation-building. While keen on embracing the goal of complete independence, they also worried about their status and the impact of proposed separate electorates for Muslims on the equilibrium of regional politics. Caught in this competition with Muslims for a privileged recognition, they too were negotiating with Congress in order to ensure themselves a secure position in provincial and national political space. Their rejection of the adoption by the Simon Commission in 1930 of communal electorates which would favour Muslim representation in the province and their demand for reservations for Sikhs on the same grounds coincided with an intensification of their claims for the inclusion of the Sikh colour on the flag.[76]

Sikh opposition to the flag designed by Gandhi in 1921, as we have seen, took shape progressively. It had been articulated as early as 1921 when Gandhi's Swaraj flag had barely taken form. When the Sikh

[74] On this production, see N. Gerald Barrier, *The Sikhs and their Literature* (Delhi, Manohar Books, 1970); J.S. Grewal, 'The Emergence of Punjabi Drama: A Cultural Response to Colonial Rule', *Journal of Regional History*, vol. 5, 1984, pp. 115–55; and *The Sikhs of the Punjab*, op. cit., esp. p. 147; the struggle for the Sikh identity is today reflected in historiography on the subject. See J.S. Grewal, *Contesting Interpretations of the Sikh Tradition* (Delhi, Manohar, 1998).

[75] Robert Taylor, *The Princely Armoury*, op. cit., p. 6.

[76] A discussion of these questions can be found in chapter 4.

League passed a resolution that the Sikh colour, henceforth identified as black, be included in the national flag, Gandhi rejected this proposition publicly in his journal *Young India*; he argued that Hindu and Muslim colours were necessary to symbolically express the reconciliation between two estranged communities; as Sikhs had no quarrel with the Hindus, there was no reason to specifically acknowledge them as a 'community apart'—as indeed there was no reason for Parsis, Christians, and Jews in India.[77] But Gandhi's reasoning, which he continued to present in the following months,[78] dominated as it was by the perspective of national unity, did not satisfy the Sikhs. They desired to affirm themselves as a separate community without rejecting a national perspective. Nevertheless, no further development took place in public debates until 1930.

During the Civil Disobedience movement Baba Kharak Singh, president of the Shiromani Gurdwara Prabandhak Committee (SGPC), refused to join Gandhi's protest in March 1930 unless the Sikh colour, faithful to their traditions, was included in the national flag. Their claim for a symbolic presence of their community was couched in defensive terms, in reaction to the recognition of Hindu and Muslim communities represented by red and green. A certain Teja Singh from Amritsar expressed a similar wish: while rejecting a communal interpretation of colours and pleading for political unity, he argued for the temporary inclusion of the Sikh colour as long as this unity did not exist.[79] Many Sikhs refused to be relegated or merged into the nebulous category of other communities or faiths. It was consistent with their struggle for separate electorates and weightage in provincial constitutional politics while the communal award arrangement was being discussed.[80] Yet, they did not have a unique strategy. In opposition to the SGPC, a central body which had the power to excommunicate Sikhs for not following its directives, other groups like the Shiromani

[77] *Young India*, 18 May 1921, p. 154.

[78] *Young India*, 4 August 1921, p. 242.

[79] *The Tribune*, 10 April 1931.

[80] The Sikhs would be disappointed when, in August 1931, the Ramsay MacDonald Award left them with only 33 seats in the Punjab Legislative Council, making them lag behind Muslims (88 seats) and Hindus (44 seats), and threatening a diminution of their political presence and influence.

Akali Dal, and the Central Sikh League threw in their lot with the Civil Disobedience movement, irrespective of Congress deliberations on the inclusion of their colour.[81]

Other Sikhs continued to protest, insisting for example on the inclusion of saffron, a colour more suitable to the Sikhs than red, chosen by Gandhi in his 1921 proposal.[82] Gandhi, in turn, attempted to diffuse Sikh pressure on Congress for a change of colours: he pointed to the flag's unofficial nature, underlining the fact that it had been produced at his own personal initiative, without any formal adoption by the party.[83] A Sardar Charan Singh Shahid from Amritsar answered Gandhi that although 'every Sikh must feel thankful for your characteristic sweetness and sincerity . . . it will not be true to say that it has completely satisfied Sikhs regarding the inclusion of the Sikh colour in the national flag', an issue which they now considered to be one of 'Panthic honour'.[84] The same month, in March 1931, over a dozen Sikh leaders met Gandhi to discuss the inclusion of a distinct colour for the Sikhs in the national flag or, alternatively, adopt a single colour for the flag. Gandhi then reassured them with promises of envisaging a review of the matter through a committee.[85]

Sikh discontent was used by other groups as an indication of the danger of admitting the principle of separate representation through colours: 'why should it be denied to the Parsis who form perhaps the most important mercantile community in the country? . . . Other minor communities conscious of their self-importance, may follow suit with the same justification.'[86] The point was more theoretical than real. Parsis had rarely expressed their political interest in a Zoroastrian flag, symbol of their faith and historical origins. The only known demonstration had occurred more than five decades earlier on their victory in the Parsi-British cricket match at the Bombay Gymkhana in

[81] J.S. Grewal, op. cit., p. 169.

[82] Sardul Singh, 'The Indian National Flag', *The Tribune*, 24 May 1931.

[83] *The Tribune*, 1 March 1931.

[84] *The Tribune*, 6 March 1931. 'Panthic' = communitarian, from 'panth', community in Punjabi.

[85] *Searchlight*, 31 March 1931.

[86] R.D. Tiwari, 'The Indian National Flag. An Inquiry into Its Colour', *The Mahratta*, 14 June 1931.

1889. Even at this moment, they never disavowed their allegiance to the Union Jack as the only possible political symbol.[87] Nonetheless, the possibility of other communities taking up the Sikh refrain could not be ruled out, as *The Mahratta*'s commentary indicated, and risked further complicating and hampering the progress of the national flag.

Thus the pressure applied by the few Sikh political groups and personalities was taken seriously by the Congress, which had resolved to officially adopt the flag before engaging in the Round Table Conference. As seen in Chapter 3, it instituted a Flag Committee in May 1931 to gather and examine public proposals for the flag. The executive committee of the Central Sikh League then submitted several propositions: a tricolour flag of saffron, green, and red; white stars indicating the number of provinces, and an indigo background; the seven colours of the rainbow; a map of India in yellow with a red boundary.[88] Whereas Sikh political organizations were quick to publicize their views on the flag's colours, the reaction from the Sikh people was comparatively lukewarm. Apart from a few letters sent to the editor in English newspapers, until June 1931 there were no Sikh proposals listed among the forty-three recommendations sent to the convener of the Flag Committee, P. Sitaramayya, and made public by him.[89] Sikh complaints were put to rest by the committee's final recommendation of one single colour, saffron. It seems to have satisfied Sikh leaders. The executive committee of the Central Sikh League unanimously approved the initiative and urged the working committee of the Indian National Congress to confirm this recommendation.[90] Even when this proposal was not retained and saffron was included only as one of the three colours of the flag, the Sikhs accepted this concession too, and considered that their demand had been heard and registered.

Sikh protests had not mobilized the Sikh people in a very significant way in the sense that they generated a limited public reaction. They remained political, intellectual demands in comparison to the passion invited by the Indian tricolour. A Sikh flag was not used in political

[87] Ramachandra Guha, *A Corner of a Foreign Field. The Indian History of a British Sport* (London, Picador, 2002), p. 33.

[88] *Bombay Chronicle*, 4 July 1931.

[89] The list was published by *The Tribune*, 17 June 1931.

[90] *The Tribune*, 19 July 1931.

rituals celebrating Sikh identity. Sikh views were aired in well-chosen platforms through their representative organizations, and before a few eminently political personalities like Gandhi, Nehru, and Patel. At no point were there public rallies around the flag, demonstrations, clashes, furore or passion for this Sikh symbol. Yet, the affront to Sikh feelings was made amply clear, systematically and persistently by their leaders, and by their success in barring Sikh participation in the Civil Disobedience movement. And the very hint of other communities like the Parsis, the Jains, and the Christians taking up the Sikh refrain was sufficient incentive to take the matter seriously. Although political differences prevented Sikh parties from adopting a common stand or political strategy on either Civil Disobedience or the communal award, they all nonetheless agreed about wanting a colour acceptable to the Sikhs on the national flag. Given the strains exercised by religious and ethnic divisions among Jats and non-Jats as well as the different merchant castes on the affirmation of a Sikh identity, this consensus was of no mean value. Finally, the inclusion of saffron in the flag reassured the Sikhs, reinforcing their political weight in the Indian firmament, and their identity as a distinct group—a preoccupation which had dogged the evolution of the Sikh community since their emergence in the fifteenth century. At the same time, it opened a path of honourable integration into the nation. By negotiating the inclusion of what they affirmed to be an acceptable colour, they had succeeded in manoeuvring themselves into a position of some strength from which they hoped to bargain with the British and the Congress for further rewards. The relatively easy resolution of the problem also proved that the Sikh people's identification with their own colours or their flag had not taken deep root. The battle was only part of the larger fight for national recognition and equality with Hindus and Muslims, within the frame of the nation, not outside it.

The emergence of the national flag in the political landscape, placed over and above all other symbols of party or community identity had some immediate implications. On the one hand it called for negotiation, a readjustment with existing traditional political symbols such as those of the princely houses. On the other hand a further adjustment was necessary with newly defined symbols of political parties and the odd community. As far as princely houses were concerned, the principal stake turned round their future power and sovereignty. It anticipated the problem that loomed on the immediate horizon and would have to be resolved at the moment of independence. And as far the political parties were concerned, the possibility of a clash that could have taken place in the 1920s, when the nationalization of the tricolour was in progress, actually receded during the 1930s. For this process of nationalizing the flag produced at least the concrete political result of making it part and parcel of the most important political movements.[91] What began as opposition to the British flag had emerged as the symbol that would replace it on India's independenc;[92] it was the centre of a large public debate and inserted in political rituals that were rituals of sovereignty. In comparison, political symbols of parties never aspired to this status, with the exception of the Muslim League flag. Ultimately, the multiplication of party political flags was not, as some British observers noted, simply a sign of Indian divisions and weakness. Although independence itself was still to be acquired, the country was already working at a massive process of politicization.

[91] On the process of the nationalization of the tricolour, see Arundhati Virmani, 'National Symbols under Colonial Domination. The Nationalization of the Indian Flag. March–August 1923', *Past & Present*, no. 164, August 1999, pp. 169–97.

[92] Arundhati Virmani, ' "Up, up with the Indian Flag, Down, down with the Union Jack!". Le drapeau indien et le ralliement à la nation, 1930–1931', dans *Les ralliements. Ralliés, traîtres et opportunistes du Moyen Age à l'époque moderne et contemporaine*. Actes du colloque tenu à la Maison des Sciences de l'Homme d'Aquitaine les 9, 10, 11 février 1995 (Bordeaux, CROCEMC, 1997), pp. 215–37.

9

The Uses of the Flag in Independent India

From the standpoint of this major political symbol, the national flag, India's independence did not appear a moment of rupture. Echoing the process already instituted in 1931, a new debate took place through the country, above all within the flag committee set up by the Constituent Assembly on 23 June 1947, whose task was to determine the new republic. The assembly that gave India its final national form decided to broadly conserve the tricolour that had accompanied the affirmation of the nation since the 1920s. If there was indeed a rupture it came later, not at the level of symbolic representation but in the uses that independent India and its citizens would make of the national flag. Symbol of a heritage, it no longer seemed to invite the political passions and emotions that had contributed to the strong mobilization and politicization in the colonial period. Subjected to constitutionally laid down norms, encapsulated in strongly codified official rituals, it appeared less and less liable to personal appropriation by Indian citizens. Fifty years were to go by before this distant and formal use of the flag was criticized and challenged, and private citizens increasingly reclaimed the flag as an object of national pride and patriotic sentiment. In the first decade of the twenty-first century it is at last open to popular usage, free to be hoisted by citizens on all occasions, even if it is impossible to decide today whether this announces a long-lasting change or is merely a conjectural development. Can it be concluded that national symbols serve principally to project what does not yet exist or create a symbolic force in times of crisis, only to retreat with the realization of the political idea they had portrayed?

The Constitutional Debate

When the United Nations acknowledged India's independence in New York on 15 August 1947 it was with the hoisting of a green, white, saffron tricolour with a wheel or chakra in the centre,[1] a newly designed flag chosen by the flag committee. This standard ceremony contrasted starkly with the climate of difficulties and tension about political symbols that had characterized the last months of British rule. Inter-flag rivalries had compounded the fundamental, deep-seated opposition between the Union Jack and the national flag. All over British India, since the beginning of the year, British officials were confronted with categorical Indian opposition to any display of the British emblem. In Madras, for example, students demanded that the Union Jack on buildings be removed and walked out of their classrooms. Before ultimatums by Indians to boycott official visits or threats to remove the Union Jack, Archibald Nye, vice-chief of the Imperial General Staff from 1941 to 1946, urged the withdrawal of the flag order that called for the hoisting of the Union Jack on occasions of visits by important representatives, viceroy, governor, or ministers.[2] The matter had become a big political flashpoint and caused so much concern that in August the British government refused an immediate symbolic expression of the transfer of power on Indian soil. 'At no point during the ceremonies relating to independence was there a symbolic transition as far as flags were concerned. The old imperial flag for India, a blue field bearing the British Union Jack and the Great seal with the Star of India was not taken down and replaced by the Indian national flag. Rather, on the viceroy's recommendation, the Union Jack went down on the evening of 14 August before the national flag went up the next morning.'[3] In Lucknow, where memories of the British residency's siege in 1857 were still strong, the British flag that had flown from the masthead of the ruined residency ever since was taken down by British sappers at night. The flagstaff was also removed and the base cemented so that no trace

[1] *New York Times*, 15 August 1947.

[2] OIOC, L/P&J/5/210, Archibald Nye to Lord Wavell, 18 January 1947.

[3] Nicholas Mansergh (ed.), *India. The Transfer of Power 1942–47*, XII, 8 July–15 August 1947 (London, HMSO, 1983), pp. 641–2.

of its location be apparent and no other emblem should fly over that historic place.[4] Greater care could not have been taken to clearly separate the two rituals, the end of an empire and the birth of a nation. As one British army officer noted, the obligatory round of official parades, ceremonies, and official gatherings that accompanied the transfer of power could have been any old official celebration that had characterized British rule in India.[5]

Mountbatten's anxiety to present the moment of British departure in a positive light as the birth of two nations and not in terms of a bloody end of empire lay behind this decision. Until the end, he did not give up all hope of establishing a symbolic continuity between India and Britain. Towards this objective he presented a flag design on 24 June 1947 to Nehru, as well as to Jinnah for Pakistan. The Indian flag would have been a tricolour with a small Union Jack in the upper canton, fitted into the exact width of the space between the stripes. Mountbatten was confident of his proposal's success, for the British symbolic presence envisaged would have been modest, the British jack occupying only one-sixth or one-ninth of the total area of the flag instead of one-quarter as, for example, in the Australian flag. Nehru answered that he would follow the matter up.[6] Mountbatten later recorded that Nehru did ask him if he would very much mind if Congress rejected the design. Although Gandhi, Patel and the others originally expressed their willingness, they finally balked before the general feeling among Congressmen that the leaders were pandering far too much to the British. That being the case, Nehru and Patel declared it was inadvisable to impose such a design in the present situation.[7] In contrast, Gandhi, true to his principles of not hating his opponents, declared in a meeting in Delhi that he saw no harm in the Union Jack occupying a corner of the flag: it would be an act of courtesy, a gesture worthy of the tradition of tolerance and love they had built up. Be that as it may,

[4] Major-General Shahid Hamid, *Disastrous Twilight* (London, Cooper, 1986), p. 224.

[5] Leonard Mosley, *The Last Days of the British Raj* (London, Weidenfeld and Nicolson, 1961), p. 239.

[6] Manmath Nath Das, *Partition and Independence of India. Inside Story of Mountbatten Days* (Delhi, East-West Publications, 1982), p. 288.

[7] OIOC, L/PO/6/123, Viceroy's Personal Report, 18 July 1947, no. 13, in Nicholas Mansergh (ed.), *India. The Transfer of Power*, XII, op. cit., pp. 230–1.

he still accepted the Congress Working Committee's decision not to include the Union Jack in their flag.[8] Mountbatten did not give up, striving hard to maintain the symbolic presence of the British empire, submitting a last proposal to hoist the Union Jack at the same time as the Indian flag on 15 August. Nehru pointed out that this was the least suitable day in the year to fly the Union Jack.[9]

At all levels, from the central government to the provincial administration, the change of state symbols was a similar object of negotiation. London followed developments closely. The secretary of state had hoped that provincial governors would fly the Union Jack, alone or with the badge of their province, as was the custom in Australia and Canada. In a secret meeting of the India and Burma committee at 10 Downing Street, Atlee, Cripps, and the Earl of Listowel agreed that the provincial governor's flags might have a different background from those used by the governors general, a dark green background for Pakistan, a saffron one for India. Flags of both types could be made and sent out in anticipation of the viceroy's agreement. Nehru, Jinnah, and the viceroy eventually agreed that provincial governors would fly flags similar to those of the governors general (a blue one with a crown and lion in gold), with the name of the province in white instead of the dominion and without the lion.[10]

Meanwhile, the nine-member flag committee debated on a national flag that would both recall the struggle for freedom and lay to rest possible criticisms of it being a party flag.[11] As the *Hindustan Times* put it—'so that something may be done to enthuse people and enable a psychological change to occur in consonance with the revolutionary change about to take place in the country's affairs'.[12] Under the chairmanship of the president of the Constituent Assembly, Rajendra Prasad, the committee included representatives of all communities: Muslim

[8] *Harijan*, 27 July 1947, p. 256.

[9] Viceroy's Personal Report, 8 August 1947, in Nicholas Mansergh (ed.), XII, op. cit., p. 596.

[10] Minute of the India and Burma Committee, ibid., pp. 381–2.

[11] This type of protest was still being made in July 1947, as expressed by a certain S. Moses who felt that the birth of a new India required a flag that was not associated with any political party: *The Statesman*, 19 July 1947, Letter to the Editor.

[12] *Hindustan Times*, 17 June 1947.

(Maulana Abdul Kalam Azad), Hindu (C. Rajagopalachari, Sarojini Naidu, K.M. Panikkar, K.M. Munshi, B.R. Ambedkar, S.N. Gupta), Christian (Frank Anthony), and Sikh (Sardar Ujjal Singh).[13] For all that, the princes still felt excluded from these deliberations. As noted in the preceding chapter, the maharaja of Bikaner wrote to Rajendra Prasad, chairman of the Constituent Assembly, suggesting the inclusion of representatives of the princely states. He argued that since the future Indian Union would consist of both British India provinces and princely states, it was only logical that national emblems such as the flag and the anthem should be decided upon in consultation with the states. As integral parts of the union, princely states too should have some symbol to represent them on the flag.[14] Although the maharaja's suggestion made little impact, it mirrored a broader current of opinion that supported a new design for the national flag capable of symbolically reshaping a lost unity.

The most pressing demands came from the Hindu parties. Since 1946 they had been advancing arguments for a uniquely saffron flag with an unmistakably Hindu design. *The Mahratta* cautioned against any conciliation with the Muslim League flag or any policy of appeasement. No country, it declared, had two national flags, not even Yugoslavia, where the antagonisms between Serbs and Croats and Slovenes were equally sharp.[15] Once the flag committee's existence was made public, *The Mahratta* welcomed the move, considering this an ideal moment to create everything brand new. In the light of growing objections to the tricolour, it was advisable to sound Indians views on the largest possible scale. What of the demands of tradition, history or society, it questioned. The 1931 flag had paid scant respect to these factors. As for the tricolour's success, it was surely partly due to 'stirring developments', the insistence of obstinate and resourceful Gandhians, and the absence of a forceful public opinion. Retracing the history of the successive flags of the freedom struggle, the article concluded by making an appeal for the saffron flag which had continuously marked

[13] B. Shiva Rao, *The Framing of India's Constitution. Select Documents*, op. cit., vol. 1, p. 492.

[14] *National Herald*, 21 June 1947.

[15] *The Mahratta*, 8 March 1946, 'Deep Intrigue for New Approach to Communal Problem', C.L.R. Shastri.

India's political and religious traditions.[16] The same sentiment was echoed by the president of the Maharashtra Hindu Sabha, G.V. Ketkar, who appealed to 'true nationalists' to demand Hindustan as the name for the national union, the Bhagwa Mahasabha flag as the national flag and *Bande Mataram* as the national anthem.[17] These suggestions for a saffron flag to represent India as a Hindu nation had already surfaced in 1931, but they acquired a sharper edge in 1947 with the imminence of Pakistan.

Some other proposals appeared in the national press during the last months preceding independence. One reader from Lucknow proposed a tricolour in deep blue, yellow, and red, with an outline map of India in black in the centre. Such a flag would not represent the symbols of any party, religion or interest, and would therefore be unobjectionable.[18] Another reader complained that the tricolour flag was neither appealing nor distinctive, for national flags with two or three-coloured stripes placed horizontally or vertically were among the commonest in the world. A national flag was destined not only for use in the native country but outside as well. It therefore had to be impressive, artistically distinctive, with suitable colours representing national character, and stand out among flags of other nations.[19]

Yet the committee considered none of these few demands or designs. In the absence of archival documents its precise deliberations are unknown, except for the presentation of a note on the flag by S.D. Kalelkar of Nagpur, until its adoption, on 22 July 1947. Kalelkar's note argued for the continuity of the flag with a replacement of the charkha because of its complicated design, lack of symmetry, and confusion between the front and reverse sides of the flag. It suggested keeping the existing tricolour adopted by the Congress in 1931, with the exception of keeping only the wheel design. This idea was credited to a Muslim, Badr-ud-Din Tyabji, son of Badruddin Tyabji, who had been president of the third Indian National Congress session in 1887, Madras.

[16] *The Mahratta*, D.V. Kale, 'In Search of a National Flag', 11 July 1947.

[17] *The Mail*, 14 July 1947.

[18] *National Herald*, 31 March 1947, Letter to the Editor, 'Our Flag', from B.S. Sitholey, Lucknow, p. 2.

[19] *The Statesman*, 9 July 1947, Letter to the Editor, 'Flag for India', by E.N. Sinclair.

Badr-ud-Din Tyabji himself was an ICS officer, artist, and art connoisseur, and in this latter capacity he was attached to the Constituent Assembly.[20] The idea of a wheel as symbol was not entirely new, having already been proposed in 1931.[21] On the new national flag, the ancient charkha (spinning wheel) proposed in 1921 by Gandhi was replaced by a 'navy blue wheel with 24 spokes' as represented on the abacus of the Sarnath lion capitol of Asoka, and known as 'the wheel of law' or dharma chakra.[22]

If this decision was not preceded by an animated, nationwide debate, its formal presentation before the Constituent Assembly invited comments and questions from members. Partisans of a 'Hindu nation', for the most part from the Central Provinces, once again pressed for a clearly Hindu orientation. H.V. Kamath from the Central Provinces & Berar proposed putting the swastika, the ancient Indian symbol, with the words 'Shantam, Shivam, Sundaram' (peace, goodness, beauty), inscribed in the centre of the white band. Seth Govind Das (also from the Central Provinces and Berar) wished the house to give a distinctive name to the flag in the manner of the British flag known as the Union Jack; he suggested Sudarshan, which meant beautiful in appearance and recalled the weapon of Lord Vishnu.[23] P.S. Deshmukh, also from the Central Provinces & Berar, wished to retain the tricolour intact with the charkha as it was the emblem of ahimsa, and of the common man, and therefore inseparably associated with the acquisition of their political freedom and with Gandhi.[24] None of these amendments were retained. The assembly members were largely in favour of the wheel.

Having refused to give India an overtly Hindu dimension, the assembly undertook to infuse the flag with its own legitimacy. This took the form of hearing deputies from the different geographical corners of India, beginning with the presentation of the flag by seventy-two

[20] Badruddin Tyabji, *Memoirs of an Egoist 1907–1956* (New Delhi, Roli Books, 1988), vol. 1, pp. 172–3.

[21] See chapter 4.

[22] B. Shiva Rao, *The Framing*, op. cit., vol. 1, p. 497.

[23] *Constituent Assembly Debates. Official Report*, 4 November 1948 to 8 January 1949 (Delhi, 1950), vol. XII, 5 November 1948, p. 223.

[24] *Constituent Assembly Debates. Official Report*, 14 July 1947 to 31 July 1947, 22 July 1947, vol. IV, p. 743.

women led by a Constituent Assembly member, Hansa Mehta. Thus, when Nehru explained the national logic in the succession of designs since 1921, he was also reaffirming the old commitment to making a nation that would transcend all parochial identifications such as caste, or boundaries of region, religion, or community for a wider sentiment of Indianness. His insistence that India's flag was a flag of freedom acquired greater force and influence at this singularly historic occasion. So too did Sarojini Naidu's nostalgic evocation of her 'most terrible moments of anguish in free countries' at India not possessing a national flag of her own, particularly at the post-World War celebration at Versailles in 1918.[25] And Radhakrishnan, the future second president of the Indian republic, but equally an authority on Indian religious traditions as well as Western philosophy, laid down the philosophical guidelines to serve as beacons of national objectives in his speech. The flag, he announced, epitomized what must be the path for India to follow, that of dharma or right action: the chakra indicated movement, eternal change, and progress; the colours saffron, white, and green indicated the spirit of renunciation and detachment, truth, purity, and fertility.[26]

Beyond these numerous predictable speeches by the main political leaders on behalf of different communities, other more modest public political figures tried to show how the flag contributed symbolically to the union of the various social classes, in particular to long-marginalized and exploited groups. V.I. Muiswami Pillai of Madras and Lakshminarayan Sahu from Orissa saw in the flag the symbol of the depressed, oppressed, and submerged classes all over the country,[27] an immediately accessible reality to millions of new citizens who did not necessarily grasp the abstract categories evoked by the others. It could thus become a tool for the political pedagogy of the new nation. In much the same spirit, Jaipal Singh from Bihar extended this argument further. Speaking for the thirty million tribals whom he considered the real owners of this country and the most ancient aristocracy of India, he presented the flag as belonging first and foremost to them who had been fighting for

[25] Ibid., 14 July –31 July 1947, p. 760.
[26] Ibid., 22 July 1947, pp. 745–6.
[27] Ibid., p. 758.

their freedom for the last 6000 years. He based this assertion on the claimed existence of the tradition of flag hoisting attributed not to the Aryans but to the tribes preceding them. He reminded the assembly that, year after year, in melas, jatras, festivals in Chota Nagpur, each tribe arrived with its flag; each village had its own unique flag, which they were ready to defend at the cost of their lives. The tribes would henceforth possess two flags, their traditional banner which they had been hoisting, and the national flag which announced their new status as citizens and the end of their ancient struggle for freedom.[28]

In comparison with the national debate on the flag in 1931, the change in 1947 gave rise to a relatively limited public discussion. Some criticism did surface about the chakra being a strong Hindu symbol as opposed to Gandhi's wheel, which had stood for a non-violent and non-sectarian nation. But it had little impact.[29] Anticipating such attacks, a few articles in Congress-backed English newspapers commented and justified the modification in order to thwart its opponents.[30] Against some religious orthodox circles which suggested that the chakra was a purely Buddhist symbol and therefore sectional in its appeal, the *National Herald* argued that, both as a material and symbolic object, it was in fact deeply rooted in Indian culture since ancient times and well beyond the decline of Buddhism. Embedded in the philosophical and literary traditions of the country, mainly as the bhava chakra (the wheel of existence), the bhagya chakra (the wheel of destiny), and the kal chakra (the wheel of time), it had all the political and symbolic virtues to become the new 'wheel of the nation' (rashtra chakra). It was the emblem of the god Vishnu, known as the wielder of the chakra—a weapon to ward off evil doers; it was also central to the Buddha's teachings, which explained change in the religious traditions as the turning of the wheel of religion (*dharma-chakra pravastana*); and during the Maurya period Kautilya had elevated it to a political concept by

[28] Ibid., pp. 742, 744, 751.

[29] *CWMG*, LXXXIX, 1 August 1947–10 November 1947 (Ahmedabad, 1987), p. 2.

[30] For example, in the *Hindustan Times*, 'Tricolour with Wheel in Foreground', 20 July 1947; 'Flag of Independent India. Unanimous Support for Nehru's Resolution', 23 July 1947; 'Freedom & Dignity of Asoka's India Recaptured', 28 July 1947.

referring to it as the wheel of the state in his political treatise *Arthashastra* (The Art of Governance).[31] Across these diverse opinions, the chakra presented itself as capable of linking different Indian traditions, thus constituting many reasons for each community to recognize in it meanings that were particular to them. It was this synthesis that one writer proposed by recalling its continuity from Vishnu's sudarshan chakra—the cosmic circle within which was included all that was animate and inanimate—to Buddha's dharma chakra—or the wheel of righteousness, the rule of right as against might—to Gandhi's charkha.[32]

If the adoption of the flag did not give rise to a large debate in 1947, it was also because it was immediately accepted. Public reactions to the spectacular initiative taken by the *Hindustan Times* less than a week after the official passage of the flag in the assembly support this conclusion. With its edition of 28 July, the newspaper distributed a national flag in reduced size (10 x 7 1/2 inches), printed on art paper, with the original colours and design adopted by the Constituent Assembly. There was no separate charge for it, the idea being to encourage each reader to familiarize himself with it and use it according to his wishes. In the days that followed the newspaper received hundreds of letters, so much so that it asked readers to describe their reactions to the flag, including any reservations they might hold and what they had done with the flag supplement. They would publish the most typical and interesting of these letters in a special column, 'Thanks for the flag'.[33] The column was continued till 14 August and readers shared their patriotic sentiments (analysed in Chapter 6), evoking their 'great joy', 'thrill', 'pride' or 'tears of emotion' on receiving the 'sacred gift' of the national flag, which was 'rooted in the heart of millions'. Letters from different provinces of India were selected for publication: Delhi of course but also Punjab, Uttar Pradesh, and Rajasthan. Readers shared the numerous private and public ways in which they were using the flag, displaying it in their homes, framing it, worshipping it during their family pujas, saluting it, carrying it to their offices, and showing

[31] *National Herald*, 6 August 1947, R.B. Pandey, 'The Symbolism of Chakra'.

[32] *Harijan*, 7 September 1947, p. 313, 'The National Flag', by Radha Kumud Mookerji.

[33] *Hindustan Times*, 5, 6, 8 August 1947.

it to colleagues, whether Muslims or Christians. Many recounted how their children had taken it to school, where its past battles were remembered and glorified. For instance, it was put up on the notice board of a college which until then had been occupied by poppies. In a significant replay of Partition, some squabbles to possess the flag supplement led to it being torn, with the fragments being preserved as a souvenir.[34]

In this conjuncture of crisis and violence that has rightly been recognized by a recent historiography of Partition,[35] these letters published by the press draw attention to quite another dimension of this moment. They could appear superficial, artificial, restricted expressions of public sentiment, even unreal before the collective trauma and experience of pain and inhumanity. Still, these testimonies cannot be ignored even if they were clearly selected by a press promoting the government vision. The difficulty lies precisely in considering these two dimensions together, and requires a deeper analysis of its own.

The formal operation of the flag's adoption, once complete, the state instituted a set of norms and rules aimed at making it a sacred object. On the model of other countries, India's flag was to invite respect both within and without. Therefore, while subscribing to international standards, the Indian state affirmed its distinctiveness through values on which it intended to build the Indian state and society. In the process it profoundly modified the practices and uses of the flag that had developed in the colonial period and imposed a restricted model that prevented a more personalized, subjective, and creative appropriation by each citizen. The situation was quite paradoxical, for at the very moment of liberation the flag was being confined in strict rules and regulations.

A Material Image of Indian Political Culture

If the decision of July 1947 had made some people fear a rupture with the Gandhian heritage, subsequent legislation fixing exclusive norms

[34] *Hindustan Times*, 2–14 August 1947.

[35] In particular, Urvashi Butalia, *The Other Side of Silence*, op. cit.; Gyanendra Pandey, *Remembering Partition* (Cambridge, Cambridge University Press, 2001); Suvir Kaul (ed.), *The Partitions of Memory. The Afterlife of the Division of India*

of production of the flag reconfirmed the continuity with Gandhi's recommendations since the 1920s. Indeed, since the very beginning Gandhi had deplored the fact that many Indians used foreign cloth instead of handspun and hand-woven khadi to make their flag. Answering those who complained against such practices that could diminish the flag's prestige, he tried to lay down some basic material standards. The proportion between the length and width should be fixed, the length being twice the width of the flag. Above all, khadi was the only cloth acceptable and worthy of being publicly displayed as a flag, symbolizing both the strength and the enduring qualities of the Indian artisan tradition and the political battle for swadeshi launched in 1905.[36] Informing the Congress Working Committee of frequent irregularities in the making of the flag, he pointed out the need for a formal resolution concerning its material qualities. He further suggested that the Congress could make the All-India Spinners' Association responsible for producing, stocking, and selling the flags on behalf of the Congress at different stores.[37]

In 1947, as far as the flag cloth and material production were concerned, this continuity with the Gandhian tradition served as a political argument to reassure the Mahatma's followers. Thus, Rajendra Prasad, one of Gandhi's close disciples, insisted on the inclusion of the resolution specifying that the cloth for making the flag be invariably handspun and hand-woven. On hearing that the Constituent Assembly had placed an order for 3000 flags with a textile mill, he ordered its cancellation; various government departments and provincial governments were instructed to use flags only of pure handspun and hand-woven khaddar.[38]

(Delhi, Permanent Black, 2001); S. Settar, Indira Baptista Gupta (eds), *Pangs of Partition, The Human Dimension* (Delhi, Indian Council of Historical Research, Manohar, 2002), 2 vols, esp. vol. 2.

36 Bernard S. Cohn, 'Cloths, Clothes and Colonialism', in *Colonialism and its Forms of Knowledge. The British in India* (Princeton, Princeton University Press, 1996), p. 106; C.A. Bayly, 'The Origins of *Swadeshi*', op. cit., pp. 285–321.

37 *Young India*, 28 February 1929.

38 Rajendra Prasad to Jawaharlal Nehru, 27 July 1947, in B. Shiva Rao, op. cit., pp. 510–11.

At the request of the ministry of home affairs and army headquarters, the Indian Standards Institution (now the Bureau of Indian Standards) brought out formal specifications for the first time in 1951. They were revised in 1964 to adapt the flag to the metric system. On 17 August 1968 these specifications were revised a second time. The National Flag of India Sectional Committee finally approved an initial draft prepared by the Textile Division Council. This committee included representatives from a wide range of ministries—defence, home affairs, state institutions like the Directorate General of Supplies and Disposals, some professional associations, the Sri Ram Institute for Industrial Research, Delhi, the Khadi and Village Industries and Dyestuffs Manufacturers Association, as well as Gandhi Ashram. It confirmed the design and structural details of the flag, including the raw material to be used, standards of spinning, weaving, testing, dyeing, and processing. Cloth, either cotton, woollen or silk, was to be hand-woven. The yarn, equally handmade, had to conform to established norms. Even the sewing threads of the three colours, i.e. white, saffron, and green, used for stitching the flag, had to be of khadi. All the sewing threads were to be well spun, evenly twisted, and free from knots, short lengths, and other defects. The spectrophotometer value of all the three colours was measured and determined by the Technical Development Establishment Laboratory in Kanpur by using the illuminant 'C' as specified by the International Commission of Illumination, 1931. The colours were to correspond, when visually examined in ordinary daylight, to the colours in the sealed standard flag presented to the Constituent Assembly on 22 July 1947, now held in the custody of the Chief Inspector of Textiles and Clothing, Kanpur.[39] Cotton had to be of one variety, i.e. Y-1, the sliver had to be procured from the Central Sliver Plant of KVIC. A periodic testing of the yarn was to be carried out by Khadi Gramodyog Prayog Samiti, Ahmedabad. To have uniform picks as well as uniform spacing of picks, cotton khadi bunting had to be woven on improved or semi-automatic looms.[40] While there was officially no embargo on the private manufacture of the national flag on all occasions for official display, only the flag conforming to these

[39] *Indian Standard Specification for the National Flag of India*, second revision (Delhi, Indian Standards Institution, 1968).

[40] *Indian Standard Specification*, op. cit., pp. 2–6.

specifications laid down by the ISI and bearing the ISI mark was to be used.[41]

Such a technical and bureaucratic document reflected more than a state-heavy approach. It disclosed a determination to separate the flag from the world of ordinary objects. A similar concern to place it beyond a commercial profit based approach led to the establishment of a monopoly in its production. For years, the charkha sangh branches had been producing the tricolour. They had to stop, but Gandhi proposed that they continue selling it until their stock was exhausted, as the meaning of the new flag was not radically different. It too was made of pure khadi.[42] The manufacture and supply of the new flag were initially accorded to the Ordnance Clothing Factory in Shahjahanpur (Uttar Pradesh). Set up in 1914 and working since 1948 under the ministry of defence, it was the largest clothing factory in the country in the 1960s.[43] At an unknown date, this factory stopped producing flags, and today there is only one firm, a unit of the Khadi and Village Industries Board in Mumbai, that manufactures the national flag according to the IBS standards and supplies it for official functions. Even now, for private citizens, only state run Khadi Bhandars are authorized to supply the flags.

The Khadi and Village Industries were set up in 1953 and took their original form in 1956 in order to promote economic rural development. They federate a great number of small workshops, which, more than sixty years after Independence, still keep Gandhian principles alive. The example of one unit of flag production illustrates the impact of this theoretical loyalty to Gandhian principles. Founded in 1954 by a few freedom fighters in Garag, a tiny village of less than 10,000 inhabitants in Dharwad district, north Karnataka, the Dharwad Taluk Garag Kshetriya Seva Sangh obtained the centre's licence to make flags. The weavers of the village, earlier engaged in making barbed wires, were now commissioned to supply the cloth for the flags to government institutions. Their flag-making unit was founded on a 'no profit, no loss' basis to keep the Gandhian tradition alive. No modern machines were

[41] K.V. Singh, *Our National Flag*, op. cit., pp. 75–7.

[42] *Harijan*, 3 August 1947, p. 263; 10 August 1947.

[43] Dharm Pal, *The Indian Army* (Delhi, Publications Division, Ministry of Information and Broadcasting, Govt of India, 1967).

used and the flags were entirely hand-woven. Ten sub-units produced the special cotton thread for the flags. An inquiry revealed that making the cloth in the 1990s involved 250 women working over seventy looms. Only khadi cloth was used, every inch having forty lines of hand-knitted thread; each flag piece of 50 mm by 200 mm was to have a capacity for supporting 40 kg on the warp side and 30 kg on the weft side; only no. 36 threads made from a special cotton stock called Jaxadhar could be used. The unit made flags at Rs 56 per metre, and the demand was double before national commemorations like Republic Day and Independence Day or Gandhi Jayanti. Each flag piece was then sent to BITRAC, a Bombay-based central government body affiliated to the Khadi and Village Industries Commission, where it was dyed saffron, green, and white and the Ashok chakra was printed on it. The flags next underwent a quality check before they were distributed throughout the country through nationalized banks. Though they could not be marketed commercially, a few flag pieces were nonetheless dyed in Garag for local functions.[44]

This procedure of production in government authorized agencies controlled sales and prevented the flag's massive diffusion among the public. It contributed for decades to maintain a restricted use of the national emblem, untouched and unaffected by change.

The Indian Flag Etiquette: A Distant Symbol

In the circumstances, this controlled process of production was coherent with the codification of practices set out in the Flag Code of India. In 1947 Rajendra Prasad had received demands for 'a distinct directive' concerning the national flag from the government for 'the significance of the national flag of India has not been fully grasped by our people . . . it is proudly aloft on the Kumbha of the temple chariot during festivals, as well as on the occasion of the ear-boring ceremony of a child.'[45] An

[44] Stephen David, 'Weavers with a Mission', *India Today*, 15 May 1996, p. 24; see also interview with Bore Gowda, Khadi and Village Industries Board CEO, on the new uses of the flag fabric made by the Dharwad Khadi Association in *The Indian Express*, 30 January 2002.

[45] S. Ramachandran, Secretary, Indian Chamber of Commerce, Penang, to Rajendra Prasad, President, Indian Constituent Assembly, Delhi, 24 January 1947, in *Dr Rajendra Prasad. Correspondence and Selected Documents, 4 January 1949–24 January 1950* (Delhi, Allied Publishers, 1988), vol. II, pp. 20–1.

alleged insult to the tricolour by a jailor of a Lucknow prison was debated in the UP assembly.[46] Letters to the editor complained that in their ignorance people did not know when and where and how to fly the national flag, when and how to bring it down. A code of conduct, they suggested, should be immediately laid down so that the Indian masses learnt the significance and importance attached to a national flag and so that it may not become a subject of ridicule in the eyes of other nations.[47] Constituent Assembly members challenged the government's policy relating to the dishonour and insult of the flag.[48] All kinds of social practices that had become the standard norm under the colonial period were now considered unacceptable. It was felt that the flag's official sanctification demanded a different treatment. With its change of status in independent India, it was no longer simply a tool of protest.

In the absence of official precedents or juridical norms, the newly created Indian Standards Institution turned to the American Standards Association as well as to the British government for information on international standards.[49] The UK High Commissioner in India, when approached, could only refer to the *Encyclopaedia Britannica*, Whitaker's Almanac (which indeed contains a page on the uses of the Union Jack), and the Flag Manual, probably John Irving's booklet, published in 1934.[50] The College of Arms possessed no official specifications either for the display,[51] or for the production of the Union Jack.[52] The consultation of a 'Memorandum respecting British regulations and Practice

[46] *National Herald*, 27 February 1947, p. 7.

[47] *National Herald*, 18 August 1947, Letter to the Editor, 'What is the Flag Etiquette?', by R.L. Singhal.

[48] *The Bombay Sentinel*, 20 August 1947.

[49] OIOC, L/I/1/1252, file no. 475, U.K. High Commissioner in India to Secretary of State for India, 19 June 1947.

[50] OIOC, L/I/1/1252, file no. 475, U.K. High Commissioner to Secretary of State for India, New Delhi, 19 June 1947; Note from the Press Office, India Office, 23 June 1947. The complete title is John Irving, *The Manual of Flag Etiquette. Reviewed and accepted as correct by the Lords Commissioners of the Admiralty, etc.* (London, Seeley, Service & Co., 1934; a revised edition was published in 1938).

[51] OIOC, L/I/1/1252, file no. 475, Press Office, India Office, 23 June 1947.

[52] NAI, L/P&J/10/139, Note from British High Commission, 26 October, 5 November 1948.

regarding the flying of the Union Jack and Royal Standard' revealed that there were no British laws or regulations governing the use of the Union Jack. Any British subject could fly it on land.[53] Even such scanty information was appreciated and considered useful, for India Office was informed that the 'Memorandum most fortunately arrived on the same day as the sub-committee of the Constituent Assembly was to sit to consider regulations for the use of the Indian flag. The Librarian of the Imperial Secretariat Library was therefore extremely grateful for our help and I am sure, must now have a very high opinion of our service.'[54]

While discussions on the rules of flag display were in progress, the British High Commission in Delhi analysed this major juridical transformation with some perspicacity. It maintained that the euphoria of the weeks preceding and following Independence Day, which had also characterized the years of struggle for freedom, was giving way to a rigorous regime of order which would place the emblem out of reach of the citizens.

> The new regulations, which are designed to bring the practice in India more into line with that prevailing in other countries are welcome and somewhat overdue. At the time of the transfer of power last August, nationalist enthusiasm not unnaturally manifested itself in profuse displays of the new national flag: though the occasion has passed, the flags have remained to face the rigours of the Indian climate and it is still a common sight to see taxis, tonga and refreshment stalls flaunting a barely recognisable tricolour. It remains to be seen how the public will accept the new restrictions; for so many years the display of the Congress tricolour (which, prior to August 1947, was always referred to as the 'National flag') has been associated in the popular mind with the 'struggle for freedom' and nationalist sentiment, that the ordinary man may find it hard to understand why he is forbidden the use of its successor symbol now that freedom has been achieved.[55]

A certain number of isolated measures were rapidly announced. In 1948 the government declared that the flag would be flown on all

[53] OIOC, L/I/1/1252, file no. 475.

[54] Ibid., J.T. Hughes, Deputy UK Publicity Office, Delhi, to G.F. Crawley, Information Department, India Office, 15 July 1947.

[55] Ibid.

occasions on important government buildings such as high courts, secretariats, commissioner's offices, collectorates, jails and offices of district boards, and municipalities; it could also be displayed on the residences of high government officials such as chief commissioners, ruling princes and Raj Pramukhs (chief ministers), and abroad, obviously by India's representatives in foreign countries and states. Only on special occasions like Independence Day celebrations, National Week, and Mahatma Gandhi's birthday, or other days of national rejoicing, its use would be unrestricted.[56] The British high commissioner in Delhi commented on this move with some scepticism, doubting that the public would respect these rules, given their long-lasting habit of its free use.[57] The AICC welcomed and supported these measures.[58] A year later, noting the persistent indiscriminate use of the emblem of the flag in advertisements, the government explicitly prohibited its use in any trade, business, or profession through section 69 of the Trade Marks Act.

Eventually the Indian government adopted a Prevention of Improper Use of Emblems and Names Act in 1950 (no. 12 of 1950), that was later reinforced by the Prevention of Insults to National Honour Act in 1971 (no. 69 of 1971).[59] The new bill linked the flag with the names or pictorial representations of Mahatma Gandhi and other national leaders, excluding them from commercial and trade purposes. Beyond this general condemnation, the entire range of uses elaborated around the flag in the 1930s and encouraged by the Congress and its leaders—on handkerchiefs and clothes, stationery and means of transport, draping statues and buildings—now ended. This codification was not derived from international standards, but could be found in earlier reflections made by Indian nationalists as in the manual of flag usage composed by N.S. Hardikar in 1931.[60]

[56] Ibid., Press Communique, Ministry of Home Affairs, 17 June 1948.

[57] NAI, L/P&J/10/139, L.A.C. Fry, High Commissioner, Delhi, to H.A.F. Rumbold, Commonwealth Relations Office, 23 June 1948.

[58] NMML, AICC Papers, P-8/1947-49, 3 November 1948.

[59] *The All India Reporter Manual. Civil and Criminal* (Nagpur, 5th edn, 1989), pp. 658–9; a section on the rules for display of the national flag is also found in P. Muthuswamy's *Swamy's Complete Manual on Establishment and Administration for Central Govt. Offices* (Madras, 2nd edn, 1988), pp. 1–9.

[60] N.S. Hardikar, 'Our National Flag', op. cit.

Accordingly, on the morrow of independence, the national flag was guaranteed a privileged position in official functions from the most obviously national celebrations like Independence Day (15 August) or Republic Day (26 January) at the central level, but also at provincial or city levels. The flag was thus sanctified in India through these restrained, carefully orchestrated displays at well-identified moments of national celebration, around the birth of the nation, the commemorations of national leaders, and the freedom movement.

In the same years the Indian government published an illustrated booklet which proposed a short history of the national flag, principally aimed at schoolchildren. Entitled *Our Flag*, it was brought out by the publications and broadcasting division of the ministry of information in 1950. The book presented some of the major projects of the flag in chronological order since the Bengal partition, along with a short explanatory text about the meanings of the colours and design. It also included the most important discourses by national leaders like Nehru, Gandhi, and Radhakrishnan, either in the form of chosen extracts or quotations. The flag's history was narrated according to two principal approaches. On the one hand these projects were linked to a limited number of authors who thus joined, if they were not already part of the pantheon of heroes and heroines of the national movement—Bhikaji Cama, Nivedita, Annie Besant, Gandhi. On the other hand the flag appeared at key moments of the anti-colonial struggle—the Bengal partition, Home Rule or civil disobedience. The national flag such as it was defined in 1931 and 1947, is here presented as the final product of more than forty years of search for a symbolic image of the nation. Obviously it is not the entire history of the freedom movement that is narrated through the flag. But this booklet tries to advance what the government considered the spirit of the movement and renders it accessible to a large public. Viewed from this vantage point, the story evokes a successful search for the unity of the Indian people, and portrays the flag as a powerful means of creating an Indian national identity. *Our Flag* was an introduction in simple language to a strong political programme that refused to build the nation on a dominantly Hindu mythological and ritual past. It showed the elimination of symbols of this ahistorical past, still present among the earliest designs, in favour of non-divisive images of the nation. It thus limited the understanding of the national emblem mainly to the anti-colonial past and to those aspects it considered as leading to a modern and secular ideal. These were the very features that Nehru, for example, had already developed in *The Discovery of India*, written between 1942 and 1945.[61] Even if the booklet on the flag was widely accessible thanks to its easy, undemanding language, its cheap price and the government's pedagogical determination to diffuse a modern narrative of the Indian nation, it could still only reach a minority as it was published in English, was not translated into other languages, and was printed only thrice during the fifty years following independence. In similar vein, the government imposed a documentary film 'Our Flag', in 1951; then, in 1955, on cinema audiences, at the end of commercial films. This formal, unimaginative political pedagogy remained perfectly coherent with the restrained regime the government instituted after 1947 for the flag.[62]

If the flag conserved a certain emotional power for Indians, it was more the consequence of unofficial practices and uses. Through the 1950s and 1960s, a popular image of the national flag was elaborated thanks largely to Hindi films and songs. Poems in regional languages on the tricolour were comparatively little known outside their linguistic community. But lines like 'world victory to our beloved tricolour, May our flag be held high' (*Vijayi vishwa tiranga pyaara, Jhanda uncha rahe hamara*), from a song composed, as we saw earlier, in 1924 by Shyamlal Gupta, or 'our tricolour' (*hamara tiranga*), became familiar to Indians through their interpretation by a very popular singer, Lata Mangeshkar, whose musical career began in 1947. She maintained the emotional feeling that had characterized the tricolour from the late 1920s onwards,

[61] In this sense, the flag was a material expression of the new relationship to the past that some nationalists were determined to advance to build a contemporary Indian society. See Bernard S. Cohn, 'The Shaping of the Civilization: Views of the Past in India', in *India. The Social Anthropology of a Civilization* (Englewood Cliffs; Hemel Hempstead, Prentice-Hall, 1971; 2nd edn, Delhi, Oxford University Press, 2000), p. 51.

[62] *Our Flag* (New Delhi, Information and Broadcasting Publications Division, 1950, 1963, 1989); G.P. Rajratnam, *Introducing Our Flag: For Our Boys and Girls*, 1949; *Significance of the Wheel of Ashoka in the Flag of Free India*, 1948; Kapila Thakore, *Our National Flag* (Bombay, Hind Kitab, 1946); K.V. Singh, *Our National Flag*, op. cit.

giving a new impulsion to the genre of patriotic songs with famous refrains like *Sare jahan se aacha, Hindustan hamara* (Our India is the best in the world), *Jaha dal dal per sone ki chidya* (At every step a golden bird dwells), *Mere desh ki dharati* (My country's soil), and *Hum sab bhartiya hain* (We are all Indians). Since 1947, the flag has been constantly present in the background of many Bollywood films set in contemporary India and its appearance is nearly always heralded by one of these patriotic songs. This combination of songs and films, that is to say music, images, and stories, proved to be an effective means of maintaining the emotional regime of the flag laboriously constructed in the 1920s and 1930s. The government accepted these depictions as they reinforced the very patriotic ethos it sought to associate exclusively with the flag.

In this context, despite the restrained regime instituted by the flag code, we can observe the simultaneous development of practices on the margins of legality, which expressed a more personal relationship with the national flag. A few examples can be mentioned and broadly analysed. For instance, a painted miniature tricolour is commonly seen displayed on the sides of trucks, on their windows, or on the rear, more often than not accompanied by a patriotic slogan. The same symbol appears on many scooters, on the front or the rear, on tongas as well as on shops or hotels, on roadside snack shops . . . It is impossible to say when exactly this usage began. It is certain that it existed during the inter-War period, when national leaders like Nehru encouraged Indians to multiply the presence of the flag in their daily habits, to the extent of saturating their environment with this emblem. From all the available evidence, the flag code did not interrupt this habit, which certainly tended to increase in times of war, during the Indo-Chinese war in 1962 and during the first conflicts with Pakistan (1965, 1971). None of these popular unofficial practices has ever provoked any negative reactions, either from the public or the government.

The Last Decade: A Flag for Each Citizen

While official statutes governed the flag's usage, there was no case of judicial action against a private use of the flag in the first fifty years following independence. During the 1990s, on the contrary, many instances showed the development of a new public sensitivity to the manner in which the flag was handled. Examples of this concern have occasionally been expressed in the press. Thus, a private individual from Calcutta registered his shock at the casualness with which the flag was handled even on official ceremonial events.

> Sir, The shameful incident of the Indian tricolour falling off its flag-post while Jyoti Basu [chief minister of West Bengal] was trying to unfurl it on Independence Day underlines the low ebb the state's work culture has sunk into. Nothing is sacrosanct anymore. The hospitals, transport system, all reflect the miserable state of the people living in Calcutta. . . . Mr Basu walked away in annoyance when he found the flag coming down instead of the flowers. Preferably, he should have asked for the flag to be properly positioned so that he could make a second attempt.[63]

In this reader's eyes, the incident reflected the degradation of the state services and the general political climate of indifference. Again, the handling of the Indian national flag at the Singer Cup cricket tournament in Sri Lanka, where the Indian tricolour was unfurled upside down at the stadium, was similarly reproved and considered a desecration of the national symbol.[64]

My brief survey in December 2002 and January 2003 among students of three schools in Delhi, one public, one Christian school, and two schools in Amritsar was also revealing. The groups consisted of 8-year-old schoolchildren at Delhi and 17-year-old school-leaving young adults at Amritsar. They manifested a clear awareness and knowledge about the flag, its history, and its official meaning. The written enquiry form of four open questions permitted students to give their personal opinion. Two of the questions concerned the national flag, as it exists today, inviting them to state what they knew about its history and meanings. The two remaining questions departed from the official track to inquire into their degree of satisfaction with the actual symbol or if they would prefer an alternative design or colours.[65] The first two questions revealed a good mastery of the standard historical knowledge

[63] Diponkor Dutt, 'Decaying Culture', *Asian Age*, 1 September 1996.

[64] 'Restoring Glory of Tricolour', *The Indian Express*, 10 September 1996.

[65] Thanks to Junior school class students of Modern School and Victoria Girls School, Delhi and Ajanta Senior Secondary School, Amritsar. I am grateful

of the flag, including the amendment of the flag code in January 2002 as found in official publications and school syllabuses.[66] All the same, the persistence of certain interpretations that had been officially rejected and condemned since the 1930s showed continuing plural approaches to the flag. For example, some answers reproduced the communal meanings of the flag's colours. For Delhi students, the history of the flag was linked to the main national figures, Gandhi and Nehru, while Amritsar students accorded an important place to Punjab nationalists in the history of the flag, including those who had chosen a more revolutionary path, like Bhagat Sigh, Sukhdev, and Rajguru. The large majority of students expressed their satisfaction with the existing flag, and showed a strong adherence to political values like unity, peace, prosperity, and freedom. A very small minority nonetheless suggested that the design could more clearly reflect India's changed status in the new millennium as an emerging technological power, expressed in an accompanying slogan *Jai kisan, jai jawan, jai vigyan* (Hail to the peasant, the soldier, and science).

This brief investigation of seventy-odd students was not done to propose a representative picture of the contemporary Indian situation. Other research enquiries into the perceptions of the nation have emphasized very different aspects in their conclusions. Krishna Kumar's examination of the teaching of history in school textbooks highlights the tensions between official ideology and personal reconstructions that result in diluting the state message.[67] And Veronique Benei, in her study of Maharashtra, found that at a state level the nation is today largely conceived through a regional, in this case Marathi, perspective, strongly tinted with Hinduism, despite the national liturgy enacted in schools according to state directives.[68] Nita Kumar, in her interviews

---

to Shadhona Ganguly and Pami Singh, Delhi, and Vikrant Kapoor, Amritsar, for arranging these encounters.

[66] Among the literature on Indian symbols destined to schoolchildren for example, see Jaiprakash Bharti, *Rashtra ke Pratik* (Delhi, Pitambar Publishing Company, 1994). Ch. 2 is devoted to 'Jhande ka Itihas', pp. 5–14.

[67] Krishna Kumar, *Prejudice and Pride: School Histories of the Freedom Struggle in India and Pakistan* (New Delhi, Viking, 2001).

[68] Véronique Bénéi, 'Teaching nationalism in Maharashtra schools', in C.J. Fuller and Véronique Bénéi (eds), *The Everyday State and Society in Modern India* (London, C. Hurst & Co., 2001), pp. 194–221.

with schoolchildren of Benares and Lucknow on the memory of Partition, noted their complete ignorance of India as a nation. She concluded that they knew of no freedom fighters, were unable to draw a map of India, and in short had no mental picture of India or its states.[69] It is evident that the strong cultural and social heterogeneity of India has not produced representations that are uniform and shared. A more precise analysis as well as a bigger sociological enquiry would be necessary to draw a broader, more comprehensive picture of contemporary perceptions of the nation. But the stakes of the flag and Partition are not the same, symbolically and politically. In many schools since the 1960s, children are made to sing a national song in public assemblies, either the official *Jana gana mana* or the first national song *Bande Mataram* as well as Iqbal's *Hindustan hamara*, and given a minimum information about the flag.

In any case, my survey confirms the new importance acquired by the flag since the beginning of the 1990s, reinforced during and after the Kargil war in May–July 1999. It is difficult to identify a precise point of departure for this large-scale phenomenon, which opposed the restricted, closed regime of the flag, increasingly seen as an abusive appropriation by the state and central authorities of a symbol that belongs to all Indians. This new tendency and desire for the liberalization of the uses of the flag can be seen as the culmination of diverse and complex processes. Among these, it would be necessary to consider the role of political conflicts of a new kind, linked among others with the rise of the Bharatiya Janata Party (BJP) and its proposition of a Hindu India, as well as the concern for presenting a stronger image of India in the context of economic liberalization after 1991 and the affirmation of new forms of patriotism by Indians working abroad, particularly in the United States.

In this context, the claim of a young industrialist from Madhya Pradesh, Navin Jindal, to fly the flag as his fundamental right can be seen as representative of this new tendency.[70] After having very legally hoisted the flag on his factory in Raigarh, Chhattisgarh, on

[69] Nita Kumar, 'Children and the Partition', in S. Kaul (ed.), *The Partitions of Memory*, op. cit., pp. 269–301, esp. pp. 283–4, 289.

[70] For a basic presentation of this affair, see K.V. Singh, *The Indian Tricolour* (Delhi, Rupa and Co., 2005), pp. 14–30.

Independence Day, 26 January 1993, he decided to keep it flying. Despite the observations of local authorities, he persisted until the superintendent of police himself removed the flag in September 1994. Having consulted prominent jurists and concluded that he had in no way broken the law—he had neither offended nor commercialized the flag—Jindal wrote to the commissioner of Bilaspur as well as to the home affairs ministry, explaining his position. Ultimately, both reminded him of the restrained regime of the flag. In February1995, he then made a writ petition to the Delhi high court that would give all Indians and institutions the right to fly the flag in a respectful manner: 'when a person flies the national flag', he pleaded, 'he rises above his religion and political affiliations and shows that he is a proud Indian. We are a diverse group of people and this is one way to bind all of us.' Even after the Delhi high court recognized this right on 22 September 1995, the Union of India challenged this decision before the supreme court in January 1996. A month later, in February 1996, the supreme court allowed Jindal to fly the tricolour on his factory while awaiting the decision about it being a fundamental right of Indian citizens.

The media importance acquired by this affair must not be understood to imply it was an isolated or even exceptional case. In the same years we can note the appearance of the flag in other working premises, on individual houses, and on private buildings.[71] The opening of a national debate provoked by Jindal reinforced this movement, which nonetheless remained limited. Some time later, celebrations of India's fiftieth anniversary of independence provided the occasion to introduce a strong historical dimension in the evocation of the flag. However, the arguments advanced in such accounts did not have a large echo in public debate.[72] In 1999 the Kargil war led to an unprecedented presence of the flag in public space and on a national scale, not seen in India since the 1930s. Media reports of the war in newspapers, and via television channels like Star and Zee TV brought scenes of coffins draped with

[71] For example, an employee of a textile factory in Delhi, an ex-serviceman has been hoisting the national flag on the premises since the late 1990s.

[72] Arundhati Virmani, 'From Charkha to Chakra', *The Sunday Statesman*, 10 August 1997, pp. 1–3; Vinay Lal, 'Idolatory of the National Tricolour', *Indian Express*, 17 January 1996.

the national flag to homes in this 'battle for hearts and minds'.[73] The movement of national support for soldiers fighting in Kargil expressed itself through the tricolour. This was not a short-lived development but continued in the aftermath of the war—in the press of course, but also in public space, in streets, market places, on vehicles and houses, in films, theatres, and dance festivals. The phenomenon sometimes attained unexpected and unprecedented dimensions in which the personal appropriation of the tricolour raised the question of respect for the national symbol. In 1999, a fashion model Malini Ramani made the headlines for wearing the tricolour as an opening one-piece knee-length outfit dress to the India Fashion Week.

More broadly, this trend was accompanied by media exposure of national feelings through short television films, music videos, and compact discs. Continuing on the lines of *Mera Bharat Mahan* (My India is Great) that had brought the tricolour into homes, Sony Music and Bharatbala Productions proposed new pop versions of *Jana Gana Mana* and *Bande Mataram*. '*Jana Gana Mana* needed a new 2000 version, we have tried to make just that', declared its music director. In 2000 a host of music directors and producers from Susmit Bose's India Unlimited to Tajdar Amrohi's *Paigam* and Annamika's *Aman ke Pujari* to Niveditha's *Dil Kurban Jan Kurban* flooded music shops with odes to the nation which were no longer classic but hip. A compact disc of the various historical versions of *Bande Mataram*, once exclusively identified with the voice of Lata Mangeshkar, now produced by Bandana Mukhopadhya, offered multiple versions of Bankimchandra's famous song, from a Rabindrasangeet rendering to the more sensual interpretation of Shubha Mudgal. The film-maker G. Bharat's lyricist Mehboob and composer A.R. Rahman proposed a more energetic version of *Mau Tujhe Salaam* (Salutations to the Mother).[74] Well-known classical singers and film singers, among them D.K. Pattammal,

[73] Dipankar Sinha analyses the portrayal of the war in two Bengali newspapers, *Amrita Bazar Patrika* and *Ganashakti*: 'Kargil Episode in Bengali Print Media', *Economic and Political Weekly*, vol. 37, no. 27, 6 July 2002, pp. 2803–9.

[74] The music album consisted of three songs in an upbeat contemporary tune with Dominic Miller on the acoustic guitar, to reflect the three colours of the Indian flag. See Srirupa Roy, 'A Symbol of Freedom', op. cit., esp. p. 519, f.n. 36.

Bhimsen Joshi, Balamurli Krishna, Lata Mangeshkar, and Bhupen Hazarika participated in this popularization. Folk-singers from Rajasthan like Sadiq Khan Langa too were included. Sony Music representative Vijay Singh called it 'an articulation of one's pride in being Indian.'[75] To cite only a few examples, Mani Ratnam's Tamil film *Roja* (1992), dealing with Kashmiri separatism, has Arvind Swamy jumping into the fire to save the Indian flag from burning. In *Dil Se*, and *1942—A Love Story*, the flag becomes the central element of the story, the apex toward which all energies and actions are directed. It not only blends with the usual ingredients and emotional pathos of Hindi films, but also heightens the sentiments of sacrifice, patriotism, solidarity and national pride.[76]

In this climate of national fervour the supreme court still not having given its final judgement, the BJP government in power set up an inter-ministerial flag committee on 18 October 2000 to examine the constitutional issue. Headed by Dr P.D. Shenoy, an additional home secretary, the committee submitted a report to the home minister in April 2001 that still bore the imprint of the strong patriotic fervour that had accompanied the Kargil war. Led to define the role of the flag, it noted: 'It is at this time of danger that this length of cloth inspires people to unite under its umbrella and urges them to defend the honour of their motherland.'[77] Predictably, it recommended the liberalization of the flag code.

The government accepted this and a new flag code was promulgated in January 2002.[78] Nine years after the opening of the case, the supreme

[75] *India Today*, 21 August 2000, 'Stereo Nation. Welcome to the India of Jana Gana Mana on Power Cords', pp. 64–5.

[76] Towards the end of the film, the British attempt to capture an Indian suspected of organizing the bomb attack against the British general. The Indians protest at an official reception of the English general in Kasauli. The Indian police commissioner's daughter joins the protest with flag in hand and her father too changes sides when his daughter is shot. He siezes the flag and tries to attack the English general, but is shot and wounded. The 'terrorist' grabs the flag and pins down the English general with it. Meanwhile, the Union Jack atop the chowki (police station) is torn down, the Indian flag is raised on a pole, the English general is hanged and comes down in the burning Union Jack.

[77] Report of the National Flag Committee, April 2001, para. 3.1.

[78] *Hindustan Times*, 17 January 2002, 'Tricolour rainbow'.

court judgement of 23 January 2004 recognized that the right to fly the national flag freely on all days was a fundamental right of citizens.[79] The press welcomed the 'end of a privilege limited to specific government offices', of a 'control-centric, military-oriented' regime that had come to characterize post-Independence India.[80] It posed the problem in larger political terms, asserting: 'In other democracies sovereignty is a popular concept: in India it is a public-sector unit',[81] and invited a more open, public and less remote definition of the republic. The sentiment was echoed in other quarters: 'Our flag has been so pious, untouchable and inaccessible to the public . . . letting citizens get familiar and comfortable with it is a step in the right direction', said fashion designer Suneet Verma.[82] That this was a widespread sentiment was reflected in the public reaction that welcomed the judgement. In Bangalore, vendors were selling the flag at traffic lights, and bikes, cars, tourist buses had jhandas that day.[83]

In the following months a large number of Indians bought their own personal flag in the Khadi Bhandars. The manager of the Ludhiana agency declared that he 'had recorded an unprecedented sale this year (2002)', leading to a shortage on the eve of Republic Day 2003, when he was unable to satisfy hundreds of customers: 'We have already sold hundreds of flags, still, people want more.'[84] Three years after the liberalization, *The Tribune* talked of the 'runaway enthusiasm' that the measure provoked. 'Soon enough the flag became a rage and went up on many rooftops. Rarely has a trend of this nature, cutting across the many divides this country is hostage to, caught on so quickly among so many. This shows the unabashed pride Indians feel in their flag. Such pride is all to the good.'[85]

Can one see these reactions as the expression of a strong, growing nationalist sentiment already nurtured by the technical success of the

[79] For details of this case, see K.V. Singh, op. cit. and the website *http://www.flagfoundationofindia.in/fight*-to-be-free-tiranga.html

[80] *India Today*, 30 April 2001, p. 5.

[81] Ibid.

[82] *Hindustan Times*, 6 July 2005.

[83] Ramachandra Guha, 'The Locality and the Nation', *The Hindu*, 31 August 2003.

[84] *Ludhiana Tribune*, 26 January 2003.

[85] *The Tribune*, 12 July 2005.

explosion of a nuclear device in Pokharan in 1998 and its political impact? Clearly, the Kargil war, as we have observed, saw the burst of a patriotic fervour which did not fizzle out, unlike earlier post-war phases. As one author put it after the Kargil war: 'Victory left the tricolour drenched in blood.'[86] It was undoubtedly in this sense different from the traditional forms of Indian nationalism and appeared as the product of a new representation of India as an important economic, and even nuclear, power. It was especially strong among the middle class and based itself on the model of a 'Bharatiya' economic growth, which was seen to have replaced the hesitant economic growth mocked by some analysts as the 'Hindu rate of growth'. The proliferation of business magazines was an important vector for this new image of India as a technical and commercial power. When Jindal and other businessmen chose their factory or office to hoist and display the national flag, they were participating in the construction of this new image. While conserving a powerful symbol of the Gandhian heritage, this movement gave it a new dimension, which inserted it strongly in the contemporary reality of a country wishing to affirm its economic strength.

The revival of the flag linked to its liberalization and its subsequent popularity has also led to its increasing politicization, that is to say its reappropriation by political parties to strengthen their position. This is noticeably the case with the BJP. For a long time members of the party had shown little interest in the flag. Thus, the chief minister of Gujarat, Narendra Modi, declared on one Republic Day during the official flag-hoisting ceremony: '*Main yahan ek kapde ke tukde ke liye nahin aya hoon*' (I am not here to unfurl a piece of cloth). Seized by the press, these dismissive remarks about the national emblem became a national issue, allowing the Congress to denounce the BJP's insensitivity to the Indian national tradition.[87] Two years later the BJP took a radically opposite stance by organizing a pilgrimage through the country in which the flag was the principal object. The sixteen-day *tiranga yatra* (tricolour pilgrimage) was launched on 10 September 2004, led

[86] M.K. Akbar, *Kargil, Cross Border Terrorism* (New Delhi, Mittal Publications, 1999), p. 306.

[87] *Hindustan Times*, 31 January 2002, 'Modi in a Spot over Alleged Insult to National Flag.'

by former Madhya Pradesh chief minister Uma Bharati from Hubli, Karnataka to Jallianwala Bagh in Punjab, to protest against her arrest on charges of rioting. The BJP announced that a nationwide call would be given to unfurl the tricolour in as many places as possible to 'rejuvenate nationalistic feeling' with the help of slogans like *Lathi, goli khayenge, tiranga jhanda ferayenge* (we will face lathis and bullets to unfurl the national flag).[88]

The demands for the liberalization of the flag cannot be confined within the parameters of these patriotic affirmations. They were equally and even more so the affirmation of a certain conception of the nation. Already in April 2001 the flag committee noted: 'The national flag stands for the whole nation, its ideals, aspirations, its hopes and achievements.'[89] In a period of religious violence since the beginning of the 1990s, of which the riots in Gujarat in February 2002 are only one example, resisting the communalization of society, the aggressive use of religious symbols (temples, festivals, processions),[90] and the corresponding retreat of civil society has acquired political urgency for many. This is reflected in the renewed interest in debates on the political uses of the past,[91] more militant cultural interventions through different art forms like theatre or music,[92] and a search for common civic values.[93]

[88] *The Hindu*, 10 September 2004; *The Telegraph*, 18 September 2004.

[89] Report of the National Flag Committee, April 2001, para. 3.1.

[90] The Ramjanmabhoomi issue, L.K. Advani's yatras, the revival of Ganesh Chaturthi and Rakhi are only some examples. Among the vast literature on the subject see, Richard H. Davis, 'The Iconography of Rama's Chariot', in David Ludden (ed.), *Contesting the Nation. Religion, Community, and the Politics of Democracy in India* (Philadelphia, University of Pennsylvania Press, 1996), pp. 27–54.

[91] S. Gopal, *Anatomy of a Confrontation. The Babri Masjid–Ram Janmabhumi Issue* (New Delhi, Viking, 1991), esp. Neeladri Bhattacharya's contribution, 'Myth, History and the Politics of Ramjanmabhumi', pp. 122–40.

[92] SAHMAT (Safdar Hashmi Memorial Trust) for example has been conducting a campaign against communalism through painting, music, and street plays since it was founded in 1989 after Safdar Hashmi died following an attack on him.

[93] See, for instance, K.N. Panikkar, *An Agenda for Cultural Action and Other Essays* (New Delhi, Three Essays, 2002).

At the same time, putting the flag in the forefront has also allowed citizens to reappropriate it and infused a new vigour into the founding principles of the Indian republic, mainly national unity and the harmonious coexistence of communities and groups. Seen from this angle, the flag appeared as a political response to counter-tendencies of factionalization of Indian politics as well as discriminatory and exclusionist religious-cultural nationalism, for it permitted the development of a more unifying political pedagogy. One example of the possibilities of educating youth on unity through the flag was provided by a music show intermingling Hindustani and Carnatic music. Entitled 'Tiranga', the production brought together musicians from all parts of India to expatiate on the colours and design of the flag. From Kashmir, Shiv Kumar Sharma on the santoor evoked the colour white, Srinivas on his mandolin green; from the south the violinist Subramaniam elaborated his raga on the chakra, and the exponent of Hindustani music, the vocalist Jasraj dwelt on saffron. Accompanied by explanations and commentaries combining Hindi and Urdu traditions, the show was staged in different cities of India after being presented before Parliament House.[94]

With a similar objective, Jindal launched a nationwide appeal for the compilation of photographs on the flag in 2005. He invited people to send photographs of the tricolour in places and situations that they considered particularly meaningful.[95] The project reached out to a larger public. It thus aimed to make evident the link between the flag and the territory of India, reviving an earlier pedagogy of the nation practised since the 1930s. It also echoed photos of Kargil soldiers planting the national flag in the threatened territory of India. These visual testimonies, sent in large numbers by people all over the country, now inserted the flag in different sites—familiar or distant—and in the various provinces of India, giving unity to the fragments of the country, which together constituted the territory of the nation.[96]

[94] *The Hindu*, 30 August 2004.

[95] *Hindustan Times*, 31 January 2005.

[96] Vijay S. Jodha & Samar S. Jodha, *Tiranga: A Celebration of the Indian Flag* (New Delhi: Newvision Publishers for Yuva Hindustani, Flag Foundation of India, 2005).

A final feature for understanding the impact of the flag's liberalization in contemporary India leads us to look beyond its political dimensions. The ambiguities of its liberalization have provoked certain practices that are immediately liable to judicial proceedings.[97] In fact, the 'liberalization' of the flag has not implied the removal of all control. The new flag code clearly prohibits any act that is an insult to the flag and ensures that it does not become a mere fashion accessory.[98] The Prevention of Insult to National Honour Act forbids the use of the tricolour on costumes, cushions, napkins, and handkerchiefs. BBC news reported on 6 July 2005 that Indians were free to wear images of their flag on their clothing but not where it hurts national sentiments—below the belt!

In recent years, a series of affairs have received media attention—such as Sachin Tendulkar wearing a helmet painted in the colours of the flag, or cricket captain Sourav Ganguly's batting gloves showing the tricolour. These provoked a home ministry decree banning cricketers and sportsmen from displaying the flag on their kit.[99] The following testimony of a non-resident Indian on the flag's place in contemporary India summarizes the uneasy transition that has taken place.

> It is amazing how much of the people of some countries identify themselves with its national colours!
>
> I was recently in Brazil and it was very interesting to note that there were more 'Brasileroes' buying the Yellow and Green than tourists.
>
> Of course, the Sao Paolo airport was full of yellow and green—anything you want from bikinis to beach sandals were available in the Brazilian colours. A lot of that can of course be attributed to the upcoming soccer tournament, but not all. I have been to Brazil a few times now and the airports are always yellow and green and I had always wondered about it . . . The same was true in the Buenos Aires airport—blue and white; and in Ireland—all shamrocks—all green. Of course, the United States surpasses everybody when it comes to displaying the flag proudly. I think it is pretty hard to go to any place in the US without seeing the flag.

[97] See Srirupa Roy, 'A Symbol of Freedom', op. cit., pp. 515–17.
[98] *Hindustan Times*, 6 July 2005.
[99] *The Telegraph*, 5 July 2005.

> I cannot but wonder are we Indians not attached to our flag? Even with the changed Flag Code, I do not see (well, I haven't been to India in almost 2 years) us Indians putting on a bashful display of the tricolour, I wanted to buy a flag last time I was in India (a small one) and I got the really bad plastic ones (which to be frank, I was ashamed to buy due to the quality). The cricket season, of course, brings out the INDIA caps and T-shirts, but is that tantamount to a proud display of the national colours? When would I be able to buy a tricolour cap or bag or shirt or jacket at the Mumbai airport? When would we able to see all houses in the country have a flag on their porch or balcony?[100]

The last element to be considered, which appears throughout the recent flag controversy, is the articulation of the flag on behalf of the individuals' fundamental claim to democracy. The American example in the US flag code and the practices of flag usage are permanently evoked by protagonists and constitute a strong reference. The United States here serves in this sense as a model of democracy. Jindal constantly referred to his experience as a student in Texas. The supreme court's decision of January 2004 compared the uses of flags in twenty-odd countries, insisting in particular on the American flag code. Demands for the liberalization of the flag appeared as a criticism of the bureaucratic and oligarchic system in which a minority had privileges that simple citizens did not enjoy. Jindal's argument included the reminder: 'Do you realize that if Mahatma Gandhi were alive today and not a minister, even he would not have been able to fly the flag?'[101] The condemnation of bureaucratic control of the flag expressed the desire to deepen democracy, to define the nation in egalitarian terms, as a whole composed of citizens, symbolized by the equal relationship they all shared with the national symbol. The idea had already been expressed at the end of the 1980s in discussions on citizenship values. Even then, the flag's potential in furthering a different political culture was being advanced: 'The U.S. model would be worth considering as another formula (for inculcating a national habit in place of the concept of self, inherent in

[100] 8 May 2006, 'Colors of a Nation'. This testimony has been taken from a blog called 'Turnpike thoughts', by a non-resident Indian (*http://capricornian.livejournal.com*).

[101] Interview with N. Jindal, 13 June 2001, reported in *The Hindu*, 24 January 2004.

the doctrine of *dharma*) where every child in school at least starts the day by a pledge to the country and the flag.'[102] One real rupture can be seen in this statement. In July 1947 Radhakrishnan had associated the flag with dharma before the Constituent Assembly, i.e. the right and just action performed by every individual guided by elements specific to him. Demands made from the perspective of the rights and duties of citizens introduce a more collective reasoning. This interpretation defines the nation not as linked to its territory but to a political body. The reflection, no doubt marginal, shows the complexity and diversity of the elements that underlie the renewed interest in the flag, which had been neutralized in the period from 1947 to the mid 1990s when the restrained regime of the flag had been imposed.

In recent years these questions have been prolonged in reflections, even debates, on the subject of citizenship and the role of civil society, in a manner relevant to the Indian context and traditions,[103] whether through grassroots movements, intermediary non-governmental associations, or individual citizen groups.[104] Partisans of this approach see civil society's emphasis on equality and individual rights to be more in concord with India's traditions of social pluralism. In their eyes, strengthening civil society can be one of the means of ensuring democracy and the individual's fundamental rights as defined in the Preamble and Article 19 of the Indian constitution, and an antidote to the rising fundamentalism of Hindu groups and caste-based *senas*. The language

[102] Shyam Ratna Gupta, Urs Schöttle and Jürgen Axel (eds), *Citizenship Values in India. Individualism and Social Imperatives (*Calcutta, Mandira, 1990), p. 11.

[103] The importance of creating a national identification which before all would be civic and accommodate healthy difference can be found in Ashis Nandy, 'Self as a Political Concept', in P.C. Chatterjee (ed.), *Self-Images, Identity and Nationality* (New Delhi, Indian Institute of Advanced Study, Shimla, in association with Allied Publishers, 1989); *Baroda Conference on Religion and Society in Contemporary India, 13 November 1994 (*Delhi, Rajiv Gandhi Institute for Contemporary Studies, 1996), pp. 5–17, esp. Dharma Kumar, 'Religion and Society in Contemporary India', p. 13; Amar Kumar Singh, 'Developing Indian National Identity', pp. 58–9.

[104] Rajni Kothari, 'The Decline of the Moderate State', in Zoya Hasan (ed.), *Politics and the State in India (*New Delhi, Sage, 2000), pp. 177–205; Sudipta Kaviraj and Sunil Khilnani (eds), *Civil Society. Historical Possibilities* (Cambridge, Cambridge University Press, 2001); Carolyn M. Elliott (ed.), *Civil Society and Democracy* (Delhi, Oxford University Press, 2003).

of citizenship is located in Gandhi's discourse since the 1940s.[105] Thus, opposition to the Narmada Valley projects has been articulated principally around the violation of citizens' rights that the constructions of dams imply.[106] While deliberations on civil society concentrate on the crisis of the modern nation state, the growth of casteism, communalism, and the exclusionist policies of political parties, some rare voices recognize the disproportionate weight given to discussing 'threadbare every aspect of social conflict' in undergraduate teaching and giving too little thought to examining the processes of construction and reinforcement of social harmony, national integration, and unity-in-diversity: 'Have these ideas become non-objects in Indian social science? Or are they, as erstwhile slogans of the secular state, as official constructions left over from the Congress Party era, merely objects of ridicule for contemporary social scientists?' So writes a college lecturer from Bangalore, struck by the absence of mechanisms in Indian society, 'to process these emotions of hatred, anger, jealousy, fear and humiliation—hence riots, those public detonations of pent-up sentiments. But riots are just one expression of the politics of sentiment.'[107]

Starting from very different realities of conflict and social tensions and violence in contemporary India, she finds one of the central processes of the construction of the nation as a whole of citizens to be precisely that very forceful expression of the 'politics of sentiment', which I have shown to be the backbone of nation-construction during the colonial period. But unlike my study of this process, at no moment does she refer to the flag or any other element that permits this non-aggressive cohesion of a people into a nation. Nonetheless, the questions she raises are the very questions raised in symbolic terms by the flag and the role some Indians attribute to it in contemporary India, when the flag is no longer the privilege of the state but an object available to all citizens.

[105] Kumkum Sangari, 'A Narrative of Restoration: Gandhi's Last Years and Nehruvian Secularism', *Social Scientist,* vol. 30, March–April 2002, pp. 3–33.

[106] Niraja Gopal Jayal, *Democracy and the State. Welfare, Secularism and Development in Contemporary India* (Delhi, Oxford University Press, 1999).

[107] Ananya Vajpeyi, 'Teaching against Communalism. Role of Social Science Pedagogy', *Economic and Political Weekly,* vol. 37, 21 December 2002, pp. 5093–7.

Conclusion

Fifteen years ago, when I started work on the Indian national flag, it was with the intention of writing a short article as part of a comparative study initiated by the French historian Maurice Agulhon of national symbols in France, England, and Canada. This project did not materialize. It made me realize that the flag was a distant, marginal object for Indian historiography, whose concerns lay elsewhere. Certainly, in the early1990s the flag was not an object that appeared central to the issues that preoccupied Indian historians. It was in fact the very symbol of a national construct that was being vehemently questioned and criticized. Contrary to the vistas opened up by what had become keywords of the national struggle—religion, community, caste, minorities, gender, violence—the flag appeared a highly and even-too-respectable political symbol, familiar and legitimate to the point of not being a historical problem at all! Apart from the obvious constitutional framework of debates and legislation, there were no prominent indicators showing up its existence in the archives; no identifiable home public or political series that one could begin by examining; no entry in the index of books dealing with colonial or national history. In short, if it qualified for an article or two, it did not 'make a book'.

These initial impressions were slowly belied by enquiries into its genesis, its colours, its progressive growth in public colonial space, as well as in the private sphere. Curiously, as they revealed the dynamics and implications of this symbol for the process of national construction, the flag was projected to centrestage in Indian political culture. These movements have in turn prompted a more academic interest today in the flag as a site for negotiation and claims of citizenship. Besides justifying my years spent on the subject, this trend underlines the importance of the issues this book has attempted to underline.

First, as analysed in recent historiography, India appears a fragile reality, torn by innumerable conflicts and divisions, racked by ongoing processes of fragmentation. The causes are multiple, stretching from communities, castes, religions, and languages, to gender, classes, and ecological stakes. Through these approaches, India constantly appears on the verge of dissolution. Yet the conflicts and the struggles which led to independence eventually produced, at least during the sixty-odd years following 1947, one of the most stable democratic nations having experienced colonization. The dominant trends in historiography skim over this striking evidence or simply take it for granted. In investigating the emotional adherence of individuals and groups to the nation that the flag permitted through its diverse uses and appropriations, the emphasis shifts to the forms of solidarity and cohesion implied by the process of nation-building. Once we leave a narrow patriotic glorification and approach it as more than a clear-cut tool of manipulation and state engineering that tends to further either the power of state regimes or their hegemony, this is what the history of the flag allows us to grasp. This investigation into the symbolic constructions of the nation under colonial rule reveals the flag to be clearly one of the symbols that could canalize feelings and passions and reinforce bonds of national cohesion and solidarity. The recent growing demand for the freedom to handle and display the national flag by private citizens proves, if nothing else, the continued relevance of a symbol of national belonging in what is characterized as a 'global age'. But it has deeper implications. The fact that today it is equally and easily accessible to all citizens in itself introduces a novel situation in the Indian system where respect for an object is intimately linked to its exclusive or restrained nature. The 'liberal regime' for the flag introduces a democratic note in a society and politics constructed around the notion of privilege, not rights.

Secondly, the history of the emergence and problematic growth of this national symbol underlines the fact that the success of a national symbol for India lay precisely in its capacity to appeal beyond the narrow, limited pulls of region, caste, community, religion, and ethnicity. This trait imposed itself at all moments of the anti-colonial struggle, during the Nagpur flag satyagraha in 1923, under the slogan 'Up, up with the National Flag, Down, down with the Union Jack' through the 1930s, down till 1947 when national cohesion and solidarity acquired a greater urgency with Partition. Its success was built on the principle of rallying and reconciling differences. This standard determined the choice and success of its colours and design in 1921, 1931, and again in 1947. To reaffirm this idea is not simply to repeat a party slogan or a national line. It is to recognize the flag as a national symbol that has since the colonial period proposed an alternative to an exclusively religious identification. Even more, it served to assert a secular vision of a country and society, as in the rejection of saffron in 1931. Can this recompense the lack of a clear, well-defined 'secular strategy'? Probably not. But it does indicate where such national strategies are to be identified.

Finally, in the present context—before the growing tendencies to withdraw into narrow groups and separate units, to advance community rights and organize movements for the defence of sectarian interests—any exercise that explores ways and possibilities which can contribute to strengthening these bonds, acquires greater importance. The adherence to a common, shared symbol such as a flag, which can provide a 'coherence of sentiments', is far from being a natural feature of modern nation states, an acquisition for ever after. On the contrary, at least in democratic systems, it can serve as a platform for a continuous process of negotiation between citizens and the state, recalling and reinforcing a contract of citizenship without extending the power and control of the state. More particularly, in the Indian context, it advances a form of cohesion that deviates significantly from the more classic forms rooted in affiliation to communities, religious, and linguistic groups. It proposes a shift from these customary operational clusters, without of course denying their importance and value. It thus disturbs the deeply embedded archetypal categories, but, as opposed to these sectarian forms of solidarity, the flag offers the possibility of an equal relationship between all Indians.

Bibliography

Manuscript Sources

National Archives of India, New Delhi

Home Department (Political) Proceedings
Home Department Public Proceedings
Foreign & Political Department Proceedings
Central Provinces Legislative Council Proceedings
Central Provinces & Berar Fortnightly Reports
Curzon Collection
Rajendra Prasad Papers
Kharpade Papers

Nehru Memorial Museum and Library, New Delhi

AICC Papers
Indian National Congress Reports
Indian National Congress proceedings
Tagore Manuscripts
M.R. Jayakar Papers
C.R. Rajagopalachari Papers
T.B. Sapru's private papers 1921–48

British Library, Oriental and India Office Collection, London

Viceroy's Fortnightly Private and Personal Correspondence with the Secretary of State for India
Selections from the Records of the Government of India
Departmental Papers: Political and Secret Files
Political and Secret Home Correspondence about Indian States

Governor's Fortnightly Correspondance with Viceroy
Local Government Reports
Compilations and Miscellaneous Records
Political and Secret Political Records
Daily News Schedules
Native Newspaper Reports

Centre for South Asian Studies, Cambridge

M.L. Darling Papers
G.P.S. Stewart Papers
Gracie Papers
Hicks Papers
Johnston Papers
Tape Recordings (J.N. Sahani, Vejubhai Shah, Sucheta Kripalani)

University Library, Cambridge

Royal Commonwealth Society Collection

Archives du Ministères des Affaires étrangères, Paris

Asie-Océanie, Inde française, no. 17, no. 24 (Chandernagor, 1946–8)
Nouvelle série, Inde, no. 6 (1907–8), no. 9 (1915–19)

Centre des Archives d'Outre-Mer, Aix-en-Provence (France)

Etablissements français en Inde:
C 727 (1907–23), Affaires politiques
F. 6-31, 'Correspondance confidentielle du gouverneur au ministre des colonies', 1902–55
H 13, nationalist agitation in Karihal, 1939–43; H17, political tracts and press reports, 1947

Printed Sources

Official Sources

Constituent Assembly Debates. Offical Report (New Delhi, Lok Sabha Secretariat, 12 vols, 1950–99)

Indian Annual Register (Calcutta, 1921–47)
Parliamentary Debates. House of Commons, Sessions 1902, 1921 (London, Wymon & Sons)
Report for Parliament. India in 1931–32 (Calcutta, Bureau of Public Information, Government of India, 1933)
Review of the Administration of the Presidencey of Bombay, 1923–24 (Bombay, 1925)

Newspapers

Aaj (in Hindi), 1920–3
Advocate, 1917
Amrita Bazar Patrika, 1905–10, 1916–18, 1920–3, 1930–2, 1946–7
Asian Age, 1996
Bombay Chronicle, 1916–17, 1920–3, 1930–1, 1947
Bombay Sentinel, 1947
Common Wheel, 1917–18
Daily Telegraph, 1901–2
Dawn, 1941–7
Deccan Chronicle, 1947
Deccan Times, 1947
Eastern Times, 1947
Harijan, 1933–9, 1947
Hindu 1906, 1917–18, 1920–3, 1930–8, 1946–7, 2003–4
Hindu Illustrated Weekly, 1930
Hindustan Review, 1935
Hindustan Times, 1924–5, 1947, 2002–5
Hitavada, 1921–3, 1930, 1947
Independent Hindustan, 1920–1
India Today, 1996, 2000–5
Indian Express, 1996, 2002
Indian People, 1904–8
Janmabhumi, 1921–3
L'Illustration (Paris), 1930
Ludhiana Tribune, 2003
Madras Mail, 1931, 1947
Madras Weekly Mail, 1930

Mahratta, 1905, 1912, 1921–3, 1930–2, 1946–7
Modern Review, 1909, 1912, 1919, 1931
Muslim Outlook, 1930
National Herald, 1947
New India, 1917–18
New York Times, 1930, 1947
People, 1931
Pioneer, 1928
Pioneer Mail & Indian Weekly News, 1930–1
Searchlight, 1920–3, 1930–1
Servant of India, 1923
Statesman, 1930, 1947, 1997
Telegraph, 2004–5
Times (London), 1900–8, 1923, 1930–1
Times of India, 1907, 1930
Tribune, 1906–7, 1918, 1930–1, 1946–7, 2004–5
Young India, 1920–47

Published Documents and Memoirs

Afzal, M. Rafique (ed.), *Speeches and Statements of Quaid-i-Millat Liaquat Ali Khan, 1941–1951* (Lahore, Research Society of Pakistan, University of Punjab, 1967)

Ahmad, Jamil-ud-din, *Historic Documents of the Muslim Freedom Movement* (Lahore, Publishers United, 1970)

Ahmed, Syed Rais Jafri (ed.), *Rare Documents* (Lahore, Muhammad Ali Academy, 1967)

Ahmad, Waheed (ed.), *Jinnah, Mahomed Ali, 1876–1948. Nation's Voice, vol. VI* (Karachi, Quaid-i-Azam Academy, 2002)

Asaf, Ali M., *Memoirs, The Emergence of Modern India* (Delhi, Ajanta, 1994)

Azad, Maulana Abul Kalam, *India Wins Freedom* (London, Sangam, 1988)

Bachchan, Harivansh Rai, *In the Afternoon of Time. An Autobiography* (Delhi, London, Viking, 1998)

Bakshi, S.R., *Documents of Home Rule Movement* (New Delhi, Criterion Publications, 1989)

Bannerjee, Surendranath, *A Nation in Making: Being the Reminiscences of Fifty Years of Public Life* (London, Humphrey Milford, 1925)

Basu, Sankari Prasad (ed.), *Letters of Sister Nivedita* (Calcutta, Nababharat Publishers, 1982)

Bhattacharya, Sabyasachi (ed.), *The Mahatma and the Poet. Letters and Debates between Gandhi and Tagore 1915–1941* (New Delhi, National Book Trust, 1997)

Besant, Annie Wood, *Under the Congress Flag* (Madras, Commonweal Office, 1916)

Besant, Annie Wood, *How India Fought for Freedom. The Story of the National Congress told from Official Records* (Adyar, Theoso-phical Publishing House, 1915)

Besant, Annie Wood, *The Future of Indian Politics: A Contribution to the Understanding of Present-Day Problems* (Adyar, Theosophical Publishing House, 1922)

Besant, Annie Wood, *India, Bond or Free? A World Problem* (London, Putnam's Sons, 1926)

Besant, Annie Wood, *The Birth of New India. A Collection of Writings and Speeches on Indian Affairs* (Adyar, Theosophical Publishing House, 1917)

Besant, Annie Wood, *Speeches and Writings* (Madras, G.A. Natesan, 1921)

Bharati, Subramania, *Chosen Poems and Prose.* English renderings of a selection from the Tamil writings (Delhi, All-India Subramania Bharati Centenary Celebrations Committee, Govt. of India, 1984)

Bhabani, Bhattacharya, *So Many Hungers* (Left Book Club, Victor Gollancz, 1947)

Bose, C., *Indian Revolutionaries Abroad 1905–1927. Select Documents* (New Delhi, Northern Book Centre, 2002)

Bose, Subhas Chandra, *An Indian Pilgrim: An Unfinished Autobiography and Some Collected Letters, 1827–1921* (Calcutta, Netaji Research Bureau, 1962)

Chatterji, Basudev (ed.), *Towards Freedom. Documents on the Movement for Independence in India, 1938* (Delhi, Indian Council of Historical Research, Oxford University Press, 1999)

Chaudhuri, Nirad C., *The Autobiography of an Unknown Indian* (London, Macmillan & Co., 1951)

Chaudhuri, Nirad C., *Thy Hand, Great Anarch: India, 1921–1952* (London, Chatto & Windus, 1987)

Chopra, P.N. (ed.), *Towards Freedom, 1937–47* (New Delhi, Indian Council of Historical Research, 1985)

Chopra, P.N. (ed.), *Collected Works of Sardar Vallabhbhai Patel, 1918–1925* (Delhi, 3 vols, 1990)

Choudhary, Valmiki, *Rajendra Prasad, Correspondence and Select Documents* (Delhi, Allied Publishers, 1984)

Darling, Sir Malcolm, *Apprentice to Power, India 1904–1908* (London, Hogarth Press, 1966)

Das, Durga (ed.), *Sardar Patel's Correspondence, 1945–1950* (Ahmedabad, Navjivan Publishing House, 1971)

Datta, Bhupendranath, *Bharater Dwitiya Swadhinatar Sangram* (Calcutta, Aprakasita Rajanitika Itihasa, 1926)

Dutta, Krishna & Robinson, Andrew (eds), *Rabindranath Tagore. An Anthology* (London, Picador, 1997)

Dwarkadas, Kanji, *Ten Years to Freedom 1938–1947* (Bombay, Popular Prakashan, 1968)

Dwarkadas, Kanji, *India's Fight for Freedom 1913–1937: An Eyewitness Story* (Bombay, Popular Prakashan, 1966)

Elwin, Edward F., *Indian Jottings. From Ten Years Experience in and Around Poona City* (London, John Murray, 1907)

Forster, E.M., *A Passage to India* (London, Penguin, 1st edn, 1924, 5th edn, 1989)

Fuller, Sir Joseph Bamfylde, *Some Personal Experiences* (London, Murray, 1930)

Gandhi, Mohandas Karamchand, *Hind Swaraj* (Madras, 1921)

Gandhi, Mohandas Karamchand, *An Autobiography or the Story of My Experiments with Truth* (Ahmedabad, Navajivan Trust, 1995, 1st edn, 1927–9)

Gandhi, Mohandas Karamchand, *India of My Dreams* (Ahmedabad, Navajivan Trust, 1st ed., 1947, 7th edn, 1999)

Gandhi, Mohandas Karamchand, *Collected Works* (Delhi, Publications Division, Ministry of Information and Broadcasting, Govt. of India, 1958–94)

Ghosh Aurobindo, *On Nationalism. Selected Writings and Speeches* (Pondicherry, Sri Aurobindo National Trust, 1996)

Gilbert, M. (ed.), *Servant of India. A Study of Imperial Rule from 1905–1910 as told through the Correspondence and Diaries of Sir James Dunlop Smith* (London, Longmans, 1966)

Gopal, Sarvepalli (ed.), *Jawaharlal Nehru. Selected Works* (Delhi, Orient Longman, 1972–82)

Gupta, Partha Sarathi (ed.), *Towards Freedom. Documents on the Movement for Independence in India: 1943–1944* (Delhi, Indian Council of Historical Research, Oxford University Press, 1997)

Hamid, Major-General Shahid, *Disastrous Twilight* (London, Cooper, 1986)

Hosain, Attia, *Sunlight on a Broken Column. A Novel* (London, Chatto & Windus, 1961)

Hutheesing, Krishna Nehru, *We Nehrus* (Bombay, Pearl Books, 1968)

Hyder, Qurratulain, *River of Fire* (1st edn, 1927, New Delhi, Kali for Women, 1998)

Ikramullah, Shaista Suhrawardy, *From Purdah to Parliament* (Karachi, Oxford University Press, 1998)

Ispahani, Mirza Abol Hassan, *Qaid-e-Azam Jinnah as I Knew Him* (Karachi, Royal Book Company, 1976)

Jayakar, Mukund Ramrao, *The Story of My Life, 1922–25* (Bombay, Asia Publishing House, 1958–9)

Joshi, Vijaya Chandra (ed.), *Lajpat Rai, Autobiographical Writings* (Delhi, Jullundur University Publishers, 1965)

Karandikar, Raghunath Pandurangh, *Letters from England, 1908* (Satara, Vithal Raghunath Karandikar, 1935)

Khurshid, Khalid Hasan (ed.), *Memoirs of Jinnah* (Karachi, Oxford University Press, 1990)

Kumar, Ravinder, Panigrahi, D.N. & Sharma, Hari Dev (eds), *Selected Works of Motilal Nehru [1899–1928]* (New Delhi, Vikas, 6 vols, 1982–95)

Mansergh, Nicolas & Moon, Penderel (eds), *Transfer of Power 1942–1947* (London, HMSO, 1974–82)

Manto, Saadat Hasan, *Kingdom's End and Other Stories* (London, Verso, 1987)

Meston, James Scorgie, *Nationhood for India* (Oxford, Oxford University Press, 1931)

Moon, Penderel, *Divide and Quit* (London, Chatto & Windus, 1961)

Moon, Penderel, *Strangers in India* (London, Faber & Faber, 1944)

Mosley, Leonard, *The Last Days of the British Raj* (London, Weidenfeld & Nicolson, 1961)

Muhammad, Shan (ed.), *Unpublished Letters of the Ali Brothers* (Delhi, Idarah-i-Adabiyat-i Delhi, 1979)

Mujahid, Sharif Al (ed.), *Muslim League Documents, 1900–1908* (Karachi, Quaid-i-Azam Academy, 1990), vol. 1

Munshi, Kanaiyalal Maneklal, *The End of an Era: Hyderabad Memories* (Bombay, Bharatiya Vidya Bhavan, 1957)

Nehru, Braj Kumar, *Nice Guys Finish Second* (Delhi, Viking, 1997)

Nehru, Jawaharlal, *Eighteen Months in India 1936–1937* (Allahabad, Kitabistan, 1938)

Nehru, Jawaharlal, *An Autobiography* (London, John Lane The Bodley Head, 1936, 9th edn, 1995)

Nehru, Jawaharlal, *A Bunch of Old Letters* (Bombay, Asia Publishing House, 1958)

Nehru, Jawaharlal, *The Unity of India: Collected Writings 1937–1940* (New York, John Day Co., 1948)

Nehru, Jawaharlal, *Selected Works*, S. Gopal (ed.), *first series* (New Delhi, Orient Longman, 15 vols, 1972–82); *second series* (New Delhi, Jawaharlal Nehru Memorial Fund and Oxford University Press, 34 vols, 1984–2004)

Pal, Bipin Chandra, *The Spirit of Indian Nationalism* (London, Hind National Agency, 1910)

Pal, Bipin Chandra, *Swadeshi & Swaraj* (Calcutta, Yugayatri Prakashak, 1954)

Pal, Bipin Chandra, *Memories of My Life and Times* (Calcutta, 2nd edn, Bipin Chandra Pal Institute, 1973)

Pandit, Vijaya Lakshmi, *The Scope of Happiness. A Personal Memoir* (London, Weidenfeld and Nicolson, 1979)

Pant, Apa, *An Unusual Raja. Mahatma Gandhi and the Aundh Experiment* (Hyderabad, Sangam Books, 1989)

Panikkar, Kavalam Madhava & Pershad, A. (eds), *The Voice of Freedom. The Speeches of Pandit Motilal Nehru* (Bombay, Asia Publishing House, 1961)

Paranjpe, Makarand, *Sarojini Naidu. Selected Letters 1890s to 1940s* (New Delhi, Kali for Women, 1996)

Phatak, N.R. (ed.), *Source Material for the History of the Freedom Movement in India* (Bombay, Maharashtra Archives, 5 vols, 1965–9)

Pirzada, Syed Sharifuddin (ed.), *Foundations of Pakistan: All-India Muslim League Documents 1906–1947* (Karachi-Dacca, National Publishing House, 2 vols, 1970)

Pirzada, Syed Sharifuddin (ed.), *Quaid-e-Azam Jinnah's Correspondence* (Karachi, Guild Publishing House, 1966; 3rd edn, Karachi, East & West Pub. Co., 1977)

Prasad, Rajendra, *India Divided* (Bombay, Hind Kitab, 1946)

Rao, B. Shiva (ed.), *The Framing of India's Constitution. Select Documents* (New Delhi, The Indian Institute of Public Administration, 1966)

Rolland, Romain, *Mahatma Gandhi* (Paris, Stock, 1924)

Roy, M.N., *Memoirs* (Bombay, Allied Publishers Private, 1964)

Roy, Subodh (ed.), *Communism in India. Unpublished Documents 1925–1934* (Calcutta, Ganasahitya Prakash, 1972)

Rushbrook, Williams L.F., *The History of the Indian Tour of H.R.H. The Prince of Wales 1911–21* (Calcutta, Superintendent of Government Printing, India, 1922)

Sahgal, Lakshmi, *A Revolutionary Life. Memoirs of a Political Activist* (Delhi, Kali for Women, 1997)

Sahgal, Nayantara (ed.), *Before Freedom: Nehru's Letters to His Sister* (New Delhi, HarperCollins Publishers, 2000)

Sahni, Bhisham, *Tamas* (New Delhi, Penguin, 1988)

Setalvad, Chimanlal H., *Recollections and Reflections. An Autobiography* (Bombay, Padma Publications, 1946)

Singh, Amar Kaur Jasbir (ed.), *Gandhi and Civil Disobedience. Documents in India Office Records 1922–46* (London, India Office Library and Records, 1980)

Sitaramayya, Bhograju Pattabhi, *The History of the Indian National Congress, 1935–1947* (Bombay, Padma Publications, 1947)

Strachey, Sir John, *India. Its Administration and Progress* (London, Kegan Paul, 1st edn, 1888, 3rd edn, 1903)

Syed, Rais Ahmad Jafri (ed.), *Rare Documents* (Lahore, Muhammad Ali Academy, 1967)

Tagore, Rabindranath, *Gora* (London, Macmillan, 1924)
Tagore, Rabindranath, *Nationalism* (London, Macmillan & Co., 1917)
Tandon, Prakash, *Punjabi Century 1857–1947* (London, Chatto & Windus, 1961)
Tandon, Prakash, *Beyond Punjab, 1937–1960* (New Delhi, Thomson Press, 1971)
Taylor, Robert, *The Princely Armoury. Being the Display of the Arms of the Ruling Chiefs of India Prepared for the Imperial Assemblage held at Delhi on the First Day of January 1877* (Calcutta, Office of the Superintendent of Government Printing, 1877; 2nd edn, Calcutta, Government of India, 1902)
Tirtha, Swami Ramananda, *Memoirs of Hyderabad Freedom Struggle* (Bombay, Popular Prakashan, 1967)
Tyabji, Badruddin, *Memoirs of an Egoist* (New Delhi, Roli Books, 1988)
Venkatarangaiya, Mamidipudi (ed.), *Freedom Struggle in Andhra Pradesh* (Andhra Pradesh State Committee, 1965)
Zaidi, Z.H. (ed.), *Quaid-i-Azam Mohammad Ali Jinnah Papers. Prelude to Pakistan, 20 February–2 June 1947* (National Archives of Pakistan, 1993)
Zelinsky, Wilbur, *Nation into State: The Shifting Symbolic Foundations of American Nationalism* (Chapel Hill, North Carolina University Press, 1988)

Secondary Works

Studies on Flags and Political Symbolism

Agaravala, S. Vasudev, *The Wheel Flag of India: Chakra Dhvaja* (Varanasi, Prithvi Prakashan, 1964)
Agulhon, Maurice, *Marianne au combat. L'imagerie et la symbolique républicaine de 1789 à 1880* (Paris, Flammarion, 1979) (English translation, *Marianne into Battle. Republican Imagery and Symbolism in France, 1789–1880*, Cambridge, Cambridge University Press, 1981)
Agulhon, Maurice, *Marianne au pouvoir. L'imagerie et la symbolique républicaines de 1880 à 1914* (Paris, Flammarion, 1989)

Agulhon, Maurice, *Les métamorphoses de Marianne. L'imagerie et la symbolique républicaine de 1914 à nos jours* (Paris, Flammarion, 2001)

Agulhon, Maurice, 'Les couleurs dans la politique française', *Ethnologie française*, 20, 1990, pp. 392–8

Agulhon, Maurice, 'Politics, Images, Symbols in Post-revolutionary France', in Wilentz, Sean (ed.), *Rites of Power: Symbolism, Ritual and Politics since the Middle Ages* (Philadelphia, University of Pennsylvania Press, 1985)

Alter, Peter, 'Symbols of Irish Nationalism', *Studia Hibernica*, no. 14, 1974, pp. 104–23

Arvidsson, Claes & Blomquist, Erik Lars, *Symbols of Power. The Esthetics of Political Legitimation in the Soviet Union and Eastern Europe* (Stockholm, Almqvist and Wiksell International, 1987)

Barraclough, E.M.C., *Flags of the World* (London, Warne, 1950)

Bodnar, John (ed.), *Bonds of Affection. Americans Define their Patriotism* (Princeton, Princeton University Press, 1996)

Bonner, Robert E., 'Flag Culture and the Consolidation of Confederate Nationalism', *The Journal of Southern History*, LXVIII, 2, 2002, pp. 293–332

Bonner, Robert E., *Colors and Blood: Flag Passions of the Confederate South* (Princeton-Oxford, Princeton University Press, 2002)

Boureau, Alain, *L'Aigle. Chronique politique d'un emblème* (Paris, Les éditions du Cerf, 1985)

Brittlebank, Kate, 'Sakti and Barakat: The Power of Tipu's Tiger. An Examination of the Tiger Emblem of Tipu Sultan of Mysore', *Modern Asian Studies*, 29, 1995, pp. 257–69

Bryson, Lucy & McCartney, Clem, *Clashing Symbols. A Report on the Use of Flags, Anthems and other National Symbols in Northern Ireland* (Belfast, Queen's University, Institute of Irish Studies, 1994)

Campbell, Gordon & Evans, I.O. *The Book of Flags* (London, Oxford University Press, 1950)

Chandra, Rai Govind, *Indian Symbolism. Symbols as Sources of Our Customs and Beliefs* (New Delhi, Munshiram Manoharlal Publishers, 1996)

Chatterji, Suniti Kumar, *The National Flag. A Selection of Papers, Cultural and Historical* (Calcutta, Mitra & Ghosh, 1944)

Firth, Raymond, *Symbols Public and Private* (New York, Cornell University Press, 1973)

Fraser, Alistair B., 'A Canadian Flag for Canada', *Journal of Canadian Studies*, xxv, 4, 1980–1, pp. 74–80

Gavelli, Mirtide, Sangiorgi, Otello, Tarozzi, Fiorenza (ed.), *Colorare la patria. Tricolore e formazione della coscienza nazionale, 1797–1914* (Florence, Vallecchi, 1996)

Ghisi, E., *Del tricolore Italiano* (Torino, 1912)

Girardet, Raoul, 'Les Trois Couleurs', in Pierre Nora (ed.), *Les Lieux de Mémoire* (Paris, Gallimard, 1984), vol. 1, pp. 5–35

Goldstein, Robert Justin, *Saving 'Old Glory': The History of the American Flag Desecration Controversy* (Boulder, Colo., Westview, 1995)

Goldstein, Robert Justin, *Burning the Flag: The Great 1989–1990 American Flag Desecration Controversy* (Kent, Ohio, Kent State University Press, 1996)

Goldstein, Robert Justin (ed.), *Desecrating the American Flag: Key Documents of the Controversy from the Civil War to 1995* (Syracuse, NY, Syracuse University Press, 1996)

Guenter, Scot M., *The American Flag, 1777–1924. Cultural Shifts from Creation to Codification* (London-Toronto, Associated American Presses, 1990)

Hulme, F.E., *The Flags of the World: Their History, Blazonry and Associations* (London, Frederick Warne & Co., 1897)

Indian Standards, *Specification for the National Flag of India* (New Delhi, Indian Standards Institution, 2nd edn, 1977)

Jha, Sadan, 'The Indian National Flag as a Site of Daily Plebiscite', 55 pp., 7th Subaltern Conference, 'Lives of Democracy: Peoples, Populations & Citizens in South Asia', 6–9 January 2004, Centre for Studies of Developing Societies, Delhi, Unpublished typescript

Jha, Sadan, 'The Mythic (Non)Presence of the Other in the Text of Indian Nation-ness', in Anna Branach-Kallas & Katarzyna Wieckowska (eds), *The Nation of the Other: Construction of Nation in Contemporary Cultural and Literary Discourses* (Torun, Wydawnictwo Uniwersytetu Mikolaja Kopernika, 2004)

Jodha, Vijay S. & Jodha, Samar S. (eds), *Tiranga: A Celebration of the Indian Flag* (New Delhi, New Vision Publishers for Yuva Hindustani, Flag Foundation of India, 2005)

Kale, Steven D., 'The Monarchy According to the King: The Ideological Content of the *Drapeau Blanc*, 1871–1873', *French History*, II (4), 1988, pp. 399–426

Kwan, Elizabeth, 'The Australian Flag: Ambiguous Symbol of Nationality in Melbourne and Sidney, 1920–1921', *Australian Historical Studies*, no. 103, 1994, pp. 280–303

Leepson, Marc, *Flag. An American Biography* (New York, St Martin's Press, 2005)

Lux-Wurm, Pierre C., *Les Drapeaux de l'Islam de Mahomet à nos jours* (Paris, Meta Editions, 2001)

Naik, Y.G., *Indian National Emblems: Their Significance* (Bombay, Visual Education Society, 1957)

Nair, Thankappan P., *Indian National Songs and Symbols* (Calcutta, Firma KLM, 1987)

Oliva, G., 'Il Tricolore', in Mario Isnenghi (ed.), *I luoghi della memoria. Simboli e miti dell'Italia unita* (Bari, Laterza, 1996), pp. 5–13

Matheson, John Ross, *Canada's Flag. A Search for a Country* (Boston, G.K. Hall, 1980)

Matthews, Roy T., 'Britannia and John Bull: From Birth to Maturity', *The Historian*, 62, no. 4, 2000, pp. 799–820

Mosse, George L., *The Nationalization of the Masses. Political Symbolism and Mass Movements in Germany from the Napoleonic Wars through the Third Reich* (New York, H. Fertig, 1975)

Pastine, Onorato, 'Il Tricolore Italiano', *Bollettino Ligustico per la storia e la Cultura Regionale*, VI, 1954, pp. 85–92

Pastoureau, Michel, 'L'Etat et son image emblématique', in *Culture et idéologie dans la genèse de l'Etat moderne* (Rome, Ecole française de Rome, 1985), pp. 145–53

Pastoureau, Michel, *Etudes d'histoire et d'anthropologie* (Paris, Le Léopard d'Or, 1989)

Pastoureau, Michel, *L'étoffe du Diable. Une histoire des rayures et des tissus rayés* (Paris, Seuil, 1991)

Pastoureau, Michel, *Dictionnaire des couleurs de notre temps. Symbolique et société* (Paris, C. Bonneton, 1992)

Pastoureau, Michel, *Traité d'héraldique* (Paris, Picard, 2nd edn, 1993)

Pastoureau, Michel, 'Genèse du drapeau', in *Genèse de l'Etat moderne en Méditerranée. Approches historiques et anthropologiques des pratiques et des représentations* (Rome, Ecole française de Rome, 1993), pp. 97–108

Pastoureau, Michel, 'L'emblême fait-il la nation? De la bannière à l'armoirie, de l'armoirie au drapeau', in Rainer Babel, Jean-Marie Moeglin (eds), *Identité régionale et conscience nationale en France et en Allemagne du Moyen Âge à l'époque moderne*, Sigmaringen, Thorbecke (Beihefte der Francia, 39), 1997, pp. 193–203

Pastoureau, Michel, *Bleu, histoire d'une couleur* (Paris, Seuil, 2000)

Pécout, Gilles, 'Les représentations officielles de l'Italie nouvelle au XIXe siècle', in Charle, Christophe, Lalouette, Jacqueline, Pigenet, Michel, Sohn, Anne-Marie (eds), *La France démocratique. Combats, mentalités, symboles. Mélanges offerts à Maurice Agulhon* (Paris, Publications de la Sorbonne, 1998)

Perera, Edward W., *Sinhalese Banners and Standards* (Colombo, Colombo Museum, 1916)

Perrin, W.G., *British Flags, Their Early History and Their Development at Sea; With an Account of the Origin of the Flag as a National Device* (Cambridge, Cambridge University Press, 1922)

Porciani, Ilaria, *La festa della nazione. Rappresentazione dello Stato e spazi sociali nell'Italia unita* (Bologna, Il Mulino, 1997)

Rajagopalachari, Chakravarti, *India's Flag* (Madras, Ganesh & Co., 1923)

Rajaratnam, G.P., *Significance of the Wheel of Asoka in the Flag of Free India* (Bangalore, Indian Institute of Culture, 1948)

Rajaratnam, G.P., *Introducing Our Flag: For Our Boys and Girls* (Bombay, Hind Kitabs, 1949)

Rangoni, L.M., *La Bandiera Tricolore e gli stati Italiani del 1848–1849* (Città di Castello, 1914)

Roy, Srirupa, ' "A Symbol of Freedom": The Indian Flag and the Transformations of Nationalism, 1906–2002', *Journal of Asian Studies*, 65 (3), 2006, pp. 495–527

Ruiz, Alain, 'Noir-rouge-or et noir-blanc-rouge. La question du drapeau national en Allemagne de Bismarck à Hitler et après', in Françoise Knopper & Alain Ruiz (eds), *Etat et nation en Allemagne au XXe siècle* (Toulouse, Presses universitaires du Mirail, 1996), pp. 25–58

Saker, Harry, *The South African Flag Controversy, 1925–1928* (Cape Town, Oxford University Press, 1980)

Sharma, Lt. Col. Gautam & Murthi, R.K., *Indian National Songs* (New Delhi, Reliance Publishing House, 1998)

Singh, K.V., *Our National Flag* (New Delhi, Publications Division, Ministry of Information & Broadcasting, Govt. of India, 1991)

Singh, K.V., *The Indian Tricolour* (New Delhi, Rupa, 2005)

Smith, Whitney, *The Bibliography of Flags of Foreign Nations* (Boston, G.K. Hall, 1965)

Stohl, Hugo Gerard, *Wappen und Flaggen des Deutchen Reiches und seiner Bundesstraten, 1871–1918* (Dortmund, 1979)

Szarota, Tomasz, *Der deutsche Michel. Die Geschichte eines Nationalen Symbols und Autostereotyps* (Osnabrück, Fibre, 1998; original edition in Polish, Warsaw, PWN, 1988)

Swan, Conrad, *Canada: Symbols of Sovereignty* (Toronto, University of Toronto Press, 1977)

Ṭhakore, Kapila, *Our National Flag* (Bombay, Padma, 1946)

Taylor, Miles, 'John Bull and the Iconography of Public Opinion in England, 1712–1929', *Past and Present*, no. 134, 1992, pp. 93–128

Thapluiyal, Uma Prasad, *The Dhvaja. Standards and Flags of India? A Study* (Delhi, B.R. Pub. Corp., 1983)

Venkayya, Pingali, *A National Flag for India* (Masulipatam, 1916)

Virmani, Arundhati, ' "Up, up with the Indian Flag, Down, down with the Union Jack!". Le drapeau indien et le ralliement à la nation, 1930–1931', in *Les ralliements. Ralliés, traîtres et opportunistes du Moyen Age à l'époque moderne et contemporaine* (Bordeaux, CROCEMC, 1997), pp. 215–37

Virmani, Arundhati, 'Drapeau colonial, drapeau national. De la 'Star of India' au 'Swaraj Flag', 1863–1921', in *La France démocratique. Combats, mentalités, symboles* (eds), Charle, Christophe, Lalouette, Jacqueline, Pigenet, Michel, Sohn, Anne-Marie (ed.) (Paris, Publications de la Sorbonne, 1998), p. 409–17

Virmani, Arundhati, 'National Symbols under Colonial Domination.

The Nationalization of the Indian Flag. March–August 1923', *Past & Present*, no. 164, 1999, pp. 169–97

Viola, Orazio, *Il Tricolore italiano. Saggio bibliografico con due appendici* (Catania, Libreria editrice C. Battiato, 1905)

Other Secondary Works

Abbot, J., *The Keys of Power: A Study of Indian Ritual and Belief* (1st edn, 1932, Delhi, Manohar, 2000)

Ahmad, Jamil-ud-din, *Is India One Nation?* (Muslim University Muslim League Publications, 1939)

Ahmed, Rafiuddin, *The Bengal Muslims 1871–1906. A Quest for Identity* (Delhi, Oxford University Press, 1981)

Alter, Joseph S., *Gandhi's Body. Sex, Diet and the Politics of Nationalism* (Philadelphia, University of Pennsylvania Press, 2000)

Amin Shahid, *Event, Memory, Metaphor. Chauri Chaura 1922–1992* (Delhi, Oxford University Press, 1995)

Anderson Benedict, *Imagined Communities: Reflections on the Origin and Spread of Nationalism* (London, Verso, 1983)

Anderson, Walter K. & Damle, Shridhar D., *The Brotherhood in Saffron: The Rashtriya Swayam Sevak Sangh and Hindu Revivalism* (London, Westview Press, 1987)

Appadurai, Arjun (ed.), *The Social Life of Things. Commodities in Cultural Perspectives* (Cambridge, Cambridge University Press, 1986)

Applegate, Celia, *A Nation of Provincials: The German Idea of Heimat* (Berkeley, University of California Press, 1990)

Assayag, Jackie, *L'Inde. Désir de Nation* (Paris, Odile Jacob, 2001)

Aziz, Khursheed Kamal, *The Making of Pakistan: A Study of Nationalism* (London, Chatto & Windus, 1967)

Aziz, Khursheed Kamal, *Muslims under Congress Rule 1937–1939. A Documentary Record* (Islamabad, National Commission on Historical and Cultural Research, 1978–9), 2 vols

Bagchee, Moni, *Bande Mataram* (Bombay, Bharatiya Vidya Bhavan, 1977)

Banerjee, Kalyan Kumar, *Indian Freedom Movement Revolutionaries in America* (Calcutta, Jijnasa, 1969)

Balandier, Georges, *Le Pouvoir sur scènes* (Paris, Balland, 1980)

Barrier, Gerald, *Banned Controversial Literature and Political Control in British India 1907–1947* (Delhi, Manohar, 1974)

Baskaran, S. Theodore, *The Message Bearers. The Nationalist Politics and the Entertainment Media in South India, 1880–1945* (Madras, Cre-A, 1981)

Basu, Tapan, Datta, Pradip, Sarkar, Sumit, Sarkar, Tanika, Sen, Samuddha, *Khaki Shorts and Saffron Flags* (Delhi, Orient Longman, 1993)

Bayly, Christopher A. (ed.), *The Raj. India and the British 1600–1947* (London, National Portrait Gallery Publications, 1990)

Bayart, Jean-François (ed.), *La greffe de l'Etat. Les trajectoires du politique*, 2 (Paris, Kartala, 1996)

Bazaz, Prem Nath, *The History of the Struggle for Freedom in Kashmir, Cultural and Political. From the Earliest Times to the Present Day* (New Delhi, Pamposh Publications, 1954)

Bloch, Maurice, *Ritual, History and Power. Selected Papers in Anthropology* (London, Athlone, 1989)

Brass, Paul, *Language, Religion and Politics in North India* (Cambridge, Cambridge University Press, 1974)

Brass, Paul & Robinson, F. (eds), *The Indian National Congress and Indian Society, 1885–1985: Ideology, Social Structure and Political Dominance* (Delhi, Chanakya Publications, 1987)

Brittlebank, Kate, *Tipu Sultan's Search for Legitimacy. Islam and Kingship in a Hindu Domain* (Delhi, Oxford University Press, 1997)

Brimnes, Niels, *Constructing the Colonial Encounter. Right and Left Hand Castes in Early Colonial South India* (Richmond, Curzon, 1999)

Brown, Emily Clara, *Har Dayal, Hindu Revolutionary and Nationalist* (Tucson, University of Arizona Press, 1975)

Brown, Judith, *Gandhi and Civil Disobedience. The Mahatma in Indian Politics 1928–34* (Cambridge, Cambridge University Press, 1977)

Butalia, Urvashi, *The Other Side of Silence. Voices from the Partition of India* (London, Hurst & Co., 2000)

Cannadine, David, *Ornamentalism. How the British Saw their Empire* (London, Penguin, 2001)

Cannadine, David & Price, Simon, *Rituals of Royalty* (Cambridge, Cambridge University Press, 1987)

Cashman, Richard, *The Myth of the Lokmanya: Tilak and Mass Politics in Maharashtra* (Berkeley, University of California Press, 1975)

Centlivres, Pierre, Fabre, Daniel, Zonabend, Françoise, *La Fabrique des Héros* (Paris, Editions de la Maison des Sciences de l'Homme, 1998)

Chakrabarti, Hiren, *Political Protest in Bengal: Boycott and Terrorism 1905–1918* (Calcutta, Papyrus, 1992)

Chandra, Bipan, *India's Struggle for Independence* (Delhi, Penguin, 1989)

Choudhary, Rahmat Ali, *Pakistan* (Cambridge, Pakistan National Liberation Movement, 1935, 3rd edn, 1947)

Chatterji, Joya, *Communal Politics and the Partition of Bengal 1932–1947* (Cambridge, Cambridge University Press, 1991)

Chatterjee, P.C. (ed.), *Self-Images, Identity and Nationality* (New Delhi, Indian Institute of Advanced Study, Shimla, Allied Publishers, 1989)

Chattopadhyay, Gautam, *Communism & Bengal's Freedom Movement, 1917–1929* (New Delhi, People's Publishing House, 1970)

Chew, Shirley and Rutherford, Anna (ed.), *Unbecoming Daughters of the Empire* (Sydney, Dungaroo Press, 1993)

Chirol, Valentine, *The Modern World. A Survey of Historical Forces, India* (London, Ernest Benn, 1926), vol. 5

Chowdhury, Indira, *The Frail Hero and Virile History. Gender and the Politics of Culture in Colonial Bengal* (Delhi, Oxford University Press, 1998)

Cohn, Bernard S., *An Anthropologist among the Historians and Other Essays* (New Delhi, Oxford University Press, 1987)

Cohn, Bernard S., *Colonialism and its Forms of Knowledge: The British in India* (Princeton, Princeton University Press, 1996)

Cohn, Bernard S., *India. The Social Anthropology of a Civilization* (Delhi, Oxford University Press, 2000)

Copland, Ian, *The British Raj & the Indian Princes: Paramountcy in Western India, 1857–1930* (London, Sangam Books, 1982)

Das, Manmath Nath, *Partition and Independence of India. Inside Story of Mountbatten Days* (Delhi, East-West Publications, 1982)

Deol, Gurdev Singh, *The Role of the Ghadar Party in the National Movement* (Jullundur, Sterling Publishers, 1969)

Eddy, John & Shreuder, Deryck (eds), *The Rise of Colonial Nationalism. Australia, New Zealand, Canada and South Africa First Assert their Nationalities, 1888–1914* (Sydney-Boston, Allen & Unwin, 1988)

Eliade, Mircea, *Sur l'érotique mystique indienne* (Paris, L'Herne, 1997)

Elliott, Carolyn M. (ed.), *Civil Society and Democracy* (Delhi, Oxford University Press, 2003)

Embree, Ainslee Thomas, *India's Search for National Identity* (New York, Alfred A. Knopf, 1972)

Embree, Ainslee Thomas, *Imagining India. Essays on Indian History* (Oxford University Press, 1989)

Foxe, Barbara, *Long Journey Home. A Biography of Margaret Noble* (London, Rider & Co., 1975)

Fuller, C.J. & Bénéï, Véronique (eds), *The Everyday State & Society in Modern India* (New Delhi, Social Science Press, 2000)

Gellner, Ernest, *Nations and Nationalism* (Oxford, Blackwell, 1983)

Ghose, Charu Chander, *The Partition of Bengal. A Plea for Reconsideration* (Calcutta, 1906)

Ghosh, Binoy Jiban, *Revolt of 1905 in Bengal* (Calcutta, G.A.E. Publishers, 1987)

Gilmartin, David, *Empire and Islam. Punjab & the Making of Pakistan* (London, I.B. Tauris & Co., 1988)

Gilmour, David, *Curzon* (London, John Murray, 1994)

Gode, Parsuram Krisna, *Studies in Indian Cultural History* (Hoshiarpur, Vishveshvaranand Vedic Research Insitutue, 1960–9)

Goodwin, Jeff, Jasper, James M., Polletta, Francesca (eds), *Passionate Politics. Emotions and Social Movements* (Chicago-London, Chicago University Press, 2001)

Gooptu, Nandini, *The Politics of the Urban Poor in Early 20th Century India* (Cambridge, Cambridge University Press, 2001)

Gopal, Sarvepalli, *The Viceroyalty of Lord Irwin 1926–1931* (Oxford, Clarendon Press, 1957)

Gopal, Sarvepalli, *Jawaharlal Nehru. A Biography* (Delhi, Oxford University Press, 1975), vol. 1

Goswami, Manu, *Producing India. From Colonial Economy to National Space* (New Delhi, Permanent Black, 2004)

Grewal, J.S., *The Sikhs of the Punjab* (Delhi, The New Cambridge History of India, II-3, 1990)

Grewal, J.S., *Contesting Interpretations of the Sikh Tradition* (Delhi, Manohar, 1998)

Gupta, Shyam Ratna, Schöttle, Urs, Axel, Jürgen (eds), *Citizenship Values in India. Individualism and Social Imperatives* (Calcutta, Mandira, 1990)

Handa, Rajendra Lal, *History of Freedom Struggle in Princely States* (New Delhi, Central News Agency, 1968)

Haithcox, John Patrick, *Communism and Nationalism in India: M.N. Roy and Comintern Policy, 1920–1939* (Princeton, Princeton University Press, 1971)

Hansen, Thomas Blom, *The Saffron Wave. Democracy and Hindu Nationalism in Modern India* (Princeton, Princeton University Press, 1999)

Hardy, Peter, *The Muslims in British India* (Cambridge, Cambridge University Press, 1972)

Hardy, Peter, *Partners in Freedom and True Muslims: The Political Thought of Some Muslim Scholars in British India, 1912–1947* (Stockholm, Scandinavian Institute of Asian Studies, 1971)

Haynes, Douglas & Prakash, Gyan (eds), *Contesting Power. Resistance and Everyday Social Relations in South Asia* (Delhi, Oxford University Press, 1991)

Hettne, Bjorn, *The Political Economy of Indirect Rule. Mysore 1881–1947* (Stockholm, Scandinavian Institute of Asian Studies, 1978)

Hasan, Mushirul, *Nationalism and Communal Politics in India, 1885–1930* (Delhi, Manohar Publications, 1991)

Hasan, Mushirul, *India's Partition. Process, Strategy and Mobilization* (Delhi, Oxford University Press, 1993)

Hasan, Mushirul, *Mohammad Ali in Indian Politics: Select Writings, 1920–23* (New Delhi, Atlantic, 1986)

Hasan, Mushirul (ed.), *Knowledge, Power and Politics. Educational Institutions in India* (Delhi, Lotus Collection, 1998)

Hasan, Mushirul, *Islam, Communities and the Nation. Muslim Identities in South Asia and Beyond* (Delhi, Manohar Publications, 1998)

Hasan, Mushirul (ed.), *India Partitioned. The Other Face of Freedom* (Delhi, Roli Books, 2 vols, 1995)

Hasan, Zoya (ed.), *Politics and the State in India* (New Delhi, Sage, 2000)

Haynes, Douglas E., *Rhetoric and Ritual in Colonial India. The Shaping of a Public Culture in Surat City, 1852–1928* (Berkeley, University of California Press, 1991)

Hintze, Andrea, *The Mughal Empire and its Decline. An Interpretation of the Sources of Social Power* (Ashgate, Variorum, 1997)

Humphrey, Caroline & Laidlaw, James A., *The Archetypal Actions of Ritual. A Theory of Ritual Illustrated by the Jain Rites of Worship* (Oxford, Clarendon Press, 1994)

Imam, Mohammad Muzaffar, *Role of Muslims in the National Movement 1912–30. A Study of Bihar* (Delhi, Mittal Publications, 1987)

Jaffrelot, Christophe, *The Hindu Nationalist Movement in India* (New York, Columbia University Press, 1996)

Jalal, Ayesha, *The Sole Spokesman: Jinnah, the Muslim League and the Demand for Pakistan* (Cambridge, Cambridge University Press 1985)

Jayal, Niraja Gopal, *Democracy and the State. Welfare, Secularism and Development in Contemporary India* (Delhi, Oxford University Press, 1999)

Jayaprasad, K., *RSS and Hindu Nationalism. Inroads in a Leftist Stronghold* (New Delhi, Deep Publications, 1991)

Jebb, Richard, *Studies in Colonial Nationalism* (London, E. Arnold, 1905)

Jeffrey, Robin (ed.), *People, Princes and Paramount Power. Society and Politics in the Indian Princely States* (Delhi, Oxford University Press, 1978)

Joshi, Naveen (ed.), *Freedom Fighters Remember* (New Delhi, Publications Division, 1997)

Kanjilal, K., *Literature on Patriotism and Patriotic Feeling in Sanskrit* (Calcutta, Sanskrit College, 1994)

Kaul, Suvir, *Poems of Nation, Anthems of Empire. English Verse in the Long 18th Century* (Delhi, Oxford University Press, 2000)

Kaur, Manmohan, *Role of Women in the Freedom Movement* (Jullundur, Sterling Publishers, 1968)

Kaviraj, Sudipta & Khilnani, Sunil (eds), *Civil Society, Historical Possibilities* (Cambridge, Cambridge University Press, 2001)

Kaye, Cecil, *Communism in India. Unpublished Documents for National Archives of India 1919–1924* (Calcutta, Editions Indian, 1971)

Keith, Arthur Berriedale (ed.), *Speeches and Documents on the British Dominions. From Self Government to National Sovereignty* (London, Oxford University Press, 1922–38), 2 vols

Ker, James Campbell, *Political Trouble in India 1907–1917* (Calcutta, Superintendent Government Printing, 1917)

Kertzer, David, *Rituals, Politics and Power* (New Haven-London, Yale University Press, 1988)

Khaled, Ahmed, *Pakistan: Behind the Ideological Mask* (Lahore, Vanguard, 2001)

Khaliquzzaman, Choudhry, *Pathway to Pakistan* (Lahore, Longmans, 1961)

Knopper, Françoise & Ruiz, Alain (eds), *Etat et nation en Allemagne au XXe siècle* (Toulouse, Presses universitaires du Mirail, 1996)

Kumar, Krishna, *Prejudice and Pride: School Histories of the Freedom Struggle in India and Pakistan* (New Delhi, Viking, 2001)

Ludden, David (ed.), *Contesting the Nation. Religion, Community and the Politics of Democracy in India* (Philadelphia, University of Pennsylvania Press, 1996)

Mackenzie, John M., *Propaganda and Empire. The Manipulation of British Public Opinion 1880–1960* (Manchester, Manchester University Press, 1986)

Mangan, J.A. (ed.), *Making Imperial Mentalities, Socialisation and British Imperialism* (Manchester, Manchester University Press, 1990)

Manor, James, *Political Change in an Indian State, Mysore 1917–1955* (New Delhi, Manohar, 1977)

Mehrotra, Sri Ram, *India and the Commonwealth 1885–1929* (London, George Allen & Unwin, 1965)

Mehta, Makrand (ed.), *Regional Roots of Indian Nationalism. Gujarat, Maharashtra and Rajasthan* (Delhi, Criterion Publications, 1990)

Menon, Dilip M., *Caste, Nationalism and Communism in South India. Malabar 1900–1948* (Cambridge, Cambridge University Press, 1994)

Metcalf, Thomas R., *An Imperial Vision. Indian Architecture and Britain's Raj* (Oxford, Oxford University Press, 1989)

Miller, John D.B., *Richard Jebb and the Problem of Empire* (London, Athlone Press, 1956)

Minault, Gail, *The Khilafat Movement. Religious Symbolism and Political Mobilization in India* (New York, Columbia University Press, 1982)

Moore, Sally F. & Meyerhoff, Barbara G. (eds), *Secular Rituals* (Assen, Van Gorcum and Co., 1977)

Mukherjee, H. & Mukherjee, V., *Bande Mataram and Indian Nationalism 1906–1908* (Calcutta, Firma K.L. Mukhopadhyay, 1957)

Mukherjee, H. & Mukherjee, V. (eds), *Sri Aurobindo & the New Thought in Indian Politics* (Calcutta, 1964)

Noman, Mohammad, *Muslim India: Rise and Growth of the All India Muslim League* (Allahabad, Kitabistan, 1942)

Nandakumar, Prema, *Subramania Bharati* (Mysore, Rao & Raghavan, 1964)

Nora, Pierre (ed.), *Les lieux de mémoire* (Paris, Gallimard, 1984–92)

Oberoi, Harjot S., *The Construction of Religious Boundaries. Culture, Identity and Diversity in the Sikh Tradition* (Delhi, Oxford University Press, 1997)

Ojha, P.N. (ed.), *History of Indian National Congress in Bihar 1885–1985* (Patna, K.P. Jayaswal Research Institute, 1985)

Ozouf, Mona, *The Pedagogy of the Nation. Festivals and the French Revolution* (Cambridge, Mass., Harvard University Press, 1991, 3rd edn, 1994)

Page, David, *Prelude to Partition. The Indian Muslims and the Imperial System of Control 1920–1932* (Delhi, Oxford University Press, 1981)

Pal, Dharm, *The Indian Army* (Delhi, Publications Division, Ministry of Information and Broadcasting, Govt. of India, 1967)

Pandey, Gyanendra, *The Ascendancy of the Congress in U.P. A Study in Imperfect Mobilization* (Delhi, Oxford University Press, 1978)

Pandey, Gyanendra, *Remembering Partition* (Cambridge, Cambridge University Press, 2001)

Patil, S.H., *The Congress Party and Princely States* (Bombay, Himalaya Publishing House, 1981)

Petrie, David, *Communism in India 1921–1927* (Calcutta, Editions Indian, 1972)

Popplewell, Richard J., *Intelligence and Imperial Defence. British Intelligence and the Defence of the Indian Empire 1904–1924* (London, Frank Cass & Co., 1995)

Prochasson, Christophe, 'Emotions et politiques: premières approches', in Audoin-Rouzeau, Stéphane & al. (ed.), *La politique et la guerre. Pour comprendre le XXe siècle européen. Hommage à Jean-Jacques Becker* (Paris, A.Vienot-Noesis, 2002), pp. 431–9

Quereshi, Ishitaq Husain, *The Struggle for Pakistan* (Karachi, University of Karachi, 1969)

Rahman, Hossainur, *Hindu–Muslim Relations in Bengal, 1905–1947. Study in Cultural Confrontation* (Bombay, Nachiketa Publications, 1974)

Rajendran, N., *National Movement in Tamil Nadu, 1905–14* (Madras, Oxford University Press, 1994)

Ramusack, Barbara, *The Princes of India in the Twilight of Empire: Dissolution of a Patron–Client System 1914–1939* (Columbus, Ohio State University Press, 1978)

Rangaswami, Vanaja, *The Story of Integration. A New Interpretation in the Context of the Democractic Movements in the Princely States of Mysore, Travancore and Cochin 1900–1947* (Delhi, Manohar, 1981)

Reddi, Ravi Narayan, *Heroic Telengana: Reminiscences & Experiences* (New Delhi, Tarun Sengupta for Communist Party of India, 1973)

Reddy, William, *Navigation of Feeling: A Framework of the History of Emotions* (Cambridge, Cambridge University Press, 2001)

Richards, Jeffrey, *Imperialism and Music. Britain 1876–1953* (Manchester, Manchester University Press, 2001)

Richards, John F. (ed.), *Kingship and Authority in South Asia* (Delhi, Oxford University Press, 1998)

Sarkar, Sumit, *Swadeshi Movement in Bengal, 1903–1908* (New Delhi, People's Publishing House, 1973)

Savarkar, Vinayak Damodar, *Hindu Rashtra Darshan* (Bombay, Laxman Ganesh Khare, 1949)

Sayeed, Khalid B., *Pakistan, The Formative Phase, 1857–1948* (London, Oxford University Press, 1968)

Sethna, K.A., *Madame Bhikhaji Rustom Cama* (New Delhi, Prakasana Vibhaga Sucana, 1992)

Settar, S. & Gupta, Indira Baptista (eds), *Pangs of Partition* (New Delhi, Manohar, 2002)

Shaikh, Farzana, *Community & Consensus in Islam. Muslim Representation in British India, 1860–1947* (Cambridge, Cambridge University Press, 1989)

Siddiqui, Kalim, *Conflict, Crisis and War in Pakistan* (London, Macmillan, 1972)

Singh, Narayan Iqbal, *The Indian National Congress. A Reconstruction*, vol. 2, *1919–23* (Delhi, Manohar, 1988)

Singh, Anita Inder, *The Origins of the Partition of India 1936–1947* (Delhi, Oxford University Press, 1987)

Symonds, Richard, *Oxford and Empire. The Lost Cause?* (Oxford, Clarendon Press, 1986)

Talbot, Ian, *Freedom's Cry. The Popular Dimension in the Pakistan Movement and Partition. Experience in Northwest India* (Karachi, Oxford University Press, 1996)

Tinker, Hugh, *Separate and Unequal. India and the Indians in the British Commonwealth 1920–1950* (London, C. Hurst, 1976)

Tiwari, Arya Ramchandra G., *Making of the Leader Sardar Vallabhbhai Patel: His Role in the Ahmedabad Municipality 1917–1922* (Gujarat State, Sardar Patel University,1967)

Tomlinson, Brian Roger, *The Indian National Congress and the Raj, 1929–1942: The Penultimate Phase* (London, Macmillan, 1976)

Vadgama, Kusoom, *India, British-Indian Campaigns in Britain for Indian Reforms, Justice and Freedom 1831–1947* (London, Banyan Tree, 1997)

Van der Veer, Peter, *Religious Nationalism. Hindus and Muslims in India* (Berkeley, University of California Press, 1994)

Waley, Sigismund David, *Edwin Montagu. A Memoir and an Account of his Visits to India* (Bombay, Asia Publishing House, 1964)

Waseem, M. (ed.), *On Becoming an Indian Muslim. French Essays on Aspects of Syncretism* (Delhi, Oxford University Press, 2003)

Wilentz, Sean (ed.), *Rites of Power: Symbolism, Ritual and Politics since the Middle Ages* (Philadelphia, University of Pennsylvania Press, 1985)

Wolpert, Stanley A., *Tilak and Gokhale. Revolution and Reform in the Making of Modern India* (Oxford, Oxford University Press, 1981)

Zaidi, Abdul Moin (ed.), *The Encyclopaedia of Indian National Congress* (New Delhi, Criterion Publications, 1989)

Zaidi, Abdul Moin, *Evolution of Muslim Political Thought in India* (New Delhi, Indian Institute of Applied Political Research, 1975)

Zaman, Mukhtar, *Students' Role in the Pakistan Movement* (Karachi, Quaid-i-Azam Academy, 1978)

Zelliot, Eleanor & Bernstein, Maxine (eds), *The Experience of Hinduism. Essays on Religion in Maharashtra* (Albany, NY, State University of New York Press, 1988)

Index